FAULTLINES

Debating the Issues in American Politics

Third Edition

FAULTLINES

Debating the Issues in American Politics

Third Edition

A brief edition of *The Enduring Debate*, Sixth Edition

David T. Canon
University of Wisconsin–Madison

John J. Coleman
University of Wisconsin–Madison

Kenneth R. Mayer
University of Wisconsin–Madison

W. W. Norton & Company
New York London

W. W. Norton & Company has been independent since its founding in 1923, when William Warder Norton and Mary D. Herter Norton first published lectures delivered at the People's Institute, the adult education division of New York City's Cooper Union. The Nortons soon expanded their program beyond the Institute, publishing books by celebrated academics from America and abroad. By mid-century, the two major pillars of Norton's publishing program—trade books and college texts—were firmly established. In the 1950s, the Norton family transferred control of the company to its employees, and today—with a staff of 400 and a comparable number of trade, college, and professional titles published each year—W. W. Norton & Company stands as the largest and oldest publishing house owned wholly by its employees.

Previous editions (1990–2002) published as Readings for AMERICAN GOVERNMENT

Composition: Bytheway Publishing Services
Book design by Anna Oler
Production manager: Jane Searle
Manufacturing by Sheridan Printing Company

Library of Congress Cataloging-in-Publication Data
Faultlines : debating the issues in American politics / David T. Canon, John J. Coleman, Kenneth R. Mayer. — 3rd ed.
       p. cm.
   "A brief edition of The Enduring Debate. 6th ed."
   Includes bibliographical references.
   ISBN 978-0-393-91206-7 (pbk.)
   1. United States—Politics and government.   I. Canon, David T.   II. Coleman, John J.,
1959–   III. Mayer, Kenneth R., 1960–   IV. Enduring debate.
   JK31.F37   2011
   320.973—dc22   2011002194

W. W. Norton & Company Inc., 500 Fifth Avenue, New York, N.Y. 10110
www.wwnorton.com
W. W. Norton & Company Ltd., Castle House, 75/76 Wells Street, London W1T 3QT

1   2   3   4   5   6   7   8   9   0

Contents

FAULTLINES

Debating the Issues in American Politics

Third Edition

1

Political Culture: What Does It Mean to Be an American?

What does it mean to be an American? This deceptively simple question is challenging to answer. Because the United States encompasses a vast array of ethnicities, religions, and cultures, it can be difficult to define "American" by reference to those criteria. The country's geography differs dramatically from area to area, and the economic way of life accordingly differs greatly as well. And in many ways, diverse groups of Americans have experienced American history differently, so a common historical identity is not obviously the answer either. One popular argument is that the United States is united by a set of political ideals. As far back as the early nineteenth century, scholars have tried to identify the nature of American political culture: Is it a commitment to individualism? A belief in equality? A shared set of values about the appropriate role of government? Openness?

Sarah Song reviews three ways in which ideals might provide what she refers to as civic solidarity. Constitutional patriotism says that the key to the American identity is fidelity and support of ideals set forth in the major texts of American political culture such as the Declaration of Independence and the Constitution. Liberal nationalism argues that adherence to a set of ideals is not sufficient for a national identity. It also must include these four features: "a shared belief among a group of individuals that they belong together, historical continuity stretching across generations, connection to a particular territory, and a shared set of characteristics constituting a national culture." Last, Song argues most strongly for "deep diversity," a multicultural understanding of the United States in which an acceptance of difference is the key idea that glues society together— the search for a common culture shared by all is set aside. In this view, acceptance and encouragement of different languages, beliefs, and values are themselves the unifying value that unites a society's understanding of itself. Song presents Canada as an example of deep diversity.

Steven Warshawsky argues that American identity centers around a commonly held set of ideas that can be considered the American way of life. This way of life includes beliefs in liberty, equality, property rights, religious freedom, limited government, and a common language for conducting political and economic life. Although we have always been a nation of immigrants, from the original settlers to the mass immigration of the late nineteenth and early twentieth centuries, Warshawsky sees assimilation into American political culture as critical to American national identity. He also notes that America, including the scope and reach of government, has changed dramatically over time. Warshawsky asks whether these changes also changed what it means to be "an American." He argues this is a difficult question but concludes that straying too far from the principles of the Founders means "we will cease to be 'Americans' in any meaningful sense of the word."

Daniel Elazar provides a different way of approaching the question of what it means to be an American. He argues that political beliefs in the United States are distributed unevenly across the country. In large part, this has to do with migration patterns. Once certain ethnic groups and nationalities predominated in a particular area, the institutions they built and the practice of politics tended to become ingrained with their political and cultural beliefs. Elazar sees three types of value systems across the country: moralism, individualism, and traditionalism. Moralism is focused on the community and engaging in politics to do good. Individualism focuses on individual rights and tends to view governing as a set of transactions among various individuals and groups. Traditionalism attempts to use the power of government to preserve existing social arrangements. These three approaches vary in their prevalence across the country, and even within states there may be variation as to which of the three predominates. Some areas have a mixture of two of these value systems, whereas other areas are more purely of one type.

Sarah Song
What Does It Mean to Be an American?

It is often said that being an American means sharing a commitment to a set of values and ideals. Writing about the relationship of ethnicity and American identity, the historian Philip Gleason put it this way:

> To be or to become an American, a person did not have to be any particular national, linguistic, religious, or ethnic background. All he had to do was to commit himself to the political ideology centered on the abstract ideals of liberty, equality, and republicanism. Thus the universalist ideological character of American nationality meant that it was open to anyone who willed to become an American.

To take the motto of the Great Seal of the United States, *E pluribus unum*—"From many, one"—in this context suggests not that manyness should be melted down into one, as in [the] image of the melting pot, but that, as the Great Seal's sheaf of arrows suggests, there should be a coexistence of many-in-one under a unified citizenship based on shared ideals.

Of course, the story is not so simple, as Gleason himself went on to note. America's history of racial and ethnic exclusions has undercut the universalist stance; for being an American has also meant sharing a national culture, one largely defined in racial, ethnic, and religious terms. * * * In this essay, I explore different ideals of civic solidarity with an eye toward what they imply for newcomers who wish to become American citizens.

Why does civic solidarity matter? First, it is integral to the pursuit of distributive justice. * * * The underlying idea is that people are more likely to support redistributive schemes when they trust one another, and they are more likely to trust one another when they regard others as like themselves in some meaningful sense.

Second, genuine democracy demands solidarity. If democratic activity involves not just voting, but also deliberation, then people must make an effort to listen to and understand one another. Moreover, they must be willing to moderate their claims in the hope of finding common ground on which to base

Published in *Daedalus*, Spring 2009.

political decisions. Such democratic activity cannot be realized by individuals pursuing their own interests; it requires some concern for the common good. A sense of solidarity can help foster mutual sympathy and respect, which in turn support citizens' orientation toward the common good.

Third, civic solidarity offers more inclusive * * * models of political community as an alternative to the racial, ethnic, or religious narratives that have permeated political life. The challenge, then, is to develop a model of civic solidarity that is "thick" enough to motivate support for justice and democracy while also "thin" enough to accommodate racial, ethnic, and religious diversity.

We might look first to [the] idea of constitutional patriotism * * *. On this view, what binds citizens together is their common allegiance to the ideals embodied in a shared political culture.

* * *

The basis of American solidarity is not any particular racial or ethnic identity or religious beliefs, but universal moral ideals embodied in American political culture and set forth in such seminal texts as the Declaration of Independence, the U.S. Constitution and Bill of Rights, Abraham Lincoln's Gettysburg Address, and Martin Luther King, Jr.'s "I Have a Dream" speech. * * *

What does constitutional patriotism suggest for the sort of reception immigrants should receive? There has been a general shift in Western Europe and North America in the standards governing access to citizenship from cultural markers to values, and this is a development that constitutional patriots would applaud. In the United States those seeking to become citizens must demonstrate basic knowledge of U.S. government and history. A newly revised U.S. citizenship test was instituted in October 2008 with the hope that it will serve, in the words of the chief of the Office of Citizenship, Alfonso Aguilar, as "an instrument to promote civic learning and patriotism." The revised test attempts to move away from civics trivia to emphasize political ideas and concepts. * * * The new test asks more open-ended questions about government powers and political concepts: "What does the judicial branch do?" "What stops one branch of government from becoming too powerful?" "What is freedom of religion?" "What is the 'rule of law'?"

Constitutional patriots would endorse this focus on values and principles. * * * All that should be expected of immigrants is that they embrace the constitutional principles as interpreted by the political culture, not that they necessarily embrace the majority's ethical-cultural forms [such as language].

Yet * * * government decisions about the language of public institutions, public holidays, and state symbols unavoidably involve recognizing and supporting particular ethnic and religious groups over others. In the United States, English language ability has been a statutory qualification for naturalization since 1906, originally as a requirement of oral ability and later as a requirement of English literacy. Indeed, support for the principles of the Constitution has been interpreted as requiring English literacy. The language requirement might be justified as a practical matter (we need some language to be the common language of schools, government, and the workplace, so why not the language of the majority?), but for a great many citizens, the language requirement is also viewed as a key marker of national identity. The continuing centrality of language in naturalization policy prevents us from saying that what it means to be an American is purely a matter of shared values.

Another misconception about constitutional patriotism is that it is necessarily more inclusive of newcomers than [other] models of solidarity. Its inclusiveness depends on which principles are held up as the polity's shared principles. * * * Consider ideological requirements for naturalization in U.S. history. The first naturalization law of 1790 required nothing more than an oath to support the U.S. Constitution. The second naturalization act added two ideological elements: the renunciation of titles or orders of nobility and the requirement that one be found to have "behaved as a man . . . attached to the principles of the constitution of the United States." This attachment requirement was revised in 1940 from a behavioral qualification to a personal attribute, but this did not help clarify what attachment to constitutional principles requires. Not surprisingly, the "attachment to constitutional principles" requirement has been interpreted as requiring a belief in representative government, federalism, separation of powers, and constitutionally guaranteed individual rights. It has also been interpreted as disqualifying anarchists, polygamists, and conscientious objectors for citizenship. In 1950, support for communism was added to the list of grounds for disqualification from naturalization—as well as grounds for exclusion and deportation. The 1990 Immigration Act retained the McCarthy-era ideological qualifications for naturalization; current law disqualifies those who advocate or affiliate with an organization that advocates communism or opposition to all organized government. Patriotism

* * * is capable of excess and pathology, as evidenced by loyalty oaths and campaigns against "un-American" activities.

In contrast to constitutional patriots, liberal nationalists acknowledge that states cannot be culturally neutral even if they tried. States cannot avoid coercing citizens into preserving a national culture of some kind because state institutions and laws define a political culture, which in turn shapes the range of customs and practices of daily life that constitute a national culture. David Miller, a leading theorist of liberal nationalism, defines national identity according to the following elements: a shared belief among a group of individuals that they belong together, historical continuity stretching across generations, connection to a particular territory, and a shared set of characteristics constituting a national culture. It is not enough to share a common identity rooted in a shared history or a shared territory; a shared national culture is a necessary feature of national identity. I share a national culture with someone, even if we never meet, if each of us has been initiated into the traditions and customs of a national culture.

What sort of content makes up a national culture? Miller says more about what a national culture does not entail. It need not be based on biological descent. Even if nationalist doctrines have historically been based on notions of biological descent and race, Miller emphasizes that sharing a national culture is, in principle, compatible with people belonging to a diversity of racial and ethnic groups. In addition, every member need not have been born in the homeland. Thus, "immigration need not pose problems, provided only that the immigrants come to share a common national identity, to which they may contribute their own distinctive ingredients."

Liberal nationalists focus on the idea of culture, as opposed to ethnicity. * * * Both nationality and ethnicity have cultural components, but what is said to distinguish "civic" nations from "ethnic" nations is that the latter are exclusionary and closed on grounds of biological descent; the former are, in principle, open to anyone willing to adopt the national culture.

Yet the civic-ethnic distinction is not so clear-cut in practice. Every nation has an "ethnic core."

* * *

Why, then, if all national cultures have ethnic cores, should those outside this core embrace the national culture? * * *

The major difficulty here is that national cultures are not typically the

product of collective deliberation in which all have the opportunity to participate. The challenge is to ensure that historically marginalized groups, as well
as new groups of immigrants, have genuine opportunities to contribute "on an
equal footing" to shaping the national culture. * * *

Cultural nationalist visions of solidarity would lend support to immigration and immigrant policies that give weight to linguistic and ethnic preferences
and impose special requirements on individuals from groups deemed to be outside the nation's "core culture." One example is the practice in postwar Germany of giving priority in immigration and naturalization policy to ethnic
Germans; they were the only foreign nationals who were accepted as permanent residents set on the path toward citizenship. They were treated not as immigrants but "resettlers" (Aussiedler) who acted on their constitutional right to
return to their country of origin. In contrast, non-ethnically German guest-
workers (Gastarbeiter) were designated as "aliens" (Ausländer) under the 1965
German Alien Law and excluded from German citizenship. Another example is
the Japanese naturalization policy that, until the late 1980s, required natural-
ized citizens to adopt a Japanese family name. The language requirement in
contemporary naturalization policies in the West is the leading remaining example of a cultural nationalist integration policy; it reflects not only a concern
with the economic and political integration of immigrants but also a nationalist
concern with preserving a distinctive national culture.

Constitutional patriotism and liberal nationalism are accounts of civic solidarity that deal with what one might call first-level diversity. Individuals have
different group identities and hold divergent moral and religious outlooks, yet
they are expected to share the same idea of what it means to be American:
either patriots committed to the same set of ideals or co-nationals sharing the
relevant cultural attributes. [A]n alternative approach [is] the idea of "deep
diversity."

* * *

What leads people to support [deep] diversity is both the desire to be a
member of the political community and the recognition of disagreement about
what it means to be a member.

* * * The United States has a need for acknowledgment of diverse modes
of belonging based on the distinctive histories of different groups. Native
Americans, African Americans, Irish Americans, Vietnamese Americans, and
Mexican Americans: across these communities of people, we can find not only

distinctive group identities, but also distinctive ways of belonging to the political community.

* * *

While attractive for its inclusiveness, the deep diversity model may be too thin a basis for civic solidarity in a democratic society. Can there be civic solidarity without citizens already sharing a set of values or a culture in the first place? * * * In contrast to liberal nationalism, deep diversity does not aim at specifying a common national culture that must be shared by all. What matters is not so much the content of solidarity, but the ethos generated by making the effort at mutual understanding and respect.

Canada's approach to the integration of immigrants may be the closest thing there is to "deep diversity." Canadian naturalization policy is not so different from that of the United States: a short required residency period, relatively low application fees, a test of history and civics knowledge, and a language exam. Where the United States and Canada diverge is in their public commitment to diversity. Through its official multiculturalism policies, Canada expresses a commitment to the value of diversity among immigrant communities through funding for ethnic associations and supporting heritage language schools. Constitutional patriots and liberal nationalists say that immigrant integration should be a two-way process, that immigrants should shape the host society's dominant culture just as they are shaped by it. Multicultural accommodations actually provide the conditions under which immigrant integration might genuinely become a two-way process. Such policies send a strong message that immigrants are a welcome part of the political community and should play an active role in shaping its future evolution.

* * *

What is now formally required of immigrants seeking to become American citizens most clearly reflects the first two models of solidarity: professed allegiance to the principles of the Constitution (constitutional patriotism) and adoption of a shared culture by demonstrating the ability to read, write, and speak English (liberal nationalism). The revised citizenship test makes gestures toward respect for first-level diversity and inclusion of historically marginalized groups with questions such as, "Who lived in America before the Europeans arrived?" "What group of people was taken to America and sold as slaves?" "What did Susan B. Anthony do?" "What did Martin Luther King, Jr. do?"

The election of the first African American president of the United States is a significant step forward. A more inclusive American solidarity requires the recognition not only of the fact that Americans are a diverse people, but also that they have distinctive ways of belonging to America.

Steven M. Warshawsky
What Does It Mean to Be an American?

"Undocumented Americans." This is how Senate Majority Leader Harry Reid recently described the estimated 12–20 million illegal aliens living in America. What was once a Mark Steyn joke has now become the ideological orthodoxy of the Democratic Party.

Reid's comment triggered an avalanche of outrage among commentators, bloggers, and the general public. Why? Because it strikes at the heart of the American people's understanding of themselves as a nation and a civilization. Indeed, opposition to the ongoing push for "comprehensive immigration reform"—i.e., amnesty and a guest worker program—is being driven by a growing concern among millions of Americans that massive waves of legal and illegal immigration—mainly from Mexico, Latin America, and Asia—coupled with the unwillingness of our political and economic elites to mold these newcomers into red-white-and-blue Americans, is threatening to change the very character of our country. For the worse.

I share this concern. I agree with the political, economic, and cultural arguments in favor of sharply curtailing immigration into the United States, as well as refocusing our immigration efforts on admitting those foreigners who bring the greatest value to—and are most easily assimilated into—American society. * * * But this essay is not intended to rehash these arguments. Rather, I wish to explore the question that underlies this entire debate: What does it mean to be an American? This may seem like an easy question to answer, but it's not. The harder one thinks about this question, the more complex it becomes.

Clearly, Harry Reid has not given this question much thought. His implicit definition of "an American" is simply: Anyone living within the geopolitical boundaries of the United States. In other words, mere physical location on

Published in *American Thinker*, July 2007.

Earth determines whether or not someone is "an American." Presumably, Reid's definition is not intended to apply to tourists and other temporary visitors. Some degree of permanency—what the law in other contexts calls "residency," i.e., a subjective intention to establish one's home or domicile—is required. In Reid's view, therefore, a Mexican from Guadalajara, a Chinese from Shanghai [sic], an Indian from Delhi, or a [fill in the blank] become "Americans" as soon as they cross into U.S. territory and decide to live here permanently, legally or not. Nothing more is needed.

This is poppycock, of course. A Mexican or a Chinese or an Indian, for example, cannot transform themselves into Americans simply by moving to this country, any more than I can become a Mexican, a Chinese, or an Indian simply by moving to their countries. Yet contemporary liberals have a vested interest in believing that they can. This is not just a function of immigrant politics, which strongly favors the Democratic Party (hence the Democrats' growing support for voting rights for non-citizens). It also reflects the liberals' (and some libertarians') multicultural faith, which insists that it is morally wrong to make distinctions among different groups of people, let alone to impose a particular way of life—what heretofore has been known as the American way of life—on those who believe, speak, and act differently. Even in our own country.

In short, diversity, not Americanism, is the multicultural touchstone.

What's more, the principle of diversity, taken to its logical extreme, inevitably leads to a *rejection* of Americanism. Indeed, the ideology of multiculturalism has its roots in the radical—and anti-American—New Left and Black Power movements of the 1960s and 1970s. Thus the sorry state of U.S. history and civics education in today's schools and universities, which are dominated by adherents of this intellectual poison. Moreover, when it comes to immigration, multiculturalists actually *prefer* those immigrants who are as unlike ordinary Americans as possible. This stems from their deep-rooted opposition to traditional American society, which they hope to undermine through an influx of non-western peoples and cultures.

This, in fact, describes present U.S. immigration policy, which largely is a product of the 1965 Immigration Act (perhaps Ted Kennedy's most notorious legislative achievement). The 1965 Immigration Act eliminated the legal preferences traditionally given to European immigrants, and opened the floodgates to immigration from less-developed and non-western countries. For example, in 2006 more immigrants came to the United States from Columbia, Peru, Vietnam, and Haiti (not to mention Mexico, China, and India), than from the

United Kingdom, Germany, Italy, and Greece. And once these immigrants arrive here, multiculturalists believe we should accommodate *our* society to the needs and desires of the newcomers, not the other way around. Thus, our government prints election ballots, school books, and welfare applications in foreign languages, while corporate America asks customers to "press one for English."

Patriotic Americans—those who love our country for its people, its history, its culture, and its ideals—reject the multiculturalists' denuded, and ultimately subversive, vision of what it means to be "an American." While the American identity is arguably the most "universal" of all major nationalities—as evidenced by the millions of immigrants the world over who have successfully assimilated into our country over the years—it is not an empty, meaningless concept. It has substance. Being "an American" is *not* the same thing as simply living in the United States. Nor, I would add, is it the same thing as holding U.S. citizenship. After all, a baby born on U.S. soil to an illegal alien is a citizen. This hardly guarantees that this baby will grow up to be *an American.*

So what, then, does it mean to be an American? I suspect that most of us believe, like Supreme Court Justice Potter Stewart in describing pornography, that we "know it when we see it." For example, John Wayne, Amelia Earhart, and Bill Cosby definitely are Americans. The day laborers standing on the street corner probably are not. But how do we put this inner understanding into words? It's not easy. Unlike most other nations on Earth, the American nation is not strictly defined in terms of race or ethnicity or ancestry or religion. George Washington may be the Father of Our Country (in my opinion, the greatest American who ever lived), but there have been in the past, and are today, many millions of patriotic, hardworking, upstanding Americans who are not Caucasian, or Christian, or of Western European ancestry. Yet they are undeniably as American as you or I (by the way, I am Jewish of predominantly Eastern European ancestry). Any definition of "American" that excludes such folks—let alone one that excludes me!—cannot be right.

Consequently, it is just not good enough to say, as some immigration restrictionists do, that this is a "white-majority, Western country." Yes, it is. But so are, for example, Ireland and Sweden and Portugal. Clearly, this level of abstraction does not take us very far towards understanding what it means to be "an American." Nor is it all that helpful to say that this is an English-speaking, predominately Christian country. While I think these features get us closer to the answer, there are millions of English-speaking (and non-English-speaking)

Christians in the world who are not Americans, and millions of non-Christians who are. Certainly, these fundamental historical characteristics are important elements in determining who we are as a nation. Like other restrictionists, I am opposed to public policies that seek, by design or by default, to significantly alter the nation's "demographic profile." Still, it must be recognized that demography alone does not, and cannot, explain what it means to be an American.

So where does that leave us? I think the answer to our question, ultimately, must be found in the realms of ideology and culture. What distinguishes the United States from other nations, and what unites the disparate peoples who make up our country, are our unique political, economic, and social values, beliefs, and institutions. Not race, or religion, or ancestry.

Whether described as a "proposition nation" or a "creedal nation" or simply just "an idea," the United States of America is defined by *our way of life*. This way of life is rooted in the ideals proclaimed in the Declaration of Independence; in the system of personal liberty and limited government established by the Constitution; in our traditions of self-reliance, personal responsibility, and entrepreneurism; in our emphasis on private property, freedom of contract, and merit-based achievement; in our respect for the rule of law; and in our commitment to affording equal justice to all. Perhaps above all, it is marked by our abiding belief that, as Americans, we have been called to a higher duty in human history. We are the "city upon a hill." We are "the last, best hope of earth."

Many immigration restrictionists and so-called traditionalists chafe at the notion that the American people are not defined by "blood and soil." Yet the truth of the matter is, we aren't. One of the greatest patriots who ever graced this nation's history, Teddy Roosevelt, said it best: "Americanism is a matter of the spirit and of the soul." Roosevelt deplored what he called "hyphenated Americanism," which refers to citizens whose primary loyalties lie with their particular ethnic groups or ancestral lands. Such a man, Roosevelt counseled, is to be "unsparingly condemn[ed]."

But Roosevelt also recognized that "if he is heartily and singly loyal to this Republic, then no matter where he was born, he is just as good an American as any one else." Roosevelt's words are not offered here to suggest that all foreigners are equally capable of assimilating into our country. Clearly, they aren't. Nevertheless, the appellation "American" is open to anyone who adopts our way of life and loves this country above all others.

Which brings me to the final, and most difficult, aspect of this question: How do we define the "American way of life"? This is the issue over which our nation's "culture wars" are being fought. Today the country is divided between those who maintain their allegiance to certain historically American values, beliefs, and institutions (but not all—see racial segregation), and those who want to replace them with a very different set of ideas about the role of government, the nature of political and economic liberty, and the meaning of right and wrong. Are both sides in this struggle equally "American"?

Moreover, the "American way of life" has changed over time. We no longer have the Republic that existed in TR's days. The New Deal and Great Society revolutions—enthusiastically supported, I note, by millions of white, Christian, English-speaking citizens—significantly altered the political, economic, and social foundations of this country. Did they also change what it means to be "an American"? Is being an American equally compatible, for example, with support for big government versus small government? the welfare state versus rugged individualism? socialism versus capitalism? And so on. Plainly, this is a much harder historical and intellectual problem than at first meets the eye.

Personally, I do not think the meaning of America is nearly so malleable as today's multiculturalists assume. But neither is it quite as narrow as many restrictionists contend. Nevertheless, I am convinced that being *an American* requires something more than merely living in this country, speaking English, obeying the law, and holding a job (although this would be a very good start!). What this "something more" is, however, is not self-evident, and, indeed, is the subject of increasingly bitter debate in this country.

Yet one thing is certain: If we stray too far from the lines laid down by the Founding Fathers and the generations of great American men and women who built on their legacy, we will cease to be "Americans" in any meaningful sense of the word. As Abraham Lincoln warned during the secession era, "America will never be destroyed from the outside. If we falter and lose our freedoms, it will be because we destroyed ourselves." Today the danger is not armed rebellion, but the slow erasing of the American national character through a process of political and cultural redefinition. If this ever happens, it will be a terrible day for this country, and for the world.

Daniel J. Elazar
The Three Political Cultures

The United States is a single land of great diversity inhabited by what is now a single people of great diversity. The singleness of the country as a whole is expressed through political, cultural, and geographic unity. Conversely, the country's diversity is expressed through its states, subcultures, and sections. In this section, we will focus on the political dimensions of that diversity-in-unity—on the country's overall political culture and its subculture.

Political culture is the summation of persistent patterns of underlying political attitudes and characteristic responses to political concerns that is manifest in a particular political order. Its existence is generally unperceived by those who are part of that order, and its origins date back to the very beginnings of the particular people who share it. Political culture is an intrinsically political phenomenon. As such, it makes its own demands on the political system. For example, the definition of what is "fair" in the political arena—a direct manifestation of political culture—is likely to be different from the definition of what is fair in family or business relationships. Moreover, different political cultures will define fairness in politics differently. Political culture also affects all other questions confronting the political system. For example, many factors go into shaping public expectations regarding government services, and political culture will be significant among them. Political systems, in turn, are in some measure the products of the political cultures they serve and must remain in harmony with their political cultures if they are to maintain themselves.

* * *

Political-culture factors stand out as particularly influential in shaping the operations of the national, state, and local political systems in three ways: (1) by molding the perceptions of the political community (the citizens, the politicians, and the public officials) as to the nature and purposes of politics and its expectations of government and the political process; (2) by influencing the recruitment of specific kinds of people to become active in government and

Published in *American Mosaic: The Impact of Space, Time and Culture on American Politics*, 1994.

politics—as holders of elective offices, members of the bureaucracy, and active political workers; and (3) by subtly directing the actual way in which the art of government is practiced by citizens, politicians, and public officials in the light of their perceptions. In turn, the cultural components of individual and group behavior are manifested in civic behavior as dictated by conscience and internalized ethical standards, in the forms of law-abidingness (or laxity in such matters) adhered to by citizens and officials, and in the character of the positive actions of government.

* * *

The national political culture of the United States is itself a synthesis of three major political subcultures. These subcultures jointly inhabit the country, existing side by side or sometimes overlapping one another. All three are of nationwide proportions, having spread, in the course of time, from coast to coast. Yet each subculture is strongly tied to specific sections of the country, reflecting the streams and currents of migration that have carried people of different origins and backgrounds across the continent in more or less orderly patterns.

Given the central characteristics that define each of the subcultures and their centers of emphasis, the three political subcultures may be called individualistic, moralistic, and traditionalistic. Each reflects its own particular synthesis of the marketplace and the commonwealth.

It is important, however, not only to examine this description and the following ones very carefully but also to abandon the preconceptions associated with such idea-words as individualistic, moralistic, marketplace, and so on. Thus, for example, nineteenth-century individualistic conceptions of minimum intervention were oriented toward *laissez-faire*, with the role of government conceived to be that of a policeman with powers to act in certain limited fields. And in the twentieth century, the notion of what constitutes minimum intervention has been drastically expanded to include such things as government regulation of utilities, unemployment compensation, and massive subventions to maintain a stable and growing economy—all within the framework of the same political culture. The demands of manufacturers for high tariffs in 1865 and the demands of labor unions for worker's compensation in 1965 may well be based on the same theoretical justification that they are aids to the maintenance of a working marketplace. Culture is not static. It must be viewed dynamically and defined so as to include cultural change in its very nature.

The Individualistic Political Culture

The *individualistic political culture* emphasizes the conception of the democratic order as a marketplace. It is rooted in the view that government is instituted for strictly utilitarian reasons, to handle those functions demanded by the people it serves. According to this view, government need not have any direct concern with questions of the "good society" (except insofar as the government may be used to advance some common conception of the good society formulated outside the political arena, just as it serves other functions). Emphasizing the centrality of private concerns, the individualistic political culture places a premium on limiting community intervention—whether governmental or nongovernmental—into private activities, to the minimum degree necessary to keep the marketplace in proper working order. In general, government action is to be restricted to those areas, primarily in the economic realm, that encourage private initiative and widespread access to the marketplace.

The character of political participation in systems dominated by the individualistic political culture reflects the view that politics is just another means by which individuals may improve themselves socially and economically. In this sense politics is a "business," like any other that competes for talent and offers rewards to those who take it up as a career. Those individuals who choose political careers may rise by providing the governmental services demanded of them and, in return, may expect to be adequately compensated for their efforts.

Interpretation of officeholders' obligations under the individualistic political culture vary among political systems and even among individuals within a single political system. Where the standards are high, such people are expected to provide high-quality government services for the general public in the best possible manner in return for the status and economic rewards considered their due. Some who choose political careers clearly commit themselves to such norms; others believe that an office-holder's primary responsibility is to serve him- or herself and those who have supported him or her directly, favoring them at the expense of others. In some political systems, this view is accepted by the public as well as by politicians.

Political life within an individualistic political culture is based on a system of mutual obligations rooted in personal relationships. Whereas in a simple civil society those relationships can be direct ones, those with individualistic political cultures in the United States are usually too complex to maintain face-to-face ties. So the system of mutual obligation is harnessed through political parties, which serve as "business corporations" dedicated to providing the organization necessary to maintain that system. Party regularity is indispensable in the individualistic political culture because it is the means for coordinating individual enterprise in the political arena; it is also the one way of preventing individualism in politics from running wild.

In such a system, an individual can succeed politically, not by dealing with issues in some exceptional way or by accepting some concept of good government and then by striving to implement it, but by maintaining his or her place in the system of mutual obligations. A person can do this by operating according to the norms of his or her particular party, to the exclusion of other political considerations. Such a political culture encourages the maintenance of a party system that is competitive, but not overtly so, in the pursuit of office. Its politicians are interested in office as a means of controlling the distribution of the favors or rewards of government rather than as a means of exercising governmental power for programmatic ends; hence competition may prove less rewarding than accommodation in certain situations.

Since the individualistic political culture eschews ideological concerns in its "business-like" conception of politics, both politicians and citizens tend to look upon political activity as a specialized one—as essentially the province of professionals, of minimum and passing concern to laypersons, and with no place for amateurs to play an active role. Furthermore, there is a strong tendency among the public to believe that politics is a dirty—albeit necessary—business, better left to those who are willing to soil themselves by engaging in it. In practice, then, where the individualistic political culture is dominant, there is likely to be an easy attitude toward the limits of the professional's perquisites. Since a fair amount of corruption is expected in the normal course of things, there is relatively little popular excitement when any is found, unless it is of an extraordinary character. It is as if the public were willing to pay a surcharge for services rendered, rebelling only when the surcharge becomes too heavy. Of course, the judgments as to what is "normal" and what is "extraordinary" are themselves subjective and culturally conditioned.

Public officials, committed to "giving the public what it wants," are normally not willing to initiate new programs or open up new areas of government activity on their own initiative. They will do so when they perceive an overwhelming public demand for them to act, but only then. In a sense, their willingness to expand the functions of government is based on an extension of the *quid pro quo* "favors" system, which serves as the central core of their political relationships. New and better services are the reward they give the public for placing them in office. The value mix and legitimacy of change in the individualistic political culture are directly related to commercial concerns.

The individualistic political culture is ambivalent about the place of bureaucracy in the political order. In one sense, the bureaucratic method of operation flies in the face of the favor system that is central to the individualistic political process. At the same time, the virtues of organizational efficiency appear substantial to those seeking to master the market. In the end, bureaucratic organization is introduced within the framework of the favor system; large segments of the bureaucracy may be insulated from it through the merit system, but the entire organization is pulled into the political environment at crucial points through political appointment at the upper echelons and, very frequently, also through the bending of the merit system to meet political demands.

* * *

The Moralistic Political Culture

To the extent that American society is built on the principles of "commerce" (in the broadest sense) and that the marketplace provides the model for public relationships, all Americans share some of the attitudes that are of great importance in the individualistic political culture. At the same time, substantial segments of the American people operate politically within the framework of two political cultures—the moralistic and traditionalistic political cultures—whose theoretical structures and operational consequences depart significantly from the individualistic pattern at crucial points.

The *moralistic political culture* emphasizes the commonwealth conception as the basis for democratic government. Politics, to this political culture, is considered one of the great human activities: the search for the good society. True, it is a struggle for power, but it is also an effort to exercise power for the betterment of the commonwealth. Accordingly, in the moralistic political culture, both the general public and the politicians conceive of politics as a public activity centered on some notion of the public good and properly devoted to the advancement of the public interest. Good government, then, is measured by the degree to which it promotes the public good and in terms of the honesty, selflessness, and commitment to the public welfare of those who govern.

In the moralistic political culture, individualism is tempered by a general commitment to utilizing communal (preferably nongovernmental, but governmental if necessary) power to intervene in the sphere of "private" activities when it is considered necessary to do so for the public good or the well-being of the community. Accordingly, issues have an important place in the moralistic style of politics, functioning to set the tone for political concern. Government is considered a positive instrument with a responsibility to promote the general welfare, although definitions of what its positive role should be may vary considerably from era to era.

As in the case of the individualistic political culture, the change from nineteenth- to twentieth-century conceptions of what government's positive role should be has been great; for example, support for Prohibition has given way to support for wage and hour regulation. At the same time, care must be taken to distinguish between a predisposition toward communal activism and a desire for federal government activity. For example, many representatives of the moralistic political culture oppose federal aid for urban renewal without in any way opposing community responsibility for urban development. The distinction they make (implicitly, at least) is between what they consider legitimate community responsibility and what they believe to be central government encroachment; or between communitarianism, which they value, and "collectivism," which they abhor. Thus, on some public issues we find certain such representatives taking highly conservative positions despite their positive attitudes toward public activity generally. Such representatives may also prefer government intervention in the social realm—that is, censorship or screening of books and movies—over government intervention in the economy, holding that the former is necessary for the public good and the latter, harmful.

Since the moralistic political culture rests on the fundamental conception that politics exists primarily as a means for coming to grips with the issues and public concerns of civil society, it embraces the notion that politics is ideally a matter of concern for all citizens, not just those who are professionally committed to political careers. Indeed, this political culture considers it the duty of every citizen to participate in the political affairs of his or her commonwealth.

Accordingly, there is a general insistence within this political culture that government service is public service, which places moral obligations upon those who participate in government that are more demanding than the moral obligations of the marketplace. There is an equally general rejection of the notion that the field of politics is a legitimate realm for private economic enrichment.

Of course, politicians may benefit economically because of their political careers, but they are not expected to *profit* from political activity; indeed, they are held suspect if they do.

Since the concept of serving the community is the core of the political relationship, politicians are expected to adhere to it even at the expense of individual loyalties and political friendships. Consequently, party regularity is not of prime importance. The political party is considered a useful political device, but it is not valued for its own sake. Regular party ties can be abandoned with relative impunity for third parties, special local parties, or nonpartisan systems if such changes are believed to be helpful in gaining larger political goals. People can even shift from party to party without sanctions if such change is justified by political belief.

In the moralistic political culture, rejection of firm party ties is not to be viewed as a rejection of politics as such. On the contrary, because politics is considered potentially good and healthy within the context of that culture, it is possible to have highly political nonpartisan systems. Certainly nonpartisanship is instituted not to eliminate politics but to improve it, by widening access to public office for those unwilling or unable to gain office through the regular party structure.

In practice, where the moralistic political culture is dominant today, there is considerably more amateur participation in politics. There is also much less of what Americans consider to be corruption in government and less tolerance of those actions considered to be corrupt. Hence politics does not have the taint it so often bears in the individualistic environment.

By virtue of its fundamental outlook, the moralistic political culture creates a greater commitment to active government intervention in the economic and social life of the community. At the same time, the strong commitment to *communitarianism* characteristic of that political culture tends to channel the interest in government intervention into highly localistic paths, such that a willingness to encourage local government intervention to set public standards does not necessarily reflect a concomitant willingness to allow outside governments equal opportunity to intervene. Not infrequently, public officials themselves will seek to initiate new government activities in an effort to come to grips with problems as yet unperceived by a majority of the citizenry. The moralistic political culture is not committed to either change or the status quo *per se* but, rather, will accept either depending upon the morally defined ends to be gained.

The major difficulty of this political culture in adjusting bureaucracy to the political order is tied to the potential conflict between communitarian principles and the necessity for large-scale organization to increase bureaucratic efficiency, a problem that could affect the attitudes of moralistic culture states toward federal activity of certain kinds. Otherwise, the notion of a politically neutral administrative system creates no problem within the moralistic value system and even offers many advantages. Where merit systems are instituted, they are rigidly maintained.

* * *

The Traditionalistic Political Culture

The *traditionalistic political culture* is rooted in an ambivalent attitude toward the marketplace coupled with a paternalistic and elitist conception of the commonwealth. It reflects an older, precommercial attitude that accepts a substantially hierarchical society as part of the ordered nature of things, authorizing and expecting those at the top of the social structure to take a special and dominant role in government. Like its moralistic counterpart, the traditionalistic political culture accepts government as an actor with a positive role in the community, but in a very limited sphere—mainly that of securing the continued maintenance of the existing social order. To do so, it functions to confine real political power to a relatively small and self-perpetuating group drawn from an established elite who often inherit their "right" to govern through family ties or social position. Accordingly, social and family ties are paramount in a traditionalistic political culture; in fact, their importance is greater than that of personal ties in the individualistic political culture, where, after all is said and done, a person's first responsibility is to him- or herself. At the same time, those who do not have a definite role to play in politics are not expected to be even minimally active as citizens. In many cases, they are not even expected to vote. In return, they are guaranteed that, outside of the limited sphere of politics, family rights (usually labeled "individual rights") are paramount, not to be taken lightly or ignored. As in the individualistic political culture, those active in politics are expected to benefit personally from their activity, though not necessarily through direct pecuniary gain.

Political parties are of minimal importance in a traditionalistic political culture, inasmuch as they encourage a degree of openness and competition that goes against the fundamental grain of an elite-oriented political order.

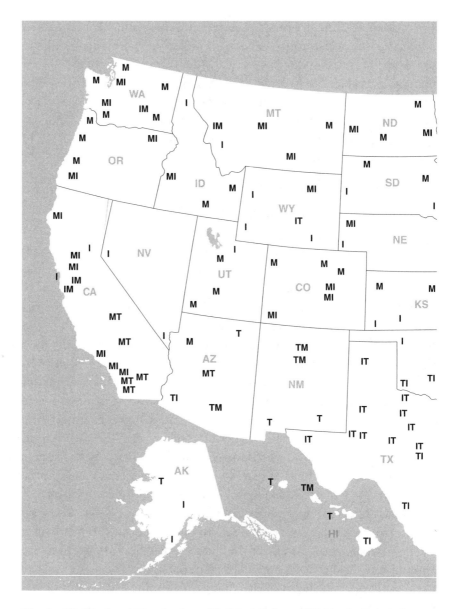

Map 1   The Regional Distribution of Political Cultures Within the States. *Source:* Daniel J. Elazar, *American Federalism: A View from the States*, 3d ed. (New York: Harper and Row Publishers, 1984), pp. 124–25. Reprinted by permission of HarperCollins Publishers.

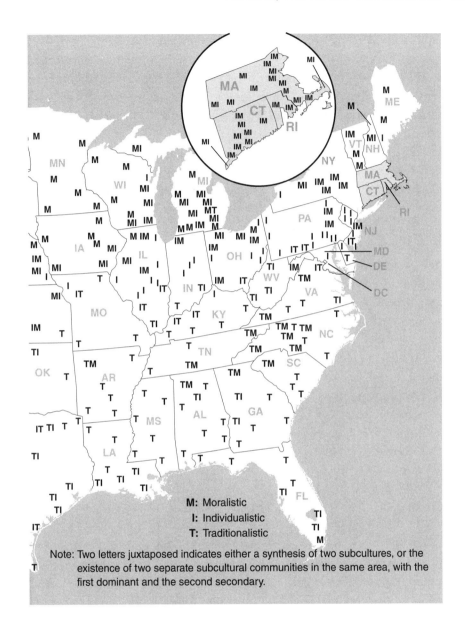

M: Moralistic
I: Individualistic
T: Traditionalistic

Note: Two letters juxtaposed indicates either a synthesis of two subcultures, or the existence of two separate subcultural communities in the same area, with the first dominant and the second secondary.

Their major utility is to recruit people to fill the formal offices of government not desired by the established power-holders. Political competition in a traditionalistic political culture is usually conducted through factional alignments, as an extension of the personalistic politics that is characteristic of the system; hence political systems within the culture tend to have a loose one-party orientation if they have political parties at all.

Practically speaking, a traditionalistic political culture is found only in a society that retains some of the organic characteristics of the pre-industrial social order. "Good government" in the political culture involves the maintenance and encouragement of traditional patterns and, if necessary, their adjustment to changing conditions with the least possible upset. Where the traditionalistic political culture is dominant in the United States today, political leaders play conservative and custodial rather than initiatory roles unless pressed strongly from the outside.

Whereas the individualistic and moralistic political cultures may encourage the development of bureaucratic systems of organization on the grounds of "rationality" and "efficiency" in government (depending on their particular situations), traditionalistic political cultures tend to be instinctively anti-bureaucratic. The reason is that bureaucracy by its very nature interferes with the fine web of informal interpersonal relation-ships that lie at the root of the political system and have been developed by following traditional patterns over the years. Where bureaucracy is introduced, it is generally confined to ministerial functions under the aegis of the established power-holders.

* * *

The Distribution and Impact of Political Subcultures

Map 1 on pages 22–23 shows how migrational patterns have led to the concentration of specific political subcultures in particular states and localities. The basic patterns of political culture were set during the period of the rural-land frontier by three great streams of American migration that began on the East Coast and moved westward after the colonial period. Each stream moved from east to west along more or less fixed paths, following lines of least resistance that generally led them due west from the immediately previous area of settlement.

* * *

Political Culture: Some Caveats

By now the reader has no doubt formed his or her own value judgments as to the relative worth of the three political subcultures. For this reason a particular warning against *hasty* judgments must be added here. Each of the three political subcultures contributes something important to the configuration of the American political system, and each possesses certain characteristics that are inherently dangerous to the survival of that system.

The moralistic political culture, for example, is the primary source of the continuing American quest for the good society, yet there is a noticeable tendency toward inflexibility and narrow-mindedness among some of its representatives. The individualistic political culture is the most tolerant of out-and-out political corruption, yet it has also provided the framework for the integration of diverse groups into the mainstream of American life. When representatives of the moralistic political culture, in their striving for a better social order, try to limit individual freedom, they usually come up against representatives of the individualistic political culture, to whom individual freedom is the cornerstone of their pluralistic order, though not for any noble reasons. Conversely, of course, the moralistic political culture acts as a restraint against the tendencies of the individualistic political culture to tolerate anything as long as it is in the marketplace.

The traditionalistic political culture contributes to the search for continuity in a society whose major characteristic is change; yet in the name of continuity, its representatives have denied African-Americans (as well as Native Americans and Latinos) their civil rights. When it is in proper working order, the traditionalistic culture has produced a unique group of first-rate national leaders from among its elites; but without a first-rate elite to draw upon, traditionalistic political-culture systems degenerate into oligarchies of the lowest level. Comparisons like these should induce caution in any evaluation of a subject that, by its very nature, evokes value judgments.

It is equally important to use caution in identifying individuals and groups as belonging to one cultural type or another on the basis of their public political behavior at a given moment in time. Immediate political responses to the issues of the day may reveal the political culture of the respondents, but not necessarily. Often, in fact, people will make what appear to be the same choices for different reasons—especially in public affairs, where the choices available at any given time are usually quite limited. Deeper analysis of what is behind those responses is usually needed. In other words, the names of the political cultures are not substitutes for the terms *conservative* and *liberal*, and should not be taken as such.

* * *

QUESTIONS

1. Making English a government's official language means that all official documents, ballots, and school instruction would be in English, with no translations provided by the government (although private organizations would be free to provide translations). Should English be the "official" language of the United States? What are the advantages and disadvantages in using only a single language for all government activity? Does having a common language foster assimilation and national unity?

2. Should the United States, as a deliberate strategy, seek to reinforce what it perceives as "shared American values"? If so, how? If not, why not? Should it take the ideology and political values of potential immigrants explicitly into account?

3. Political scientists and historians often refer to "American exceptionalism," or the idea that the United States is unique. For example, compared to other democratic countries, Americans place more emphasis on individual rights and much greater decentralization of political power across the branches and levels of government. Do these outcomes require the kind of shared beliefs discussed by Warshawsky? Or could they arise under the alternative scenarios presented by Song and Elazar?

4. Consider the definitions Elazar presents in his analysis. What would you say are the fundamental differences and similarities among the three approaches?

5. A visitor from another country asks you, "What does it mean to be an American?" What do you say?

2

Constructing the Government: Should the Constitution Be Fundamentally Changed?

Veneration for the Constitution is a classic American value; indeed, it is often said that the essence of being an American is a set of shared values and commitments expressed within the four corners of that document, most notably equality and liberty. The Constitution is the embodiment of those values, celebrated as the first, and most enduring, written constitution in human history. We celebrate the first words of the preamble, "We the people," salute the Framers as men of historic wisdom and judgment, and honor the structures and processes of government.

We also note the practical wisdom of the Framers, in their ability to reconcile competing tensions in creating a government powerful enough to function, but not at the risk of giving majorities the right to trample minority rights. Political theory at the time held that efforts to create democracies inevitably devolved into one of two end results: either mob rule, as majorities took control and used their power to oppress political minorities; or autocracy, as elites assumed control and did not give it up. The many carefully considered elements of constitutional structure—bicameralism, the balance between federal and state power, the equilibrium of checks and balances—have lasted for more than two centuries. And apart from one exceptional period of civil war, the structures have channeled political conflict peacefully.

Is that veneration truly warranted? Sanford Levinson, a professor at the University of Texas Law School, thinks not. He considers the Constitution to be a seriously flawed document in need of fundamental change. As originally written, the Constitution came nowhere near the aspirations of the Preamble, explicitly allowing slavery, and even after amendments retains several antidemocratic elements, including the electoral college; the vastly unequal representation in the Senate, in which Wyoming (population 544,000) has the same voting power as California (population 37 million, over sixty times as large); and lifetime tenure for judges. These features fail to live up to the Preamble, which Levinson considers to be the foundation of the rest of the Constitution—the whole point of the constitutional enterprise. Levinson points out that several key figures of the American founding—Thomas Jefferson especially—believed that the Constitution would require frequent updating. This was the purpose of Article V, which sets out the process for amending the document. And, Levinson notes, many of the features of the Constitution that we venerate were not thought through but were instead the product of pure compromise, in which the Framers took vastly inconsistent positions when necessary in order to secure sufficient support for ratification. So, far from being a philosophically perfect document or system, the Constitution created a cumbersome and inequitable system, one that no other democratic system has chosen to copy since.

The problem with amending the Constitution is that the features Levinson considers most offensive—especially the unequal representation in the Senate—are virtually impossible to change. Article V specifies that no state can be deprived of its equal representation in the Senate without its consent (something that no state could ever be expected to do). The only recourse is a constitutional convention, in which delegates would consider fundamental reform. Levinson regards this as essential in order to allow the national government to respond to the challenge of modern economic and political times.

Eric Lane and Michael Oreskes take the more traditional stance that the Constitution is fine as it is; they argue that it is the people who must change. The key problem is that people do not understand the purpose of checks and balances or other features of the Constitution that frustrate their policy demands. But the Constitution is not just a mechanism for giving each of us what we want: the Constitution, they argue, is a vehicle for protecting liberty and providing the opportunity for individuals to pursue what they want through political and economic freedom. Instead of evaluating our legislators by how well they fulfill their constitutional duties, we base our evaluation on how much pork they can deliver to the folks at home. We are looking for an institutional fix through constitutional change when the problem is that our own fidelity to constitutional principles is waning. Evidence that the Constitution got it right comes from the fact that it produced the richest, freest, and most powerful country that has ever existed.

If there is one area of agreement between Levinson and Lane and Oreskes, it is that democracy is fragile, though they arrive at that conclusion for different reasons: Levinson because government fails to give the public what it wants, Lane and Oreskes because we are using our power to demand the wrong things.

Sanford Levinson

The Ratification Referendum: Sending the Constitution to a New Convention for Repair

The U.S. Constitution is radically defective in a number of important ways. Unfortunately, changing the Constitution is extremely difficult, for both political and constitutional reasons. But the difficulty of the task does not make it any less important that we first become aware of the magnitude of the deficiencies in the current Constitution and then turn our minds, as a community of concerned citizens, to figuring out potential solutions. This [reading] is organized around the conceit that Americans in 2008 will have the opportunity to vote on the following proposal: "Shall Congress call a constitutional convention empowered to consider the adequacy of the Constitution, and, if thought necessary, to draft a new constitution that, upon completion, will be submitted to the electorate for its approval or disapproval by majority vote? Unless and until a new constitution gains popular approval, the current Constitution will continue in place."

Although such a referendum would be unprecedented with regard to the U.S. Constitution, there is certainly nothing "un-American" about such a procedure. As Professor John J. Dinan has noted in his recent comprehensive study of what he terms "the American state constitutional tradition," fourteen American states in their own constitutions explicitly give the people an opportunity

Published in *Our Undemocratic Constitution: Where the Constitution Goes Wrong (And How We the People Can Correct It)*, 2006.

"to periodically vote on whether a convention should be called." Article XIX of the New York Constitution, for example, provides that the state electorate be given the opportunity every twenty years to vote on the following question: "Shall there be a convention to revise the constitution and amend the same?" Should the majority answer in the affirmative, then the voters in each senate district will elect three delegates "at the next ensuring general election," while the state-wide electorate "shall elect fifteen delegates-at-large." It should occasion no surprise that one author has described such a "mandatory referendum" as a means of "enforcing the people's right to reform their government."

It is no small matter to give people a choice with regard to the mechanisms—as well as the abstract principles—by which they are to be governed. The imagined referendum would allow "We the People of the United States of America," in whose name the document is ostensibly "ordain[ed]," to examine the fit between our national aspirations, set out in the Preamble to the Constitution, and the particular means chosen to realize those goals.

I am assuming that those reading this * * * are fellow Americans united by a deep and common concern about the future of our country. * * * I hope to convince you that, as patriotic Americans truly committed to the deepest principles of the Constitution, we should vote yes and thus trigger a new convention. My task is to persuade you that the Constitution we currently live under is grievously flawed, even in some ways a "clear and present danger" to achieving the laudable and inspiring goals to which this country professes to be committed, including republican self-government.

I believe that the best way to grasp the goals of our common enterprise is to ponder the inspiring words of the Preamble to the Constitution:

> We the People of the United States, in Order to form a more perfect Union, establish Justice, insure domestic tranquility, provide for the common defence, promote the general Welfare, and secure the Blessings of Liberty to ourselves and our Posterity, do ordain and establish this Constitution for the United States of America.

It is regrettable that law professors rarely teach and that courts rarely cite the Preamble, for it is *the single most important part* of the Constitution. The reason is simple: It announces the *point* of the entire enterprise. The 4,500 or so words that followed the Preamble in the original, unamended Constitution were all in effect merely means that were thought to be useful to achieving the great aims set out above. It is indeed the ends articulated in the Preamble that justify the means of our political institutions. And to the extent that the means turn out to be counterproductive, then we should revise them.

It takes no great effort to find elements in the original Constitution that run counter to the Preamble. It is impossible for us today to imagine how its authors squared a commitment to the "Blessings of Liberty" with the toleration and support of chattel slavery that is present in various articles of the Constitution. The most obvious example is the bar placed on Congress's ability to forbid the participation by Americans in the international slave trade until 1808. The most charitable interpretation of the framers, articulated by Frederick Douglass, is that they viewed these compromises with the acknowledged evil of slavery as temporary; the future would see its eradication through peaceful constitutional processes.

One might believe that the Preamble is incomplete because, for example, it lacks a commitment to the notion of equality. Political scientist Mark Graber has suggested that the reference to "*our* Posterity" suggests a potentially unattractive limitation of our concerns *only* to members of the American political community, with no notice taken of the posterity of other societies, whatever their plight. Even if one would prefer a more explicitly cosmopolitan Preamble, I find it hard to imagine rejecting any of the overarching values enunciated there. In any event, I am happy to endorse the Preamble as the equivalent of our creedal summary of America's civil religion.

There are two basic responses to the discovery that ongoing institutional practices are counterproductive with regard to achieving one's announced goals. One is to adjust the practices in ways that would make achievement of the aims more likely. This is, often, when we mean by the very notion of rationality: One does not persist in behaviors that are acknowledged to make more difficult the realization of one's professed hopes. Still, a second response, which has its own rationality, is to adjust the goals to the practices. Sometimes, this makes very good sense if one comes to the justified conclusion that the goals may be utopian. In such cases, it is a sign of maturity to recognize that we will inevitably fall short in our aims and that "the best may be enemy of the good" if we are tempted to throw over quite adequate, albeit imperfect, institutions in an attempt to attain the ideal.

Perhaps one might even wish to defend the framer's compromises with slavery on the ground that they were absolutely necessary to the achievement of the political union of the thirteen states. One must believe that such a union, in turn, was preferable to the likely alternative, which would have been the creation of two or three separate countries along the Atlantic coast. Political scientist David Hendrickson has demonstrated that many of the framers—and many other theorists as well—viewed history as suggesting a high probability that such separate countries would have gone to war with one another and made impossible any significant measure of "domestic tranquility." Hendrickson well describes the Constitution as a "peace pact" designed to prevent the possibility of war. If there is one thing we know, it is that unhappy compromises must often be made when negotiating such pacts. Of course, American slaves—and their descendants—could scarcely be expected to be so complacently accepting of these compromises, nor, of course, should *any* American who takes seriously the proclamation of the Pledge of Allegiance that ours is a system that takes seriously the duty to provide "liberty and justice for all."

Not only must we restrain ourselves from expecting too much of any government; we must also recognize that the Preamble sets out potentially conflicting goals. It is impossible to maximize the achievement of all of the great ends of the Constitution. To take an obvious example, providing for the "common defence" may require on occasion certain incursions into the "Blessings of Liberty." One need only refer to the military draft, which was upheld in 1918 by the Supreme Court against an attack claiming that it constituted the "involuntary servitude"—that is, slavery—prohibited by the Thirteenth Amendment. We also properly accept certain limitations on the freedom of the press with regard, say, to publishing certain information—the standard example is troop movements within a battle zone—deemed to be vital to American defense interests. The year 2005 ended with the beginning of a great national debate about the propriety of warrantless interceptions of telephone calls and other incursions on traditional civil liberties in order, ostensibly, to protect ourselves against potential terrorists.

Even if one concedes the necessity of adjusting aims in light of practical realities, it should also be readily obvious that one can easily go overboard. At the very least, one should always be vigilant in assessing such adjustments lest one find, at the end of the day, that the aims have been reduced to hollow shells. It is also necessary to ask if a rationale supporting a given adjustment that might well have been convincing at time A necessarily continues to be present at time B. Practical exigencies that required certain political compromises in 1787 no longer obtain today. We have long since realized this about slavery.

It is time that we apply the same critical eye to the compromise of 1787 that granted all states an equal vote in the Senate.

To criticize that particular compromise—or any of the other features of the Constitution that I shall examine below—is not necessarily to criticize the founders themselves. My project—and, therefore, your own vote for a new convention, should you be persuaded by what follows—requires no denigration of the founders. They were, with some inevitable exceptions, an extraordinary group of men who performed extraordinary deeds, including drafting a Constitution that started a brand-new governmental system. By and large, they deserve the monuments that have been erected in their honor. But they themselves emphasized the importance—indeed, necessity—of learning from experience.

They were, after all, a generation that charted new paths by overturning a centuries-long notion of the British constitutional order because it no longer conformed to their own sense of possibility (and fairness). They also, as it happened, proved ruthlessly willing to ignore the limitations of America's "first constitution," the Articles of Confederation. Although Article XIII of that founding document required unanimous approval by the thirteen state legislatures before any amendment could take affect, Article VII of the Constitution drafted in Philadelphia required the approval of only nine of the thirteen states, and the approval was to be given by state conventions rather than by the legislatures.

The most important legacies handed down by the founding generation were, first, a remarkable willingness to act in bold and daring ways when they believed that the situation demanded it, coupled with the noble visions first of the Declaration of Independence and then of the Preamble. Both are as inspiring—and potentially disruptive—today as when they were written more than two centuries ago. But we should also be inspired by the copious study that Madison and others made of every available history and analysis of political systems ranging from ancient Greece to the Dutch republic and the British constitutional order. We best honor the framers by taking the task of creating a republican political order as seriously as they did and being equally willing to learn from what the history of the past 225 years, both at home and abroad, can teach us about how best to achieve and maintain such an order. At the time of its creation, we could legitimately believe that we were the only country committed to democratic self-governance. That is surely no longer the case, and we might well have lessons to learn from our co-ventures in that enterprise.

To the extent that experience teaches us that the Constitution in significant aspects demeans "the consent of the governed" and has become an impediment to achieving the goals of the Preamble, we honor rather than betray the founders by correcting their handiwork.

Overcoming Veneration

* * * I suspect * * * that at least some readers might find it difficult to accept even the possibility that our Constitution is seriously deficient because they venerate the Constitution and find the notion of seriously criticizing it almost sacrilegious.

In an earlier book, *Constitutional Faith*, I noted the tension between the desire of James Madison that Americans "venerate" their Constitution and the distinctly contrasting views of his good friend Thomas Jefferson that, instead, the citizenry regularly subject it to relentless examination. Thus, whatever may have been Jefferson's insistence on respecting what he called the "chains" of the Constitution, he also emphasized that the "Creator has made the earth for the living, not the dead." It should not be surprising, then, that he wrote to Madison in 1789, "No society can make a perpetual constitution, or even a perpetual law."

Jefferson and Madison might have been good friends and political associates, but they disagreed fundamentally with regard to the wisdom of subjecting the Constitution to critical analysis. Jefferson was fully capable of writing that "[w]e may consider each generation as a distinct nation, with a right, by the will of its majority, to bind themselves, but none to bind the succeeding generation, more than the inhabitants of another country." His ultimate optimism about the Constitution lay precisely in its potential for change: "Happily for us, that when we find our constitutions defective and insufficient to secure the happiness of our people, we can assemble with all the coolness of philosophers, and set it to rights, while every other nation on earth must have recourse to arms to amend or restore their constitutions." * * *

Madison, however, would have none of this. He treated 1787 almost as a miraculous and singular event. Had he been a devotee of astrology, he might have said that the stars were peculiarly and uniquely aligned to allow the drafting of the Constitution and then its ratification. Though Madison was surely too tactful to mention this, part of the alignment was the absence of the famously contentious Jefferson and John Adams. Both were 3,000 miles across the sea, where they were serving as the first ambassadors from the new United States to Paris and London, respectively. Moreover, it certainly did not hurt that Rhode Island had refused to send any delegates at all and therefore had no opportunity to make almost inevitable mischief, not to mention being unable to vote in an institutional structure where the vote of one state could make a big difference. And, if pressed, Madison would presumably have agreed that the Constitutional Convention—and the ratifying conventions thereafter—would never have succeeded had the delegates included American slaves, Native Americans, or women in the spirit of Abigail Adams. She had famously—and altogether unsuccessfully—told her husband that leaders of the new nation should "remember the ladies." One need not see the framers in Philadelphia as an entirely homogeneous group—they were not—in order to realize that the room was devoid of those groups in America that were viewed as merely the *objects*, and not the active *subjects*, of governance.

Madison sets out his views most clearly in the *Federalist*, No. 49, where he explicitly takes issue with Jefferson's proposal for rather frequent constitutional conventions that would consider whether "alter[ation]" of the constitution might be desirable. Madison acknowledges the apparent appeal, in a system where "the people are the only legitimate fountain of power," of "appeal[ing] to the people themselves." However, "there appear to be insuperable objections against the proposed recurrence to the people." Perhaps the key objection is that *"frequent appeal to the people would carry an implication of some defect in the government [and] deprive the government of that veneration which time bestows on every thing, and without which perhaps the wisest and freest governments would not possess the requisite stability."* Only "a nation of philosophers" can forgo this emotion of veneration—and, therefore, feel free of guilt-ridden anxiety about the idea of constitutional change. However, "a nation of philosophers is as little to be expected as the philosophical race of kings wished for by Plato."

Madison is thus fearful of "disturbing the public tranquillity by interesting too strongly the public passions." The success of Americans in replacing a defective Articles of Confederation with a better Constitution does not constitute a precedent for future action. We should "recollect," he says, "that all the existing constitutions were formed in the midst of a danger which repressed the passions most unfriendly to order and concord." Moreover, the people at large possessed "an enthusiastic confidence . . . in their patriotic leaders," which, he says, fortunately "stifled the ordinary diversity of opinions on great national questions."

He is extremely skeptical that the "future situations in which we must expect to be usually placed" will "present any equivalent security against the danger" of an excess of public passion, disrespect for leaders, and the full play of diverse opinions. In case there is any doubt, he writes of his fear that the "*passions*, therefore, not the *reasons*, of the public would sit in judgment."

Madison's view of his fellow Americans was far closer to that of Alexander Hamilton, with whom he had coauthored the *Federalist*. One can doubt that Madison expressed any reservations when hearing Hamilton, addressing his fellow delegates to the Philadelphia convention on June 18, 1787, denounce the conceit that "the voice of the people" is "the voice of God." On the contrary, said Hamilton: "The people are turbulent and changing; they seldom judge or determine right." Although Madison was not opposed to constitutional amendment as such, he clearly saw almost no role for a public that would engage in probing questions suggesting that there might be serious "defects" in the Constitution. Only philosophers (like himself?) or, perhaps, "patriotic leaders" could be trusted to engage in dispassionate political dialogue and reasoning. In contrast, the general public should be educated to feel only "veneration" for their Constitution rather than be encouraged to use their critical faculties and actually assess the relationship between the great ends set out in the Preamble and the instruments devised for their realization.

* * *

This is a mistake. To the extent that we continue thoughtlessly to venerate, and therefore not subject to truly critical examination, our Constitution, we are in the position of the battered wife who continues to profess the "essential goodness" of her abusive husband. To stick with the analogy for a moment, it may well be the case that the husband, when sober or not gambling, is a decent, even loving, partner. The problem is that such moments are more than counterbalanced by abusive ones, even if they are relatively rare. And he becomes especially abusive when she suggests the possibility of marital counseling and attendant change. Similarly, that there are good features of our Constitution should not be denied. But there are also significantly abusive ones, and it is time for us to face them rather than remain in a state of denial.

Trapped Inside the Article V Cage

The framers of the Constitution were under no illusion that they had created a perfect document. The best possible proof for this proposition comes from

George Washington himself. As he wrote to his nephew Bushrod two months after the conclusion of the Philadelphia convention over which he had presided, *"The warmest friends and the best supporters the Constitution has do not contend that it is free from imperfections*; but they found them unavoidable and are sensible if evil is likely to arise there from, the remedy must come here-after." Sounding a remarkably Jeffersonian note, Washington noted that the "People (for it is with them to Judge) can, as they will have the advantage of experience on their Side, decide with as much propriety on the alteration[s] and amendment[s] which are necessary." Indeed, wrote the man described as the Father of Our Country, "I do not think we are more inspired, have more wisdom, or possess more virtue, than those who will come after us."

Article V itself is evidence of the recognition of the possibility—and inevitable reality—of imperfection, else they would have adopted John Locke's suggestion in a constitution that he drafted for the Carolina colonies that would have made the document unamendable. It is an unfortunate reality, though, that Article V, practically speaking, brings us all too close to the Lockean dream (or nightmare) of changeless stasis.

As University of Houston political scientist Donald Lutz has conclusively demonstrated, the U.S. Constitution is the most difficult to amend of any constitution currently existing in the world today. Formal amendment of the U.S. Constitution generally requires the approval of two-thirds of each of the two houses of our national Congress, followed by the approval of three-quarters of the states (which today means thirty-eight of the fifty states). Article V does allow the abstract possibility that amendments could be proposed through the aegis of a constitutional convention called by Congress upon the petition of two-thirds of the states; such proposals, though, would still presumably have to be ratified by the state legislatures or, in the alternative, as was done with regard to the Twenty-first Amendment repealing the prohibition of alcohol required by the Eighteenth Amendment, by conventions in each of the states. As a practical matter, though, Article V makes it next to impossible to amend the Constitution with regard to genuinely controversial issues, even if substantial—and intense—majorities advocate amendment.

As I have written elsewhere, some significant change functionally similar to "amendment" has occurred informally, outside of the procedures set out by Article V. One scholar has aptly described this as a process of "constitutional change off-the-books." Yale law professor Bruce Ackerman has written several brilliant books detailing the process of "non-Article V" amendment, and I warmly commend them to the reader. Yet it is difficult to argue that such informal amendment has occurred, or is likely to occur, with regard to the basic *structural* aspects of the American political system with which this book is primarily concerned.

It is one thing to argue, as Ackerman has done, that the New Deal worked as a functional amendment of the Constitution by giving Congress significant new powers to regulate the national economy. Similarly, one could easily argue that the president, for good or for ill, now possesses powers over the use of armed forces that would have been inconceivable to the generation of the framers. Whatever the text of the Constitution may say about the power of Congress to "declare war" or whatever the original understanding of this clause, it is hard to deny that many presidents throughout our history have successfully chosen to take the country to war without seeking a declaration of war (or, in some cases, even prior congressional approval of any kind). Ackerman and David Golove have also persuasively argued that the Treaty Clause, which requires that two-thirds of the Senate assent to any treaty, has been transformed through the use of "executive agreements." Although such agreements are unmentioned in the text of the Constitution, presidents have frequently avoided the strictures of the Treaty Clause by labeling an "agreement" what earlier would have been viewed as a "treaty." Thus, the North American Free Trade Agreement did not have to leap the hurdles erected by the Treaty Clause; instead, it was validated by majority votes of both the House of Representatives and the Senate.

These developments are undoubtedly important, and any complete analysis of our constitutional system should take account of such flexibility. But we should not overemphasize our system's capacity to change, and it is *constitutional stasis* rather than the potential for adaptation that is my focus.

* * *

* * * One cannot, as a practical matter, litigate the obvious inequality attached to Wyoming's having the same voting power in the Senate as California. Nor can we imagine even President George W. Bush, who has certainly not been a shrinking violet with regard to claims of presidential power, announcing that Justice John Paul Stevens—appointed in 1976 and embarking on this fourth decade of service on the Supreme Court at the age of eighty-six—is simply "too old" or has served "long enough," and that he is therefore nominating, and asking the Senate to confirm, a successor to Justice Stevens in spite of the awkward fact that the justice has not submitted his resignation.

In any event, * * * the Constitution makes it unacceptably difficult to achieve the inspiring goals of the Preamble and, therefore, warrants our disapproval. * * *

Although I am asking you to take part in a hypothetical referendum and to vote no with regard to the present Constitution, I am *not* asking you to imagine simply tearing it up and leaping into the unknown of a fanciful "state of nature." All you must commit yourself to is the proposition that the Constitution is sufficiently flawed to justify calling a new convention authorized to scrutinize all aspects of the Constitution and to suggest such changes as are felt to be desirable. The new convention would be no more able to bring its handiwork into being by fiat than were the framers in Philadelphia. All proposals would require popular approval in a further national referendum. This leaves open the possibility that, even after voting to trigger the convention, you could ultimately decide that the "devil you know" (the present Constitution) is preferable to the "devil you don't" (the proposed replacement). But the important thing, from my perspective, is to recognize that there are indeed "devilish" aspects of our present Constitution that should be confronted and, if at all possible, exorcised. To complete this metaphor, one might also remember that "the devil is in the details." * * *

Eric Lane and Michael Oreskes

We

We live in a remarkable political age. More people than ever before in history, possibly a majority of all the people on earth, live under governments that could reasonably be described as democracies. The enormity of this can only be grasped by going back * * * to that moment in the late 1700s when democracy as we now know it barely existed in the world. Indeed, the word *democracy* was essentially an insult, a synonym for *mob rule*. Yes, there were places where the king had ceded some measure of power to aristocracies or even to semirepresentative parliaments. There were also commercial cities in Europe that had allowed considerable popular participation in decision making.

But nowhere was there anything like what a group of men, desperately

Published in *The Genius of America: How the Constitution Saved Our Country and Why It Can Again*, 2007.

trying to save their fledgling country, invented in Philadelphia in the summer of 1787. They wrote "a Constitution which . . . has brought such a happy order out of so gloomy a chaos," James Madison said of his handiwork many years later. They wrote a Constitution that invented a new kind of representative government. It ushered in what we can now see as the Age of Democracy in which "representative government bottomed on the principle of popular sovereignty . . . has become the political norm." In a recent book on the rise of democracy, the British scholar John Dunn finds Madison's pride understandable given the far-reaching effects of his invention: "It secured the new Republic extremely effectively, and, as we now know, for a very long time. In doing so, it turned the United States into the most politically definite, the best consolidated and the most politically self-confident society on earth. It also, over time . . . opened the way for it to become overwhelmingly the most powerful state in human history."

Quite an impressive summer's work.

But where are we in the life span of this invention? The American experiment has now lasted longer than any democracy in history. (Athens, for example, lasted only around 170 years as a democracy.) It has also spawned and inspired many others to pursue democracy. After much spillage of words and blood across the twentieth century, there is no longer even a serious intellectual challenger to representative democracy as the best and most legitimate way to organize government. What a long way we have come from 1787! "The United States is now the oldest enduring republic in world history, with a set of political institutions and traditions that have stood the test of time," wrote the historian Joseph J. Ellis.

The framers would have been stunned by this success. They knew the lessons of history were against them. They had learned from experience that individuals set free pursued their own interests. Large numbers of individuals pursuing their own interests led to chaos. Chaos invited dictators, homegrown or external, to intervene to restore order, snuffing out the very liberty people had fought to establish. They understood this cycle from their reading and, more, from the first eleven years of their own nation, which by 1787 seemed to them to be descending into the gloomy chaos Madison wrote of later.

That is why they saw democracy as "fragile."

Fragile because the framers had come to understand that in pursuit of their self-interests, Americans, like everyone else, would be willing to trample the "democracy" of others thus endangering their own.

Fragile because it was dependent on the broad participation of Americans in the nation's political processes.

Fragile because it was dependent on the willingness of Americans to acquiesce to the results of such a process.

Fragile because of the Constitution's delicate arrangement of checks and balances.

Fragile because it was a system for institutionalizing compromise. There would always be citizens searching for a more perfect system, some system that promised more wealth, or more security, or more equality, or a more glorious future, or just more of whatever it is they particularly wanted.

That was the challenge the framers confronted in 1787. People wanted what they wanted for themselves. The framers' solution, wonderfully modern and, in 1787, totally original, was to adopt a more realistic view of people and adapt their design for government to that view. They enlisted vice "on the side of virtue." They set out to prove how a representative democracy could operate without special public virtue, how "an avaricious society can form a government able to defend itself against the avarice of its members." In other words, this was not a government as good as its people. It was a government designed to produce results better than the desires of each individual person! And that is how the people ensured their own liberty. Out of many one, *E Pluribus Unum.*

To accept democracy as it emerged from Philadelphia meant to accept, as Franklin said, that this was no perfect system, just the closest to perfection a human design could come.

The framers worried that their new democracy would last only a few years. But amazingly it succeeded. Two hundred and twenty years later, the many offshoots of modern representative democracy have triumphed around the world. How ironic, then, that its original American version, with its complicated checks and balances, faces meaningful challenge in the place where it was born.

This is not the first such challenge in American history, of course, and we hope not the last. It won't be if we face it, as previous generations faced their constitutional challenges. The challenge takes new forms each time. But at heart the issue is always the same: We want what we want, and we are convinced that the system that is stopping us is wrong, flawed, broken or outmoded.

This is the essence of our present challenge. The bond between government and governed has become strained. Americans are deeply frustrated with the workings of their government. They see it as unresponsive, unrepresentative, ineffective, crippling. Can you image even a handful of Americans acknowledging today that the purpose of their government is to produce results better than the desires of the people as individuals? Not likely.

We Americans love the framers. We consume books about them and revere their words. But we have lost our connection to what they actually invented and how that invention over time created in us what we have come to call a Constitutional Conscience. We have lost the narrative thread that connects us to the story of our constitutional democracy. That story tells us two things. First, how the framers learned a series of lessons between 1776 and 1787 and used these lessons to craft our government, the blueprint for which became the Constitution. And second, how we, the people, created a Constitutional Conscience from the essential meaning of that Constitution—its freedoms and its processes and tradeoffs—and guided by these principles were then able to adapt time and again through our history to an evolving America.

This narrative thread is vital to us. It is the story that makes us Americans, ties us to our government and ties our government to us. Without it we have begun, without being totally conscious of what we are doing, to drift away from our constitutional system. We are drifting away because our knowledge of our system has grown thin. From the 1960s onward, according to Derek Bok, civic education has been declining and by the 1980s had nearly vanished. "It is striking how little energy is devoted to trying to engage citizens more actively in the affairs of government. Civic education in the public schools has been almost totally eclipsed by a preoccupation with preparing the workforce of a global economy. Most universities no longer treat the preparation of citizens as an explicit goal of their curriculum."

Reports have documented this steady decline in civic understanding. In 1998, the Department of Education found that 75 percent of high school seniors were "not proficient in civics; one third lacked even a basic comprehension of how the government operates, while only 9 percent could give two reasons why citizens should participate in the democratic process." A report in 2002 concluded "that the nation's citizenry is woefully under-educated about the fundamentals of our American Democracy."

This lack of connection is producing a dangerous spiral of frustration and disenchantment. On the one hand, Americans take the existence of our democracy for granted, while, on the other hand, being frustrated with its workings. This produces a dangerous spiral of frustration and disenchantment. Observed

Bok: "Americans have expectations for politics and the political process that are often unrealistic. Convinced that presidents can often accomplish more than is humanly possible, that legislators should be able to arrive at sensible decisions without prolonged disagreement or controversy, and that politicians should refrain from pandering to the voters yet still reflect the views of their constituents, the public seems fated to endure repeated disappointment over the government and those who run it."

Some Americans respond to this disappointment by demanding changes in the system, others by distancing themselves from the system, which leaves those who stay engaged more powerful to push for the agenda they want.

Those demands for change come in two basic forms, although proponents of each argue that their proposals would make the system more democratic by shifting power. There are the Lloyd Cutlers, Oliver Norths and Dick Cheneys who want to shift more power to the president so he can either force the rest of the government to respond or just act without being fettered by the process. And there are others who want to shift more power directly to citizens so they can force government to respond, or simply go around the process. That they want such changes is within their rights. But any meaningful argument for them must occur in the context of the lessons the framers learned long ago. Without this context, we risk making changes that dismantle what has been proven right about our system and even endanger the freedoms it was built to guarantee.

It might be helpful to restate those lessons, in a simple form that everyone can paste on their refrigerator.

The framers boiled their experience down to a Constitution. We have boiled their experience down to these five lessons.

1. Everyone is selfish. This is not to say that people cannot act well or perform acts of great nobility. But essentially people act to achieve their own self-interest, particularly at the level at which government operates: regulating conduct and redistributing wealth. People are, however, willing to trade one benefit for another and sometimes even sacrifice a narrow interest for a broader one that they feel will ultimately do them more good. The government's job is to find those areas of common ground. That is where we can build a common good.

2. Government is the steam valve of society. It funnels and relieves the pressures that build from competing interests.

3. Political process is more important than product. Consensus around a flawed plan can still produce great progress. (The Constitution itself is the best example.) But a "perfect plan" without consensus will only produce conflict and deadlock. (The Clinton health care debacle is one example.) Respect for the system is thus a vital prerequisite for progress. When respect is in such short supply, it is no surprise that progress is, as well.

4. The strength of consensus is directly related to the breadth of representation and the depth of deliberation. A sound-bite society where civic education has vanished has little basis for forging strong consensus.

5. Every interest is a special one. The founders would no doubt be amazed by the scale and power of modern corporations and trade unions. But they would have no difficulty at all with the idea that everyone has wants and desires and that these drive their views and their allegiances to groups and factions. To them, the only meaningful definition of the *common good* would be the agreement that emerged from an inclusive political and legislative process to resolve competing (special) interests.

Our world is very different from that of the framers. People have powers now they could not have dreamed of then. Information, the lifeblood of democracy, moved then at the speed of sail. It moves now at the speed of light.

But there is no evidence that people have changed. Therefore, we see no reason to abandon the lessons the framers formed about people or the system they built from those lessons. Indeed, some of the changes, most particularly the speed with which society can now move, only reinforce the need for care in our political deliberations and for the speed bumps in the process that prevent us from rushing to judgment. That is what the framers built for us.

Recent experience reminds us that we make mistakes as a country when we move away from how our system was built to work. When people say now they wish the Congress and the media had done more to question the march to war in Iraq, they are saying, too, that they wish the leaders of Congress and of the press had done more to assert their authority, and fulfill their responsibilities, under, respectively, Article I and the First Amendment to the Constitution. Even many proponents of the war concede now that the checks and balances did not work well. We believe this failure was due to the weakening of our sense of constitutional roles, of our Constitutional Conscience.

We as Americans need to continue to remind ourselves of the framers' concern that democracy was fragile.

So far, unlike in the past, no one is openly arguing for an abandonment of democracy. Indeed, what many Americans think we need is what they see as more democracy. Both the proponents of strengthened presidential power and the proponents of direct democracy argue that their proposals would make the system more representative of the general public: the president as the only nationally elected official, and direct democracy as the only means to involve Americans more directly in the decision-making processes. Either way, the argument is for a more direct engagement and less entanglement in Washington process. We understand those feelings. They rise historically from a treasured strain of American belief running back to, at least, Tom Paine, the Declaration of Independence and the Articles of Confederation.

But we must not forget the warning of the framers that the most likely undoing of democracy would be in the name of more democracy.

That thought is why we wrote this book. We wanted to pick up the dropped narrative thread of the American democratic story, to remind ourselves that the democratic thinking of 1776 is only the first half of our legacy. The second half was born of Madison and his colleagues in 1787. The framers in 1787 saw liberty and direct democracy is inadequate on their own to ensure the very democracy they purported to further. For in the real world in which government works, this directly democratic perspective translates into one group getting its way over the interest of other groups or one branch, whether a powerful legislature or monarchical president, getting too much power over everyone else.

The framers' ideas transformed the thirst for liberty into a real nation. Madison and his colleagues invented a form of government whose purpose, as the historian Gordon Wood summed it up, was not to transcend our differences but to reconcile them.

Americans' current frustration and anger with their government is sapping their commitment to the principles that have made the country work. Rather than drift away from the Constitution, we should renew our connection to it. We should remember that consultation and process and debate are good things, even when they slow and complicate decisions. Most of all, we should remind each other that compromise is a show of strength, not weakness. Reaffirming these constitutional principles will actually address our frustration better than inventing something different, or more accurately, returning to what did not work between 1776 and 1787.

People say that what they want is compromise and consensus. The framers believed in that. It is why the most important and radical word in the Constitution was the first word, *We*. The government was the people and is the people. The power of each branch of government is a grant from the people, and each branch to one degree or another is accountable to them. Nothing like this had ever been created before. One British political leader, comparing the evolution of Britain's unwritten constitution to the seemingly overnight drafting of the U.S. Constitution, called the latter "the most wonderful work ever struck off at a given time by the brain and purpose of man."

But Americans in practice, in the grind of life, are no longer seeing it this way. For one thing, they do not connect their desire for consensus with the Constitution's governmental design. For another, they routinely, and predictably, define the consensus they want as the achievement of their own goals, not something larger. Americans' demands on government are today broad and deeply diverse. And when they are in an uncompromising mood, when they are divided fifty-fifty, red from blue, their representative government reflects this division, and it stalls.

The problem is not that government is unrepresentative. The problem, if you want to call it that, is that the government is very representative. The message we are hearing is that our government does not work. The message we should be hearing is that our government is a reflection of our own divisions. What we need is not a new system of government. We need a renewed willingness to work out our differences and find compromises, consensus and that other now-popular phrase, common ground.

The purpose of American-style democracy is not to guarantee each of us what we want individually. It is to give each of us as large an opportunity as possible to pursue what we want within the limits the Constitution and our Constitutional Conscience impose on us. This tension between individual liberty and community restraint has over time produced a great deal of good for a great many people and worked better than any alternative yet tried. It is still the best system for our sprawling, complicated nation.

To say that ours is the best system is not to say that it is a perfect system. It is not and never will be perfect. It can't be. It is composed of we, the people, with all our flaws. That is the point. We make it work. Our drive.

Our demands. Our participation! In 1888, the poet and editor James Russell Lowell remarked on the "splendid complacency" he found among his fellow Americans who were "neglectful" of their "political duties." He traced this neglect back to a widespread but mistaken belief that the framers of the Constitution had "invented a machine that would go of itself." Lowell said he admired the ability of Americans to let "confidence in our luck" and "absorption with material interests" subsume attention to the state of our democracy.

* * *

These problems have been building for years. By the end of the 1980s, politicians in Washington were in open despair that the political system was unable to deal with the problems facing the country.

The political deterioration has grown steadily worse. Not surprisingly, since it is our most representative branch of government, the dysfunction is most visible in the Congress. In a nation of citizens so lacking in an understanding of our system, it is hardly surprising that, increasingly, the men and women they send to Washington don't make an adherence to constitutional principles an important part of their daily work. "People revere the Constitution yet know so little about it—and that goes for some of my fellow senators," said the Senate's top institutionalist, Robert Byrd of West Virginia.

The framers counted on a balance of power between Congress and the president. They were, critically, intended to watch each other. But * * * Congress has wavered in the exercise of its constitutional duty.

The weakness of the legislature throws off the whole design of the system. The strong reassertions of presidential prerogatives would not have surprised the framers. They would have expected this, although some may have been surprised at the degree. "You must . . . oblige [the government] to control itself," Madison wrote. The American system counts on each branch asserting its authority, just as it counts on each individual to press his or her wishes. Balance is essential to the framers' design, but to find the right balance each participant has to push and pull. The danger comes when one branch pushes and the other folds.

* * *

The imbalance we refer to here is far more than the common instinct of members of Congress trying to protect a president of the same party. To some extent, this will always happen. But American history is marked with examples of members of Congress of each party asserting their institutional, constitutional role and challenging a president of their own party. Senator Harry S. Truman investigated President Roosevelt's administration, and Senator Lyndon B. Johnson investigated president Truman's administration. It was a Republican senator, Howard Baker, whose incessant questions crystallized the belief that a Republican president knew more about Watergate than he had told. And it was a Democratic senator, Daniel Patrick Moynihan, who blocked the Democratic president and his wife from their plan to overhaul American health care. Moynihan's critique was a classic defense of constitutional process. The Clintons drafted their plan, Moynihan complained, behind closed doors and failed to consult the Congress or build a consensus. And a few Republican legislators had begun challenging President George W. Bush's Iraq policy by the end of 2006.

But over the last few years on Capitol Hill, the Republican leadership seemed to disown the institutional role in the constitutional design. * * * Without amending the Constitution, both Senator Bill Frist and Speaker Dennis Hastert effectively gave President Bush the parliamentary type of system that Lloyd Cutler had so desperately wanted for President Carter. They operated as the president's floor leaders in the Congress, rather than as his separate and coequal partners in government.

Congress of course is not a piece of machinery. It is 535 individual members. They are the ones who decide how assertive to be. The single most important factor in that decision is the question of how assertive American voters expect them to be. Senator Frist and Speaker Hastert followed their path because it was easy, because they did not feel political pressure to assert their institutional roles under the Constitution. We can blame the voters for not pressuring the leaders. Or we can blame the leaders for not leading the citizens. Both are true. If two of the top elected figures in the country have such little regard for the institutional obligations handed down to them, how can we expect ordinary Americans to pay attention to the Constitution? Yet it is also hard to ask politicians to exercise institutional responsibilities that we give them no credit for exercising.

Both sides of the problem are an outgrowth of how far we have fallen away from an intimate knowledge of or connection to our Constitutional Conscience. We judge our politicians heavily by what we want and how well they deliver. We measure them in the present tense alone. We don't praise honest men and women for taking clear stands on constitutional principle or exercising those institutional responsibilities. We want to know what they have done for us lately; not what they have done to faithfully exercise the responsibilities given them by the Constitution. And how could it be otherwise, for we have little idea what those responsibilities are. * * *

The 2006 election sent a message to the incumbents in Congress. In very much the way the Federalists were tossed out in 1800, after President Adams failed to stop a Federalist Congress from plunging forward with the reviled Sedition Act, the Republicans were tossed out of Congress in 2006 for failing to check a Republican president's plunge into an unpopular war. Elections, as vital as they are, are in effect a last resort—the voters passing judgment after the fact. The system was designed to produce better results before the fact, when it is allowed to work. Whether you in the end supported or opposed American entry into Iraq, that decision, and more particularly the decision of the president and Congress, would have been stronger and more effective if it had been subject to more oversight in Congress and more debate in public. Perhaps you think the more effective policy would have been to stay out of war. Or perhaps you wish the war and its aftermath had been more effectively executed. As it turned out, Congress did not watch over the president, and the country got neither peace nor effective war. In both 1800 and 2006, the election produced dramatic shifts because classic checks and balances failed and thus produced policies that angered the voters. The election results were a punishment. But punishment by itself did not correct the more basic reasons the system of checks and balances failed.

The downward spiral will continue unless we get to the root of the problem. And what is the root of the problem? All of us, Americans, and each of us. A public opinion survey once asked Americans to "suppose the President and Congress have to violate a Constitutional principle to pass an important law the public wanted. Would you support them in this action?" Only 49 percent of the public said no. The other half were a mix of yes (22 percent) and undecided or neither (29 percent). Even on a simple statement of a bedrock principle of our system, we are divided. That is a shaky foundation on which to rest the most important government on earth.

Why does our constitutional commitment seem so thin? At one level, we have come to mistake longevity for permanence. We take for granted the existence of what not so long ago was remarkable and revolutionary. We assume that because we have been a free and successful democracy for our lifetimes and our parents' and grandparents' lifetimes that we will remain such for our children's and our children's children's lifetimes, too. That alone would be worrisome. When citizens take their democracy for granted, they undermine its most basic tenet. Democracy dissolves without the commitment to it of its citizens. That loss of commitment is what the framers most feared.

In our own time, the historian Sean Wilentz put it this way: "Democracy is never a gift bestowed by benevolent, far seeing rulers who seek to reinforce their own legitimacy. It must always be fought for, by political coalitions that cut across distinctions of wealth, power, and interest. It succeeds and survives only when it is rooted in the lives and expectations of its citizens and continually reinvigorated in each generation. Democratic successes are never irreversible."

But instead of reinvigorating our representative government, current generations are disparaging it. We are not fighting for it. Instead, we as a people are frustrated with the day-to-day workings of government and restlessly search for some "fix" for the system.

Perhaps our confidence in the permanence of our democracy has left us feeling free to attack its workings. To a point, that is healthy. The system was built for robust debate, and it has survived a great deal of it. But robust debate requires engagement and information. It requires the debaters to have some context, some sense of shared ground.

Where do we find that common ground? By looking behind the trouble signs. We said that taking our democracy for granted while also being frustrated with our government seems almost contradictory. We said "almost" because in fact we believe they rise from the same source.

Americans don't know their own government anymore. They don't know their own history. We take our democracy for granted because we don't understand how hard it was to build it, how much courage (not just on the battlefield) it took to preserve it, and how close it came to failure on several occasions from the Alien and Sedition Acts, through the Civil War to the Great Depression. And we are frustrated with how it works today because no one is explaining that how it works (most of time) is how the framers, benefiting from the real-life experience of the early nation, designed it to work. Defending the system is not a politically popular thing to do. And in our hurry-up society, no one wants to sit still long enough to hear explanations of the system, let alone defenses. This is frightening. The framers expected flaws to emerge in their design. They expected fixes to be needed.

What is dangerous now is that the debate over the system has lost the context of how the system got to be what it is. In an environment where citizens do not particularly understand the system's basic design, many of the fixes are actually challenges to the overall design. Madison and his colleagues envisioned the Senate, with its members chosen for longer terms from entire states, as a balance and a check to the House, with its larger membership with shorter terms from narrower constituencies. Together they would check the president, with a term halfway between that in the House and that in the Senate. Yet today former senator Gravel is running for president on the express platform of creating a national system of referendum to circumvent the Congress. His campaign is welcome to the extent that it encourages a debate that teaches Americans about the design of the Constitution. Americans are free to change that design. But they should understand what they are doing and what they are abandoning if they do.

We hope the result will be an embrace of improvements, rather than a dismantling of constitutional principles. But if only 49 percent of the country is willing to speak up for a fundamental constitutional principle, we are perilously close to undoing the system itself. The wrong crisis at the wrong moment could push us over the edge before we realize what we have done. Indeed, all that protects us in this situation is the framers' prescience in creating a system where a majority of one is not enough to make radical changes. But then of course we become frustrated that we can't get the change we want, and the spiral starts all over again.

Thomas Jefferson said that the tree of liberty needs to be refreshed from time to time with the blood of patriots and tyrants. What a wonderful bit of Jeffersonian poetry. But we think something less dramatic, but perhaps harder in its own way, is needed right now. We as Americans need to tend our own garden. We need to renew not just our faith in but our understanding of the system the framers gave us. That understanding requires more than some sound bites about liberty and freedom. We need to embrace that our liberty and freedom flow directly from less glamorous but still vital ideas, such as compromise, and checks and balances, and representation and process. A dash of humility would not hurt either.

Two of our most important modern presidents, Franklin Roosevelt and Ronald Reagan, each saw the importance of renewing our understanding of American constitutional government.

Roosevelt became president in the middle of the worst crisis of American democracy since the Civil War. The link between the American political system and its economic success had snapped. Around the world, dictatorships of the left and the right were on the rise. There were people who came to FDR—serious, important people—to advise him that he might have to take authoritarian powers himself. Looking back, we came much closer than many people realize to the loss of our democracy. But we did not lose it, thanks to the resolve of FDR and the strength in the American people of what we have come to describe as our Constitutional Conscience. Four years later, Roosevelt, in his first fireside chat of his second term as president, said he hoped the American people had reread their Constitution in the last few weeks. "Like the Bible," he said "it ought to be read again and again." Ironically, Roosevelt made this remark in a speech in which he argued for a plan to weaken the Supreme Court and strengthen the power of the presidency and the Congress by putting more of his appointees on the Court. It is a testament to the strength of our Constitutional Conscience that Roosevelt's way of arguing for this plan was to present it as a defense of the Constitution, not an infringement of it. The system stopped him anyway, and even without those expanded powers he guided the country out of the Depression. The Court-packing plan he outlined in that fireside chat has vanished into history. It turns out that the more important notion of that speech was Roosevelt's insistence that we reconnect with the Constitution regularly.

Half a century later, Ronald Reagan was saying farewell after eight years as president. He had come to office in the midst of a crisis of confidence. Watergate, stagflation, the Iran hostage crisis, the residue of the 1960s had combined to shake Americans' faith in their country. Reagan had worked with considerable success to rebuild that faith. As he said farewell, he took pride in that accomplishment. But he recognized that the job was only partly done: "This national feeling is good, but it won't count for much and it won't last unless it is grounded in thoughtfulness and knowledge. An informed patriotism is what we want. And are we doing a good enough job teaching our children what America is and what she represents in the long history of the world? Those of us who are over thirty five or so years of age grew up in a different America. We were taught, very directly, what it means to be an American. And we absorbed, almost in the air, a love of country and an appreciation of its institutions."

But as America prepared to enter the 1990s, Reagan warned, the fashion had changed. "Younger parents aren't sure that an unambivalent appreciation of America is the right thing to teach modern children. And as for those who create the popular culture, well-grounded patriotism is no longer the style. Our spirit is back, but we haven't reinstitutionalized it."

Roosevelt and Reagan are the touchstone presidents of the American Century. In some ways they could not represent more different political moments. The first brought a powerful centralized federal government into our domestic lives. The other drew the line to limit it. Yet across the half century that separated them, they each affirmed the centrality of connecting Americans to their democratic heritage.

"So we've got to teach history based not on what's in fashion but what's important," said Reagan. He concluded: "If we forget what we did, we won't know who we are. Let's start with some basics: more attention to American history and a greater emphasis on civic ritual."

We agree. Indeed, we think we owe it to the framers and all succeeding Americans who have struggled for the Constitution to renew our connection to our own history. But even more, we owe it to the future, which will be shaped by our actions.

There is a strong sense that we have become selfish and self-involved as a people. It is hard to say whether we are more self-interested than Americans at the time the Constitution was written. It was written because the framers thought we were very selfish, and they decided they could not fight human nature, only harness it. That was the genius of their system. It accepted us for who we are and yet still offered the optimistic vision that we could, as a nation, compromise our differences to agree to do great things.

We are all for ideas to make us less selfish or self-interested. But we are with the framers in doubting that human nature can be fundamentally changed.

They were right that our more selfish impulses can be channeled. Americans throughout their history have understood that it was in their own interest, ultimately, to preserve this system that balanced everyone's demands. That understanding is what we mean by our Constitutional Conscience. It is what Sean Wilentz is talking about when he describes coalitions that cut across lines of wealth, power and interest. It is noble to try to make people different. We admire those who try. But politics is the art of the possible. The framers made it possible for us to live together in liberty and community. The 220-year history of our Constitution is a history of Americans repeatedly rekindling their belief that their own interests are served by this system that grants extensive liberty in exchange for a willingness to compromise and tolerate differences. We Americans need to rekindle that belief once more.

If this [reading] has one message, it is that there is nothing about our past success that guarantees our future success. Each generation must do that for itself. Nevertheless, this is a hopeful message, because we are not alone in our struggle. We have been given a great gift and with it a great responsibility. We are the inheritors of the longest democratic tradition in the world. We still hold in great respect the men who began that tradition and the men and women who carried it forth and bequeathed it to us. That respect is a resource for us now. The struggles we are having, the frustrations we are feeling, are exactly the struggles and frustrations the framers anticipated when they designed our democracy. We can lean on them and their experience. By reaching backward to them and their ideas, we can move forward.

QUESTIONS

1. Most of the time, people become critical of the Constitution when they don't get the policy results they want. When Congress fails to pass legislation because of the power of small-state senators, when the Supreme Court issues a ruling they oppose, when the president makes a decision regarding the use of force that they oppose, the immediate impulse is to blame the system and call for change that would make the preferred policies more likely. Is this a valid reason for wanting the system to change?

2. The Constitution was written over two hundred years ago by a group of white men who had very "unmodern" views about democracy and equality. On what basis should we be bound by the decisions that they made? What is the foundation of constitutional fidelity? What would be the result if each generation were permitted to remake the rules?

3. Often, opinions about the Constitution divide along philosophical lines. On one side are people who believe that the most important purpose of a constitution is to limit government size and power. On the other are people who believe that the Constitution must protect rights and promote equality (which almost always involves expanding the size and power of government). Who has the better case? Why?

3

Federalism: Nullifying Health Care Reform

For many years, federalism was viewed as a relatively sleepy, unexciting part of American politics. Certainly, it was important to understand federalism's role in the American political system, Madison's "double security," and how intergovernmental relations have evolved. But relations between the national government and the states had settled into a stable system of cooperative federalism in most policy areas, so there were not many new and exciting developments. That all has changed in the past couple of decades. The Supreme Court has generally been shifting power from the national government to the states (with some exceptions). New struggles with "coercive federalism" have emerged as the national government tries to shape policy in the states. From education policy to the environment, immigration, welfare, gun rights, and now health care, the states are often at odds with Washington, D.C.

The states have raised the stakes of this intergovernmental struggle in recent years by reviving the early nineteenth century idea of "nullification." As the historian Sean Wilentz explains, the idea was developed by Thomas Jefferson in response to the Alien and Sedition Acts' limits on the First Amendment and asserts that the states can ignore national laws that they believe are unconstitutional. Jefferson used the term "interposition" to describe states interposing themselves between the unconstitutional acts of the national government and the people. John C. Calhoun developed this idea as a justification for southern opposition to a protective tariff, as a broad statement of states' rights, and ulti-mately the rationale for southern secession over the issue of slavery. This view also played a prominent role in the "massive resistance" to the integration of southern public schools after the *Brown v. Board of Education* decision in 1954.

States have recently applied nullification to federal policies concerning medi-cal marijuana, gun control, immigration, and most prominent-ly, health care. In each instance, states have passed laws or statewide referenda that contradict federal law. Attorneys general from twenty states have filed lawsuits challenging the constitutionality of Obama's health care reform, arguing that the federal gov-ernment does not have the power to compel individuals to purchase health insur-ance; many of these suits also claim that the federal government cannot force states to fund expanded Medicaid coverage or administer health insurance ex-changes (markets where individuals can purchase insurance). One of the lead attorneys in the lawsuit, David Rivkin, calls it "the most important constitutional challenge in our generation, and one of the two or three most important in our history." At least thirty-nine states have initiated legislation to overturn parts of the law. Three states have passed legislation voiding the individual mandate, and four more have put the issue to voters in a referendum on a constitutional amend-ment. One example of the latter is a proposed amendment to the Arizona consti-tution that says, "A law or rule shall not compel, directly or indirectly, any person, employer, or health care provider to participate in any health care system."

Will these challenges to the national health care law succeed? Most constitu-tional experts give the state challenges little chance of success because of broad congressional powers recognized by the U.S. Supreme Court under the com-merce clause, the necessary and proper clause, and Congress's taxing and spending powers. However, several federal district court judges have ruled in favor of the challenges, meaning that the question may well be left to the Supreme Court to resolve.

Timothy Jost agrees that these are not frivolous arguments but asserts that the "argument that the mandate [that individuals buy health insurance] is consti-tutional is overwhelming." Instead, he sees the push for nullification being driven by politics. Its real significance is that it is "an invitation to civil disobedience" to ignore the federal mandate, much like the current battle over medical marijuana and the historical "massive resistance" to the integration of southern schools discussed by Wilentz.

Clint Bolick defends the Health Care Freedom Act on several grounds. He sidesteps the question of nullification (by arguing that the Arizona amendment would not nullify part of the federal statute because people would still have the right to participate—they simply would not be forced to do so). He points out that national supremacy does not automatically mean that the national government can do whatever it wants: the national government would have to justify its right to require people to buy health insurance. He outlines a series of Supreme Court cases in which the states' position was upheld over the national government's regulatory and commerce powers. Whether the Court agrees with the states on the Health Care Freedom Act remains to be seen, but these are serious constitutional arguments.

Sean Wilentz

States of Anarchy: America's Long, Sordid Affair with Nullification

Historical amnesia is as dangerously disorienting for a nation as for an individual. So it is with the current wave of enthusiasm for "states' rights," "interposition," and "nullification"—the claim that state legislatures or special state conventions or referendums have the legitimate power to declare federal laws null and void within their own state borders. The idea was broached most vociferously in defense of the slave South by John C. Calhoun in the 1820s and '30s, extended by the Confederate secessionists in the 1850s and '60s, then forcefully reclaimed by militant segregationists in the 1950s and '60s. Each time it reared its head, it was crushed as an assault on democratic government and the nation itself—in Abraham Lincoln's words, "the essence of anarchy." The issue has been decided time and again, not least by the deaths of more than 618,000 Americans on Civil War battlefields. Yet there are those who now seek to reopen this wound in the name of resisting federal legislation on issues ranging from gun control to health care reform. Proclaiming themselves heralds of liberty and freedom, the new nullifiers would have us repudiate the sacrifices of American history—and subvert the constitutional pillars of American nationhood.

The origins of nullification date back to the stormy early decades of the republic. In 1798, a conservative Federalist Congress, fearing the rise of a political opposition headed by Thomas Jefferson, passed the Alien and Sedition Acts, which outlawed criticism of the federal government. Coming before the

Published in *The New Republic*, April 2010.

Supreme Court had assumed powers of judicial review, the laws, signed by President John Adams, were steps toward eradicating political dissent. In a panic, Jefferson and his ally, James Madison, wrote sets of resolutions duly passed by the legislatures of Virginia and Kentucky, which called upon the state governments to resist and, as Madison put it, "interpose" themselves between the federal government and the citizenry. But the other state legislatures either ignored or repudiated the resolutions as affronts to the Constitution, and the crisis was ended by the democratic means of an election when Jefferson won the presidency two years later—the wholly peaceable and constitutional "revolution of 1800."

The concept was revived by John C. Calhoun, who expanded it into a theory of nullification and Southern states' rights in 1828. The specific issue at stake was a protective tariff that Southerners believed unfair to their section, but behind it lay a growing fear that the federal government might interfere with the institution of slavery. Calhoun declared that, as "irresponsible power is inconsistent with liberty," individual states had the right to nullify laws they deemed unconstitutional. He asserted further that, should the federal government try to suppress nullification, individual states had the right to secede from the Union. In 1832, the South Carolina legislature passed a formal ordinance nullifying the tariff. But President Andrew Jackson proclaimed nullification pernicious nonsense. The nation, Jackson proclaimed, was not created by sovereign state governments—then, as now, a basic misunderstanding propagated by pro-nullifiers. Ratified in order "to form a more perfect union," the Constitution was a new framework for a nation that already existed under the Articles of Confederation. "The Constitution of the United States," Jackson declared, created "a government, not a league."

Although state governments had certain powers reserved to them, these did not include voiding laws duly enacted by the people's representatives in Congress and by the president. Calhoun and South Carolina were isolated by Jackson's firm stand. The aging James Madison sided with the president, deploring "the strange doctrines and misconceptions" of the South Carolinians, charging that they were a perversion of the Virginia Resolutions and insisting that the "Constitution & laws of the U.S. should be the supreme law of the Land." (Madison also wrote of nullification that "[n]o man's creed was more opposed to such an inversion of the Repubn. order of things" than Thomas Jefferson's.) Other Southern states refused to join in the nullification movement, and Congress approved a compromise tariff bill.

Calhoun's radical ideas about states' rights resurfaced during the sectional crisis over slavery in the 1850s. The Civil War began as a struggle over democracy and U.S. government, focused on a key question: Could the slave interests in individual states, dissatisfied with the outcome of a presidential election, declare that election null and void and secede from the Union? Lincoln, like Jackson before him, declared such extreme views of state sovereignty a direct attack on democratic republican government.

After four years of the Civil War, in a "new birth of freedom" that resurrected the Union, Calhoun's states' rights doctrines were utterly disgraced—but they did not disappear forever. Nearly a century later, they were exhumed to justify the so-called "massive resistance" of the segregationist South against civil rights and, in particular, the Supreme Court's ruling on *Brown v. Board of Education* in 1954. The current rage for nullification is nothing less than another restatement, in a different context, of musty neo-Confederate dogma.

Following the *Brown* decision, James J. Kilpatrick, the prosegregationist editor of *The Richmond News Leader*, dressed up nullification under the milder sounding "interposition," borrowed from Madison's Virginia Resolutions. Kilpatrick hoped that adopting lofty Madisonian language would lift resistance to *Brown* "above the sometimes sordid level of race and segregation." Despite his rhetorical sleight of hand, his intent was radical—supporting resistance not only to acts of Congress or the outcome of a presidential election, but also to the decisions of the ultimate court. Not surprisingly, not a single Supreme Court justice then or since, including the fiercest advocates of states' rights, has ever ruled the concept a valid response to federal law or judicial rulings. All have recognized that nullification under any name would leave controversial laws or court decisions open to state-by-state popular referendums—a recipe for chaos that would undercut judicial review, the cornerstone of American constitutional jurisprudence. And the justices have recognized the explicit language of Article VI of the Constitution, that federal laws made in pursuance of the Constitution "shall be the supreme Law of the Land; and the Judges of every State shall be bound thereby." Yet, in their last-ditch efforts to save Jim Crow, segregationists like Kilpatrick grasped and distorted the words of James Madison from 1798. In the spirit of John C. Calhoun and the Confederacy, they then vaunted their idea of "interposition" above the words of the Constitution, of which Madison is considered the father.

Kilpatrick's gambit caught on among his fellow white supremacists in Southern state governments—most notably Virginia's—and they passed resolutions of interdiction in defiance of the *Brown* decision. (The Alabama legislature went further, bluntly declaring *Brown*, "as a matter of right, null, void, and of no effect.") Those resolutions came to lie at the heart of what Senator Harry F. Byrd of Virginia announced in February 1956 as a policy of "massive resistance" to *Brown*. For several years, the strategy succeeded in fending off federal authority, resulting in mob violence against blacks and federal officials, as well as the closure of entire public school systems in the South—including the shutdown of public education in Virginia's Prince Edward County for five years, beginning in 1959. But determined efforts by the administrations of Dwight D. Eisenhower, John F. Kennedy, and Lyndon B. Johnson eventually broke the back of the segregationist campaign. And, as early as January 1960, state and federal courts negated the Virginia nullification laws meant to implement massive resistance. Segregationists found other temporary means to preserve racial separation in the schools, including, for a time, the creation of private "segregation academies." But, in time, Virginia, as well as the rest of the South, finally acceded to the legitimacy of the *Brown* decision. The repudiated doctrines of interposition and nullification were repudiated once more.

Less than a year ago, on July 16, 2009, the *Richmond Times-Dispatch* ran an editorial apologizing for its role and that of its sister newspaper, the *News Leader*, in instigating and supporting massive resistance, which it called "a dreadful doctrine." It is all the more ironic that the legal fictions used to justify that doctrine should now be reappearing in new circumstances. "Who is the sovereign, the state or the federal government?" demanded state Representative Chris N. Herrod, a Republican, amid a recent session of the Utah legislature that affirmed it had the power to nullify heath care reform. Last month, Governor Mike Rounds of South Dakota, a Republican, signed into law a bill that invalidated all federal regulation of firearms regarding weapons manufactured and used in South Dakota. The day before, Wyoming's governor, Dave Freudenthal, a Democrat, signed similar legislation for his state. Meanwhile, the Oklahoma House of Representatives resolved that Oklahomans should be permitted to vote on a state constitutional amendment that would allow them to ignore the impending reform of the health care system. And, in Virginia, the home of massive resistance, Attorney General Ken Cuccinelli, a Republican, has argued that a recently enacted state law prohibiting the government from requiring the people to buy health insurance counters federal health care reform, which, he insists, is unconstitutional.

Now, as in the 1860s and 1960s, nullification and interposition are pseudo-constitutional notions taken up in the face of national defeat in democratic politics. Unable to prevail as a minority and frustrated to the point of despair, its militant advocates abandon the usual tools of democratic politics and redress, take refuge in a psychodrama of "liberty" versus "tyranny," and declare that, on whatever issue they choose, they are not part of the United States or subject to its laws—that, whenever they say so, the Constitution in fact forms a league, and not a government. Although not currently concerned with racial supremacy, the consequence of their doctrine would uphold an interpretation of the constitutional division of powers that would permit the majority of any state to reinstate racial segregation and inequality up to but not including enslavement, if it so chose.

That these ideas resurfaced 50 years ago, amid the turmoil of civil rights, was as harebrained as it was hateful. But it was comprehensible if only because interposition and nullification lay at the roots of the Civil War. Today, by contrast, the dismal history of these discredited ideas resides within the memories of all Americans who came of age in the 1950s and '60s—and ought to, on that account, be part of the living legacy of the rest of the country. Only an astonishing historical amnesia can lend credence to such mendacity.

Arizona House Concurrent Resolution 2014: A Concurrent Resolution Proposing an Amendment to the Constitution of Arizona; Amending Article XXVII, by Adding Section 2, Constitution of Arizona; Relating to Health Care Services

Section 2.

A. To preserve the freedom of Arizonans to provide for their health care:
  1. A law or rule shall not compel, directly or indirectly, any person, employer or health care provider to participate in any health care system.
  2. A person or employer may pay directly for lawful health care services and shall not be required to pay penalties or fines for paying directly for lawful health care services. A health care provider may accept direct payment for lawful health care services and shall not be required to pay penalties or fines for accepting direct payment from a person or employer for lawful health care services.

B. Subject to reasonable and necessary rules that do not substantially limit a person's options, the purchase or sale of health insurance in private health care systems shall not be prohibited by law or rule.

C. This section does not:
   1. Affect which health care services a health care provider or hospital is required to perform or provide.
   2. Affect which health care services are permitted by law.
   3. Prohibit care provided pursuant to Article XVII, Section 8 of this constitution or any statutes enacted by the legislature relating to worker's compensation.
   4. Affect laws or rules in effect as of January 1, 2009.
   5. Affect the terms or conditions of any health care system to the extent that those terms and conditions do not have the effect of punishing a person or employer for paying directly for lawful health care services or a health care provider or hospital for accepting direct payment from a person or employer for lawful health care services.

D. For the purposes of this section:
   1. "Compel" includes penalties or fines.
   2. "Direct payment or pay directly" means payment for lawful health care services without a public or private third party, not including an employer, paying for any portion of the service.
   3. "Health care system" means any public or private entity whose function or purpose is the management of, processing of, enrollment of individuals for or payment for, in full or in part, health care services or health care data or health care information for its participants.
   4. "Lawful health care services" means any health-related service or treatment to the extent that the service or treatment is permitted or not prohibited by law or regulation that may be provided by persons or business otherwise permitted to offer such services.
   5. "Penalties or fines" means any civil or criminal penalty or fine, tax, salary or wage withholding or surcharge or any named fee with similar effect established by law or rule by a government established, created or controlled agency that is used to punish or discourage the exercise of rights protected under this section.

Timothy S. Jost

Can the States Nullify Health Care Reform?

On February 1, the Virginia Senate passed a bill stating that "No resident of this Commonwealth . . . shall be required to obtain or maintain a policy of individual insurance coverage." In considering this legislation, Virginia joins numerous other states with pending legislation aimed at limiting, changing, or opposing national health care reforms. What is going on here?

Whereas states generally adopt laws to achieve a legal effect, nullification laws are pure political theater. On its face, the Virginia bill exempts residents of the Commonwealth from having to comply with a law requiring the purchase of heath insurance. Although the bill is phrased in the passive voice, its intent is clearly to block the implementation of a federal mandate requiring all individuals to carry health insurance. But achieving this aim is constitutionally impossible.

The Supremacy Clause of the United States Constitution (article VI, clause 2) states, "This Constitution, and the Laws of the United States . . . shall be the supreme Law of the Land; . . . any Thing in the Constitution or Laws of any State to the Contrary notwithstanding." Indeed, one of the primary reasons for adopting our Constitution in place of the Articles of Confederation was to establish the supremacy of national over state law. Our only civil war was fought over the question of whether national or state law was ultimately supreme.

Within the past 60 years, the most important confrontation between federal law and states' rights concerned school desegregation. Faced with federal law commanding the desegregation of its schools, Arkansas amended its constitution to prohibit integration. In *Cooper v. Aaron* (1958), the only Supreme Court opinion I know of that was signed individually by each of the Court's nine justices, the Court decisively reaffirmed the supremacy of federal law and rejected the state's claimed right to nullification. More recently, a number of federal courts have rejected claims that a state could refuse Medicaid coverage of abortions in cases of rapes and incest after the Hyde amendment (which originally prohibited the use of federal funds for coverage of abortion except

Published in *The New England Journal of Medicine*, March 2010.

when the mother's life was at risk) was changed to permit federal funding for abortions under these circumstances. These decisions held that state constitutional provisions must yield even to federal regulations. State law cannot nullify federal law. This principle is simply beyond debate, and state legislators, many of them lawyers, know that.

The purpose of these laws, therefore, is not legal but rather political. The Virginia bill is a second-generation nullification statute. Earlier proposals in other states, including a constitutional amendment proposed by the Arizona legislature, are worded differently. These bills protect a right to pay health care providers directly for services and to purchase private health insurance. In other words, they were proposed to oppose a single-payer system or mandatory public option, neither of which has ever been part of the current federal reform legislation. These antireform bills were based on model legislation put forward by the American Legislative Exchange Council, an organization funded by wealthy right-wing foundations to support conservative state legislative causes, which was reportedly aided in this endeavor by the insurance industry. Because these bills were not aimed at any actual federal legislation, they seem to have simply been part of a larger campaign to mischaracterize federal legislative efforts and stir up opposition to any federal health care reform.

The Virginia bill, in contrast, is aimed at an actual provision of the federal health care reform bill—the individual mandate. As the legislative findings that accompany the individual mandate in the Senate bill emphasize, the mandate is fundamental to the legislation. The government cannot require insurers to take all comers, regardless of health status and preexisting conditions, unless the healthy as well as the unhealthy are required to purchase health insurance. We will not be able to reduce providers' burden of uncompensated care or the alarming rate of medical bankruptcies unless all Americans who can afford health insurance buy it.

The individual mandate, however, is uniquely vulnerable. First, it is strongly opposed by conservatives and libertarians. The fact that five of the Virginia Senate's Democrats voted for the state senate bill sends a clear message to Virginia's congressional delegation that a federal bill containing such a mandate is going to be very unpopular with many of their constituents.

Second, the individual mandate is somewhat vulnerable constitutionally. Although the argument that the mandate is constitutional is overwhelming, as Balkin noted in a recent issue of the *Journal*, it is hard to think of a direct precedent for it. And the argument against it is not frivolous, unlike most of the other constitutional arguments that have been raised against the pending legislation. The state bills can be read as briefs to the Supreme Court on this issue.

Third, the mandate is particularly vulnerable from an enforcement perspective. It essentially imposes a tax penalty (to begin in 2014 and to be fully phased in by 2016) on uninsured individuals who do not purchase health insurance, subject to a number of exceptions for those who cannot afford health insurance or who oppose it for religious reasons. Individuals are supposed to pay this penalty with their annual income taxes, but the Senate bill waives criminal penalties and prohibits the Internal Revenue Service (IRS) from imposing liens or levies on a taxpayer's property for failure to pay. Compliance will, therefore, be largely voluntary (although the IRS can still make a tax resister's life miserable, whether or not it can ultimately collect). The state bills can thus be seen as invitations to civil disobedience that counsel state citizens to "violate the federal law, wave this statute in their face, and dare them to come after you."

I know of two other significant state campaigns—one ongoing, one historical—to rally or support state citizens in resisting federal law. In the ongoing effort, more than a quarter of the states have now legalized medical marijuana in the face of a federal prohibition. Although the Supreme Court has emphatically upheld the authority of the federal government to outlaw medical marijuana, the Justice Department announced last fall that the prosecution of users of the medical marijuana was not "an efficient use of limited federal resources." It is possible that the federal government will eventually conclude that it is not possible to enforce the individual mandate for health insurance. But if individuals successfully resist accepting responsibility for being insured, there will be no way of expanding affordable coverage in a system that depends on private insurers. If government funding of health care must therefore be increased, it may not be the result resisters want.

In the historical effort, demagogues such as the late Senator Harry Byrd (D-VA) mounted the Campaign for Massive Resistance to school desegregation in Virginia and other states during the 1950s and 1960s. Virginia passed a series of statutes intended to maintain the strict segregation of its schools, even going so far as to close the public schools in one county for 6 years. The legislation was held unconstitutional by the federal courts, and the campaign eventually collapsed. Today, most Virginians regard the whole episode as an embarrassment. The state legislature has even adopted reparations legislation to help people who were denied an education during the campaign. Perhaps if health care reform is successfully implemented and Americans come to fully appreciate its benefits, they will look back at the current efforts with similar embarrassment.

These resistance efforts are not about law—they are about politics. But of course at this point, health care reform is only about politics, except insofar as it is still about the morality of equal treatment for all.

Clint Bolick

The Health Care Freedom Act: Questions & Answers

The Health Care Freedom Act will appear as a proposed constitutional amendment on Arizona's 2010 election ballot, and similar measures are under consideration in more than 30 other states. With the possibility that Congress will enact some sort of national health insurance legislation, questions are being raised about the scope of the Health Care Freedom Act and its effect should a federal bill become law. In the following pages, Clint Bolick, who helped to author the Health Care Freedom Act, answers frequently asked questions.

Q: What is the Health Care Freedom Act?

A: The Health Care Freedom Act is a proposed amendment to the Arizona Constitution that would preserve certain existing rights that individuals have regarding health care. It was initially proposed by two Arizona physicians, Dr. Eric Novack and Dr. Jeffrey Singer, with drafting assistance from the Goldwater Institute. The measure qualified as a voter initiative on the 2008 ballot, and despite a well-financed opposition campaign, it was defeated by less than one-half of 1 percent of the vote. Changes were made to address concerns raised by the opponents, and the Arizona Legislature voted to refer the revised version to the 2010 ballot.

The American Legislative Exchange Council adopted model legislation based on the Arizona measure, and activists and legislators in at least 35 additional states are pursuing constitutional amendments or statutes based on the Arizona model.

Q: What are the key provisions?

Published by the Goldwater Institute, February 2010.

A: Although the precise language varies from state to state, the Health Care Freedom Act seeks to protect two essential rights. First, it protects a person's right to participate or not in any health care system, and prohibits the government from imposing fines or penalties on that person's decision. Second, it protects the right of individuals to purchase—and the right of doctors to provide—lawful medical services without government fine or penalty. The Health Care Freedom Act would place these essential rights in the state constitution (or, in some states, it would protect them by statute).

Q: What motivated the Health Care Freedom Act?

A: No one questions the need for serious health care reform. However, the proponents of the Health Care Freedom Act believe that regardless of how such reform is fashioned, either at the state or federal level, the essential rights protected by the Health Care Freedom Act should be preserved. Many advocates of a larger government role in regulating or providing health insurance support a mandate that would compel individuals to join a government-approved health insurance plan, whether or not they can afford it and whether or not the system best fits their needs. In some countries in which government plays a large role in providing health insurance, medical services are rationed and individuals are prevented or discouraged from obtaining otherwise lawful medical services. Supporters of the Health Care Freedom Act have a variety of perspectives on the form that health care reform should take. But they agree that no matter what legislation is passed, it should not take from Americans their precious right to control their own medical affairs.

Q: By what authority can states pass the Health Care Freedom Act?

A: It is well-established that the U.S. Constitution provides a baseline for the protection of individual rights, and that state constitutions may provide additional protections—and all of them do. For instance, some states provide greater protections of freedom of speech or due process rights. Because the Health Care Freedom Act offers greater protection than the federal constitution, states are allowed to enact it.

Q: Does it matter whether the Health Care Freedom Act is passed as a statute or as a constitutional amendment?

A: A state constitution is the organic law of the state, reflecting the most fundamental values shared by the citizens of the state. Moreover, a state constitutional amendment will ensure that state legislature can never infringe upon the protected rights. So a constitutional amendment is preferable, especially to protect against legislative tinkering. However, for purposes of a federalism defense against excessive federal legislation, it should not matter whether the people of the state have acted through their constitution or by statute.

Q: Does the Health Care Freedom Act attempt to "nullify" federal health insurance legislation?

A: Absolutely not. If federal legislation is enacted, individuals would still have the option to participate in federal health insurance programs. This act simply protects a person's right not to participate.

Q: To the extent that the Health Care Freedom Act conflicts with provisions of federal legislation, isn't the state law automatically preempted by the Supremacy Clause of the U.S. Constitution?

A: No. In any clash between state and federal provisions, at least four federal constitutional provisions are relevant. The Supremacy Clause establishes the Constitution as the supreme law of the land and provides that federal laws prevail over conflicting state laws where Congress has the legitimate authority to enact the legislation and where it does not impermissibly tread upon state sovereignty. The federal government will have to demonstrate that its legislation legitimately is derived from congressional authority to regulate interstate commerce. It will also have to show the legislation does not violate the 10th Amendment, which reserves to the states all government power not expressly delegated to the national government; and the 11th Amendment, which protects states from being used as mere instrumentalities of the national government. This constitutional construct is known as federalism.

Q: Are certain provisions of proposed federal health care legislation vulnerable to constitutional challenge without the Health Care Freedom Act?

A: Yes, in at least three ways. First, to the extent that the legislation purports to regulate transactions that do not directly affect interstate commerce, such as mandating insurance for individuals. Congress may lack authority to do so under the Commerce Clause. Several relatively recent decisions by the U.S. Supreme Court have invalidated federal legislation on this basis. In *U.S. v. Lopez* (1995), the Court struck down federal laws that restricted guns in school zones; and in *U.S. v. Morrison*, it struck down a federal statute involving violence against women. In both cases, the Court found the subject matter of the federal laws did not "substantially affect" interstate commerce, so Congress had no power to regulate it under the circumstances presented.

Second, to the extent the legislation interferes with the individual's right to choose health insurance providers, doctors, or lawful medical services, it may violate the right to medical self-determination recognized under the U.S.

Constitution. As the Court declared in *Griswold v. Connecticut* (1965), "We have recognized that the special relationship between patient and physician will often be encompassed within the domain of private life protected by the Due Process Clause." Several of the early abortion cases involved what Justice William O. Douglas, concurring in *Doe v. Bolton* (1973), described as the "right to seek advice on one's health and the right to place reliance on the physician of one's choice." Whether or not one agrees with those abortion rulings, they establish a strong basis for challenging certain federal and state intrusions.

Third, several recent decisions have invalidated federal laws that "commandeer" state governments to do their bidding. In *New York v. United States* (1992), for instance, the Court struck down federal rules requiring states to take ownership of certain radioactive waste and to expose themselves to liability. Speaking for the Court, Justice Sandra Day O'Connor ruled that "no matter how powerful the federal interest involved, the Constitution simply does not give Congress the authority to require the States to regulate." Tellingly, she added "the Constitution protects us from our own best intentions: It divides power among sovereigns . . . precisely so that we may resist the temptation to concentrate power in one location as an expedient solution to the crisis of the day." To the extent that federal health insurance legislation forces states to implement its provisions, it could be subject to robust constitutional challenge.

Q: Could the Health Care Freedom Act provide additional protection against federal health insurance legislation that violates protected rights?

A: Yes. Although the federal government usually prevails in federalism clashes, the current U.S. Supreme Court is the most pro-federalism Court in decades. There are no cases precisely on point, but the Court under Chief Justice John Roberts has sided with the states in at least three major recent federalism clashes. In the case most closely on point, *Gonzales v. Oregon* (2006), the Court upheld the state's "right-to-die" law, which was enacted by Oregon voters, over the objections of the U.S. Attorney General, who argued that federal law pre-empted the state law. Applying "the structure and limitations of federalism," the Court observed that states have great latitude in regulating health and safety, including medical standards, which are primarily and historically a matter of local concern. Holding that the attorney general's reading of the federal statute would mark "a radical shift of authority from the States to the Federal Government to define general standards of medical practice in every locality," the Court interpreted the statute to allow Oregon to protect the rights of its citizens.

Horne v. Flores (2009) considered a measure adopted by Arizona voters to require English immersion as the state's educational policy for students for whom English is a second language. Lower federal courts had imposed an injunction based on a finding that Arizona was failing to comply with federal bilingual education requirements. The Supreme Court held that injunctions affecting "areas of core state responsibility, such as public education," should be lifted as quickly as circumstances warrant. It observed that "federalism concerns are heightened when . . . a federal court decree has the effect of dictating state or local budget priorities." The Court remanded the case to lower courts to reconsider the injunction.

In *Northwest Austin Municipal Utility District No. 1 v. Holder* (2009), the Court examined a challenge to section 5 of the Voting Rights Act, which places certain states and localities in a penalty box, requiring them to obtain "preclearance" by the U.S. Department of Justice for any changes that impact voting. The Court was sharply critical of the "federalism costs" imposed upon the covered jurisdictions. It avoided the constitutional question by applying the federal law in a way that allowed the utility district to "bail out" from pre-clearance requirements under section 5.

In each of these cases, the Court sided with states in federalism disputes with the federal government.

Q: Will the Health Care Freedom Act affect future state legislation regarding health insurance?

A: Yes. If it is passed as a constitutional amendment, it would prevent any future legislation that infringes upon the rights protected by the amendment.

Q: Won't this be really expensive for the states to defend in court?

A: The Goldwater Institute has offered to defend the constitutionality of the Health Care Freedom Act at no cost to any state. Because legal challenges would involve purely constitutional issues and would not require expensive trials, to the extent that states become involved in litigation, they should be able to do so within existing Attorney General litigation budgets. Moreover, depending on the details of national health insurance legislation, the cost of federal mandates is likely to far exceed the cost of litigation.

Q: Even if the states and individuals did not prevail in a challenge to intrusive federal health insurance legislation, would there be reasons to support the Health Care Freedom Act?

A: Yes. First, if these rights are given additional protection under state constitutions, they will create an absolute barrier to future state legislation that violates those rights. Moreover, efforts to enact the Health Care Freedom Act send a powerful message to our nation's capitol that people at the grassroots take these rights very seriously and intend to protect them.

* * *

QUESTIONS

1. When should the national government direct policy? When should it step back and let the states have their way? Should the national government have the power to compel people to buy health insurance (while providing subsidies to those who cannot afford it)?

2. Sean Wilentz argues that if states can simply ignore national laws they disagree with, this would be a recipe for anarchy. Do you agree? Are there any instances in which the states should be able to ignore national laws? What about assisted suicide, medical marijuana, or gun rights?

3. Do you agree with Timothy Jost that the most important implications of the legal challenges by the states are political, rather than legal? If so, will "massive resistance" to the law be a problem?

4. Are you convinced by Clint Bolick's case for the legal arguments in favor of the Arizona state constitutional amendment on health care? On which points, if any, do you think the health care law is vulnerable to constitutional challenge?

4

Civil Liberties: Corporate and Labor Spending in Campaigns and the First Amendment

The First Amendment says that "Congress shall make no law . . . abridging the freedom of speech." The Supreme Court must define the boundaries of what that broad prohibition means: Does it apply to pornography, commercial speech, or speech that advocates the overthrow of the government or incites violence? Political advertising and campaign spending generate a difficult set of questions. The Court has recognized a government interest in promoting fair elections that are free from corruption, so some regulation of campaign speech is warranted. But the question is where to draw the line between permissible speech and corrupting speech.

Most of you are probably familiar with the saying "Money talks." With the recent Supreme Court decision in *Citizens United v. Federal Election Commission* (FEC), the speaking power of money just got much stronger. In this decision, the Court decided that the First Amendment protects the right of corporations, non-profit groups, and labor unions to spend directly in political campaigns, rather than having to set up political action committees to run so-called electioneering ads (that specifically call for the election or defeat of a candidate). One controversial aspect of this decision was that corporations, not just individuals, have free-speech rights.

Ronald Dworkin, a law professor at New York University, says the decision "threatens democracy" because it will create "an avalanche of negative political commercials financed by huge corporate wealth." He also is concerned that the decision has "generated open hostilities among the three branches of our government," pointing to comments from President Obama in his 2010 State of the Union message and the subsequent negative reaction from Supreme Court Justices Alito and Roberts. Dworkin argues that this radical a decision cannot be grounded in any theory of the First Amendment, ignored relevant precedent (despite the conservative majority's avowed belief in judicial restraint), and opened American electoral campaigns to influence from foreign corporations. Dworkin concludes with a plea for stronger disclosure laws and public financing for congressional elections.

Bradley Smith, a former chair of the Federal Election Commission, strongly disagrees. He calls the decision a "wonderful affirmation of the primacy of political speech in First Amendment jurisprudence." Furthermore, he says, the impact of the decision is almost certainly overstated: Twenty-eight states already allow corporations to advertise in state elections, and most large corporations are unlikely to start spending huge amounts of money because they prefer lobbying to spending money in elections. Also, the decision empowers not only corporations but also labor unions, which are more likely to want to spend in elections. Though downplaying the radical nature of the decision, Smith clearly indicates (and hopes) that it may be a foot in the door for more significant changes down the road such as allowing unlimited corporate donations to candidates and more corporate spending against "tax and spend, pro-regulatory politicians."

Ronald Dworkin

The Decision That Threatens Democracy

No Supreme Court decision in decades has generated such open hostilities among the three branches of our government as has the Court's 5–4 decision in *Citizens United v. FEC* in January 2010. The five conservative justices, on their own initiative, at the request of no party to the suit, declared that corporations and unions have a constitutional right to spend as much as they wish on television election commercials specifically supporting or targeting particular

Published in *The New York Review of Books*, May 2010.

candidates. President Obama immediately denounced the decision as a catastrophe for American democracy and then, in a highly unusual act, repeated his denunciation in his State of the Union address with six of the justices sitting before him.

"With all due deference to separation of powers," he said, "last week the Supreme Court reversed a century of law that I believe will open the floodgates for special interests—including foreign corporations—to spend without limit in our elections." As he spoke one of the conservative justices, Samuel Alito, in an obvious breach of decorum, mouthed a denial, and a short time later Chief Justice John Roberts publicly chastised the President for expressing that opinion on that occasion. The White House press secretary, Robert Gibbs, then explained Obama's remarks: "The President has long been committed to reducing the undue influence of special interests and their lobbyists over government. That is why he spoke out to condemn the decision and is working with Congress on a legislative response." Democrats in Congress have indeed called for a constitutional amendment to repeal the decision and several of them, more realistically, have proposed statutes to mitigate its damage.

The history of the Court's decision is as extraordinary as its reception. At least since 1907, when Congress passed the Tillman Act at the request of President Theodore Roosevelt, it had been accepted by the nation and the Court that corporations, which are only fictitious persons created by law, do not have the same First Amendment rights to political activity as real people do. In 1990, in *Austin v. Michigan Chamber of Commerce*, the Court firmly upheld that principle. In 2002, Congress passed the Bipartisan Campaign Reform Act (BCRA) sponsored by Senators John McCain and Russell Feingold, which forbade corporations to engage in television electioneering for a period of thirty days before a primary for federal office and sixty days before an election. In 2003, in *McConnell v. Federal Election Commission (FEC)*, the Court upheld the constitutionality of that prohibition.

In the 2008 presidential primary season a small corporation, Citizens United, financed to a minor extent by corporate contributions, tried to broadcast a derogatory movie about Hillary Clinton. The FEC declared the broadcast illegal under the BCRA. Citizens United then asked the Supreme Court to declare it exempt from that statute on the ground, among others, that it proposed to broadcast its movie only on a pay-per-view channel. It did not challenge the constitutionality of the act. But the five conservative justices—Chief Justice Roberts and Justices Samuel Alito, Anthony Kennedy, Antonin Scalia, and

Clarence Thomas—decided on their own initiative, after a rehearing they themselves called for, that they wanted to declare the act unconstitutional anyway.

They said that the BCRA violated the First Amendment, which declares that Congress shall make no law infringing the freedom of speech. They agreed that their decision was contrary to the *Austin* and *McConnell* precedents; they therefore overruled those decisions as well as repealing a century of American history and tradition. Their decision threatens an avalanche of negative political commercials financed by huge corporate wealth, beginning in this year's midterm elections. Overall these commercials can be expected to benefit Republican candidates and to injure candidates whose records dissatisfy powerful industries. The decision gives corporate lobbyists, already much too influential in our political system, an immensely powerful weapon. It is important to study in some detail a ruling so damaging to democracy.

The First Amendment, like many of the Constitution's most important provisions, is drafted in the abstract language of political morality: it guarantees a "right" of free speech but does not specify the dimensions of that right—whether it includes a right of cigarette manufacturers to advertise their product on television, for instance, or a right of a Ku Klux Klan chapter publicly to insult and defame blacks or Jews, or a right of foreign governments to broadcast political advice in American elections. Decisions on these and a hundred other issues require interpretation and if any justice's interpretation is not to be arbitrary or purely partisan, it must be guided by principle—by some theory of why speech deserves exemption from government regulation in principle. Otherwise the Constitution's language becomes only a meaningless mantra to be incanted whenever a judge wants for any reason to protect some form of communication. Precedent—how the First Amendment has been interpreted and applied by the Supreme Court in the past—must also be respected. But since the meaning of past decisions is also a matter of interpretation, that, too, must be guided by a principled account of the First Amendment's point.

A First Amendment theory is therefore indispensable to responsible adjudication of free speech issues. Many such theories have been offered by justices, lawyers, constitutional scholars, and philosophers, and most of them assign particular importance to the protection of political speech—speech about candidates for public office and about issues that are or might be topics of partisan political debate. But none of these theories—absolutely none of them—justifies the damage the five conservative justices have just inflicted on our politics.

The most popular of these theories appeals to the need for an informed electorate. Freedom of political speech is an essential condition of an effective democracy because it ensures that voters have access to as wide and diverse a range of information and political opinion as possible. Oliver Wendell Holmes Jr., Learned Hand, and other great judges and scholars argued that citizens are more likely to reach good decisions if no ideas, however radical, are censored. But even if that is not so, the basic justification of majoritarian democracy—that it gives power to the informed and settled opinions of the largest number of people—nevertheless requires what Holmes called a "free marketplace of ideas."

Kennedy, who wrote the Court's opinion in *Citizens United* on behalf of the five conservatives, appealed to the "informed electorate" theory. But he offered no reason for supposing that allowing rich corporations to swamp elections with money will in fact produce a better-informed public—and there are many reasons to think it will produce a worse-informed one. Corporations have no ideas of their own. Their ads will promote the opinions of their managers, who could publish or broadcast those opinions on their own or with others of like mind through political action committees (PACs) or other organizations financed through voluntary individual contributions. So though allowing them to use their stockholders' money rather than their own will increase the volume of advertising, it will not add to the diversity of ideas offered to voters.

Corporate advertising will mislead the public, moreover, because its volume will suggest more public support than there actually is for the opinions the ads express. Many of the shareholders who will actually pay for the ads, who in many cases are members of pension and union funds, will hate the opinions they pay to advertise. Obama raised a great deal of money on the Internet, mostly from small contributors, to finance his presidential campaign, and we can expect political parties, candidates, and PACs to tap that source much more effectively in the future. But these contributions are made voluntarily by supporters, not by managers using the money of people who may well be opposed to their opinions. Corporate advertising is misleading in another way as well. It purports to offer opinions about the public interest, but in fact managers are legally required to spend corporate funds only to promote their corporation's own financial interests, which may very well be different.

There is, however, a much more important flaw in the conservative justices' argument. If corporations exercise the power that the Court has now given them, and buy an extremely large share of the television time available for political ads, their electioneering will undermine rather than improve the public's political education. Kennedy declared that speech may not be restricted just to make candidates more equal in their financial resources. But he misunderstood why other nations limit campaign expenditures. This is not just to be fair to all candidates, like requiring a single starting line for runners in a race, but to create the best conditions for the public to make an informed decision when it votes—the main purpose of the First Amendment, according to the marketplace theory. The Supreme Court of Canada understands the difference between these different goals. Creating "a level playing field for those who wish to engage in the electoral discourse," it said, " . . . enables voters to be better informed; no one voice is overwhelmed by another."

Monopolies and near monopolies are just as destructive to the marketplace of ideas as they are to any other market. A public debate about climate change, for instance, would not do much to improve the understanding of its audience if speaking time were auctioned so that energy companies were able to buy vastly more time than academic scientists. The great mass of voters is already very much more aware of electoral advertising spots constantly repeated, like beer ads, in popular dramatic series or major sports telecasts than of opinions reported mainly on public broadcasting news programs. Unlimited corporate advertising will make that distortion much greater.

The difference between the two goals I distinguished—aiming at electoral equality for its own sake and reducing inequality in order to protect the integrity of political debate—is real and important. If a nation capped permissible electoral expenditure at a very low level, it would achieve the greatest possible financial equality. But it would damage the quality of political debate by not permitting enough discussion and by preventing advocates of novel or unfamiliar opinion from spending enough funds to attract any public attention. Delicate judgment is needed to determine how much inequality must be permitted in order to ensure robust debate and an informed population. But allowing corporations to spend their corporate treasure on television ads conspicuously fails that test. Judged from the perspective of this theory of the First Amendment's purpose—that it aims at a better-educated populace—the conservatives' decision is all loss and no gain.

A second popular theory focuses on the importance of free speech not to educate the public at large but to protect the status, dignity, and moral development of individual citizens as equal partners in the political process. Justice John Paul Stevens summarized this theory in the course of his very long but irresistibly powerful dissenting opinion in *Citizens United*. Speaking for himself and Justices Stephen Breyer, Ruth Ginsburg, and Sonia Sotomayor, he said that "one fundamental concern of the First Amendment is to 'protec[t] the individual's interest in self-expression.'" Kennedy tried to appeal to this understanding of the First Amendment to justify free speech for corporations. "By taking the right to speak from some and giving it to others," he stated, "the Government deprives the disadvantaged person or class of the right to use speech to strive to establish worth, standing, and respect for the speaker's voice." But this is bizarre. The interests the First Amendment protects, on this second theory, are only the moral interests of individuals who would suffer frustration and indignity if they were censored. Only real human beings can have those emotions or suffer those insults. Corporations, which are only artificial legal inventions, cannot. The right to vote is surely at least as important a badge of equal citizenship as the right to speak, but not even the conservative justices have suggested that every corporation should have a ballot.

A third widely accepted purpose of the First Amendment lies in its contribution to honesty and transparency in government. If government were free to censor its critics, or to curtail the right to a free press guaranteed in a separate phrase of the First Amendment, then it would be harder for the public to discover official corruption. The Court's *Citizens United* decision does nothing to serve that further purpose. Corporations do not need to run television ads in the run-up to an election urging votes against particular candidates in order to report discoveries they may make about official dishonesty, or in order to defend themselves against any accusation of dishonesty made against them. And of course they have everyone else's access to print and television reporters.

Though the Court's decision will do nothing to deter corruption in that way, it will do a great deal to encourage one particularly dangerous form of it. It will sharply increase the opportunity of corporations to tempt or intimidate congressmen facing reelection campaigns. Obama and Speaker Nancy Pelosi had great difficulty persuading some members of the House of Representatives to vote for the health care reform bill, which finally passed with a dangerously thin majority, because those members feared they were risking their seats in the coming midterm elections. They knew, after the Court's decision, that they might face not just another party and candidate but a tidal wave of negative ads financed by health insurance companies with enormous sums of their shareholders' money to spend.

Kennedy wrote that there is no substantial risk of such corrupting influence so long as corporations do not "coordinate" their electioneering with any candidate's formal campaign. That seems particularly naive. Few congressmen would be unaware of or indifferent to the likelihood of a heavily financed advertising campaign urging voters to vote for him, if he worked in a corporation's interests, or against him if he did not. No coordination—no role of any candidate or his agents in the design of the ads—would be necessary.

Kennedy's naiveté seems even stranger when we notice the very substantial record of undue corporate influence laid before Congress when it adopted the BCRA. Before that act, corporations and other organizations were free to broadcast "issue" ads that did not explicitly endorse or oppose any candidates. The district court judge who first heard the *Citizens United* case found that, according to testimony of lobbyists and political consultants, at least some "Members of Congress are particularly grateful when negative issue advertisements are run by these organizations . . . [that] . . . use issue advocacy as a means to influence various Members of Congress." That influence can be expected to be even greater now that the Court has permitted explicit political endorsements or opposition as well. Kennedy's optimism went further: he denied that heavy corporate spending would lead the public to suspect that form of corruption. But the district court judge had reported that

> 80 percent of Americans polled are of the view that corporations and other organizations that engage in electioneering communications, which benefit specific elected officials, receive special consideration from those officials when matters arise that affect these corporations and organizations.

So the radical decision of the five conservative justices is not only not supported by any plausible First Amendment theory but is condemned by them all. Was their decision nevertheless required by the best reading of past Supreme Court decisions? That seems initially unlikely because, as I said, the decision overruled the two most plainly pertinent such decisions: *Austin* and *McConnell*. Nothing had happened to the country, or through further legislation, that cast any doubt on those decisions. The change that made the difference was simply Justice Sandra Day O'Connor's resignation in 2006 and President George W. Bush's appointment of Alito to replace her.

Overruling these decisions is itself remarkable, particularly for Roberts and Alito, who promised to respect precedent in their Senate confirmation hearings. One of the reasons that Kennedy offered to justify his decision is alarming.

He said that since the conservative justices who dissented in those past cases and who remain on the Court had continued to complain about them, the decisions were only weak precedents. "The simple fact that one of our decisions remains controversial," he announced, "is, of course, insufficient to justify overruling it. But it does undermine the precedent's ability to contribute to the stable and orderly development of the law." In other words, if the four more liberal justices who dissented in this case continue to express their dissatisfaction with it, they would be free to overrule it if the balance of the Court shifts again. That novel view would mean the effective end of the doctrine of precedent on the Supreme Court.

* * *

* * * [T]he central issue in *Citizens United* * * * is whether corporations are entitled to the First Amendment protection that individuals and groups of individuals have. We have already noticed a variety of arguments that they do not. Very few individuals have anything like the capital accumulation of any of the Fortune 500 corporations, the smallest of which had revenues of $5 billion (the top of the list—Exxon Mobil—had $443 billion) in 2008. Individuals speak and spend for themselves, together or in association with other individuals, while corporations speak for their commercial interests and spend other people's money, not their own. Individuals have rights, on which their dignity and standing depend, to play a part in the nation's government; corporations do not. No one thinks corporations should vote, and their rights to speak as institutions have been limited for over a century. * * *

* * *

Two Democrats—Senator Charles Schumer of New York and Representative Chris Van Hollen of Maryland—have announced proposals for legislation to protect the country from the Court's ruling. The Court might reject some of their proposals—forbidding corporate advertising by TARP recipients who have not paid back the government's loan, for example—as unconstitutional attempts to ban speech according to the speaker's identity. Kennedy left open the possibility, however, that Congress might constitutionally accept another of their proposals: banning electioneering by corporations controlled by foreigners.

He also explicitly recognized the constitutionality of another of the Democrats' proposals: he said that Congress might require public disclosure of a corporation's expenses for electioneering. (Thomas dissented from that part of

Kennedy's ruling.) Congress should require prompt disclosures on the Internet so that the information could be made quickly available to voters. It would be even more important for Congress to provide for ample disclosure within a television advertisement itself. The disclosure should name not only fronting organizations, like Citizens United, but also at least the major corporate contributors to that organization. Congress should also require that any corporation that wished to engage in electioneering obtain at least the annual consent of its stockholders to that activity and to a proposed budget for it, and that the required disclosure in an ad report the percentage of stockholders who have refused that blanket consent. Finally, Congress should require that the CEO of the major corporate contributor to any ad appear in that ad to state that he or she believes that broadcasting it is in the corporation's own financial interests.

The conservative justices might object that such disclosure requirements would unduly burden corporate speech and impermissibly target one type of speaker for special restriction. They might say, to use one of Kennedy's favorite terms, that these requirements would "chill" corporate speech. But we must distinguish measures designed to deter speech from those designed to guard against deception. The in-ad disclosures I describe need not take significantly more broadcast time than the "Stand By My Ad" rule that now requires a candidate to declare in his campaign's ad that he approves it. If several corporations finance an ad together, much of the required information—the amount of shareholder dissent, for instance—could be disclosed as an aggregate figure. If these requirements discourage a corporation's speech not because of the expense but for the different reason that managers are unwilling to report shareholder opposition or to acknowledge their fiduciary duty to act only in the financial interests of their own company, then their fear only shows the pertinence of Kennedy's own claim that "shareholder democracy" is the right remedy to protect shareholders who oppose a corporation's politics.

* * *

The Supreme Court's conservative phalanx has demonstrated once again its power and will to reverse America's drive to greater equality and more genuine democracy. It threatens a step-by-step return to a constitutional stone age of right-wing ideology. Once again it offers justifications that are untenable in both constitutional theory and legal precedent. Stevens's remarkable dissent in this case shows how much we will lose when he soon retires. We must hope that Obama nominates a progressive replacement who not only is young enough to endure the bad days ahead but has enough intellectual firepower to help construct a rival and more attractive vision of what our Constitution really means.

Bradley A. Smith

Citizens United We Stand

March 24, 2009, was a turning point in the long-running battle to restrict political speech, aka "campaign finance reform." On that day, the Supreme Court heard oral argument in *Citizens United v. Federal Election Commission*, in which the conservative activist group Citizens United challenged the provisions of the McCain-Feingold law that had prohibited it from airing a documentary film, *Hillary: The Movie*, through video on demand within 30 days of any 2008 Democratic presidential primary.

In the course of the argument, Deputy Solicitor General Malcolm Stewart, an experienced Supreme Court litigator, argued that a 1990 precedent, *Austin v. Michigan Chamber of Commerce*, gave the government the power to limit any political communication funded by a corporation, even a nonprofit such as Citizens United. Justice Samuel Alito asked Stewart if that power would extend to censoring political books published by corporations. Stewart responded—consistent with the government's position at all stages of the case—that yes, it would. There was an audible hush—if such a thing is possible—in the court. Then Justice Alito, appearing to speak for the room, merely said, "I find that pretty incredible."

Incredible or not, that was, and had been for many years, the position of the U.S. government. But until that moment, it seemed to have never quite sunken in with the justices. Americans are willing to accept far more abridgements of free speech than we sometimes like to believe, but the idea of banning books strikes an emotional chord that something described simply as "prohibitions and limits on campaign spending" does not. Americans may not always live up to the Bill of Rights, but Americans do not ban books. A stunned Court eventually asked the parties to reargue the case, to consider whether *Austin* should be overruled.

Published in *The American Spectator*, May 2010.

On reargument last September, Solicitor General Elena Kagan tried to control the damage, arguing that the government never actually had tried to censor books, even as she reaffirmed its claimed authority to do just that. She also stated that "pamphlets," unlike books, were clearly fair game for government censorship. (Former Federal Election Commissioner Hans von Spakovksy has noted that in fact the FEC has conducted lengthy investigations into whether certain books violated campaign finance laws, though it has not yet held that a book publisher violated the law through publication. And the FEC has attempted to penalize publishers of magazines and financial newsletters, only to be frustrated by the courts.) With the endgame of "campaign finance reform" finally laid out plainly, the Supreme Court's decision seemed a foregone conclusion. Sure enough, in January, the Court ruled that corporations, as associations of natural persons, have a right to spend funds from their general treasuries to support or oppose political candidates and causes—including through the publication or distribution of books and movies.

Though this ruling is obviously a correct interpretation of the First Amendment, reaction to the Court's decision in *Citizens United* has been loud, often disingenuous, and in some cases nearly hysterical. President Obama used his State of the Union address to publicly scold the Court, in the process so mischaracterizing the Court's decision that he prompted Judge Alito's now famous, spontaneous rejoinder, "Not true."

Meanwhile, Democrats in Congress and the states have been working overtime to come up with "fixes," ranging from the absurd (a Vermont legislator proposed forcing corporate sponsors to be identified every five seconds during any broadcast ad), to the merely pernicious (such as proposals that seek to immobilize corporate speech by forcing corporations to hold a majority vote of shareholders before each and every expenditure). The fact that virtually all of these proposed "fixes" have been sponsored by Democrats, with the aim of silencing what they perceive to be the pro-Republic voices of the business community, merely illustrates once again the basic problem with campaign finance reform that *Citizens United* sought to alleviate: the desire to manipulate the law for partisan purposes.

Citizens United is at once both a potential game-changer and a decision whose "radicalism" has been widely overstated. Why overstated? Well, to start, one would never guess from the left's hysteria that even prior to *Citizens United*, 28 states, representing roughly 60 percent of the U.S. population, already allowed corporations and unions to make expenditures promoting or opposing candidates for office in state elections; in 26 states, such corporate and union expenditures were unlimited. Moreover, while the first bans on corporate spending were enacted more than a century ago, prior to the 1990 *Austin* decision, the Supreme Court had never upheld a ban, or even a limitation, on independent expenditures supporting or opposing a political candidate. It was the misleading contention that the decision overturned "100 years of law and precedent," that appears to have evoked Justice Alito's "not true" response to the president's State of the Union comments.

The president also stated, again misleadingly, that the decision would open the door for foreign corporations to spend unlimited sums in American elections. In fact, another provision of federal law, not at issue in the case, already prohibits any foreign national, including foreign corporations, from spending money in any federal campaign. FEC regulations, which have the force of the law, further prohibit any foreign national from playing any role in the political spending decisions of any U.S. corporation, political action committee, or association. And the Court specifically stated that *Citizens United* was not addressing these laws at all. So while some states may tweak their state rules in the wake of *Citizens United* to limit the ability of U.S. incorporated and headquartered subsidiaries of foreign corporations to spend money in campaigns, the "foreign corporation" bogeyman is little more than leftist demagoguery.

What is much more alarming than the prospect of U.S. corporations with some foreign ownership participating in campaigns is the fact that the four most liberal justices on the Supreme Court would have upheld the *Austin* precedent, and with it the authority of the federal government to censor books and movies published, produced, or distributed by U.S. corporations. But by affirming the rights of citizens to speak out on political issues, even when organized through the corporate form, the Supreme Court quite rightly put political speech back at the core of the First Amendment.

After four decades in which the Court had given greater First Amendment protection to such activities as topless dancing, simulated child pornography, Internet porn, flag burning, and the transfer of stolen information than to political speech, *Citizens United* is a wonderful reaffirmation of the primacy of political speech in the First Amendment jurisprudence. In that respect, the case has already been a constitutional game-changer. Future litigation is sure to follow, building on the success of *Citizens United* to free up the political system and strike down the still extensive web of regulation that envelops political speech.

Some of these challenges are already well under way. For example, under current federal law, an individual such as George Soros is free to spend $20 million to promote his favored candidates, but if two or more individuals get together to do the same thing, neither can contribute more than $5,000 to the effort. It is hard to see what anti-corruption purpose such a dichotomy serves, and in *SpeechNow.org v. FEC*, argued before the U.S. Court of Appeals for the District of Columbia Circuit in January, plaintiffs argue that if it is not corrupting for one person to spend unlimited sums on independent expenditures, it is not corrupting if two or more people combine their resources to promote the candidates of their choice. A decision is expected soon. Expect, too, legal challenges to the federal prohibition on contributions by corporations directly to candidates—if a $2,300 contribution from a corporate CEO or PAC is not corrupting, it is hard to see how a $2,300 contribution directly from a corporate treasury is corrupting.

Much less clear is whether *Citizens United* will be a game-changer in electoral politics. The general consensus is that *Citizens United* favors Republicans, based on the widely held perception that corporations are more likely to support Republicans than Democrats. But this perception may not be true. Even before *Citizens United*, the federal government and most states also allowed corporations to operate political action committees (PACs), which could then solicit the corporation's managers and shareholders for voluntary contributions to the PAC, which in turn could contribute limited amounts to candidates or make independent expenditures to support candidates. But whereas corporate PACs typically gave about two-thirds of their contributions to Republicans during the 1990s and the first part of the last decade, peaking in the 2004 cycle at nearly 10 to 1 for the GOP, over the past three years corporate PACs have devoted a slim majority of the contributions to Democrats.

More importantly, there is good reason to doubt that *Fortune 500* companies are going to start making large expenditures in political campaigns. As noted, even before *Citizens United*, 28 states allowed corporate and union spending on state and local political races, yet large-scale corporate spending was very rare in those states. Another sign that corporations are not eager to jump headfirst into political spending comes from the relatively low level of activity by corporate PACs. Among the *Fortune 500*—huge corporations that are all heavily regulated by the government—only about 60 percent actually maintained PACs.

These PACs are subject to extensive regulation, which runs up operating costs to the point that the operating costs of PACs often total more than half of their total revenue. Corporations can, however, pay these operating costs directly from their corporate treasuries. Yet roughly half of these PACs' operating expenses were paid not by the corporations that established them, but out of funds donated to the PACs. In other words, even before *Citizens United*, corporate America could have roughly doubled the amount of money available in their PACs to use for political expenditures simply by paying the administrative and legal costs of operating the PAC from their general treasuries. Yet they did not. And only about 10 percent of PACs contributed the maximum legal amount in any election. All this suggests a lack of interest in political participation.

The truth is, the *Fortune* 500 prefer lobbying to campaigning. Even prior to McCain-Feingold, when corporations could support parties with "soft money," the *Fortune* 500 spent roughly 10 times as much money on lobbying as on political expenditures. As Edward Kangas, former chairman of Deloitte Touche Tohmatsu and of the Committee for Economic Development said in the *New York Times*, explaining his support for McCain-Feingold, "We have lobbyists."

But if large corporations may be reluctant to spend on political races, Big Labor is not. Labor unions also benefit from the *Citizens United* decision, and have historically been much more partisan in their political activity than has big business. The relatively small number of unions makes it easier for them to coordinate their activity. Add in the lack of any need to avoid offending a portion of their customer base, and unions are well positioned to take advantage of *Citizens United*. Indeed, within weeks of the *Citizens United* decision, three unions pledged to spend $1 million each to try to defeat U.S. senator Blanche Lincoln in the Democratic primary in Arkansas, finding her insufficiently dedicated to Big Labor's agenda.

Thus, if *Citizens United* ultimately works to favor conservatives, it may be less due to the *Fortune* 500 than to the small business community. These small and midsized companies usually cannot afford the high administrative costs of maintaining a PAC, and often don't have enough employees eligible for solicitation to make forming a PAC worthwhile in any case. Moreover, unlike *Fortune* 500 companies, small businesses typically do not maintain permanent large lobbying operations in Washington, and because they are less likely to be heavily regulated or engaged in government contracting, their contact with Washington is likely to be more sporadic. For these companies, the ability to speak directly to the public is potentially a great benefit.

This small business community is generally much more conservative in its politics than is the *Fortune 500*, and in particular much more hostile to government regulation. But these small companies are unlikely to undertake major campaigns on their own. Thus it may be up to trade associations and business groups, such as chambers of commerce, to organize business efforts.

Meanwhile, managers and executives, particularly of large, publicly traded companies, will need to do some serious rethinking about their obligations to shareholders. Do they have an obligation to their shareholders to try to maximize long-term value by opposing tax and spend, pro-regulatory politicians, and working to elect officials who appreciate pro-growth policies? Or do they play it safe, avoid political activity, and hope that the regulators will eat them last? The decisions they make may ultimately determine the real importance of *Citizens United*.

QUESTIONS

1. How should the Supreme Court balance the need for elections that are free from corruption and the First Amendment's protection for political speech?

2. Do you agree with Dworkin's argument that none of the five theories of the First Amendment apply to corporate speech? Which of the five would have the strongest basis for justifying a First Amendment protection for corporate speech?

3. Should corporations be treated as people for purposes of political speech? If yes, why isn't it sufficient that the individuals who work for the corporations can spend their own money independently in elections? If not, why should individuals give up their free speech rights just because they incorporate?

4. Setting aside for now the First Amendment questions, whose arguments about the implications of the decision do you find more compelling? Do you agree with Dworkin, who sees it as a threat to democracy? Or Bradley, who thinks the consequences are exaggerated?

5

Congress: Pork-Barrel Politics

In an era of enormous budget deficits, federal spending is under intense scrutiny. One type of spending—"pork-barrel" policies that are targeted to a specific district or project—is especially controversial because it raises questions about the capacity of Congress to deal effectively with national problems and priorities. However, the debate over pork-barrel politics illustrates the difficulties of defining national interests as opposed to parochial, or local, interests and the role of Congress in policy making.

Pork may take many forms. The most common legislative vehicle for distributing pork is the "earmark," which identifies specific, targeted spending, usually as part of a larger bill. Transportation bills and water projects are two of the traditional outlets for pork-barrel spending, but in recent years even bills funding the war against terrorism, homeland security, and the wars in Iraq and Afghanistan have been full of pork. For example, charges of wasteful spending have been made concerning the rebuilding of Iraq as contractors received "no-bid" contracts for securing and restoring oil fields, among other lucrative projects.

The Cato Institute is a libertarian think tank that is highly critical of wasteful government spending. The selection from the Cato Handbook provides a general example of how special interests win over the general interests, specific instances of pork in recent years (including grants for the Shedd Aquarium in Chicago and the Rock and Roll Hall of Fame in Cleveland), and the broader implications of pork for the policy-making process. Cato's overall critique of pork is that the American taxpayer should not be funding these programs. Rather, the private sector should provide funding (if any). Pork contributes to the ballooning federal deficit and debt and is the "currency of corruption." The selection ends with a call for more transparency in pork spending and its eventual elimination.

Where Cato sees waste and abuse of the nation's resources, however, James Inhofe, a Republican senator from Oklahoma, and Jonathan Rauch see many positive virtues. In an interview with Brian Friel, Inhofe characterizes earmark reform as a phony issue. Inhofe sees earmarks as maintaining Congress's control over spending. Otherwise, the power to decide which projects get funded would shift to unelected bureaucrats. Also, Inhofe argues that national interests can be served by allowing local interests to dip into the pork barrel. Although Inhofe has vowed to fight any ban on earmarks, one possible area of common ground between him and earmark reformers would be limiting earmarks to spending that has been authorized by a congressional committee (rather than just tacked on to a spending bill).

Rauch agrees that the power of the purse should remain with Congress rather than the executive branch, but also points out that a recent bill that was criticized as being "full of pork" had less than 2 percent of the offending spending. (Overall, pork accounts for less than 1 percent of federal spending.) Furthermore, much of the accountability and transparency Cato calls for is already in place: it isn't that easy to get an earmark, and earmark sponsors are made public. Other supporters of pork have called it the "glue" of legislating. If it takes a little pork for the home district or state to get important legislation through Congress, so be it. Also, one person's pork could be another person's essential spending. Members of Congress are best able to determine that need.

Corporate Welfare and Earmarks, from *Cato Handbook for Policymakers*

When considering budget issues, federal policymakers are supposed to have the broad public interest in mind. Unfortunately, that is not how the federal budget process usually works in practice. Many federal programs are sustained by

Published in the *Cato Handbook for Policymakers*, 2009.

special-interest groups working with policymakers seeking narrow benefits at the expense of taxpayers and the general public.

* * *

How can special interests regularly triumph over the broad public interest in our democracy? For one thing, recipients of federal handouts have a strong incentive to create organizations to lobby Congress to keep the federal gravy train flowing. By contrast, average citizens have no strong incentive to lobby against any particular subsidy program because each program costs just a small portion of their total tax bill.

When average citizens do speak out against particular programs, they are usually outgunned by the professionals who are paid to support programs. Those professionals have an informational advantage over citizens because the workings of most federal programs are complex. The lobby groups that defend subsidy programs are staffed by top program experts, and they are skilled at generating media support. One typical gambit is to cloak the narrow private interests of subsidy recipients in public interest clothing, and proclaim that the nation's future depends on increased funding.

Another reason it is hard to challenge spending programs is that lobby groups, congressional supporters, and federal agencies rarely admit that any program is a failure. Washington insiders become vested in the continued funding of programs because their careers, pride, and reputations are on the line, and they will battle against any cuts or reforms.

How do dubious spending programs get enacted in the first place? Table 1 shows how Congress can pass special-interest legislation in which the costs

TABLE 1

Majority Voting Does Not Ensure That a Project's Benefits Outweigh Costs

Legislator	Vote	Benefits Received by Constituents	Taxes Paid by Constituents
Clinton	Yea	$12	$10
Cochran	Yea	$12	$10
Collins	Yea	$12	$10
Carper	Nay	$2	$10
Coburn	Nay	$2	$10
Total	Pass	$40	$50

TABLE 2

Logrolling Allows Passage of Subsidies That Benefit Minorities of Constituents

| Legislator | Project A | | Project B | | Vote on a Bill Including Projects A and B |
	Benefits Received by Constituents	Taxes Paid by Constituents	Benefits Received by Constituents	Taxes Paid by Constituents	
Clinton	$15	$10	$8	$10	Yea
Cochran	$15	$10	$8	$10	Yea
Collins	$4	$10	$20	$10	Yea
Carper	$3	$10	$2	$10	Nay
Coburn	$3	$10	$2	$10	Nay
Total	$40	$50	$40	$50	Pass

outweigh the benefits. The table assumes that legislators vote in the narrow interest of their districts. The hypothetical project shown creates benefits of $40 and costs taxpayers $50, and is thus a loser for the nation. Nonetheless, the project gains a majority vote. The program's benefits are more concentrated than its costs, and that is the key to gaining political support.

The pro-spending bias of Congress is strengthened by the complex web of vote trading, or logrolling, that often occurs. Table 2 shows that because of logrolling, projects that are net losers to society can pass even if they do not have majority support. Because Projects A and B would fail with stand alone votes, Clinton, Cochran, and Collins enter an agreement to mutually support the two projects. That is, they logroll. The result is that the two projects get approved, even though each imposes net costs on society and benefits only a minority of voters.

The popularity of logrolling means that programs that make no economic sense and have only minimal public support are enacted all the time.

* * *

Earmarks

The federal budget practice of "earmarking" has exploded during the last 15 years. Earmarks are line items in spending bills inserted by legislators for specific projects in their home states. Some infamous earmarks funded a

$50 million indoor rain forest in Iowa and a $223 million "bridge to nowhere" in Alaska. Earmarks can provide recipients with federal grant money, contracts, loans, or other types of benefits. Earmarks are often referred to as "pork" spending.

* * * [T]he number of pork projects increased from fewer than 2,000 annually in the mid-1990s to almost 14,000 in 2005. Various scandals and the switch to Democratic control of Congress then slowed the pace of earmarking for a couple of years. But earmarking is on the rise again. The fiscal year 2008 omnibus appropriations bill was bloated with 11,610 spending projects inserted by members of Congress for their states and districts.

Earmarked projects are generally those that have not been requested by the president and have not been subject to expert review or competitive bidding. Thus, if the government had $1 billion to spend on bioterrorism research, it might be earmarked to go to laboratories in the districts of important politicians, rather than to labs chosen by a panel of scientists. Earmarking has soared in most areas of the budget, including defense, education, housing, scientific research, and transportation.

The main problem with earmarking is that most spending projects chosen by earmark are properly the responsibility of state and local governments or the private sector, not the federal government. The rise in earmarks is one manifestation of Congress's growing intrusion into state affairs, . . . Consider these earmarks from the FY08 omnibus appropriations bill:

1. $1,648,850 for the private Shedd Aquarium in Chicago, which is also awash with corporate funding;
2. $787,200 for "green design" changes at the Museum of Natural History in Minneapolis;
3. $492,000 for the Rocky Flats Cold War Museum in Arvada, Colorado;
4. $1,950,000 for a library and archives at the Charles B. Rangel Center for Public Service at the City College of New York;
5. $2,400,000 for renovations to Haddad Riverfront Park in Charleston;
6. $500,000 for upgrades to Barracks Row, a swank Capitol Hill neighborhood;
7. $742,764 for fruit fly research, partly conducted in France;
8. $188,000 for the Lobster Institute in Maine; and
9. $492,000 for fuel cell research for Rolls-Royce Group of Canton, Ohio.

Projects 1 to 3 give taxpayer money to groups that should be funding their own activities from admissions fees and charitable contributions. Interestingly, the nonprofit Shedd Aquarium has spent hundreds of thousands of dollars on lobbyists to secure federal earmarks, and its chief executive earned a huge $600,000 salary in 2006. Or consider that the Rock and Roll Hall of Fame in Cleveland has received federal grants, even though there are thousands of music industry millionaires who should be footing the bill.

Projects 4 to 6 are examples of items that state and local governments should fund locally. Unfortunately, state and local officials are increasingly asking Washington for handouts, and lobby groups such as Cassidy and Associates are helping them "mine" the federal budget for grants.

Projects 7 to 9 fund activities that should be left to the private sector. Industries should fund their own research, which is likely to be more cost-effective than government efforts. Besides, successful research leads to higher profits for private businesses, and it makes no sense for taxpayers to foot the bill for such private gains.

Earmarks' Erosion of Fiscal Responsibility

Defenders of earmarks argue that they are no big deal since they represent just a small share of overall federal spending. The problem is that earmarking has contributed to the general erosion in fiscal responsibility in Washington. Earmarks have exacerbated the parochial mindset of most members, who spend their time appeasing state and local interest groups rather than tackling issues of broad national concern. Many politicians complain about the soaring federal deficit, yet their own staff members spend most of their time trying to secure earmarks in spending bills.

The rise in earmarking has encouraged a general spendthrift attitude in Congress. Why should rank-and-file members restrain themselves when their own leaders are usually big recipients of pork? Sen. Tom Coburn (R-OK) is right that the problem with earmarks is "the hidden cost of perpetuating a culture of fiscal irresponsibility. When politicians fund pork projects they sacrifice the authority to seek cuts in any other program." Similarly, Rep. Jeff Flake (R-AZ) concludes that "earmarking . . . has become the currency of corruption in Congress. . . . Earmarks are used as inducements to get members to sign on to large spending measures."

Reforms to Increase Transparency and Downsize the Government

A first step toward eliminating earmarks, corporate welfare, and other special-interest spending is to further increase transparency in the congressional and agency spending processes. Under pressure from reformers, the government has set up a searchable database of federal grants and contracts at www.usaspending.gov. A second step is for citizens to use this website and other tools to research federal spending, and then to call their members of Congress and tell them what programs should be cut.

Citizens should also ask their members to support reforms to the budget process. One idea for cutting corporate welfare is to set up a commission akin to the successful military base–closing commissions of the 1990s. It would draw up a list of current subsidies and present it to Congress, which would vote on the cuts as a package without amendment. To make the package a political winner, all budget savings would go toward immediate tax cuts for families.

Ultimately, earmarking and corporate welfare should be abolished, and spending on activities that are legitimate federal functions should be determined by a system of competitive bidding and expert review. Of course, it will not be easy to reform the spending practices of Congress. Members often feel committed to expanding spending in their districts and on their favored programs. But taxpayers fund all those programs, and they need to do a better job of convincing their members to cut unneeded programs and pass much leaner federal budgets.

—Prepared by Chris Edwards and Jeff Patch

Brian Friel

Inhofe: Earmarks Are Good for Us

Sen. James Inhofe, R-Okla., the ranking member on the Senate Environment and Public Works Committee, spent the past eight years battling liberals over climate change and arguing that predictions of catastrophic global warming are a "hoax." Now Inhofe is taking on what he describes as another "phony"

Published in *National Journal*, March 2010.

issue—earmark reform. But this crusade puts him at odds with fellow conservatives in his own party.

In recent years, taxpayer watchdog groups and anti-pork-barrel lawmakers—including Sens. John McCain, R-Ariz.; Jim DeMint, R-S.C.; and Inhofe's home-state colleague and fellow Republican, Tom Coburn—have turned earmarks into a dirty word. They contend that lawmakers' long-standing practice of earmarking funding for pet projects promotes waste, big spending, and corruption. The Senate foes regularly offer floor amendments attempting to strip earmarks from legislation.

Inhofe, who ranked as the most conservative senator in *National Journal's* 2009 vote ratings, launched a campaign this week to recast earmarks as a tool that conservatives should embrace, not deride. He noted that most people took global warming as a fact eight years ago, and he contended that he has effectively shown that it is not. His earmark battle is aimed at showing that what everyone believes about earmarks is also untrue, he said.

"They're winning on the phrase," Inhofe said of anti-earmarkers, in an interview. "It's fraudulent."

Elected to the House in 1986 and to the Senate in 1994, Inhofe says that his efforts on global warming ultimately led to the recent demise of cap-and-trade climate-change legislation. To environmentalists and many congressional Democrats, he is a villain. Dan Lashof, the climate center director of the Natural Resources Defense Council, calls Inhofe "the Senate's chief spokesman for climate deniers." But the Oklahoman has become a star in conservative circles for his outspoken and often lonely fight on the issue.

Armed with those bona fides, Inhofe is planning to take his pro-earmark campaign to rank-and-file conservatives. He said he was inspired, in part, by a column that Jonathan Rauch wrote in this magazine. . . . Inhofe is slated to speak to a "tea party" group in Jacksonville, Fla., later this month, where he expects to test-drive his message. He has drafted an op-ed outlining his views on the "phony issue of earmarks." He also hopes to convince conservative talk-radio hosts that their frequent earmark-bashing misses the more important goal: reducing overall spending to ensure greater fiscal responsibility in Washington.

"You don't save anything by cutting earmarks," Inhofe said. He maintained that eliminating lawmakers' earmarks doesn't shrink the overall budget; it just leaves it to federal agencies—currently controlled by the Democratic Obama administration—to decide how to distribute the money. "These non-elected bureaucrats are the ones who are making the decisions."

As an example, Inhofe pointed to a transportation program that pays for low-budget initiatives such as bike trails, streetscapes, and congestion mitigation. In 2008, Congress distributed the millions of dollars in program funding through earmarks that boosted 102 projects in 35 states. The year before, when no earmarks were permitted, the Transportation Department funded projects through a grant competition in just five big cities—Miami, Minneapolis-St. Paul, New York City, San Francisco, and Seattle.

Inhofe argues that earmarks have funded many programs that conservatives support, particularly in national defense. As the second-ranking Republican on the Armed Services Committee, behind McCain, Inhofe notes that Congress has used earmarks to keep several military programs chugging along despite executive branch objections, including additional C-17 cargo planes that President Obama fought against last year. McCain offered an amendment to the Defense appropriations bill that would have nixed the funds for the extra planes, but Inhofe and 63 other senators defeated it.

Instead of imposing an earmark moratorium, Inhofe proposes a freeze in nonsecurity appropriations at fiscal 2008 levels, a move that he says would save $600 billion more than Obama's proposal in February to freeze such spending at fiscal 2010 levels. He also maintains that individual projects should be assessed on their merits, not on whether they are deemed to be earmarks.

Opponents counter, though, that earmarked congressional projects have become a symbol of what is wrong with Washington.

"I think there is a justifiable argument for earmarks, that we as legislators probably know better in some instances than bureaucrats in Washington about how money should be spent," Sen. George LeMieux, R-Fla., conceded. "But earmarks are, unfortunately, the engine that drives the train that gets us into these huge spending problems. If I put an earmark in a particular appropriations bill, and then that appropriations bill is 15 percent more than it was last year, and I say I can't support that, they'll say, well, your earmark is in there. So the earmark is what buys you into bigger spending."

"Railing against earmarks helps those who vote for the billion-dollar spending bills seem more conservative than they really are."
—James Inhofe

While not naming names, Inhofe argues that some Republican senators use their anti-earmark credentials as a fig leaf to cover their votes to authorize massive spending programs. As examples, he cited the $700 billion bank bailout in

October 2008; the Fannie Mae and Freddie Mac takeover in July 2008; and a bill the same month to increase funding for HIV/AIDS programs in Africa from $15 billion to $50 billion.

"If you look at those three things, you're well over a trillion dollars," he said. "And you look at the Republicans who voted for them. They've been able to use earmarks to distract people."

DeMint voted with Inhofe against all three measures. McCain voted for the bank bailout; and Coburn voted for both the bank bill and the AIDS legislation. DeMint, McCain, and Coburn are among the sponsors of earmark-moratorium legislation introduced last month.

Inhofe said that if Congress bans earmarks, his fallback position is that they should be defined only as projects that receive appropriations without having been previously authorized by Congress. Inhofe is a chief authorizer—for transportation programs at the Environment and Public Works Committee and for military programs at the Armed Services Committee. He and other authorizers regularly struggle for power with appropriators, who often have their own ideas about which projects to fund in their annual spending bills.

In a brief interview, McCain defended his anti-earmark stance. "My record is very clear," he said. "For 20 years I've fought against earmarks and their corruption. They breed corruption, and they've bred corruption."

McCain said he believes that the root of the problem is unauthorized appropriations. "You've got to get the definition of an earmark: that is, an unauthorized appropriation. If you authorize it, even if I disagree with it, that's the right process," he said. "What [earmarks] have done is totally circumvent what we should be doing: that is, authorizing and *then* appropriating."

Sen. Saxby Chambliss, R-Ga.—the ranking member on the Senate Agriculture, Nutrition, and Forestry Committee, another key authorizing panel—said that giving authorizers more power to say where money should be spent could be one part of earmark reform. He is a co-sponsor of the earmark moratorium. "I hope we get some sort of meaningful earmark reform as a result of continuing to stir that issue up," Chambliss said.

Inhofe's pro-earmark campaign will certainly cause a stir among his colleagues. Some House and Senate Republicans have urged the party to unilaterally adopt an earmark moratorium to paint a strong contrast to the Democrats. Inhofe counters that doing so would simply give more money to Obama to spend on liberal-supported projects and that it would distract attention from the core issues that the GOP can ride to victory in November.

"The Republican Party has the greatest issues ever in the history of politics in America—health care, cap-and-trade, closing Gitmo—that's terrorists coming into the United States, and the deficit, and the debt," Inhofe said. "Making an issue out of earmarks serves to only mislead voters by providing cover for big spenders. Railing against earmarks helps those who vote for the billion-dollar spending bills seem more conservative than they really are."

Jonathan Rauch
Earmarks Are a Model, Not a Menace

Naturally, when a gigantic omnibus appropriations bill came to the Senate floor last week, 98 percent of it got almost no attention. "Member projects—aka earmarks or 'pork'—account for less than 2 percent of spending in the $410 billion omnibus bill on the floor of the Senate this week, but they're drawing most of the opposition fire," *The Christian Science Monitor* reported. Less than 2 percent! Of course, this orgy of waste offended me for the same reason it offended everyone else: I was not getting an earmark.

I decided to get an earmark. Seemed easy enough. Just call someone in a congressional office, make a silly request—propose converting pig vomit into drywall, that sort of thing—and voila, I would have my very own "pet project."

So I called my congressman, Rep. Jim Moran, D-Va., who, handily enough, is a member of the Appropriations Committee. Imagine my shock when I got a staffer who insisted that I would have to *apply*.

Apply? For a *pet project*? Right. There was a form. As in, paperwork. The exact form would depend on which Appropriations subcommittee has jurisdiction. And I would need to meet with legislative aides to explain why my project deserved funding. And they would probably vet my request with the relevant federal agency.

Oh. But then I'm in, right?

Not quite. Moran told me he will get a thousand earmark applications this year. "It actually goes up every year." He will accept only the best hundred or so.

But *then* I'm in?

Published in *National Journal*, March 2009.

No, then the relevant Appropriations subcommittee further whittles the list. About three dozen of Moran's earmarks will get funded, he figures.

So my chances of scoring boodle were on the order of only 3 percent. I didn't fill out the form, even though it was only a page long. Down in Norfolk, Rep. Bobby Scott, D-Va., requires earmark applicants to fill out a seven-page form that looks like my tax return—and I itemize. "Please check *all* that apply: . . . This project is largely for EPA consent decree. . . . Preliminary planning and engineering design is completed." Really, it takes all the thrill out of pet projects.

Beating up on earmarks is fun. But if you interrupt the joy long enough to take a closer look, you may discover that the case against earmarks has pretty much evaporated over the past few years. In fact, reformers seem to want to hound out of existence a system that actually works better than much of what Washington does.

When former Rep. Jim Kolbe, R-Ariz., entered Congress in 1985, "there were no earmarks," he told me recently. Perhaps, you say, this was because appropriators were indifferent to how much federal money flowed to their districts? Sorry, bad guess.

In those days, according to Kolbe (an Appropriations Committee member who retired in 2007), appropriators felt little need to write earmarks into law. Instead, subcommittee chairmen and ranking members just dropped money into program accounts. Then they called up executive branch bureaucrats with advice on how to spend it.

"Most agencies didn't need to be threatened if the chairman of their subcommittee called," says Scott Lilly, a former House Appropriations Committee staff director and now a senior fellow with the Center for American Progress. Sometimes, Lilly says, "you'd increase the entire national program in order that it would have a better chance that it would spill into your state."

In the 1980s and 1990s, the once-sequestered system cracked open. The number of earmarks increased by a factor of 25 between 1991 and 2005. Earmarks were often invisible, at least until after they were enacted. "The bill would be passed before people even started digging into what was in there," Lilly says. Public outrage swelled.

On its heels, however, came reform, notably in the last couple of years. Every earmark request now must be made public before Congress votes on it. The sponsoring member, the amount and nature of the request, and the name and address of the beneficiary must all be disclosed. You can find all this stuff online. As I was miffed to discover, many congressional offices have formalized the application procedure. Getting an earmark now is a lot like applying for a grant.

As transparency has taken over, the case against earmarks has melted away. Their budgetary impact is trivial in comparison with entitlements and other large programs. Obsessing about earmarks, indeed, has the perverse, if convenient, effect of distracting the country from its real spending problems, thus substituting indignation for discipline.

Earmarks are often criticized for rewarding political clout rather than merit. If earmarks were merit-based, says Steve Ellis of the watchdog group Taxpayers for Common Sense, you wouldn't see them flowing disproportionately to Appropriations Committee members. And earmarks, he adds, reflect parochial rather than national priorities. "There's no way the Appropriations Committee is able to vet the thousands of earmarks worth billions of dollars."

Fair enough. But if you think that executive branch decisions are strictly apolitical and merit-based, I have two words for you: Karl Rove. "The idea that the only politicians in the government are in the Congress is just false," Lilly says. If you think that executive branch decision-making is transparent, I have two more words for you: Dick Cheney.

And if you think Congress is parochial, take it up with Mr. Madison. He wrote the Constitution, which says, in terms that leave no room for quibbling, that the power of the purse belongs to Congress. The Founders' notion was that accountability to local voters was the best safeguard for the people's money. "The idea that unless something is in the president's budget Congress shouldn't consider it turns the Constitution on its head," Kolbe says.

"The problem with a lot of federal programs is that they have to take a cookie-cutter approach," Moran says. Big, conventionally authorized programs, with their funding formulas and contracting rules and national purview, may be too slow to meet urgent local needs, too rigid to support innovation, too formulaic to finance a one-shot project.

Kolbe recalls an earmark that sped up an approved but languishing highway project in Arizona. "It was desperately needed; there were huge backups on the interstate," he says. "Seeing the growing need, not anticipated at the time of its initial approval, we simply jumped it up on the priority list."

Political discretion can be abused, and one would certainly not want most federal spending to be subject to it. But, provided that transparency is assured, shouldn't there be a place in government for elected officials to exercise judgment in the use of taxpayer money? In fact, if you wanted to create a non-bureaucratic, transparent system of rapid-response grants for pressing local concerns, you would come up with something very much like today's earmarking system (and you'd call it "reinventing government").

Some earmark spending is silly, but then so is some non-earmark spending, and there is a lot more of the latter. Competition for funding, combined with flexibility and local knowledge, makes earmarks "often some of the best expenditures the federal government makes in a particular area," Lilly says. "I would say, on the whole, earmarks probably provide as much value-added as non-earmarked federal spending."

And earmark spending today is, if anything, more transparent, more accountable, and more promptly disclosed than is non-earmark spending. Indeed, executive agencies could stand to emulate some of the online disclosure rules that apply to earmarks.

These days, the problem is not so much with earmarking as with Congress's and the public's obsession with it. "It just takes too damn much time," Lilly says. "Congress is spending an inordinate amount of time on 1 percent of the budget and giving the executive branch much too free a rein on the other 99 percent."

Reformers who want to ban earmarking might think again. "You're never going to abolish earmarks," Moran says. "What you'll wind up abolishing is the transparency, the accountability." If unable to earmark, legislators will inveigle executive agencies behind the scenes, fry bureaucrats at hearings, and expand or rewrite entire programs to serve parochial needs. This, of course, is the way things worked in the bad old days. "I think you'll wind up going back to that system," Kolbe cautions.

A better approach is to improve transparency and further routinize the earmarking process, as President Obama proposed on Wednesday when he signed the omnibus spending bill. But here is a reform that would help much more: Declare earmarking an ex-problem and move on. Next time you come across someone who looks at a giant federal spending bill and sees only the 2 percent that happens to be earmarked, tell that person to get over it.

QUESTIONS

1. How would you define pork-barrel projects? Are all pork projects contrary to the national interest? How do we distinguish between local projects that are in the national interest and those that are not?

2. Consider Cato's list of examples of pork. If you were a member of Congress, which of these would you clearly support? Which would you clearly oppose? Which would you want to find out more about before deciding?

3. Members of Congress face strong incentives to serve constituent needs and claim credit for delivering federal dollars. Pork-barrel projects provide the means to do just that. What changes in Congress or the political process might be made to alter legislative behavior, or to change the incentives legislators face when securing re-election? Do we want members of Congress to be focused primarily on broad national issues rather than local priorities?

6

The Presidency: Is Obama a Transformational President?

When Barack Obama announced his presidential campaign in January 2007, the odds seemed long. Yet he defeated New York State Senator Hillary Clinton in one of the most closely contested presidential nomination contests in decades, and then went on to defeat the far more experienced Republican senator John McCain to win the presidency.

Throughout the campaign, Obama dazzled audiences with soaring rhetoric about "changing Washington," announcing that his campaign was about "hope and change." "It's time for us to change America," Obama said as he accepted his party's nomination for president, time to "cast off the worn-out ideas and politics of the past." Obama presented himself as a transformational president, someone who would introduce a new kind of politics. All presidents promise change—that's the main reason for running against incumbents or the incumbent political party. But Obama held out the prospect of a fundamental alteration of political arrangements and incentives, a shift in who held political power. As the first African American president, Obama certainly represented symbolic change in the kind of person who could get elected. Would he be able to deliver? Would he truly change the way politics operated and change the distribution of political power? Progressives and liberals were euphoric, certain that their time had come after eight years of George W. Bush's conservatism and wartime policy.

Conservatives were alarmed that Obama would usher in a major expansion of government's role in the economy and weaken national security policy.

What can we now say about President Obama? Will he be compared to Andrew Jackson, Franklin Roosevelt, Thomas Jefferson, or Abraham Lincoln, presidents who fundamentally altered political arrangements and power? Will he be just another president who promised big and failed to deliver? Or is there a middle ground?

David Greenberg occupies the middle ground in this debate. The soaring hopes of January 2009 have dissipated in the face of the realities of governing, which has always been much, much harder than campaigning. But, Greenberg argues, that is inevitable, because "in the modern age, presidents are never able to meet" the expectations of transformative change. Presidents always confront limits and, given the expectations generated during the campaign, they must always disappoint. But that is hardly synonymous with failure, and Greenberg notes that other historic presidents—including Lincoln, Roosevelt, Kennedy—and Reagan, although Greenberg doesn't mention him—had rough early days.

Writing from the left, Katrina Vanden Heuvel and Robert L. Borosage express disappointment, especially over Obama's policies toward the financial sector, which they see as enriching Wall Street bankers while leaving families behind, and his surge in troop commitments in Afghanistan. "Many wonder," they write, "what happened to the transformational presidency." They argue that the president, despite his promises, has not been bold enough in confronting entrenched interests and has proven reluctant to mobilize his liberal base in the face of conservative obstructionism. The result has been timid compromises on health care reform and a reluctance to confront conservative arguments head on. These authors urge the president to move sharply to the left. They also call on progressives to organize large-scale protests that take advantage of the same enthusiasm that motivated many supporters during the 2008 campaign.

Richard Lowry and Ramesh Ponnuru see Obama as transformative, but not in a positive way. In their view, Obama is the first president explicitly to reject the notion of American exceptionalism—the idea that the United States is historically unique and has always differed from other democracies. They claim that liberals have always been uncomfortable with this notion, and that the Left is more likely to see the United States as the source of many of the world's problems, not its best hope. And Obama, in their eyes, embodies this rejection of American exceptionalism. They note his efforts to expand greatly the size and scope of government regulatory power, his "hesitance to advocate American ideals," and his defensiveness in the international arena. They claim that Obama's problems stem from the public's repudiation of his principal policies.

David Greenberg

The Honeymooners

The promise and selling point of Barack Obama's 2008 campaign—breaking with the past, delivering something new—was the oldest promise in American politics. Since European settlers crossed the Atlantic imagining (mistakenly) a "new world" without history, Americans have rewarded talk of new beginnings. The early colonists sought to create a society de novo in ways that Europe—with its religious wars, social stratification, and finitude of land—made impossible. To the Revolutionary generation, the acts of declaring independence and drafting a constitution seemed to ratify this mythology. And in every era since, Americans have fallen, starry-eyed, for leaders who speak of a future unencumbered by history's weight. Theodore Roosevelt's New Nationalism, Woodrow Wilson's New Freedom, FDR's New Deal, JFK's New Frontier, even George H. W. Bush's New World Order—all began with the promise of the new.

Of course, after the flush of a campaign, both voters and presidents have invariably discovered that history imposes constraints. After the Civil War, a cohort of young intellectuals invested hope in Ulysses S. Grant, only to see rampant corruption persist and the dream of reconstructing the South dissolve. After World War I, the crash-and-burn of Wilson's noble quest for "peace without victory" soured Americans on an energetic executive for a decade. Bill Clinton's New Covenant, a dead-on-arrival slogan, presaged the letdown that came as his followers realized that liberalism's revival would require more than a few token compromises.

Obama in 2008 was just the latest aspirant to talk of beginning anew. He bested Hillary Clinton for the Democratic nomination in part by saddling her with the record of not one but two past presidents: the residual regret over her

Published in *The Atlantic*, January/February, 2010.

husband's supposedly small-bore and blandly centrist Third Way agenda, and the collective buyers' remorse over the Iraq War. In contrast to the dreaded "incrementalism" of the Clintons, Obama's candidacy tantalized voters with a chance for what he called "transformational" or "fundamental" change.

One year later, transformation looks like a fleeting dream. No one knows whether Obama can deliver massive change on the scale of Lincoln, Wilson, FDR, or LBJ. But right now, the opportunity that loomed last fall seems to have passed. Conservatives—uncharacteristically mute last winter—have regained their voice, nearly derailing Obama's health-care plan and keeping the administration on defense in the daily media wars. Meanwhile, liberals and leftists, who largely muffled their doubts when Obama had a presidency to win, are suddenly seething over his moderation and compromises—keeping suspected terrorists jailed indefinitely, countenancing his treasury secretary's coziness with financial CEOs, letting center-right senators weaken his health-care plan. Washington pundits, for their part, intoned throughout 2009 that in taking on health care, energy, and financial reform in his first year, the president was attempting "too much."

Yet the now-prevalent pessimism about Obama's presidency is surely unwarranted. True, we can no longer expect Obama to be the agent of a postpartisan politics, or an uncorrupted anti-politician incapable of spin or triangulation, or America's most civil-libertarian president, or a socialist. But in the modern age, presidents are never able to meet such expectations. Our hunger for presidential intervention, leadership, and salvation now exceeds any individual's capacities. So the eclipse of these campaign-trail fantasies about Obama's presidency hardly signals its death. On the contrary, it marks the true beginning.

"If there is anything that history has taught us," John F. Kennedy said on the campaign trail in 1960, "it is that the great accomplishments of Woodrow Wilson and of Franklin Roosevelt were made in the early days, months, and years of their administrations. That was the time for maximum action." But Kennedy was wrong—unless you choose to focus exclusively on the word *years* instead of *days* and *months*. As rich in opportunity as presidential honeymoons can be—and the best executives have used them to get important things done—a president's real work doesn't occur when he has what Obama calls the righteous wind at his back. It occurs when he has to soldier on into a fight, despite blustery headwinds.

Like the unit of 100 days, the benchmark of a president's first year matters a lot to journalists but relatively little to historians. The 100-days concept itself, which originated with Roosevelt's flurry of activity in early 1933, soon devolved into a transparent public-relations gimmick, as media-age presidents sweated over how to boost their grades on what soon came to be recognized as the president's initial report card. Similarly, the now-ritualized year-one evaluation, though harmless as an exercise in journalistic stock-taking, offers a weak basis for predicting future performance. Indeed, none of the three presidents Obama has taken as his role models—Lincoln, FDR, and Kennedy—enjoyed a first year that foretold the direction of his presidency. Transformation doesn't happen overnight.

Abraham Lincoln is Obama's favorite president and his aspirational model. In 2007, the senator from Illinois launched his bid for the Oval Office in Lincoln's shadow, on the steps of the Springfield Old State Capitol. With his message of national conciliation, Obama often echoed Lincoln's second inaugural address. Even when he attacked his rivals, he suggested that he was merely combating their retrogressive politics while he was summoning the better angels of our nature. At times, the Lincoln comparisons taxed credulity: Obama's devotees even pointed to Lincoln's one-term service in Congress—and his subsequent rise to become America's greatest president—to answer the charge that Obama hadn't accomplished enough in his career to earn him the White House. It was no surprise when, in January 2009, the incoming president took his inaugural oath on the Bible Lincoln had used, and presided over festivities branded as "A New Birth of Freedom."

Yet as Obama surely knows, Lincoln—a transformative president if there ever was one—started his administration on a shaky note. His inaugural address fumblingly extended on olive branch to the seceding states of the South, promising (to no avail) that he would enforce the fugitive-slave law and uphold slavery in the states where it was legal. The Confederate attack on Fort Sumter forced Lincoln to change course. But on the crucial matter of slavery, the president—who had never considered himself an abolitionist—remained fairly conservative. "If I could save the Union without freeing *any* slave I would do it, and if I could save it by freeing *all* the slaves I would do it," he wrote to Horace Greeley in 1862, "and if I could save it by freeing some and leaving others alone I would also do that." Few foresaw that his presidency would end with the abolition of slavery and a redefinition of freedom, union, and equality.

Lincoln also needed time to gain his footing as commander in chief. Unsure of himself in military affairs, he was at the mercy of his generals, including the aging and detached Winfield Scott. Dispiriting defeats—notably at the First Battle of Bull Run, in July 1861—emboldened the South. Even after Lincoln mustered the wisdom to replace Scott, George B. McClellan, his new top commander, frustrated the president by declining to advance against Confederate forces. As for his domestic agenda, Lincoln, like most 19th-century presidents, followed Congress's lead. But even there, despite a Republican leadership eager to exploit the sudden absence of Southerners, major laws—the Homestead Act, the Pacific Railway Act, and the Morrill Land Grant Act—didn't get the president's signature until 1862.

No one could say that Franklin Roosevelt began his first year in office hesitantly. His first 100 days were indeed a whirlwind of legislative and executive feats. But FDR geared his first-year efforts almost entirely toward recovery—a necessary but hardly transformative goal.

Certain measures—like solving the banking crisis, which had reached catastrophic proportions on the eve of his inauguration—made a palpable difference. But the core elements of FDR's "First New Deal" turned out to be, on the whole, ineffectual or unconstitutional—or both. The National Recovery Administration, the centerpiece of it all, which relied on industry leaders to agree to production codes, was flawed in both conception and execution, and it failed miserably. When the Supreme Court unanimously ruled it unconstitutional, Roosevelt's aide Robert Jackson called the decision a blessing in disguise, since it spared the president from having to watch Congress decline to renew the act. The Agricultural Adjustment Act, which regulated farm production through central planning, was also struck down. And then there was Roosevelt's Economy Act, a misguided effort in budget balancing taken up before Washington discovered the wisdom of deficit spending.

Most of the New Deal's lasting elements didn't come until 1935. Only after taking a beating on the airwaves from demagogic populists like Senator Huey Long of Louisiana and the radio priest Charles Coughlin did FDR sign on to the Social Security Act, which created unemployment insurance, old-age pensions, and a safety net for the disabled. And not until his second term did his administration embrace a Keynesian strategy of aggressive spending to lift the economy out of crisis. If Roosevelt's first year was historic for its activist spirit and purposeful intervention, its economic philosophy left little mark.

While Obama styled himself Lincolnian in his rhetoric of reconciliation, and Rooseveltian in his steadfastness in the face of economic distress, he just as often summoned the Kennedy mystique, presenting himself as the telegenic, inspirational torchbearer of an ascendant generation. Obama suggested that he wanted to "move the country in a fundamentally different direction," as he believed Kennedy had. Just as Kennedy's election shattered the anti-Catholic taboo in presidential politics, Obama's promised to topple an age-old wall of racial prejudice. The Baby Boomers who flocked to Obama's candidacy said he brought back memories of JFK. The claim was echoed most tellingly by the fallen president's own brother, who anointed Obama as JFK's successor after perceiving a slight to the family name in Hillary Clinton's assertion that the skill of Lyndon Johnson—she didn't mention Jack—had been instrumental in passing the 1964 Civil Rights Act.

In fact, on civil rights, as in other areas, Kennedy's first-year performance dismayed his enthusiasts. As a candidate, he had vowed to desegregate federal housing with "a stroke of the presidential pen." But once in office, he demurred; fearful of alienating powerful southern Democrats whose support he needed on other issues, he focused instead on foreign-policy problems. Not until he'd cleared the 1962 midterm elections did Kennedy issue the housing proclamation. Caution likewise informed his response to the Freedom Riders—the activists who rode buses across the South starting in May 1961 to force the government to uphold the Supreme Court's desegregation of interstate travel. When white southerners brutally beat the activists, Kennedy and his aides, unprepared, at first tried to stop the rides, sending in federal marshals only when it seemed that the violence might turn deadly.

In foreign policy, too, the biggest developments of JFK's debut year yielded little positive transformation. The Bay of Pigs invasion, all ill-conceived CIA scheme hatched under Dwight Eisenhower, redounded to Kennedy's benefit only because he had the sense not to duck responsibility. At his June summit in Vienna with Nikita Khrushchev, the new president felt he was verbally pummeled by the Soviet premier, in what Kennedy called the "roughest thing in my life." Kennedy's tepid response may have encouraged Khrushchev to erect the Berlin Wall that fall. When that happened, too, JFK was slow to act (KENNEDY: YOU CAN'T STOP TANKS WITH WORDS, read one West Berliner's protest sign), and even his decision to send retired General Lucius Clay and Vice President Johnson to West Berlin to boost morale did nothing to deter the Soviets. At the end of 1961, Kennedy's aide Ted Sorensen mentioned that two reporters were considering writing books about the year gone by. Kennedy was mystified: "Who would want to read a book on disasters?"

The presidency that Obama's resembles most so far isn't any of these but, ironically, that of Bill Clinton—ironic because Obama, speaking in January 2008 about what makes a good president, implicitly denigrated Clinton even as he praised Ronald Reagan for having "changed the trajectory of America" and "put us on a fundamentally different path." Obama, many speculated at the time, may have been playing head games with his peevish predecessor, goading him into another outburst that would thrill the press pack. Even so, it was a strange reading of history. Reagan's election, after all, did not initiate but culminated a long conservative effort to gain control of the levers of power; his decisions as president moved his party to the right, but they also introduced fissures and frustrations into the conservative alliance. Clinton's tenure, in contrast, began a new era for the Democrats, and after his eight years, virtually all of the party's leading lights embraced what had been controversial stands in 1992: an internationalist foreign policy, growth-centered economics, and a willingness to link social policies to family values.

The point would be trivial had Obama not reached for Clinton's 1992 playbook during the fall 2008 campaign. Obama's battle with John McCain, which centered on the hard-pressed middle class, showed that Obama represented less a repudiation of Clinton (as the primaries had suggested) than a continuation. His rhetoric wafted to earth to focus on everyday economic concerns. His convention speech opened, after the preliminaries, not with soaring visions of postpartisan unity, but with issue-based, it's-the-economy-stupid plain language:

> Tonight, more Americans are out of work and more are working harder for less. More of you have lost your homes and even more are watching your home values plummet. More of you have cars you can't afford to drive, credit-card bills you can't afford to pay, and tuition that's beyond your reach.

Obama discovered this idiom just in time for the financial chaos and the debates with McCain.

Obama's successes and struggles in his first year bear striking resemblances to Clinton's. Both men were elected with similar mandates—Clinton won 370 electoral voles, Obama 365—and majorities in both houses of Congress. Both opened their first years well by signing a few queued-up executive orders and bills—including the Family and Medical Leave Act, for Clinton, and the Lilly Ledbetter Fair Pay Act and the expansion of the Children's Health Insurance Program, for Obama. And both made economic revival their first priority. Both men also entered office facing tooth-and-nail resistance from a right wing that had just lost the presidency. The right imagined Clinton, as it does Obama, to be far more radical than he really was, and it thus tried to delegitimize him. A short line connects the "Who shot Vince Foster?" conspiracy theories to those surrounding Obama's citizenship.

Republicans also forced Clinton to pass his first economic plan without their support, much as they tried to scuttle Obama's stimulus package. And despite losing the legislative battle, they succeeded in shaping public perception of these economic bills after their passage. Clinton's 1993 budget—which not only set the government on course for a record surplus, but also cut taxes for millions while raising them on very few—was nonetheless portrayed, and viewed by most Americans, as a tax hike. In parallel fashion, economic evidence suggests that Obama's spring stimulus bill has already done some appreciable good. But according to an August Gallup poll, Americans consider it too big and are uncertain about its benefits. And while Obama seems likely, as of this writing, to emerge from his first health-care fight with more to show for it than Clinton did from his, the final bill probably won't be more than an incremental step or two forward—less like Medicare than like the 1996 Kennedy-Kassebaum Act, a now-forgotten consolation prize that Clinton garnered later in his presidency.

The reassertion of political limits and the deflation of campaign-season euphoria make it unlikely that Obama's presidency will be "transformational" in the sense that he spoke of on the campaign trail—Lincolnian in its boldness, Rooseveltian in its activism, or Kennedyesque in its uplift. More likely, it will resemble Clinton's presidency, with eight years of muddling through, frequent bouts of sharp partisan opposition, fluctuating poll ratings, and dashed hopes.

This should be no cause for distress. Obama could do worse than to emulate Clinton, who, at the end of day, left the country better off than when he took office. Clinton's record remains undervalued, partly because a misleading narrative took hold (that his impeachment cost him the chance to do more), and partly because many of his gains were achieved not through the big-ticket stand-alone legislation that journalists recite in their year-end summaries but through less visible allocations within the interstices of the federal budget. No single law or presidential order gave us the longest economic expansion in history, the lowest unemployment rates in three decades, or the declines in poverty, crime, and teen pregnancy. Nor does Clinton deserve sole credit for these feats. But all were accomplished during his eight years.

Twenty-five years ago, the political scientist Theodore Lowi published a book called *The Personal President*. It argued that the increasingly large responsibilities placed on the president since Franklin Roosevelt's time—of regulation, social provision, and economic management, to say nothing of the leadership of the free world—have exploded into impossible expectations. Every postwar chief executive, Lowi noted—and the observation still holds—has begun his presidency with high approval ratings and left office with the public chastened of its early optimism, if not disillusioned altogether. (The president who has exited the White House with the highest approval ratings, post-FDR, is Clinton.)

It is easy to propose that we lower our expectations for our new presidents—even, or perhaps especially, for presidents who come bearing lofty promises of transformation. But we can't correct the problem, Lowi's diagnosis suggested, simply by resolving to demand less from our chief executives or by vowing to learn from the past. The problem is rooted in nothing less than the presidency's assumption of immense powers, and of a central role in our imagination. Candidates have no better path to victory than by inspiring us with dreams of a new political era, and presidents have no choice but to attempt "too much." In doing so, however, they can only disappoint us.

Katrina Vanden Heuvel and Robert L. Borosage
Change Won't Come Easy

President Obama hailed the healthcare reform bill coming out of the Senate as the "most important piece of social legislation since the Social Security Act passed in the 1930s." Former Democratic Party chair Howard Dean denounced it as a "giveaway to insurance companies."

Published in *The Nation*, February 2010.

Larry Summers, Obama's lead economic adviser, described the $780 billion recovery plan as the largest stimulus plan in the country's history. Economists like Nobel laureate Joseph Stiglitz warned from the beginning that it was too small to lift us out of the Great Recession.

The president described the administration's financial reform package as a "sweeping overhaul," a "transformation on a scale not seen since . . . the Great Depression." Former Federal Reserve chair Paul Volcker warned that the proposed "safety net" for big banks would encourage much greater "risk taking."

Congressman Ed Markey, chair of the House Select Committee on Energy Independence, hailed the energy bill that was passed by the House as "the most important energy and environmental bill in our nation's history." Environmental leaders were underwhelmed; some considered it worse than the current law.

The discordant reality of these times is that these conflicting statements are all essentially true. "I want you to be ready," Bill Clinton warned bloggers about healthcare reform at the Netroots Conference in August, to "accept less than a full loaf." He could easily have been talking about the Obama presidency itself. Progressives must determine how to respond now that the fierce resistance to change has revealed itself.

The euphoria of a year ago is dissipating. Then, in the wake of a calamitous and discredited conservative government, Americans voted for change, electing a stunningly gifted leader and large Democratic majorities in both houses of Congress. A mobilized activist base appeared ready to throw itself into the fray, and an emerging majority coalition suggested the potential for a long-term realignment.

Now the struggles of the first year of the Obama administration are generating increasing demoralization and anger. Disappointment about reforms in motion—healthcare, jobs, climate change—marks those who care the most. The recovery plan, which has revived Wall Street but not working families, is fueling dangerous right-wing populism. Substituting an unwinnable "good war" in Afghanistan for the unwinnable "bad war" in Iraq, along with a military budget exceeding that of George W. Bush, is a recipe for failure. The administration's foreign policy—despite the promise in Cairo of engaging the Muslim world and in Prague of embracing disarmament—is increasingly described by neocons as providing more continuity than change from the Bush years. Democrats cringe at prospects for the fall elections. Despite all the obvious eloquence and intelligence of the new president, many wonder what happened to the transformational presidency.

It Ain't Easy; Everything's Broken

Turns out, Obama is not the Messiah, and those who thought so were always fooling themselves. The disappointments of Obama's first year are less the product of his failures than of the balance of forces he faces in Washington and in the country. Many progressives thought we had taken back America with the election of 2008, but in reality the work had only just begun.

In fact, the president has been bolder than many expected, summoning the country to address fundamental challenges it can no longer afford to ignore. Yet the ambition of Obama's vision has been accompanied by a marked caution in conception and execution. Obama clearly aspires to a historic presidency, one that defines a new era as FDR's or Reagan's did. But he has never been a movement progressive the way Reagan was a movement conservative. He has surrounded himself with the brightest and best of the Democratic establishment, drawn inevitably from those marinated in the Clinton years. Many of his leading advisers—from Larry Summers and Timothy Geithner to Robert Gates—were directly implicated in the decisions that helped to drive us off the cliff. These voices are not advocates of transformation.

So the reform proposals that emerge from the administration often fall short not only of the hopes of progressives but of the objectives the president himself defines and the change the country needs. Obama outlined a new foundation for the economy in his "Sermon on the Mount," but the big banks were rescued, not reorganized, and no industrial policy accompanied the commitment to a new economy. Bankers were chastised for their bonuses, but there was no drive to hold executives accountable and empower workers, both central to an economy that sustains a broad middle class. The president shelved Bush's failed cowboy bellicosity, but the decision to escalate in Afghanistan accedes to the Bush folly of waging war against terrorism rather than intensifying global law enforcement.

Most surprising has been the reluctance to engage the right boldly in the war of ideas. Reagan consolidated the conservative era in part by bludgeoning reigning liberalism with a relentless conservative critique. He attacked and retreated on policy when necessary, but his ideological assault never faltered. Obama has a rare ability to frame the contrast with the right, to counter its market fundamentalism and virulent nihilism with a compelling statement of our shared values, with government as the necessary instrument of our common purpose.

But for much of the year, Democrats have been having policy debates—on the public opinion, on cap and trade, on systemic risk regulation—while Republicans and the resurgent right have been waging an argument about values and ideas, on liberty and free markets, freedom and small government. Although the administration has reminded Americans of the catastrophic legacy left by the Bush years, it has seldom indicted the conservative ideas that were the source of the calamity. Instead the president prefers to blame the process—"partisanship . . . politics . . . ever quickening news cycles . . . endless campaigns focused on scoring points instead of meeting our common challenges."

That default complements an insider Congressional strategy that prefers backroom compromise to public mobilization. This president enunciates the elements of his reform proposals and then lets Congress and his aides to do their work off-stage. But that cedes the terrain to the legions of the old order that are mobilized to fend off real reform.

The past months have exposed the elements of that resistance—the cynical Republican strategy of lockstep obstruction, the Senate rules that empower a handful of small-state conservatives and the embittered Joe Lieberman. (It is worth remembering that there were majorities in both houses of Congress for a bolder stimulus and far better healthcare reform.)

And of course, at the heart of the opposition are the entrenched corporate complexes that feed off public subsidies and a corrupt Congress. These have been boom times for Democratic lobbyists and former officeholders. The commercial banks deployed nearly 417 registered lobbyists in 2009. The insurance and drug lobbies spent about $1.4 million a day, with 350 former legislators and staffers lined up to weaken healthcare reform. Legislators in both parties succumbed to the pervasive corruptions of our money politics.

The result is that even when historic reforms like healthcare emerge, they are so battered that supporters end up dispirited. Democrats face going into the 2010 midterm elections with double-digit unemployment, rescued bankers awarding themselves million-dollar bonuses, rising casualties in Afghanistan, the right mobilized and progressive activists dismayed. If Republicans score major victories in the election, that will make everything harder; the administration will become more cautious, not less. Clearly, if we are not to squander the best opportunity for progressive reform in thirty years, something will have to change.

Going Grassroots

The president warned that change wouldn't come easy. From the start, the administration devoted energy and resources to organizing a unified base of activists. Organizing for Obama promised use of an unmatched list of activists and supporters built during the campaign. Donors were tapped to set up new entities—Common Purpose Project, Unity '09, etc.—to coordinate messages and field operations. Significant resources went to coalitions to help drive healthcare, climate change and immigration reform. The administration's argument was and is compelling. This is a reform moment with the most liberal president in memory. It is time to unite, provide support for his leadership and help drive reform.

Progressives and grassroots networks across the country rallied to that call. Remarkable work has been done. Broad coalitions were built, arming activists with more capacity and better coordination in the process of lobbying legislators. New constituencies—the faith community, young people and small business owners—have been enlisted. Resources were devoted to conservative districts and states where key swing votes had to be won.

These efforts have propelled the president's key reforms. When tea-baggers threatened to torpedo heathcare reform, progressives—led by Health Care for America Now, unions and MoveOn—mobilized and soon overwhelmed them in town hall meetings.

But there were costs associated with channeling progressive energy through the administration. Obama aides, led by Chief of Staff Rahm Emanuel, argued fiercely against going after the Democrats—Blue Dogs and New Dems—who were impeding reform, and the White House chose not to mobilize its base to pressure them. Groups were often blindsided by backroom deals like the one with the drug companies that sustained the ban on negotiating lower drug prices.

One unintended consequence was that populist anger has been channeled by the right, not the left. Tea-baggers, well funded by established interests, turned rage against those trying to dig out of the hole rather than those who got us into it. Their voice was inchoate, but at the core was a fury at Big Government, Big Banks and Big Business, which were taking their jobs, pocketing public subsidies and helping "those people" while raising their taxes. On the left, there has been no movement comparable to the labor and socialist demonstrations in the '30s or the civil rights movement in the '60s that forced the pace of change.

Moving Forward: Ideas Matter

Cynicism is the cheap coin of politics. The left blogosphere is rife with the complaints of the disillusioned (denouncing politicians as crooks, the government as corrupt and Obama as compromised) and threats to give up and stay home. That would be a profound mistake. This country is enmeshed in a fierce debate about its future. Can we summon up the will and the majorities needed to meet the critical challenges we face? Or will we continue our decline, ceding ground to the entrenched corporate cronyism that profits from conservative misrule?

Winning this debate requires new thinking as well as independent organizing. Progressives should be moving outside the Beltway, working to organize protest movements for social justice and giving voice to the displaced and the unemployed. We should be helping to chart a new course while exposing the false idols and powerful interests that stand in the way.

And we should be directly joining the argument with the resurgent right. One basic lesson must be repeated and elaborated upon: the mess that we are in results not from inaction or partisan stalemate but from the failure of conservative policies and ideas in action. Only by coming together to demand an accountable democratic government on our side, free from the special interests that feed off it, can we build a stronger, more just and more vibrant America.

Reform Matters

A renewed focus on building protest movements can bolster, not weaken, reform efforts. National debates over fundamental reforms will provide the grist for such organizing. In 2010, assuming healthcare finally passes, the legislative agenda will turn to jobs and financial accountability, two issues that are vital to building the new economy. Politically, the fall elections will likely depend on which candidates and which party can convince skeptical voters that they are on the side of working people and for curbing Wall Street's excesses.

Here progressive organizing and protests that challenge the limits of the current debate are essential. On jobs, the fundamental questions are whether a commitment will be made of sufficient scale to meet the deepening jobs crisis and whether that initiative will be sufficiently targeted to impact those areas most devastated. Republicans and Blue Dog Democrats are already declaiming against any new program. The administration, badgered about deficits and believing the economy is on the road to recovery, it likely to support a face-lift when reconstructive surgery is needed.

The stakes here couldn't be higher. If Democrats don't deliver on jobs, the economy won't recover, and the 2010 election may well snuff out any chance for reforms. At the very least, they have to show Americans that they're fighting for jobs. Independent organizing that gives voice to the unemployed, already begun by labor unions and civil rights groups, is essential. The House Progressive Caucus can play a major role in raising the bar and forcing the issue.

Similarly, the debate on financial reform should provide the context for progressive protest organizing. The White House plans to pick a fight with the banking lobby over the proposed Consumer Financial Protection Agency, which would create an independent cop to police banks and protect consumers from financial frauds and abuses. In the House, Republicans voted with the banks against reform. In contrast, progressives are pushing sweeping reforms that go to the heart of the financial excesses of the past years—auditing the Federal Reserve; breaking up the big banks; taxing windfall profits, excess bonuses and speculation; outlawing exotic instruments; and limiting usurious interest rates.

Independent organizing can tap into a wellspring of public fury. Muckraking is needed to detail and broadcast the systemic frauds and corruptions. Creative demonstrations can embarrass the bank lobby and the legislators on the take. It is only if the big banks' money becomes toxic that there is any hope of gaining the reforms needed to curb their power. Here is where the creativity and energy of the Obama activists, many frustrated by the timidity of Organizing for America, can find expression.

Pundits predict that the other issues on the president's agenda—climate change, immigration reform, employee free choice—will have a difficult time getting a hearing before the 2010 elections. Progressives will have to push hard to ensure that these reforms—vital to both the new economy and to consolidating the emerging progressive majority—are not shunted to the side.

Because of the botched terrorist attempt to bomb a plane on Christmas Day, the administration enters the year on the defensive on terrorism. The furor will add to bipartisan support for an enlarged military budget and for military escalation in Afghanistan, Yemen and elsewhere. The president will sound more bellicose notes on terrorism. The opposition to escalation in Afghanistan, which probably still enjoys majority support among Democrats in the House, will have to redouble its work, educating Americans about the costs and the stakes and offering common-sense alternative strategies to meet the threat of terrorism.

Challenge Those Who Stand in the Way

Democratic prospects look grim for the fall elections. In low-turnout midterm elections, the passion of base supporters plays a large role. Clearly, the right will be mobilized. Progressives will have to confound the widespread expectation that they will not match the right's fervor.

The elections will turn into a national referendum on the country's direction. Will Americans punish those pushing for reform, or those standing in the way? The clear focus must be to make certain that Republicans pay for their irresponsible strategy of obstruction. Here the GOP's opposition to creating jobs and curbing banks should provide a clear picture of what side they are on.

But this cannot be a purely partisan effort. Democrats who have consistently opposed or weakened vital reforms should not get a free pass. Progressives should be organizing primary challenges against the most egregious Blue Dogs—exemplified by Representative Melissa Bean, who gilded her campaign war chest by leading the banks' lobby efforts to weaken financial reform. It would be best to do this in districts or states where Democrats are strong, so the seats are not lost; but that may not be possible. Organizing formidable challenges in a couple of districts will send an important message.

The Audacity of Hope

As Frederick Douglass taught, "power concedes nothing without a demand. It never did and never will." Digging out of the hole that conservatives left Americans in can't be done overnight. The president has called on the country to face daunting challenges. Every step of reform is contested by powerful interests. Ruinous policies—such as our commitment to policing the world—have broad bipartisan support. Yet we haven't had this kind of moment since the 1960s. With persistence, work, rededication and struggle, we can issue the demands that change requires. This is a time for neither the innocent nor the cynical. It is a time for passion, for tenacity and, yes, for hope.

Richard Lowry and Ramesh Ponnuru
An Exceptional Debate

It's almost commonplace on the left that conservatives are "nihilists" for their opposition to President Obama. It's opposition for opposition's sake, an unprincipled exercise in partisan obstruction—mindless, toxic, destructive. When directed at Obama, "no" is an indefensible word, devoid of philosophical content.

Another, different charge has traditionally been leveled at conservatives—that they are "radicals." This criticism was made of *National Review* right at the beginning. Conservatives want to tear down the state, overturn precedent, reverse the direction of history. They are imprudent and incautious in their pursuit of a blinkered ideological agenda, in other words, fundamentally unconservative.

So conservatives get it coming and going. Our opposition to the Left is deemed nihilistic and our affirmative agenda radical. These dueling critiques point to a paradox at the heart of American conservatism. We aren't Tories, concerned with preserving the prerogatives of an aristocratic elite or defending tradition at all costs. Instead, we're advocates of the dynamism of an open society. Through most of human history and still in many places in the world, that would make us the opposite of conservatives. Not in America.

What do we, as American conservatives, want to *conserve*? The answer is simple: the pillars of American exceptionalism. Our country has always been exceptional. It is freer, more individualistic, more democratic, and more open and dynamic than any other nation on earth. These qualities are the bequest of our Founding and of our cultural heritage. They have always marked America as special, with a unique role and mission in the world: as a model of ordered liberty and self-government and as an exemplar of freedom and a vindicator of it, through persuasion when possible and force of arms when absolutely necessary.

The survival of American exceptionalism as we have known it is at the heart of the debate over Obama's program. It is why that debate is so charged. In his first year, Obama tried to avoid the cultural hot buttons that tripped up

Published in *National Review*, March 2010.

Bill Clinton and created the "gays, guns, and God" backlash of 1994. But he has stoked a different type of cultural reaction. The level of spending, the bailouts, and the extent of the intervention in the economy contemplated in health-care and cap-and-trade legislation have created the fear that something elemental is changing in the country. At stake isn't just a grab bag of fiscal issues, but the meaning of America and the character of its people: the ultimate cultural issue.

* * *

Liberty is the most important element of the creed. To secure it, the Founders set about strictly limiting government within carefully specified bounds. Immediately upon the collapse of British government in America, the states drew up written constitutions and neutered their executives. They went as far as they could possibly go to tame the government—indeed, they went farther, and had to start over to get a functioning state. But even this second try produced a Constitution that concentrated as much on what government could not do as on what it could.

The Founders knew what men were capable of, in the positive sense if their creative energies were unleashed and in the negative sense if they were given untrammeled power over others. "It may be a reflection on human nature," Madison wrote in a famous passage in *Federalist* No. 51 describing the checks in the Constitution, "that such devices should be necessary to control the abuses of government. But what is government itself, but the greatest of all reflections on human nature? If men were angels, no government would be necessary. If angels were to govern men, neither external nor internal controls on government would be necessary."

The Constitution's negative character reflected its basic goal: to protect people in their liberty. In stark contrast, European constitutions, even prior to World War II, established positive rights to government benefits. As Mary Ann Glendon notes, these differences "are legal manifestations of divergent, and deeply rooted, cultural attitudes toward the state and its functions."

This framework of freedom made possible the flourishing of the greatest commercial republic in history. * * *

* * *

In a telling coincidence, the publication of Adam Smith's world-changing free-market classic, *The Wealth of Nations*, coincided with the Declaration of

Independence in 1776. Many of the Founders read the book. Without the medieval encumbrances and the powerful, entrenched special interests that plagued other countries, the United States could make Smith's ideas the basis of its economic dispensation. Gordon writes, "The United States has consistently come closer to the Smithian ideal over a longer period of time than any other major nation."

In the latitude provided by this relatively light-handed government, a commerce-loving, striving, and endlessly inventive people hustled its way to become the greatest economic power the world has ever known.

In America, there really hasn't been a disaffected proletariat—because the proletariat has gotten rich. Friedrich Engels had it right when he carped that "America is so purely bourgeois, so entirely without a feudal past and therefore proud of its purely bourgeois organization."

The traditional Marxist claim about the U.S. was that it was governed by the executive committee of the bourgeoisie. This was not intended as a compliment, but it was largely true. Look at the archetypal American, Benjamin Franklin, whose name comes from the Middle English meaning freeman, someone who owns some property. Napoleon dismissed the British as "a nation of shopkeepers"; we are a nation of Franklins.

Abraham Lincoln, a de facto Founding Father, is an exemplar of this aspect of America. "I hold the value of life," Lincoln said, "is to improve one's condition." There are few things he hated more than economic stasis. He couldn't abide Thomas Jefferson's vision of a nation of yeoman farmers living on their land forevermore, blissfully untouched by the forces of modern economic life. (Appropriately enough, Jefferson died broke.) Lincoln captured the genius of American life when he said, "The man who labored for another last year, this year labors for himself and next year he will hire others to labor for him."

That sentiment is at the heart of the American economic gospel. American attitudes toward wealth and its creation stand out within the developed world. Our income gap is greater than that in European countries, but not because our poor are worse off. In fact, they are better off than, say, the bottom 10 percent of Britons. It's just that our rich are phenomenally wealthy.

This is a source of political tension, but not as much as foreign observers might expect, thanks partly to a typically American attitude. A 2003 Gallup survey found that 31 percent of Americans expect to get rich, including 51 percent of young people and more than 20 percent of Americans making less than

$30,000 a year. This isn't just cockeyed optimism. America remains a fluid society, with more than half of people in the bottom quintile pulling themselves out of it within a decade.

And so we arrived in the 21st century still a country apart. Prior to its recent run-up, total government spending was still only about 36 percent of GDP in the U.S. In Europe, the figure was much higher—44 percent in Britain, 53 percent in France, and 56 percent in Sweden. (The difference is starker when only nondefense spending is compared.)

Politically, we have always been more democratic, more populist than other countries. Edmund Burke said of the low-church Protestants who flocked here, "They represent the dissidents of dissent and the protest wing of the Protestant religion." The Scotch-Irish who settled the hinterlands were even more cussed. It wasn't very easy to tell any of these people what to do, as colonial governors learned to their regret.

* * *

Today, we still have more elections for more offices more often than other countries. Even many judges and law-enforcement officials are elected. In the federal government, political appointees have greater sway over the civil service than is the case in other developed countries. As Edward C. Banfield and James Q. Wilson have written, "There is virtually no sphere of 'administration' apart from politics."

* * *

We have managed to preserve a remarkable national spirit. At over 70 percent, more Americans express pride in their country than Western Europeans do in theirs. In terms of demography, we are the youngest advanced country in the world, and our population continues to grow as that of Western Europe is projected to decline.

Americans are more religious than Europeans. In the 18th century, American religious dissenters supported overthrowing state-supported churches because it would allow them to compete on an even playing field with other denominations. In that competition, America saw an explosion of religious feeling and became the most evangelical country in the world.

Religion gained authority and vitality from its separation from the state, and religion-inspired reform movements, from abolitionism to the civil-rights movement, have been a source of self-criticism and renewal. Today, 73 percent of Americans believe in God, compared with 27 percent of Frenchmen and 35 percent of Britons, according to a 2006 *Financial Times* survey.

All of this means that America has the spirit of a youthful, hopeful, developing country, matched with the economic muscle of the world's most advanced society and the stability of its oldest democratic institutions.

* * *

None of this is to say, of course, that America is perfect. No nation can be. But one can only regard with wonderment what America stands for and all that it has accomplished in its amazing, utterly distinct adventure in liberty.

There have always been those who take exception to American exceptionalism. Europeans developed a cottage industry in travel writing about America, most of it—although not all, with Tocqueville the most important exception—scandalized by the riotous freedoms of these restless, stubborn, commerce-crazy, God-soaked barbarians. The America of these portraits was simultaneously primitive and decadent: "grotesque, obscene, monstrous, stultifying, stunted, leveling, deadening, deracinating, roofless, uncultured," as James Ceaser summarizes the critique in *Reconstructing America*. Many of America's European critics hoped that, over time, America would lose its distinctiveness. It would become just another developed Western country: more centralized, more elitist, more secular, less warlike, and less free. In short, a *quieter*, more *civilized* place.

The American Left has shared this maddened perplexity at its country's character and this hope for its effacement. Marxists at home and abroad were always mystified by the failure of socialism in the U.S. They thought that, as the most advanced capitalist society, we would have had the most restive proletariat. Instead we have had a broad and largely satisfied middle class. Even our unions, in their early history, were anti-statist, their radicalism anarchistic rather than socialist. * * *

* * *

New Deal intellectuals gushed over Bolshevism in the 1930s. FDR Brain Truster Stuart Chase enthused, "Why should Russians have all the fun of remaking a world?" His statement captured the utopian underpinnings of the progressive project and the yearning for the kind of radical remaking of society that was readily attainable only in countries that gave themselves over entirely to the state. The other model was Italian fascism, which New Dealers studied closely and in important respects aped.

The New Deal was a watershed, but America didn't lurch all the way to socialism. The power of the central government increased, a welfare state was born, and unionization advanced. But even in the midst of the Great Depression, typically American attitudes still prevailed. In a 1935 Gallup survey, Americans by a wide margin thought the government was spending too much.

After World War II, a Left that had been gaining strength in Europe for decades finally realized its social-democratic ambitions. The U.S. followed a different course. In the academy, a perverse version of American exceptionalism took root: an exceptionalism of criminality, conquest, and oppression. America was special only in its misdeeds and failings; all cultures were to be celebrated except our own. The exceptionalism of Howard Zinn and Noam Chomsky, in milder form, occupied the commanding heights of our education system. It has worked to trash our Founding, to wipe out our historical memory, and to create a guilty conscience among our ruling elite.

In politics, however, the country's progress away from its character continued to be "unaccountably slow." American government continued to grow, particularly during the Johnson and Nixon years; the states became ever more one of the federal government's key client groups rather than checks on its power. But the individualistic American character began to reassert itself after its mid-century dormancy. Americans saw the stagflation of the 1970s as an indictment of Big Government rather than a crisis of capitalism. Ronald Reagan won the presidency of a nation that, by European standards, was still a freewheeling cowboy economy and democracy—and made it even freer.

Deregulation exposed unions to competitive pressures that they could not survive. The U.S. quickly came out of its post-Vietnam defensive crouch. And religion, rather than fading away, became more publicly assertive in response to perceived threats. Bill Clinton's Democratic presidency did more to confirm than to alter these trends.

The Left's search for a foreign template to graft onto America grew more desperate. Why couldn't we be more like *them*—like the French, like the Swedes, like the Danes? Like any people with a larger and busier government overawing the private sector and civil society? You can see it in *Sicko*, wherein Michael Moore extols the British national health-care system, the French way of life, and even the munificence of Cuba; you can hear it in all the admonitions

from left-wing commentators that every other advanced society has government child care, or gun control, or mass transit, or whatever socialistic program or other infringement on our liberty we have had the wisdom to reject for
decades.

President Obama's first year in office should be seen in the context of contemporary liberalism's discomfort with American exceptionalism.

The president has signaled again and again his unease with traditional
American patriotism. As a senator he notoriously made a virtue of not wearing
a flag pin. As president he has been unusually detached from American history:
When a foreign critic brought up the Bay of Pigs, rather than defend the country's honor he noted that he was a toddler at the time. And while acknowledging that America has been a force for good, he has all but denied the idea that
America is an exceptional nation. Asked whether he believed in American exceptionalism during a European trip last spring, Obama said, "I believe in
American exceptionalism, just as I suspect that the Brits believe in British exceptionalism and the Greeks believe in Greek exceptionalism." (Is it just a coincidence that he reached for examples of former hegemons?)

In this respect the president reflects the mainstream sentiment of American
liberals. We do not question the sincerity of his, or their, desire to better the lot
of his countrymen. But modern liberal intellectuals have had a notoriously difficult time coming up with a decent account of patriotism even when they have
felt it. * * *

Given the liberal gestalt, it is perhaps unsurprising that every important
aspect of American exceptionalism has been under threat from President Obama and his allies in Washington. Obama has frankly and correctly described
their project as to change the country fundamentally.

* * *

Already we are catching up to the European norm for government power.
In 2010, government spending in the U.S. will reach an estimated 44 percent of
GDP. With entitlements for the elderly on a path to explode with the retirement
of the Baby Boomers, the trend is toward more convergence. In a strange rever-
sal, last year it was an American president urging *continental Europeans* to
spend more to combat the recession. Two if his highest priorities would drastically, and probably irreversibly, expand the government's footprints.

American liberals have long been embarrassed about our country's supposedly retrograde policies on health care and energy, especially compared with Europe's nationalized health insurance and carbon rationing. So they tried to use their unprecedented power after the 2008 elections to bring the U.S. into line. They sought to limit carbon emissions. That legislation would simultaneously represent a massive indirect tax increase, an extension of the tentacles of government regulation into every sector of the economy, and an empowerment of new bureaucratic instruments to control and direct economic development.

Obama's health-care policy would change the relationship of people to government, probably forever, by further nationalizing our system. It would have the federal government, for the first time, order all Americans to purchase a specified product. And socialized health-care systems in other lands have become endless warrants for more taxing and spending, as both are justified as necessary to delivering adequate health care. Once the public is hooked on government health care, its political attitudes shift leftward. (The system's flaws, such as rationing, tend to be attributed to underfunding, so that even discontent with it ends up entrenching it.)

Free labor markets have been an expression of American individualism and a contributor to American dynamism. But President Obama has attempted to upend seven decades of American labor law in order to make it easier for unions to collect new members. Democrats hope to reverse the unions' decline. Tellingly, after the United Auto Workers helped wreck GM and Chrysler, the Obama administration handed it a large share of control over the two companies.

Corporations, meanwhile, are also becoming more dependent on government handouts. Rivalry between business and political elites has helped to safeguard American liberty. What we are seeing now is the possible emergence of a new political economy in which Big Business, Big Labor, and Big Government all have cozy relations of mutual dependence. The effect would be to suppress both political choice and economic dynamism.

The retreat from American exceptionalism has a legal dimension as well. Obama's judicial nominees are likely to attempt to bring our Constitution into line with European norms. Here, again, he is building on the work of prior liberals who used the federal courts as a weapon against aspects of American exceptionalism such as self-government and decentralization. Increasingly, judicial liberals look to putatively enlightened foreign, and particularly European, opinion as a source of law capable of displacing the law made under our Constitution.

Liberal regulators threaten both our dynamism and our self-government. They are increasingly empowered to make far-reaching policy decisions on their own—for instance, the EPA has the power to decide, even in the absence of cap-and-trade legislation passed by Congress, how to regulate carbon emissions. The agency thus has extraordinary sway over the economy, without any meaningful accountability to the electorate. The Troubled Asset Relief Program has turned into a honeypot for the executive branch, which can dip into it for any purpose that suits it. Government is increasingly escaping the control of the people from whom it is supposed to derive its powers.

Inevitably, the transformation of America at home is being accompanied by a shift in its policies toward the rest of the world. Since the 1940s America has been the crucial undergirding of the international order. Its power and sway are a stabilizing influence in every region of the world, and it provides international public goods, from the policing of sea lanes to humanitarian interventions. It is also, in keeping with its missionary history, the chief exponent of liberty in the world.

Obama is turning his back both on the overarching vision of freedom and on the prudence, and mislabeling his approach "realism." He has been positively allergic to the word "democracy." His administration has shown very little interest in defending human rights around the world, whether in China or in Cuba. During the Iranian election crisis, he was even cooler to the protesters in the streets than the Europeans were.

His hesitance to advocate American ideals is not a return to the realpolitik of Nixon or the first Bush. A deep naïveté informs his policy. He believes that our enemies can be persuaded, merely through sweet talk and blandishments, to abandon their cold-blooded interests and their most deeply held ambitions. This is impossible without developing the kind of leverage over them in which Obama seems to have little interest. Yes, Reagan negotiated with the Soviets, but only when they had a leader who was a reformer and the arms build-up and the prospect of SDI had tilted the correlation of forces—to use the Marxist argot—in our direction. Under the sway of Obama's anti-idealism, the U.S. is less interested in serving as a champion of liberty; his policies will also reduce our power, and thus our effectiveness should we choose to wield it again.

In many of Obama's performances overseas (the Nobel acceptance speech is an exception), there has been a dismaying defensiveness. It's almost as though he doesn't think we deserve to stand up for our ideals or for our interests, and believes that our record of sins, hypocrisies, and affronts makes a posture of apologetic passivity the only appropriate one. This posture raises a disturbing possibility: that the waning of America's civilizational self-confidence is part and parcel of the change Obama is effecting.

In Europe, we see a civilization that is not willing to defend itself: nations that will surrender their sovereignty, cultures that will step aside to be supplanted by an alien creed, peoples that will no longer make the most meaningful investment in the future by reproducing. There is a sense that history is over and Europeans are just waiting for someone to turn out the last light in the last gallery of the Louvre.

The popular revolt against Obama's policies is a sign that Americans are not prepared to go gentle into that good night. Other factors are of course in play—most important, the weak economy—but the public is saying "No" to a rush to social democracy.

Although the conservatives, libertarians, and independents who oppose Obama's health-care initiative may not put it in quite these terms, they sense that his project will not just increase insurance premiums but undermine what they cherish about America. Those Americans who want to keep our detention facility at Guantanamo Bay think it necessary to protect our security—but they also worry, more profoundly, that our leaders are too apologetic to serve our interests. Americans may want change, even fundamental change, but most of them would rather change our institutions than our national character.

It is madness to consider President Obama a foreigner. But it is blindness to ignore that American exceptionalism has homegrown enemies—people who misunderstand the sources of American greatness or think them outdated. If they succeed, we will be less free, less innovative, less rich, less self-governing, and less secure. We will be less.

As will the world. The Europeans can afford a foreign policy devoted nearly exclusively to "soft power" because we are here to defend them and mount the forward defense of freedom. Who is going to do that for us, when we are no longer doing it for ourselves? Who will answer the call when America is no longer home?

If our politics seems heated right now, that is because the central question before us is whether to abandon our traditional sense of ourselves as an exceptional nation. To be exceptional is of course not to be perfect. The old anti-imperialist saying—"My country right or wrong; if right, to be kept right; if wrong, to be set right"—has considerable wisdom. But Americans are right not to want to become exceptional only in the 230-year path we took to reach the same lackluster destination as everyone else.

QUESTIONS

1. If you were David Axelrod, President Obama's main political advisor, what political strategy would you urge? Would you recommend that Obama tack left and push hard on the progressive agenda? Or move to the center with a more moderate agenda? What would influence your recommendations: the 2010 midterm election results, reelection, maintaining popularity, getting policies through Congress, or some other consideration?

2. Greenberg argues that the problem is our expectations. The public *says* it wants a president who will shake things up, but when faced with the prospect of major change, we retreat to a more centrist posture, content with "muddling through" and nervous about dramatic change. Is he right?

3. When a president announces a desire to "change politics," what does that mean? Does it mean that political power will shift to groups currently outside the walls of power? That Democrats will call the shots instead of Republicans (or vice versa)? Something more fundamental? Or is it simply rhetoric designed to impress but without much substance? What evidence would you use to decide?

7

Bureaucracy: Policy "Czars" and Presidential Control of the Bureaucracy

All presidents want the federal bureaucracy—meaning executive branch agencies—to be responsive to presidential policies and preferences. Bringing agencies into line, however, is a difficult challenge. Not only do agencies or, more properly, the people in the agencies, seek to please multiple entities, including Congress, the courts, interest groups, and clientele groups who interact with various agencies on regulatory or benefit issues, but bureaucracies are also inherently resistant to change. The scale of the executive branch makes this task even harder, because it is difficult to monitor and assess the thousands of programs in the many different departments, regulatory agencies, government corporations, boards, and commissions.

The president appoints the people at the top of federal agencies. Most of them serve at the pleasure of the president, meaning that the president can fire them without giving a reason. Other agency leaders, particularly in the independent regulatory agencies such as the Federal Reserve Board or the Securities and Exchange Commission, are insulated from political pressure, and the president can only remove them under certain conditions. Even those whom the president has the option to fire can, in Washington lingo, "go native," meaning that they advocate the agency's views more than the president's.

Eventually, every president becomes frustrated with a lack of responsiveness among the agencies. Different presidents have come up with a variety of ways of combating this phenomenon, but the one common feature is that presidents increasingly centralize policy-making control within the White House. Rather than relying on agencies to create policy, presidents come to rely on White House personnel and processes to devise, implement, and monitor policy.

One of President Obama's tools in policy centralization is the use of so-called czars, presidential advisors who work in the White House on a particular policy area, and answer only to the president. Some of these czars occupy positions created by statute. The most noteworthy is the head of the White House Office of National Drug Control Policy, usually referred to as the drug czar. President Obama has made extensive use of these positions, relying on these advisors across a wide range of policy—environment, green energy, financial industry oversight, the automobile industry, and Afghanistan.

The readings provide three perspectives on the czar position. James Pfiffner, a presidential scholar, notes that the controversy over Obama's use of these advisors is nothing new and reflects the long-standing tension between administrative neutrality and responsiveness to presidential policy preferences. Presidents want to control policy, and that means having people who answer only to the president responsible for crafting and monitoring policy proposals.

Matthew Spalding offers a less sanguine take, noting that the existence of czars reflects a much broader debate over how policy should be made: by technical experts who do not have to answer to the public, or by elected representatives. Like Pfiffner, Spalding connects the use of czars to the long-standing presidential desire for bureaucratic control. But unlike many critics of Obama's extensive use of czars, Spalding sees their proliferation as a sign of deeper trouble: the increasing difficulty of controlling a bureaucracy that is, apart from the judiciary, the least accountable institution in the national government. The real problem, as Spalding sees it, is the fact that government has grown so large, intrusive, and potentially uncontrollable.

Finally, Will Englund provides three examples of policy czar types, noting the conditions under which they will succeed or fail. He argues that there have been some quiet successes, especially the coordinating effort carried out by the Clinton Y2K (year 2000) czar John Koskinen. For those of you too young to remember, there was a good deal of nervousness about how computers would respond when 1999 turned into 2000. Many older computers could store only two-digit dates, meaning that on January 1, 2000, they might read a date as 00 and interpret that to mean 1900, which could have caused problems with software involved with everything from electrical utilities to finance to aircraft flight management. Ultimately, January 1, 2000, came and went without incident.

James P. Pfiffner
Presidential Use of White House "Czars"

The term "czar" has no generally accepted definition within the context of American government. It is a term loosely used by journalists to refer to members of a president's administration who seem to be in charge of a particular policy area. For my purposes, the term "czar" refers to members of the White House staff who have been designated by the president to coordinate a specific policy that involves more than one department or agency in the executive branch; they do not hold Senate-confirmed positions, nor are they officers of the United States.

Article II Section 2 of the Constitution says that the president "shall nominate, and by and with the Advice and Consent of the Senate, shall appoint . . . Officers of the United States." The positions held by these officers are created in law and most of them exercise legal authority to commit the United States government to certain policies (within the law) and expend resources in doing so.

In contrast, members of the White House staff are appointed by the president without Senate confirmation. They are legally authorized only to advise the president; they cannot make authoritative decisions for the government of the United States. There is a parallel between the concepts of "line" and "staff" in the U.S. military. Staff personnel can advise line officers, but only line officers can make authoritative decisions, such as hiring and firing personnel or committing budgetary resources.

For practical purposes, however, staff personnel may have considerable "power" or influence, as opposed to authority. But this power is derivative from the line officer for whom they work. Thus White House staffers may communicate orders from the president, but they cannot legally give those orders themselves. In the real world, of course, White House staffers often make important decisions, but the weight of their decisions depends entirely on the willingness of the president to back them up.

Growth of the White House Staff

Both the advantages and disadvantages of White House czars are illustrated by the significant growth of the White House staff in the Modern Presidency [*sic*]. Although presidents have always had advisers and confidants in the White House, the formal White House staff was established in 1939 when Congress gave Franklin Roosevelt authority to create the Executive Office of the President and hire six formal White House staffers. The expected role of the White House staff was articulated by the classic statement of Franklin Roosevelt's Brownlow Committee in 1937:

> These aides would have no power to make decisions or issue instructions in their own right. They would not be interposed between the president and the heads of his departments. They would not be assistant presidents in any sense. . . . They would remain in the background, issue no orders, make no decisions, emit no public statements. . . . [T]hey would not attempt to exercise power on their own account. They should be possessed of high competence, great physical vigor, and a passion for anonymity.

Despite the fact that these precepts have gone by the wayside and the White House staff now includes hundreds of people, some of whom enjoy high public visibility and wield significant power, the norms established in the Brownlow Committee Report still define the ideal for White House aides.

Over the following decades, presidents initiated major changes in the size and scope of their staffs. Dwight Eisenhower created the position of chief of staff to the president and began to institutionalize the White House. John Kennedy, after the Bay of Pigs debacle, told McGeorge Bundy to put together "a little State Department" in the White House that would consider national security policy from his own perspective rather than through the narrower lenses of the Departments of State and Defense. The Assistant to the President for National Security Affairs, (national security advisor) has played major roles in every presidential administration since then. It reached its zenith of power when Henry Kissinger held that position at the same time he was Secretary of State in the Nixon Administration.

When Richard Nixon came to office, his distrust of the executive branch bureaucracies led him to expand considerably the White House staff. In addition to increasing the number of White House staffers in the White House Office, he created the position of domestic policy adviser and designated John Ehrlichmann to be its director. Subsequent presidents have continued to use these White House positions and to create new ones to meet their needs.

A certain amount of the centralization of policy control through expanding staff in the White House was inevitable and useful. Executive branch departments and cabinet secretaries necessarily and reasonably view national policy from their own perspective, and they often clash with other departments over the formulation and implementation of presidential policies. These conflicts and differing perspectives must be resolved and integrated by presidents, but someone short of the president must be able to narrow the range of alternatives for the president to consider. This coordination role is the most important role of the White House staff; and talented people are necessary to do the job. That being said, too much centralization and too many White House staffers can impair effective presidential leadership. White House staffers are ambitious people, and may try to use the president's power as their own. Thus the White House staff must be carefully policed and kept on a short leash.

The Appropriate Role of Czars

This brings the focus back to White House czars. Presidents designate czars in order to coordinate policy making across different departments and agencies. They thus play essential roles and lift the burden of coordination from the president. They help reduce the range of options to the essentials necessary for presidential decision. But if the number of czars proliferates, they can clog and confuse the policy making process. In addition to coordinating policy among departments and agencies, someone then must coordinate the czars and their access to the president. Czars may also create layers of aides between the president and departmental secretaries. Too many czars can result in managerial overload.

From the president's perspective, a proliferation of czars replicates the divisions already present in the departments and agencies of the executive branch. A large White House staff with many czars must be disciplined and coordinated by the president's chief of staff, a position used by every president since the Nixon administration. Perhaps the greatest challenge that the use of czars presents to coherent policy making is the question: who is in charge of this policy area short of the president? Conflict will abound, and members of Congress as well as other national leaders may be confused as to the locus of authoritative decisions. When this happens in foreign policy, as it has at times in recent decades, foreign leaders do not know who speaks for the president. In addition, a too active czar can pull problems into the White House that could be settled at the cabinet level. Only those issues that are central to a president's policy agenda should be brought into the White House; others should be delegated to the cabinet secretaries who have responsibility for their implementation.

From the czar's perspective, the title can be a mixed blessing. The czar enjoys the prestige and perks of being on the White House staff. He or she gets national news coverage and has the opportunity to exercise leadership and sometimes power. On the other hand, czars are often frustrated because they are supposed to be in charge of policy, yet they do not have authority commensurate with their responsibilities. While a czar may have the spotlight and the president's ear in the short term, he or she cannot enforce decisions on departments and agencies. Unlike cabinet secretaries, czars control neither personnel appointments nor budgets. For these they must depend on cabinet secretaries, and if they disagree with the cabinet secretary, they are at a disadvantage. They might appeal to the president to back up their decisions, but presidents have limited time, and czars can go back to that well only so many times. Persons who have been designated the "drug czar," the director of the Office of National Drug Control Policy, have thus had mixed success in their efforts to coordinate harmful substances policy across the executive branch. The Secretary of Homeland Security has more resources at her command than does the Assistant to the President for Homeland Security.

From the perspective of the department secretary, the presence of White House czars is most often frustrating. Throughout the modern presidency White house staffers have been the natural enemy of cabinet secretaries. Each vies for the president's ear, and each resents the other's "interference." White House staffers enjoy proximity to the president and can drop everything else in order to focus on whatever policy the president is considering. Cabinet secretaries, in contrast, must worry about managing their departments and the many policies for which they are responsible. Absent a close relationship with the president, cabinet secretaries are often at a disadvantage in securing presidential attention, and they often resent a czar who is interposed between them and the president.

Managing the Presidency

In the real world, presidents must balance their desire for centralized control with the managerial imperatives for delegation. No president can do an effective job without talented people on the White House staff. Yet if the president allows White House staffers to shut out cabinet secretaries, he or she will not be exposed to the crucial perspectives that cabinet secretaries provide: institutional memory, an operational point of view, and a broader political sensitivity than a single czar can provide. Thus the question of the best balance comes down to presidential judgment and managerial insight. Some czars, such as the National Security Advisor, are clearly necessary. And major presidential policy priorities must be coordinated out of the White House. Secondary issues should be pushed down to the departmental level.

A czar, seen as a symbol of presidential priorities, can be useful for that purpose and not pose an impediment to clear lines of policy making. But a czar who is charged with policy coordination and who uses his or her influence to undercut cabinet secretaries can create confusion and undermine effective policy making. So the real question of the impact of czars must be judged by the roles they play and their approach to their responsibilities rather than merely counting their numbers.

Thus insofar as President Obama's czars take active roles in policy making (as opposed to advising), attempt to shut out cabinet secretaries, and exercise power in their own right, they dilute authority and confuse the chain of command. But if they work closely with cabinet secretaries and help coordinate policy advice to the president, they can be very useful. So the effect of czars and their usefulness depends on their behavior. That said, the larger the White House staff and the more czars that the president designates, the more likely the White House will be difficult to manage, and relations between cabinet secretaries and White House staff will be strained.

Congressional Oversight of Executive Branch Policy

Members of Congress are sometimes frustrated in their attempts to oversee executive branch policies and chafe at presidential attempts to circumvent Congress in its legitimate policy making role and responsibilities for oversight of the executive branch. And it is possible that presidents may use their White House staffs to frustrate legitimate congressional participation. Presidents often resist requests for White House staff to testify before Congress and they use claims of executive privilege, sometimes legitimately, sometimes not. Thus Congress can be frustrated when it seems that the president is refusing to let it exercise legitimate oversight of executive branch policy and actions. But Congress is not without constitutional authority to oversee the executive branch.

* * *

Congress has alternatives other than calling White House staffers to testify. Policy making in the executive branch is the responsibility of the president, who is accountable to Congress and the public. If Congress is concerned with policies or their implementation, it can call cabinet secretaries (or subordinate officers of the government) to testify about policy making and implementation. Congress can exercise its power of the purse and authorization power to curb or direct policy implementation. Executive branch departments and agencies exist and are authorized only in law, and Congress can change those laws. As a matter of comity, the president is entitled to the confidentiality of his or her staff, just as members of Congress are entitled to confidentiality of their staff and Supreme Court Justices are entitled to confidentiality of their clerks.

If Congress suspects that White House staffers are illegitimately interfering with policy making or implementation, it can call in cabinet secretaries to explain the policies or programs for which they are responsible. If White House staffers seem to be actually implementing policies, there is certainly cause for concern and Congress has a right to demand explanations. But the keys to congressional control are its authorization and appropriation powers.

In my judgment, there are much more significant threats to congressional constitutional authority than the existence of czars in the White House. The explosion of the use of signing statements to imply that the president may not faithfully execute the law presents a fundamental threat to the constitutional role of Congress, which possesses "All legislative powers" granted in the Constitution.

If presidents create secret programs that effectively nullify or circumvent the laws, they are placing themselves above the law and claiming the authority to suspend the laws, which the Framers of the Constitution explicitly rejected.

If presidents use the state secrets privilege to avoid the disclosure of or accountability for their actions, the role of the courts can be undercut.

If presidents claim the right to suspend *habeas corpus*, they are treading on Article I of the Constitution.

Although some presidents have abused their power by making extraordinary claims to constitutional authority, it is also the duty of Congress as a co-equal branch of government to assert its own constitutional prerogatives. Congress has all the authority it needs to ensure effective oversight of executive branch implementation of policy. The use of czars by presidents presents serious questions of policy making and management, but the constitutional prerogatives of Congress are more seriously undermined by the claims of presidents to have the right to set aside the laws in favor of their own policy priorities.

Matthew Spalding

Examining the History and Legality of Executive Branch Czars

Let me begin by commending the Senate Judiciary Committee, and especially Senator Feingold, for calling this hearing and giving serious consideration to this issue. Who would have thought that over 200 years after the Declaration of Independence indicted George III for having "erected a multitude of New Offices, and sent hither swarms of Officers to harass our people and eat out their substance" we would be debating the number and proliferation of "czars" in the administration of American government?

The very word, of course, is itself a significant part of the problem. An endless source of humor, it is both confusing and revealing. It is a confusing term because no one officially holds the title; it is a shorthand popularization used by the media and commentators, as well as individuals in government, to describe certain individuals in the administration who seem to be coordinating national policy and particular policy issues across agencies and programs. We don't know how many there are, as there is no official list. Complicating the matter further is that, of those who have been dubbed "czars," some are in positions created by Congress and have been confirmed by the Senate while others are not in such positions and have not been confirmed.

Yet the term is also revealing. While it is a clever label meant to simplify the proliferation of long, formal job titles, it clearly was meant as well to imply in certain positions a breadth of authority and level of status beyond the particulars of the formal title, and seemingly beyond the confines of the normal administrative process. Americans have always bristled at such claims of undefined authority, and calling it by a title historically associated with lawlessness and despotism only serves to underscore the problem.

The use of the term is not new, of course. [President] Nixon seems to have had the first in the modern era, and there were a couple under both Ronald Reagan and George Herbert Walker Bush and President Clinton had a few more. But there seems to have been a proliferation of the title in the previous and the current administration. I say "seems" because there is significant information we do not know about these positions, their duties and responsibilities, and their line of authority. This is why Congress—and here I note the letters from Senator Feingold, as well as a letter from Representatives Issa and Smith—is absolutely correct in asking for more information about the activities and authority of several of the individual czars.

My guess is that there are actually many more individuals that could fairly be called "czars" in the administration. I say that because the problem is not in the title *per se,* or who made or didn't make the czar list, but with the activities associated with the particular position, and whether there is a general trend toward a centralization of czar power in the White House. Congress, both in terms of preserving its own powers and checking those of the executive as well as encouraging open deliberation and responsibility in government, ought to be keenly interested in this question.

The issue is not whether the proliferation of "czars" amounts to a usurpation of power by the executive branch. Rather, the fundamental issue is how the rise of modern administrative government has put us in an unsolvable dilemma: whether policy should be made by technical experts, insulated from public accountability and control, or whether policy should be made by our elected representatives in Congress and the executive branch. The rise of government by bureaucrats—due to the delegation of power from Congress to administrative agencies, combined with the removal of those agencies from the President's control—has given rise to efforts by Presidents from both parties to get the bureaucratic state under control through various mechanisms. The rise of "czars" in the current administration is just another manifestation—albeit, an unfortunate one—of this phenomenon.

To understand this argument, a quick synopsis of some background history is necessary. During the late nineteenth and early twentieth centuries (also known as the "Progressive Era"), leading intellectuals and politicians sought to transform American government, which they believed was set up to circumvent the public interest for the sake of narrow and parochial interests.

The problem, in their view, was that policy was being made politically—that is, by inexpert officials chosen by the people, who were unfamiliar with the practicalities of modern society. The solution they devised was to transfer policymaking authority to administrative experts, removed from day-to-day politics and political control, who would be social scientists, educated at top universities and trained to apply cutting-edge scientific research to modern problems. As one leading Progressive, John Dewey, argued, "the question of method in formation and execution of policies is the central thing in liberalism. The method indicated is that of maximum reliance upon intelligence."

Technical intelligence, rather than the will of the people expressed through elected representatives, would be the basis for policymaking in the Progressives' new state. Authority to make policy would have to be transferred *out* of the elected branches of government and *into* newly created administrative boards and commissions, which would be staffed with these experts and tasked with making policy appropriate for a modern society.

The result of this movement was to transfer the authority to make law from Congress, filled with inexpert politicians, to administrative experts housed in administrative agencies. But politics would still exert a pernicious influence on these agencies unless they were also insulated from the control of the President, who was also an elected official and tied to the political impulses of his constituency. Therefore, two things had to be achieved: the delegation of legislative power to agencies, and the removal of presidential control over these new institutions. Both were achieved before and during the New Deal, with the creation of "independent regulatory commissions" which were not located within the executive branch. Rather, they would be outside of the traditional branches of government and not directly accountable to any of those traditional branches.

In practice, this meant that the expansion of administrative agencies *appeared* to involve an expansion of executive power, but it actually resulted in a decline of executive control and responsibility for administrative policy. This led to the paradox of the expansion of administrative agencies, but the decline of presidential control over those agencies. Harry Truman famously predicted the difficulty that Dwight Eisenhower would have in setting policy priorities for the administration: "He will sit here and he will say, 'Do this!, Do that!' And nothing will happen. Poor Ike—it won't be a bit like the Army." It was President Truman who breathlessly complained, "I thought I was the President, but when it comes to these bureaucrats, I can't do a damn thing." The Progressive impulse to put technical experts in charge of national policy led to the unfortunate consequence of popularly elected Presidents being unable to change national policy. The ideal of scientific policy had been elevated over the principle of the consent of the governed.

This created a fundamental dilemma: how can the bureaucratic state the Progressives created be organized and controlled? Is it destined to result in a collection of disconnected, uncoordinated independent agencies that each pursue a focused goal such as workplace safety or the regulation of communications? How will these bureaucrats be held accountable to the people, if they do not answer to the President?

From the perspective of the domestic policy agenda of the President, the story of the twentieth century is the history of attempts by individual Presidents to regain control of agencies which are ostensibly executive and which are primarily staffed with officials that the President cannot remove.

Nearly every President, from both parties, has devised a plan for bringing the bureaucracy under the control of the chief executive. Congress has always had several tools for controlling administrative officials—most notably the powers to authorize and fund agencies. But without the power to remove administrative officials, how can the vast administrative state be controlled?

Presidents have tried many devices for bringing agencies under their supervision. Administrative re-organization was a prominent agenda, employed both by the FDR and Nixon Administrations. The President's control over the administration was expanded by Presidents Carter and Reagan, most notably in the latter's creation of a regulatory review process in the Office of Information and Regulatory Analysis (OIRA), which is now headed by the legal scholar Cass Sunstein, otherwise known as President Obama's "regulatory czar." (Incidentally, Sunstein's nomination was approved by the Senate, despite the "czar" moniker.) Elena Kagan, the former Solicitor General, wrote a famous law review article outlining the ways in which President Clinton had established a firmer grip on administrative agencies.

President Obama's attempt to centralize control over administrative agencies is therefore nothing new, nor is it peculiar to one of the two major parties in America. It is a symptom of a much more serious sickness—the fact that Congress has transferred a great deal of its authority to administrative agencies, and neglected to put anyone in charge of the whole structure. This entire framework is in tension with the original Constitution, but the Constitution nevertheless can give us some basic principles for thinking about the question of "czars" in the White House.

The United States Constitution does not create or *require* a cabinet under the executive branch, though it clearly anticipates the managerial structure and recognizes the significance of department heads to assist the President in overseeing the executive branch. From the very beginning, every President has used such a structure to manage the executive branch. The most recent example of strong cabinet government, revived after the failed executive models of the Nixon administration's heavy-handed centralization of White House authority as well as the Carter administration's small-minded micromanaging style, was the presidency of Ronald Reagan, who regularly turned to cabinet secretaries directly for advice and to carry out policy and who created "cabinet councils" to coordinate the activities of the cabinet and respective departments. Presidents since, however, seem to be moving away from the cabinet structure and more in the direction of centralizing more authority directly in the Executive Office of the President.

The President has the authority to appoint his own staff and advisors to assist in the work of his office. It is perfectly legitimate for presidential staff to advance the president's policy objectives within the administration as a matter of course, and Presidents often appoint particular advisors to advance particular, high-level policies. The executive has this authority as a separate and independent matter from officers created by the legislature to carry out the law, and Congress cannot infringe on that authority.

Nevertheless, through its legislative and oversight functions, and more specifically through the Senate's participation in the appointment of officers under Article II, Congress also has significant responsibilities over the general activities of the administration in carrying out the operations of the federal government. With this legislative power in mind, a number of Senators have focused their attention on eighteen czar positions in the administration that may overstep Congress's express statutory assignment of responsibility and its oversight responsibilities.

Where can the line be drawn between executive privilege and legislative responsibility? If executive authority is being used as a subterfuge to thwart confirmation requirements and accountability, and so evade constitutional requirements for individuals performing operational and managerial functions normally the responsibility of cabinet secretaries and department and agency executives that require Senate confirmation, that would certainly violate the spirit and probably the letter of the Constitution. A possible example of this problem may be Climate Czar Carol Browner who, according to reports, was the lead negotiator in establishing new automobile emissions standards, stemming from the Supreme Court's interpretation of the Clean Air Act. In addition to seeming to be beyond congressional legislative intent, it also seems to circumvent the authority of the EPA [Environmental Protection Agency] administrator.

As the number of czars expands, and the President's policy staff grows, and there are more and more individuals acting more and more as administrative heads rather than advisors, Congress should raise questions as to whether those individuals should be subject to executive privilege or can be compelled to testify before Congress. The President cannot have it both ways.

In addition to the constitutional questions, I would also like to note concerns about the administrative problems inherent in this new executive management paradigm. Having policy operations run out of the White House causes confusion of responsibility for one thing. Who is in charge of health care reform: Kathleen Sebelius, the Secretary of Health and Human Services, or Nancy DeParle, the health care czar? In general, running operations out of the White House can become very problematic: recall again the Nixon Administration, and the activities of Mr. Haldeman and Mr. Erlichman. More recently, the Tower Commission warned against White House staff acting outside of the regular structure of policy decision-making. There will always be a temptation to use White House authority—real or implied—to exercise political influence over normal departmental activities. As long as that influence is not accountable, and thus responsible—which seems to have been the case in recent stories concerning a conference call with the National Endowment for the Arts encouraging policy-oriented art or the issuance of curricula to accompany the President's recent speech to students—it is more likely than not to be inappropriate.

In all of these cases, congressional oversight would serve as an important and legitimate check on executive authority. But additional oversight, with the requirement for approval of and testimony from as many presidential staff as possible, will not solve the fundamental problem behind the current czar wars, which I think has more to do with the general nature of modern administrative government and a growing popular concern about the limits (or lack thereof) on its activities.

For some time now, Congress has developed the habit of delegating vast amounts of authority to the executive branch to address a problem and after the fact looks to manage the exercise of that authority, as opposed to writing clear and detailed laws to be executed by the President. The Troubled Asset Relief Program (TARP), meant to purchase assets and equity from financial institutions as a way to address the subprime mortgage crisis, is a perfect example. Unbounded delegations allowed the Secretary of the Treasury to spend up to $700 billion at will to purchase "troubled" assets of any financial institution. Lo and behold, the United States is now majority owner of General Motors and there is a Car Czar. Setting aside the wisdom of the policy, can it fairly be said that this was the intention of Congress?

And in some cases the delegation of czar-like authority is even clearer. The health care legislation in the House of Representatives creates a "Health Choices Commissioner" at the head of a new Health Choices Administration. This duly created, and presumably Senate confirmed, Health Insurance Czar would exercise enormous control over the nation's insurance industry, an enormous concentration of power in one person.

The modern executive, on the other hand, increasingly attempts to get control of the vast bureaucracy under their authority and, in the most recent iteration of the battle, appoints *uber*-bureaucrats to shift that bureaucracy in the President's policy directions. This is partly a misconception of executive authority that seems to see cabinet officers as independent of that authority, or at least an unwillingness to exert authority over executive branch policy through the cabinet. But it also seems to be a general attempt to circumvent congressional oversight (or interference, depending on how you look at it) in shaping policies within the discretion of the executive branch. An executive desire to do more and more things outside of legislative authority, and with vast sums of money appropriated by Congress to do more and more things, makes matters all the worse.

The combination of these two trends creates a situation where more and more laws—in the form of rulemaking, regulations, and policy pronouncements—are made by administrative agents not only outside of the open and transparent requirements of responsible government, and without congressional approval and oversight, but generally beyond the principle that legitimate government arises out of the consent of the governed. And the more government regularly operates as a matter of course outside of popular consent, the more we become clients rather than rulers of a vast and distant government, the less we are self-governing, and the less we control our own fate. And that, as Alexis de Tocqueville warned in *Democracy in America,* is the recipe for a benign form of despotism that truly imperils our democratic experiment.

Will Englund

Czar Wars

The way the people around Obama describe it, his system of multiple czars is intended to ensure that agencies are on the same page, that consequences that an individual department wouldn't normally consider are taken into account, that policies are drawn up with contributions from all involved, that follow-up isn't neglected. They argue that the administration has useful precedents to replicate—if [Bush's Homeland Security Advisor Frances] Townsend, for instance, didn't think of herself as a "czar," that's fine, because what matters is the way she went about doing her job. Some White House veterans think that the Obama people have a case.

"If you look back, just to give you a couple of reference points, the idea that the White House is the place to coordinate interagency policy and drive decisions of the president is a long-standing tradition, most strongly embedded in the creation of the National Security Council in 1947," says John Podesta, who was chief of staff for President Clinton and headed Obama's transition team. He mentions Clinton's use of the National Economic Council as a mechanism inside the White House where ideas were generated and policy was coordinated.

"It doesn't displace the very strong or important role that Cabinet secretaries play. But when you have problems that really cut across a swath of agencies, it's very important with respect to the president's priorities to have a strong central place within the White House where people can get on the same strategy and that actions are keyed up and accountability exists. That has proven to be an effective way of doing business in the federal government on security policy, on economic policy."

And now, Podesta says, the administration will be extending it to other realms. Back in imperial Russia, there was only one true czar (a word derived from "caesar"); Washington is about to experience life with a whole kingdom of czars.

But success, as Podesta describes it, requires relentlessly good communica-

Published in *National Journal*, February 2009.

tion, suppression of egos, presidential support, and agreement on basic issues. None of that is guaranteed. These qualities also don't fit the image of a czar as an autocrat. That, in fact, is one of two models the Obama White House would probably want to avoid.

The Imperial Czar

This is the czar who brooks no challenge and shares no responsibility. Henry Kissinger, when he was national security adviser to President Nixon, probably came closest to the type. The State Department was shut out of foreign policy. "He and Nixon decided the issues and let people know about them when they needed to know about them," says Mac Destler, a foreign-policy expert at the University of Maryland. They had their victories, "but they alienated a large share of the rest of the government." And their way of working reinforced the corrosive atmosphere of suspicion that pervaded the Nixon administration.

Zbigniew Brzezinski, President Carter's national security adviser, tried to wield the same sort of clout, Destler says, but more openly. His failing was that he pushed vigorously, and in public, for policies (such as a harder line against the Soviet Union) that no one else in the administration, including Carter, wanted. It undercut his effort to portray himself as an honest broker, and "that led to very big problems."

Hillary Rodham Clinton directed health reform in 1993 without much input from HHS [Health and Human Services], and the effort ran aground in Congress. The most recent imperial czar was Vice President Cheney, whose office shoved aside at various times the departments of State, Defense, Justice, Interior, and Commerce, not to mention the Environmental Protection Agency [EPA]. History will judge whether his tenure was a success.

The Figurehead Czar

This is the other type to avoid, personified by the various drug czars. William Bennett was the first drug czar, under George H.W. Bush, and he acknowledged being frustrated by a lack of authority. Gen. Barry McCaffrey was drug czar under Bill Clinton, and although by law he had some role in budget-setting, in practice the Office of Management and Budget [OMB] didn't give him a seat at the table, according to Winograd. "If it doesn't include the budget, it doesn't mean anything in Washington," Winograd says—and although others say that's not always true, it was nevertheless the case that McCaffrey had no clout. The agencies he was supposed to be coordinating resisted him at every turn.

When, a few years later, the administration and Congress were debating the role of homeland-security adviser, McCaffrey said he worried that Ridge would have the same problems he had had. "Six months from now," McCaffrey warned, "there's a danger that he will turn into little more than the speaker's bureau for homeland defense."

For at least a handful of Obama's czars, that will not be a risk. Carol Browner, Lawrence Summers, and retired Gen. James Jones are formidable players; the new health reform czar, taking the position created for Daschle, may be one, as well. That's not to say that they will have no-drama tenures; but none of them is likely to disappear into irrelevancy.

Look, nonetheless, for "consensus-building" to be more of a mantra than "marching orders." Many applaud the job that Robert Rubin did as head of the National Economic Council [NEC] in the Clinton administration. He organized internal debate while conscientiously keeping the Treasury Department, OMB, and the Council of Economic Advisers in the loop through the NEC. As Maryland's Destler describes it, Rubin then forced presidential decisions on key issues. It was openness and purpose at the same time.

A true czar is something more than an honest broker. The aide who simply presents options to the president, even if he's whispering them in the president's ear, performs a useful service, but it's not what a czar does. A czar has to drive those he's working with toward a plan to present to the president. That was Rubin's strength. Summers, the new head of the NEC, has a dominating personality, coupled with credibility as a thinker. He won't be a neutral figure, and he's likely to see his mandate as Rubinesque. Timothy Geithner, at Treasury, is very much on the same wavelength as Summers, although his tax troubles may have given Summers the opportunity to grab a little more clout early on than he otherwise would have. They both have plenty to do. How they'll get along with Paul Volcker, who has his own panel for thinking about financial reform, is more problematic.

Condoleezza Rice played the role of honest broker, or at least gatekeeper, as national security adviser in Bush's first term and got steamrolled. Her cerebral but understated successor, Stephen Hadley, gained a reputation as someone who lacked the political muscle or strength of personality to force coordinated execution of the president's policies. The result was a Bush administration penchant for grand designs and plans, and poor, disjointed execution.

Obama's pick, Jones, is a former Marine commandant and supreme allied commander of NATO [North Atlantic Treaty Organization] and seems intent on regaining the czarist orb for the national security adviser. NATO command has taught him how to cajole coordinated action out of a multitude of players, and he has been in close contact with a number of think tanks and experts on the Joint Chiefs of Staff and elsewhere who are pushing reforms designed to repair what is seen as a dysfunctional interagency process that failed miserably in Iraq and Afghanistan.

An empowered adviser is essentially the president's alter ego on matters of national security. By virtue of its longevity and its statutory existence, the job comes with plenty of prestige (although it should be mentioned that the drug czar's position is also long-lived and spelled out by law). The president, as head of state and commander-in-chief, has a personal role to play in foreign affairs, and that adds to the heft of the national security czar's position.

Other Obama czars start with neither a formal council to provide structure nor an institutional history. The administration's health reform project is already under way, even with no one to lead it. Jeanne Lambrew, who was going to be Daschle's deputy at the White House, has been at work, and she knows the subject as well as Daschle does. If she is picked to be health czar, the question will be whether she can succeed without the clout and reputation that he enjoyed.

Carol Browner is the energy and climate-change czar, and her position raises the question of what, exactly, gets left to the departments. The departments have the budgets. They also, in many cases, have responsibilities peripheral to the czar's concern. HHS, for instance, has plenty to take care of, even as a White House health czar is drawing up a reform program, and the delineation should be fairly clear. It's a bit muddier with the AIDS czar. And what about EPA or Interior functions that have to do with pollution but not climate-change pollution? Jeff Ruch, executive director of Public Employees for Environmental Responsibility, worries that Browner will be concerned with trying "to accomplish two or three things, and everything is going to be bent to serve those two or three objectives."

Townsend, the former homeland-security adviser, asks where the accountability will lie. No accountability means no czar, in her book. If the role of these new White House coordinators is to look out across the government, spot gaps, assign responsibility for filling them, set priorities, and keep accountability within departments—then that sounds like their jobs will resemble hers, and that means they're not czars.

"I Guess I Ought to Go to That"

Maybe this is just a matter of definition. Czars, by whatever name you call them, can get it right. A czar whose reign was peaceful and successful was John Koskinen, the Y2K czar. (And no smirking, please—he argues persuasively that there's a reason the year 2000 arrived uneventfully, although the low-level wind detectors at the nation's airports and communications links with defense intelligence satellites did go down. Moreover, he says it was because of the Y2K preparations that stock markets were able to reopen on the Monday after September 11, 2001, with assurances that transactions would be properly handled.)

An element of Koskinen's success was the specific task he faced, and the unmovable deadline. It helped that no agency really wanted to crash on December 31, 1999, if, as feared, computers—old mainframe computers in particular, with which the government was well supplied—misread the date and went haywire. Koskinen was able to direct agencies toward a $2 billion fund that OMB handled, but he succeeded without any real budgetary authority.

"I kind of knew everybody," recalls Koskinen, who recently became chairman of the board at Freddie Mac. He had been a deputy director at OMB and had overseen the two government shutdowns in 1995; as a result he was acquainted with a broad swath of executive branch officeholders. "So that was a big advantage."

Koskinen began his czardom in 1998 with three people working for him. But he presided over a council of about 25 from around the government to coordinate the policy. Koskinen asked each Cabinet secretary, in person, to appoint a representative to the council who would know the full sweep of issues in that department, and who would have the authority to make decisions on the spot.

He had what he calls "convening authority" rather than "dictating authority," but that was no small thing. "If someone says we have a meeting at the White House, you're going to say, 'Well, I guess I ought to go to that.'"

Koskinen knew he wouldn't be effective if he handed out orders to the council. That would elicit mild expressions of interest and little more. Instead, he says, "you have to pull people together around the problem, and make them feel like they're part of the solution. They'll have far more information than you'll ever have. And once people understand what needs to be done, they will work with you to get it done. If you get a group of people, they will always come up with a better answer than any individual can."

The first order of business, Koskinen says, is to sit the participants down and ask, "What are the easiest things to do? Where can we get leverage? What do we need? What's working and not working?" People in the agencies know that sort of thing. Of course there will be recalcitrants, but "once it starts moving, people want to be a part of it." At one point, he says, Vice President Gore chaired a meeting of agency heads at which those who had been a little slow on the year 2000 conversion were asked to explain why. "That was effective." One Cabinet secretary, whom Kos-kinen declined to identify, remained difficult to the end; Koskinen instead forged a relationship with his deputy.

People knew Koskinen could, if he had to, ask the president to make a call. He never had to.

Another Clinton-era czar who had a well-defined task, and pulled it off, was William Daley, who was the "NAFTA czar" before he became Commerce secretary. That assignment involved riding herd on the departments (including Commerce) with an interest in the agreement and organizing the approach to Congress, where the chief opposition came from organized labor. Once the North American Free Trade Agreement was signed, the job was done.

In one sense, Koskinen's czardom could be seen as a precursor for the technology czardom that Obama has promised to create. Its purview will be arcane but will cut across the whole government. Is there a private-sector model? Companies and universities have chief technology officers to make the organizations' computers, software, and databases blend together, and to help increase transparency, efficiency, and productivity. These CTOs sometimes succeed, especially if the CEO and the company culture are aligned with the technology, and especially if the goals are modest.

But the government is different, because the technology is varied and each department and agency is self-interested. The Defense Department probably poses the biggest challenge for the tech czar; it has its own variety of CTOs, cultures, and needs. But every agency, and every department in every agency, will resist to some degree because none wants to have its central nervous system—with all of its decisions, reports, mistakes, inefficiencies, secrets, and game-playing—displayed to rivals and superiors and even outsiders. Agencies already resist rules requiring them to disclose their goals and performance to the White House and Congress, and a tech czar would be far more intrusive than any congressional panel.

In a different sense—that of the limited, specified mandate—Koskinen's and Daley's tenures could have a parallel in the auto czar. This job, created in December [2008] by Treasury Secretary Henry Paulson Jr., comes with a jurisdiction that cuts across several departments and executive agencies: Treasury, because the money that Detroit receives comes from the TARP funds; Energy, because the czar reviews the automakers' compliance with the advanced vehicle loan program, administered by the Energy Department; Labor, which has to sign off on the compensation reductions called for by the bailout; and EPA and Transportation, which share jurisdiction over fuel-economy standards while EPA administers automotive emissions regulations, both of which are covered by the auto restructuring plans. It's a potential minefield.

But Greg Martin, General Motors' spokesman in Washington, says that there is an advantage to having someone close to the president immersed in the industry's issues. "We genuinely see it as an opportunity to build a constructive working relationship with this position and to create a strong, deep knowledge of our industry within the administration," he says. What frustrates the automakers is the prolonged delay in filling the position.

The car czar structure differs from the nearest precedent: The Chrysler bailout of 1979 was administered not by a czar but by a board, chaired by the Treasury secretary and including the Federal Reserve Board chairman and the U.S. comptroller general, with the secretaries of Labor and Transportation as nonvoting members. Brock says that in a less formal way this sort of council setup, headed by a lead Cabinet officer, was typical in the Reagan administration, and he argues that it often worked well. When Chrysler paid back its loans seven years ahead of time, in 1983, the government made a profit.

The statutory power of the car czar, like the power of the Chrysler board earlier, is mostly directed outward, toward the car companies, suppliers, dealers, and unions. In this, it is an exception to the usual experience of White House czars, who tend to have much more general, and thus much less well-defined, mandates.

* * *

QUESTIONS

1. One criticism of the widespread use of informal advisors is that they are not subject to Senate consent; therefore very little is known about them. Should there be some formal vetting process for presidential advisors? Would this conflict with the president's constitutional prerogative to organize advisory networks as he or she sees fit?

2. What methods can you think of to make executive branch agencies more responsive to presidential policy preferences?

3. In 1900 there were seven Cabinet agencies and 240,000 civilian federal government employees. In 1940, nine agencies and 1 million employees. In 2010, there are fifteen Cabinet agencies, five agencies or boards with Cabinet status, dozens of other agencies, boards, and commissions, and 2.7 million civilian employees. Are there any limits to the size of government?

8

The Federal Judiciary:
Interpreting the Constitution—
Originalism or a Living Constitution?

Debates over the federal judiciary's role in the political process often focus on the question of how judges should interpret the Constitution. Should judges apply the document's original meaning as stated by the Framers, or should they use a framework that incorporates shifting interpretations across time? This debate intensified during Earl Warren's tenure as Chief Justice (1953–69), because of Court decisions that expanded the scope of civil liberties and criminal rights far beyond what "originalists" thought the Constitution's language authorized. The debate continues in the current, more conservative Court. The two readings in this section offer contrasting viewpoints from two sitting Supreme Court justices.

Antonin Scalia, the intellectual force behind the conservative wing of the Court, argues that justices must be bound by the original meaning of the document, because that is the only neutral principle that allows the judiciary to function as a legal body instead of a political one. The alternative is to embrace an evolving or "Living Constitution," which Scalia criticizes as allowing judges to decide cases on the basis of what seems right at the moment. He says that this "evolutionary" approach does not have any overall guiding principle and therefore "is simply not a practicable constitutional philosophy." He provides several examples of how the Living Constitution approach had produced decisions that stray from the meaning of the Constitution in the areas of property rights, the right to bear arms, and the right to confront one's accuser. This last example is especially provocative, given that it concerned the right of an accused child molester to confront the child who accused him of the crime. Scalia also challenges the notion that the Living Constitution approach produces more individual freedoms. Instead, he says, this approach has led to a variety of new restrictions on practices that had previously been allowed in the political process.

Stephen Breyer argues for the Living Constitution approach, and places it within a broader constitutional and theoretical framework. He argues for a "consequentialist" approach that is rooted in basic constitutional purposes, the most important of which is "active liberty," which he defines as "an active and constant participation in collective power." Breyer applies this framework to a range of difficult constitutional issues, including freedom of speech in the context of campaign finance and privacy rights in the context of rapidly evolving technology. He argues that the plain language of the Constitution does not provide enough guidance to answer these difficult questions. He turns the tables on Scalia, arguing that it is the literalist or originalist position that will, ironically, lead justices to rely too heavily on their own personal views, whereas his consequentialist position is actually the view that is more likely to produce judicial restraint. Breyer goes on to criticize the originalist position as fraught with inconsistencies. It is inherently subjective, despite its attempt to emphasize the "objective" words of the Constitution. By relying on the consequentialist perspective, which emphasizes democratic participation and active liberty, justices are more likely to reach limited conclusions that apply to the facts at hand, while maximizing the positive implications for democracy.

Linda Greenhouse, an observer of the Supreme Court, summarized the debate between Scalia and Breyer in these terms: "It is a debate over text versus context. For Justice Scalia, who focuses on text, language is supreme, and the court's job is to derive and apply rules from the words chosen by the Constitution's framers or a statute's drafters. For Justice Breyer, who looks to context, language is only a starting point to an inquiry in which a law's purpose and a decision's likely consequences are the more important elements."

Antonin Scalia

Common-Law Courts in a Civil-Law System: The Role of United States Federal Courts in Interpreting the Constitution and Laws

I want to say a few words about the distinctive problem of interpreting our Constitution. The problem is distinctive, not because special principles of interpretation apply, but because the usual principles are being applied to an unusual text. Chief Justice Marshall put the point as well as it can be put in *McCulloch v. Maryland*:

> A constitution, to contain an accurate detail of all the subdivisions of which its great powers will admit, and of all the means by which they may be carried into execution, would partake of the prolixity of a legal code, and could scarcely be embraced by the human mind. It would probably never be understood by the public. Its nature, therefore, requires, that only its great outlines should be marked, its important objects designated, and the minor ingredients which compose the objects be deduced from the nature of the objects themselves.

In textual interpretation, context is everything, and the context of the Constitution tells us not to expect nit-picking detail, and to give words and phrases an expansive rather than narrow interpretation—though not, of course, an interpretation that the language will not bear.

Take, for example, the provision of the First Amendment that forbids abridgment of "the freedom of speech, or of the press." That phrase does not list the full range of communicative expression. Handwritten letters, for example, are neither speech nor press. Yet surely there is no doubt they cannot be censored. In this constitutional context, speech and press, the two most common forms of communication, stand as a sort of synecdoche for the whole. That is not strict construction, but it is reasonable construction.

It is curious that most of those who insist that the drafter's intent gives meaning to a statute reject the drafter's intent as the criterion for interpretation of the Constitution. I reject it for both. I will consult the writings of some men who happened to be Framers—Hamilton's and Madison's writings in the *Federalist*, for example. I do so, however, not because they were Framers and therefore their intent is authoritative and must be the law; but rather because their writings, like those of other intelligent and informed people of the time, display how the text of the Constitution was originally understood. Thus, I give equal weight to Jay's pieces in the *Federalist*, and to Jefferson's writings, even though neither of them was a Framer. What I look for in the Constitution is precisely what I look for in a statute: the original meaning of the text, not what the original draftsmen intended.

But the Great Divide with regard to constitutional interpretation is not that between Framers' intent and objective meaning; but rather that between *original* meaning (whether derived from Framers' intent or not) and *current* meaning. The ascendant school of constitutional interpretation affirms the existence of what is called the "Living Constitution," a body of law that (unlike normal statutes) grows and changes from age to age, in order to meet the needs of a changing society. And it is the judges who determine those needs and "find" that changing law. Seems familiar, doesn't it? Yes, it is the common law returned, but infinitely more powerful than what the old common law ever pretended to be, for now it trumps even the statutes of democratic legislatures. Recall the words I quoted earlier from the Fourth-of-July speech of the avid codifier Robert Rantoul: "The judge makes law, by extorting from precedents something which they do not contain. He extends his precedents, which were themselves the extension of others, till, by this accommodating principle, a whole system of law is built up without the authority or interference of the legislator." Substitute the word "people" for "legislator," and it is a perfect description of what modern American courts have done with the Constitution.

If you go into a constitutional law class, or study a constitutional-law casebook, or read a brief filed in a constitutional-law case, you will rarely find the discussion addressed to the text of the constitutional provision that is at issue, or to the question of what was the originally understood or even the originally intended meaning of that text. Judges simply ask themselves (as a good common-law judge would) what *ought* the result to be, and then proceed to the task of distinguishing (or, if necessary, overruling) any prior Supreme Court cases that stand in the way. Should there be (to take one of the less controversial examples) a constitutional right to die? If so, there is. Should there be a constitutional right to reclaim a biological child put out for adoption by the other parent? Again, if so, there is. If it is good, it is so. Never mind the text that we are supposedly construing; we will smuggle these in, if all else fails, under the Due Process Clause (which, as I have described, is textually incapable of containing them). Moreover, what the Constitution meant yesterday it does not necessarily mean today. As our opinions say in the context of our Eighth Amendment jurisprudence (the Cruel and Unusual Punishments Clause), its meaning changes to reflect "the evolving standards of decency that mark the progress of a maturing society."

This is preeminently a common-law way of making law, and not the way of construing a democratically adopted text. I mentioned earlier a famous English treatise on statutory construction called *Dwarris on Statutes*. The fourth of Dwarris's Maxims was as follows: "An act of Parliament cannot alter by reason of time; but the common law may, since *cessante ratione cessat lex*." This remains (however much it may sometimes be evaded) the formally enunciated rule for statutory construction: statutes do not change. Proposals for "dynamic statutory construction," such as those of Judge Calabresi and Professor Eskridge that I discussed yesterday, are concededly avant-garde. The Constitution, however, even though a democratically adopted text, we formally treat like the common law. What, it is fair to ask, is our justification for doing so?

One would suppose that the rule that a text does not change would apply *a fortiori* to a constitution. If courts felt too much bound by the democratic process to tinker with statutes, when their tinkering could be adjusted by the legislature, how much more should they feel bound not to tinker with a constitution, when their tinkering is virtually irreparable. It surely cannot be said that a constitution naturally suggests changeability; to the contrary, its whole purpose is to prevent change—to embed certain rights in such a manner that future generations cannot take them away. A society that adopts a bill of rights is skeptical that "evolving standards of decency" always "mark progress," and that societies always "mature," as opposed to rot. Neither the text of such a document nor the intent of its framers (whichever you choose) can possibly lead to the conclusion that its only effect is to take the power of changing rights away from the legislature and give it to the courts.

The argument most frequently made in favor of the Living Constitution is a pragmatic one: Such an evolutionary approach is necessary in order to provide the "flexibility" that a changing society requires; the Constitution would have snapped, if it had not been permitted to bend and grow. This might be a persuasive argument if most of the "growing" that the proponents of this approach have brought upon us in the past, and are determined to bring upon us in the future, were the *elimination* of restrictions upon democratic government. But just the opposite is true. Historically, and particularly in the past thirty-five years, the "evolving" Constitution has imposed a vast array of new constraints—new inflexibilities—upon administrative, judicial, and legislative action. To mention only a few things that formerly could be done or not done, as the society desired, but now cannot be done:

> admitting in a state criminal trial evidence of guilt that was obtained by an unlawful search;
> permitting invocation of God at public-school graduations;
> electing one of the two houses of a state legislature the way the United States Senate is elected (i.e., on a basis that does not give all voters numerically equal representation);
> terminating welfare payments as soon as evidence of fraud is received, subject to restoration after hearing if the evidence is satisfactorily refuted;
> imposing property requirements as a condition of voting;
> prohibiting anonymous campaign literature;
> prohibiting pornography.

And the future agenda of constitutional evolutionists is mostly more of the same—the creation of *new* restrictions upon democratic government, rather than the elimination of old ones. *Less* flexibility in government, not *more*. As things now stand, the state and federal governments may either apply capital punishment or abolish it, permit suicide or forbid it—all as the changing times and the changing sentiments of society may demand. But when capital punishment is held to violate the Eighth Amendment, and suicide is held to be protected by the Fourteenth Amendment, all flexibility with regard to those matters will be gone. No, the reality of the matter is that, generally speaking, devotees of the Living Constitution do not seek to faciliate social change but to *prevent* it.

There are, I must admit, a few exceptions to that—a few instances in which, historically, greater flexibility *has been* the result of the process. But those exceptions only serve to refute another argument of the proponents of an evolving Constitution, that evolution will always be in the direction of greater personal liberty. (They consider that a great advantage, for reasons that I do not entirely understand. All government represents a balance between individual freedom and social order, and it is not true that every alteration of that balance in the direction of greater individual freedom is necessarily good.) But in any case, the record of history refutes the proposition that the evolving Constitution will invariably enlarge individual rights. The most obvious refutation is the modern Court's limitation of the constitutional protections afforded to property. The provision prohibiting impairment of the obligation of contracts, for example, has been gutted. I am sure that We the People agree with that development; we value property rights less than the Founders did. So also, we value the right to bear arms less than the Founders (who thought the right of self-defense to be absolutely fundamental), and there will be few tears shed if and when the Second Amendment is held to guarantee nothing more than the State National Guard. But this just shows that the Founders were right when they feared that some (in their view misguided) future generation might wish to abandon liberties that they considered essential, and so sought to protect those liberties in a Bill of Rights. We may *like* the abridgment of property rights, and *like* the elimination of the right to bear arms; but let us not pretend that these are not a *reduction* of *rights*.

Or if property rights are too cold to get your juices flowing, and the right to bear arms too dangerous, let me give another example: Several terms ago a case came before the Supreme Court involving a prosecution for sexual abuse of a young child. The trial court found that the child would be too frightened to testify in the presence of the (presumed) abuser, and so, pursuant to state law, she was permitted to testify with only the prosecutor and defense counsel present, the defendant, the judge, and the jury watching over closed-circuit television. A reasonable enough procedure, and it was held to be constitutional by my Court. I dissented, because the Sixth Amendment provides that "[i]n *all* criminal prosecutions" (let me emphasize the word "all") "the accused shall enjoy the right . . . to be confronted with the witnesses against him." There is no doubt what confrontation meant—or indeed means today. It means face-to-face, not watching from another room. And there is no doubt what one of the major purposes of that provision was: to induce *precisely* that pressure upon the witness which the little girl found it difficult to endure. It is difficult to accuse someone to his face, particularly when you are lying. Now no extrinsic factors have changed since that provision was adopted in 1791. Sexual abuse existed then, as it does now; little children were more easily upset than adults, then as now; a means of placing the defendant out of sight of the witness existed then as now (a screen could easily have been erected that would enable the defendant to see the witness, but not the witness the defendant). But the Sixth Amendment nonetheless gave *all* criminal defendants the right to *confront* the witnesses against them, because that was thought to be an important protection. The only significant thing that *has* changed, I think, is the society's sensitivity to so-called psychic trauma (which is what we are told the child witness in such a situation suffers) and the society's assessment of where the proper balance ought to be struck between the two extremes of a procedure that assures convicting 100 percent of all child abusers, and a procedure that assures acquitting 100 percent of those who have been falsely accused of child abuse. I have no doubt that the society is, as a whole, happy and pleased with what my Court decided. But we should not pretend that the decision did not *eliminate* a liberty that previously existed.

My last remarks may have created the false impression that proponents of the Living Constitution follow the desires of the American people in determining how the Constitution should evolve. They follow nothing so precise; indeed, as a group they follow nothing at all. Perhaps the most glaring defect of Living Constitutionalism, next to its incompatibility with the whole anti-evolutionary purpose of a constitution, is that there is no agreement, and no chance of agreement, upon what is to be the guiding principle of the evolution. *Panta rhei* [all things are in constant flux] is not a sufficiently informative principle of constitutional interpretation. What is it that the judge must consult to determine when, and in what direction, evolution has occurred? Is it the will of the majority, discerned from newspapers, radio talk shows, public opinion polls, and chats at the country club? Is it the philosophy of Hume, or of John Rawls, or of John Stuart Mill, or of Aristotle? As soon as the discussion goes beyond the issue of whether the Constitution is static, the evolutionists divide into as many camps as there are individual views of the good, the true, and the beautiful. I think that is inevitably so, which means that evolutionism is simply not a practicable constitutional philosophy.

I do not suggest, mind you, that originalists always agree upon their answer. There is plenty of room for disagreement as to what original meaning was, and even more as to how that original meaning applies to the situation before the court. But the originalist at least knows what he is looking for: the original meaning of the text. Often, indeed I dare say usually, that is easy to discern and simple to apply. Sometimes (though not very often) there will be disagreement regarding the original meaning; and sometimes there will be disagreement as to how that original meaning applies to new and unforeseen phenomena. How, for example, does the First Amendment guarantee of "the freedom of speech" apply to new technologies that did not exist when the guarantee was created—to sound trucks, or to government-licensed over-the-air television? In such new fields the Court must follow the trajectory of the First Amendment, so to speak, to determine what it requires—and assuredly that enterprise is not entirely cut-and-dried, but requires the exercise of judgment.

But the difficulties and uncertainties of determining original meaning and applying it to modern circumstances are negligible compared with the difficulties and uncertainties of the philosophy which says that the Constitution *changes*; that the very act which it once prohibited it now permits, and which it once permitted it now forbids; and that the key to that change is unknown and unknowable. The originalist, if he does not have all the answers, has many of them. The Confrontation Clause, for example, requires confrontation. For the evolutionist, however, every question is an open question, every day a new day. No fewer than three of the Justices with whom I have served have maintained that the death penalty is unconstitutional, *even though its use is explicitly contemplated in the Constitution.* The Due Process Clause of the Fifth and Fourteenth Amendments say that no person shall be deprived of life without due process of law; and the Grand Jury Clause of the Fifth Amendment says that no person shall be held to answer for a capital crime without grand jury indictment. No matter. Under the Living Constitution the death penalty may have *become* unconstitutional. And it is up to each Justice to decide for himself (under no standard I can discern) when that occurs.

In the last analysis, however, it probably does not matter what principle, among the innumerable possibilities, the evolutionist proposes to determine in what direction the Living Constitution will grow. For unless the evolutionary dogma is kept a closely held secret among us judges and law professors, it will lead to the result that the Constitution evolves the way the majority wishes. The people will be willing to leave interpretation of the Constitution to a committee of nine lawyers so long as the people believe that it is (like the interpretation of a statute) lawyers' work—requiring a close examination of text, history of the text, traditional understanding of the text, judicial precedent, etc. But if the people come to believe that the Constitution is *not* a text like other texts; if it means, not what it says or what it was understood to mean, but what it *should* mean, in light of the "evolving standards of decency that mark the progress of a maturing society," well then, they will look for qualifications other than impartiality, judgment, and lawyerly acumen in those whom they select to interpret it. More specifically, they will look for people who agree with *them* as to what those evolving standards have evolved to; who agree with *them* as to what the Constitution *ought* to be.

It seems to me that that is where we are heading, or perhaps even where we have arrived. Seventy-five years ago, we believed firmly enough in a rock-solid, unchanging Constitution that we felt it necessary to adopt the Nineteenth Amendment to give women the vote. The battle was not fought in the courts, and few thought that it could be, despite the constitutional guarantee of Equal Protection of the Laws; that provision* did not, when it was adopted, and hence did not in 1920, guarantee equal access to the ballot, but permitted distinctions on the basis not only of age, but of property and of sex. Who can doubt that, if the issue had been deferred until today, the Constitution would be (formally) unamended, and the courts would be the chosen instrumentality of change? The American people have been converted to belief in the Living Constitution, a "morphing" document that means, from age to age, what it ought to mean. And with that conversion has inevitably come the new phenomenon of selecting and confirming federal judges, at all levels, on the basis of their views regarding a whole series of proposals for constitutional evolution. If the courts are free to write the Constitution anew, they will, by God, write it the way the majority wants; the appointment and confirmation process will see to that. This, of course, is the end of the Bill of Rights, whose meaning will be committed to the very body it was meant to protect against: the majority. By trying to make the Constitution do everything that needs doing from age to age, we shall have caused it to do nothing at all.

---

*Scalia is referring to the "equal protection clause" of the Fourteenth Amendment, which states, "No state shall . . . deny to any person within its jurisdiction the equal protection of the laws" [*Editors*].

Stephen Breyer

Our Democratic Constitution

I shall focus upon several contemporary problems that call for governmental action and potential judicial reaction. In each instance I shall argue that, when judges interpret the Constitution, they should place greater emphasis upon the "ancient liberty," i.e., the people's right to "an active and constant participation in collective power." I believe that increased emphasis upon this active liberty will lead to better constitutional law, a law that will promote governmental solutions consistent with individual dignity and community need.

At the same time, my discussion will illustrate an approach to constitutional interpretation that places considerable weight upon consequences—consequences valued in terms of basic constitutional purposes. It disavows a contrary constitutional approach, a more "legalistic" approach that places too much weight upon language, history, tradition, and precedent alone while understating the importance of consequences. If the discussion helps to convince you that the more "consequential" approach has virtue, so much the better.

Three basic views underlie my discussion. First, the Constitution, considered as a whole, creates a framework for a certain kind of government. Its general objectives can be described abstractly as including (1) democratic self-government, (2) dispersion of power (avoiding concentration of too much power in too few hands), (3) individual dignity (through protection of individual liberties), (4) equality before the law (through equal protection of the law), and (5) the rule of law itself.

The Constitution embodies these general objectives in particular provisions. In respect to self-government, for example, Article IV guarantees a "republican Form of Government;" Article I insists that Congress meet at least once a year, that elections take place every two (or six) years, that a census take place every decade; the Fifteenth, Nineteenth, Twenty-fourth, and Twenty-sixth Amendments secure a virtually universal adult suffrage. But a general constitutional objective such as self-government plays a constitutional role beyond the interpretation of an individual provision that refers to it directly. That is because constitutional courts must consider the relation of one phrase to another. They must consider the document as a whole. And consequently the document's handful of general purposes will inform judicial interpretation of many individual provisions that do not refer directly to the general objective in question. My examples seek to show how that is so. And, as I have said, they will suggest a need for judges to pay greater attention to one of those general objectives, namely participatory democratic self-government.

Second, the Court, while always respecting language, tradition, and precedent, nonetheless has emphasized different general constitutional objectives at different periods in its history. Thus one can characterize the early nineteenth century as a period during which the Court helped to establish the authority of the federal government, including the federal judiciary. During the late nineteenth and early twentieth centuries, the Court underemphasized the Constitution's efforts to secure participation by black citizens in representative government—efforts related to the participatory "active" liberty of the ancients. At the same time, it over-emphasized protection of property rights, such as an individual's freedom to contract without government interference, to the point where President Franklin Roosevelt commented that the Court's Lochner-era decisions had created a legal "no-man's land" that neither state nor federal regulatory authority had the power to enter.

The New Deal Court and the Warren Court in part reemphasized "active liberty." The former did so by dismantling various Lochner-era distinctions, thereby expanding the scope of democratic self-government. The latter did so by interpreting the Civil War Amendments in light of their purposes and to mean what they say, thereby helping African-Americans become members of the nation's community of self-governing citizens—a community that the Court expanded further in its "one person, one vote" decisions.

More recently, in my view, the Court has again underemphasized the importance of the citizen's active liberty. I will argue for a contemporary reemphasis that better combines "the liberty of the ancients" with that "freedom of governmental restraint" that Constant called "modern."

Third, the real-world consequences of a particular interpretive decision, valued in terms of basic constitutional purposes, play an important role in constitutional decision-making. To that extent, my approach differs from that of judges who would place nearly exclusive interpretive weight upon language, history, tradition and precedent. In truth, the difference is one of degree. Virtually all judges, when interpreting a constitution or a statute, refer at one time or another to language, to history, to tradition, to precedent, to purpose, and to consequences. Even those who take a more literal approach to constitutional interpretation sometimes find consequences and general purposes relevant. But the more "literalist" judge tends to ask those who cannot find an interpretive answer in language, history, tradition, and precedent alone to rethink the problem several times, before making consequences determinative. The more literal judges may hope to find in language, history, tradition, and precedent objective interpretive standards; they may seek to avoid an interpretive subjectivity that could confuse a judge's personal idea of what is good for that which the Constitution demands; and they may believe that these more "original" sources will more readily yield rules that can guide other institutions, including lower courts. These objectives are desirable, but I do not think the literal approach will achieve them, and, in any event, the constitutional price is too high. I hope that my examples will help to show you why that is so, as well as to persuade some of you why it is important to place greater weight upon constitutionally-valued consequences, my consequential focus in this lecture being the affect of a court's decisions upon active liberty.

To recall the fate of Socrates is to understand that the "liberty of the ancients" is not a sufficient condition for human liberty. Nor can (or should) we replicate today the ideal represented by the Athenian agora or the New England town meeting. Nonetheless, today's citizen does participate in democratic self-governing processes. And the "active" liberty to which I refer consists of the Constitution's efforts to secure the citizen's right to do so.

To focus upon that active liberty, to understand it as one of the Constitution's handful of general objectives, will lead judges to consider the constitutionality of statutes with a certain modesty. That modesty embodies an understanding of the judges' own expertise compared, for example, with that of a legislature. It reflects the concern that a judiciary too ready to "correct" legislative error may deprive "the people" of "the political experience and the moral education that come from . . . correcting their own errors." It encompasses that doubt, caution, prudence, and concern—that state of not being "too sure" of oneself—that Learned Hand described as the "spirit of liberty." In a word, it argues for traditional "judicial restraint."

But active liberty argues for more than that. I shall suggest that increased recognition of the Constitution's general democratic participatory objectives can help courts deal more effectively with a range of specific constitutional issues. To show this I shall use examples drawn from the areas of free speech, federalism, privacy, equal protection and statutory interpretation. In each instance, I shall refer to an important modern problem of government that calls for a democratic response. I shall then describe related constitutional implications. I want to draw a picture of some of the different ways that increased judicial focus upon the Constitution's participatory objectives can have a positive effect.

*　*　*

I begin with free speech and campaign finance reform. The campaign finance problem arises out of the recent explosion in campaign costs along with a vast disparity among potential givers. * * * The upshot is a concern by some that the matter is out of hand—that too few individuals contribute too much money and that, even though money is not the only way to obtain influence, those who give large amounts of money do obtain, or appear to obtain, too much influence. The end result is a marked inequality of participation. That is one important reason why legislatures have sought to regulate the size of campaign contributions.

The basic constitutional question, as you all know, is not the desirability of reform legislation but whether, how, or the extent to which, the First Amendment permits the legislature to impose limitations or ceilings on the amounts individuals or organizations or parties can contribute to a campaign or the kinds of contributions they can make. * * *

One cannot (or, at least, I cannot) find an easy answer to the constitutional questions in language, history, or tradition. The First Amendment's language says that Congress shall not abridge "the freedom of speech." But it does not define "the freedom of speech" in any detail. The nation's founders did not speak directly about campaign contributions. Madison, who decried faction, thought that members of Congress would fairly represent all their constituents, in part because the "electors" would not be the "rich" any "more than the poor." But this kind of statement, while modestly helpful to the campaign reform cause, is hardly determinative.

Neither can I find answers in purely conceptual arguments. Some argue, for example, that "money is speech"; others say "money is not speech." But neither contention helps much. Money is not speech, it is money. But the expenditure of money enables speech; and that expenditure is often necessary to communicate a message, particularly in a political context. A law that forbids the expenditure of money to convey a message could effectively suppress that communication.

Nor does it resolve the matter simply to point out that campaign contribution limits inhibit the political "speech opportunities" of those who wish to contribute more. Indeed, that is so. But the question is whether, in context, such a limitation abridges "the freedom of speech." And to announce that this kind of harm could never prove justified in a political context is simply to state an ultimate constitutional conclusion; it is not to explain the underlying reasons.

To refer to the Constitution's general participatory self-government objective, its protection of "active liberty" is far more helpful. That is because that constitutional goal indicates that the First Amendment's constitutional role is not simply one of protecting the individual's "negative" freedom from governmental restraint. The Amendment in context also forms a necessary part of a constitutional system designed to sustain that democratic self-government. The Amendment helps to sustain the democratic process both by encouraging the exchange of ideas needed to make sound electoral decisions and by encouraging an exchange of views among ordinary citizens necessary to encourage their informed participation in the electoral process. It thereby helps to maintain a form of government open to participation (in Constant's words "by all citizens without exception").

The relevance of this conceptual view lies in the fact that the campaign finance laws also seek to further the latter objective. They hope to democratize the influence that money can bring to bear upon the electoral process, thereby building public confidence in that process, broadening the base of a candidate's meaningful financial support, and encouraging greater public participation. They consequently seek to maintain the integrity of the political process—a process that itself translates political speech into governmental action. Seen in this way, campaign finance laws, despite the limits they impose, help to further the kind of open public political discussion that the First Amendment also seeks to encourage, not simply as an end, but also as a means to achieve a workable democracy.

For this reason, I have argued that a court should approach most campaign finance questions with the understanding that important First Amendment-related interests lie on both sides of the constitutional equation and that a First Amendment presumption hostile to government regulation, such as "strict scrutiny" is consequently out of place. Rather, the Court considering the matter without benefit of presumptions, must look realistically at the legislation's impact, both its negative impact on the ability of some to engage in as much communication as they wish and the positive impact upon the public's confidence, and consequent ability to communicate through (and participate in) the electoral process.

The basic question the Court should ask is one of proportionality. Do the statutes strike a reasonable balance between their electoral speech-restricting and speech-enhancing consequences? Or do you instead impose restrictions on that speech that are disproportionate when measured against their corresponding electoral and speech-related benefits, taking into account the kind, the importance, and the extent of those benefits, as well as the need for the restrictions in order to secure them?

The judicial modesty discussed earlier suggests that, in answering these questions, courts should defer to the legislatures' own answers insofar as those answers reflect empirical matters about which the legislature is comparatively expert, for example, the extent of the campaign finance problem, a matter that directly concerns the realities of political life. But courts cannot defer when evaluating the risk that reform legislation will defeat the very objective of participatory self-government itself, for example, where laws would set limits so low that, by elevating the reputation-related or media-related advantages of incumbency to the point where they would insulate incumbents from effective challenge.

I am not saying that focus upon active liberty will automatically answer the constitutional question in particular campaign finance cases. I argue only that such focus will help courts find a proper route for arriving at an answer. The positive constitutional goal implies a systemic role for the First Amendment; and that role, in turn, suggests a legal framework, i.e., a more particular set of questions for the Court to ask. Modesty suggests where, and how, courts should defer to legislatures in doing so. The suggested inquiry is complex. But courts both here and abroad have engaged in similarly complex inquiries where the constitutionality of electoral laws is at issue. That complexity is demanded by a Constitution that provides for judicial review of the constitutionality of electoral rules while granting Congress the effective power to secure a fair electoral system.

I next turn to a different kind of example. It focuses upon current threats to the protection of privacy, defined as "the power to control what others can come to know about you." It seeks to illustrate what active liberty is like in modern America, when we seek to arrive democratically at solutions to important technologically-based problems. And it suggests a need for judicial caution and humility when certain privacy matters, such as the balance between free speech and privacy, are at issue.

First, I must describe the "privacy" problem. That problem is unusually complex. It has clearly become even more so since the terrorist attacks. For one thing, those who agree that privacy is important disagree about why. Some emphasize the need to be left alone, not bothered by others, or that privacy is important because it prevents people from being judged out of context. Some emphasize the way in which relationships of love and friendship depend upon trust, which implies a sharing of information not available to all. Others find connections between privacy and individualism, in that privacy encourages non-conformity. Still others find connections between privacy and equality, in that limitations upon the availability of individualized information lead private businesses to treat all customers alike. For some, or all, of these reasons, legal rules protecting privacy help to assure an individual's dignity.

For another thing, the law protects privacy only because of the way in which technology interacts with different laws. Some laws, such as trespass, wiretapping, eavesdropping, and search-and-seizure laws, protect particular places or sites, such as homes or telephones, from searches and monitoring. Other laws protect not places, but kinds of information, for example laws that forbid the publication of certain personal information even by a person who obtained that information legally. Taken together these laws protect privacy to different degrees depending upon place, individual status, kind of intrusion, and type of information.

Further, technological advances have changed the extent to which present laws can protect privacy. Video cameras now can monitor shopping malls, schools, parks, office buildings, city streets, and other places that present law left unprotected. Scanners and interceptors can overhear virtually any electronic conversation. Thermal imaging devices can detect activities taking place within the home. Computers can record and collate information obtained in any of these ways, or others. This technology means an ability to observe, collate and permanently record a vast amount of information about individuals that the law previously may have made available for collection but which, in practice, could not easily have been recorded and collected. The nature of the current or future privacy threat depends upon how this technological/legal fact will affect differently situated individuals.

These circumstances mean that efforts to revise privacy law to take account of the new technology will involve, in different areas of human activity, the balancing of values in light of prediction about the technological future. If, for example, businesses obtain detailed consumer purchasing information, they may create individualized customer profiles. Those profiles may invade the customer's privacy. But they may also help firms provide publicly desired products at lower cost. If, for example, medical records are placed online, patient privacy may be compromised. But the ready availability of those records may lower insurance costs or help a patient carried unconscious into an operating room. If, for example, all information about an individual's genetic make-up is completely confidential, that individual's privacy is protected, but suppose a close relative, a nephew or cousin, needs the information to assess his own cancer risk?

Nor does a "consent" requirement automatically answer the dilemmas suggested, for consent forms may be signed without understanding and, in any event, a decision by one individual to release or to deny information can affect others as well.

Legal solutions to these problems will be shaped by what is technologically possible. Should video cameras be programmed to turn off? Recorded images to self-destruct? Computers instructed to delete certain kinds of information? Should cell phones be encrypted? Should web technology, making use of an individual's privacy preferences, automatically negotiate privacy rules with distant web sites as a condition of access?

The complex nature of these problems calls for resolution through a form of participatory democracy. Ideally, that participatory process does not involve legislators, administrators, or judges imposing law from above. Rather, it involves law revision that bubbles up from below. Serious complex changes in law are often made in the context of a national conversation involving, among others, scientists, engineers, businessmen and -women, the media, along with legislators, judges, and many ordinary citizens whose lives the new technology will affect. That conversation takes place through many meetings, symposia, and discussions, through journal articles and media reports, through legislative hearings and court cases. Lawyers participate fully in this discussion, translating specialized knowledge into ordinary English, defining issues, creating consensus. Typically, administrators and legislators then make decisions, with courts later resolving any constitutional issues that those decisions raise. This "conversation" is the participatory democratic process itself.

The presence of this kind of problem and this kind of democratic process helps to explain, because it suggests a need for, judicial caution or modesty.

That is why, for example, the Court's decisions so far have hesitated to preempt that process. In one recent case the Court considered a cell phone conversation that an unknown private individual had intercepted with a scanner and delivered to a radio station. A statute forbid the broadcast of that conversation, even though the radio station itself had not planned or participated in the intercept. The Court had to determine the scope of the station's First Amendment right to broadcast given the privacy interests that the statute sought to protect. The Court held that the First Amendment trumped the statute, permitting the radio station to broadcast the information. But the holding was narrow. It focused upon the particular circumstances present, explicitly leaving open broadcaster liability in other, less innocent, circumstances.

The narrowness of the holding itself serves a constitutional purpose. The privacy "conversation" is ongoing. Congress could well rewrite the statute, tailoring it more finely to current technological facts, such as the widespread availability of scanners and the possibility of protecting conversations through encryption. A broader constitutional rule might itself limit legislative options in ways now unforeseeable. And doing so is particularly dangerous where statutory protection of an important personal liberty is at issue.

By way of contrast, the Court held unconstitutional police efforts to use, without a warrant, a thermal imaging device placed on a public sidewalk. The device permitted police to identify activities taking place within a private house. The case required the Court simply to ask whether the residents had a reasonable expectation that their activities within the house would not be disclosed to the public in this way—a well established Fourth Amendment principle. Hence the case asked the Court to pour new technological wine into old bottles; it did not suggest that doing so would significantly interfere with an ongoing democratic policy conversation.

The privacy example suggests more by way of caution. It warns against adopting an overly rigid method of interpreting the constitution—placing weight upon eighteenth-century details to the point where it becomes difficult for a twenty-first-century court to apply the document's underlying values. At a minimum it suggests that courts, in determining the breadth of a constitutional holding, should look to the effect of a holding on the ongoing policy process, distinguishing, as I have suggested, between the "eavesdropping" and the "thermal heat" types of cases. And it makes clear that judicial caution in such matters does not reflect the fact that judges are mitigating their legal concerns with practical considerations. Rather, the Constitution itself is a practical document—a document that authorizes the Court to proceed practically when it examines new laws in light of the Constitution's enduring, underlying values.

My fourth example concerns equal protection and voting rights, an area that has led to considerable constitutional controversy. Some believe that the Constitution prohibits virtually any legislative effort to use race as a basis for drawing electoral district boundaries—unless, for example, the effort seeks to undo earlier invidious race-based discrimination. Others believe that the Constitution does not so severely limit the instances in which a legislature can use race to create majority-minority districts. Without describing in detail the basic argument between the two positions, I wish to point out the relevance to that argument of the Constitution's democratic objective.

That objective suggests a simple, but potentially important, constitutional difference in the electoral area between invidious discrimination, penalizing members of a racial minority, and positive discrimination, assisting members of racial minorities. The Constitution's Fifteenth Amendment prohibits the former, not simply because it violates a basic Fourteenth Amendment principle, namely that the government must treat all citizens with equal respect, but also because it denies minority citizens the opportunity to participate in the self-governing democracy that the Constitution creates. By way of contrast, affirmative discrimination ordinarily seeks to enlarge minority participation in that self-governing democracy. To that extent it is consistent with, indeed furthers, the Constitution's basic democratic objective. That consistency, along with its more benign purposes, helps to mitigate whatever lack of equal respect any such discrimination might show to any disadvantaged member of a majority group.

I am not saying that the mitigation will automatically render any particular discriminatory scheme constitutional. But the presence of this mitigating difference supports the view that courts should not apply the strong presumptions of unconstitutionality that are appropriate where invidious discrimination is at issue. My basic purpose, again, is to suggest that reference to the Constitution's "democratic" objective can help us apply a different basic objective, here that of equal protection. And in the electoral context, the reference suggests increased legislative authority to deal with multiracial issues.

The instances I have discussed encompass different areas of law—speech, federalism, privacy, equal protection, and statutory interpretation. In each instance, the discussion has focused upon a contemporary social problem—campaign finance, workplace regulation, environmental regulation, information-based technological change, race-based electoral districting, and legislative politics. In each instance, the discussion illustrates how increased focus upon the Constitution's basic democratic objective might make a difference—in refining doctrinal rules, in evaluating consequences, in applying practical cautionary principles, in interacting with other constitutional objectives, and in explicating statutory silences. In each instance, the discussion suggests how that increased focus might mean better law. And "better" in this context means both (a) better able to satisfy the Constitution's purposes and (b) better able to cope with contemporary problems. The discussion, while not proving its point purely through logic or empirical demonstration, uses example to create a pattern. The pattern suggests a need for increased judicial emphasis upon the Constitution's democratic objective.

My discussion emphasizes values underlying specific constitutional phrases, sees the Constitution itself as a single document with certain basic related objectives, and assumes that the latter can inform a judge's understanding of the former. Might that discussion persuade those who prefer to believe that the keys to constitutional interpretation instead lie in specific language, history, tradition, and precedent and who fear that a contrary approach would permit judges too often to act too subjectively?

Perhaps so, for several reasons. First, the area of interpretive disagreement is more limited than many believe. Judges can, and should, decide most cases, including constitutional cases, through the use of language, history, tradition, and precedent. Judges will often agree as to how these factors determine a provision's basic purpose and the result in a particular case. And where they differ, their differences are often differences of modest degree. Only a handful of constitutional issues—though an important handful—are as open in respect to language, history, and basic purpose as those that I have described. And even in respect to those issues, judges must find answers within the limits set by the Constitution's language. Moreover, history, tradition, and precedent remain helpful, even if not determinative.

Second, those more literalist judges who emphasize language, history, tradition, and precedent cannot justify their practices by claiming that is what the Framers wanted, for the Framers did not say specifically what factors judges should emphasize when seeking to interpret the Constitution's open language. Nor is it plausible to believe that those who argued about the Bill of Rights, and made clear that it did not contain an exclusive detailed list, had agreed about what school of interpretive thought should prove dominant in the centuries to come. Indeed, the Constitution itself says that the "enumeration" in the Constitution of some rights "shall not be construed to deny or disparage others retained by the people." Professor Bailyn concludes that the Framers added this language to make clear that "rights, like law itself, should never be fixed, frozen, that new dangers and needs will emerge, and that to respond to these dangers and needs, rights must be newly specified to protect the individual's integrity and inherent dignity." Instead, justification for the literalist's practice itself tends to rest upon consequences. Literalist arguments often seek to show that such an approach will have favorable results, for example, controlling judicial subjectivity.

Third, judges who reject a literalist approach deny that their decisions are subjective and point to important safeguards of objectivity. A decision that emphasizes values, no less than any other, is open to criticism based upon (1) the decision's relation to the other legal principles (precedents, rules, standards, practices, institutional understandings) that it modifies and (2) the decision's consequences, i.e., the way in which the entire bloc of decision-affected legal principles subsequently affects the world. The relevant values, by limiting interpretive possibilities and guiding interpretation, themselves constrain subjectivity, indeed the democratic values that I have emphasized themselves suggest the importance of judicial restraint. An individual constitutional judge's need for consistency over time also constrains subjectivity. That is why Justice O'Connor has explained that need in terms of a constitutional judge's initial decisions creating "footprints" that later decisions almost inevitably will follow.

Fourth, the literalist does not escape subjectivity, for his tools, language, history, and tradition, can provide little objective guidance in the comparatively small set of cases about which I have spoken. In such cases, the Constitution's language is almost always nonspecific. History and tradition are open to competing claims and rival interpretations. Nor does an emphasis upon rules embodied in precedent necessarily produce clarity, particularly in borderline areas or where rules are stated abstractly. Indeed, an emphasis upon language, history, tradition, or prior rules in such cases may simply channel subjectivity into a choice about: Which history? Which tradition? Which rules? It will then produce a decision that is no less subjective but which is far less transparent than a decision that directly addresses consequences in constitutional terms.

Finally, my examples point to offsetting consequences—at least if "literalism" tends to produce the legal doctrines (related to the First Amendment, to federalism, to statutory interpretation, to equal protection) that I have criticized.

Those doctrines lead to consequences at least as harmful, from a constitutional perspective, as any increased risk of subjectivity. In the ways that I have set out, they undermine the Constitution's efforts to create a framework for democratic government—a government that, while protecting basic individual liberties, permits individual citizens to govern themselves.

To reemphasize the constitutional importance of democratic self-government may carry with it a practical bonus. We are all aware of figures that show that the public knows ever less about, and is ever less interested in, the processes of government. Foundation reports criticize the lack of high school civics education. Comedians claim that more students know the names of the Three Stooges than the three branches of government. Even law school graduates are ever less inclined to work for government—with the percentage of those entering government (or nongovernment public interest) work declining at one major law school from 12% to 3% over a generation. Indeed, polls show that, over that same period of time, the percentage of the public trusting the government declined at a similar rate.

This trend, however, is not irreversible. Indeed, trust in government has shown a remarkable rebound in response to last month's terrible tragedy [September 11]. Courts cannot maintain this upward momentum by themselves. But courts, as highly trusted government institutions, can help some, in part by explaining in terms the public can understand just what the Constitution is about. It is important that the public, trying to cope with the problems of nation, state, and local community, understand that the Constitution does not resolve, and was not intended to resolve, society's problems. Rather, the Constitution provides a framework for the creation of democratically determined solutions, which protect each individual's basic liberties and assures that individual equal respect by government, while securing a democratic form of government. We judges cannot insist that Americans participate in that government, but we can make clear that our Constitution depends upon it. Indeed, participation reinforces that "positive passion for the public good," that John Adams, like so many others, felt a necessary condition for "Republican Government" and any "real Liberty."

That is the democratic ideal. It is as relevant today as it was 200 or 2000 years ago. Today it is embodied in our Constitution. Two thousand years ago, Thucydides, quoting Pericles, set forth a related ideal—relevant in his own time and, with some modifications, still appropriate to recall today. "We Athenians," said Pericles, "do not say that the man who fails to participate in politics is a man who minds his own business. We say that he is a man who has no business here."

QUESTIONS

1. Critics of the originalist perspective often point to ambiguities in the language of the Constitution. Justice Breyer outlines several of these in his speech. What are some other examples of ambiguous language in the Constitution? (Look at the Bill of Rights as a start.) What alternative interpretations can you develop?

2. Critics of the Living Constitution, such as Justice Scalia, often argue that judges substitute their own reading of what they think the law should be for what the law is. Do you think it is possible for justices to avoid having their own views shape their decisions? How could they protect against this happening?

3. Should judges take public opinion or changing societal standards into account when ruling on the constitutionality of a statute or practice? If so, what evidence of public opinion or societal standards should matter? Surveys? Laws enacted in states? If not, what are the risks in doing so?

4. Consider Scalia's list of activities that are no longer allowed by the Court (the list begins with using illegally obtained evidence in a criminal trial). How would Breyer's approach of active liberty decide these cases? Which do you think is the better outcome?

9

The Mass Media: The Future of Political Journalism

From the 1960s through the 1980s, when people thought of media and news, they thought of newspapers and, increasingly, the broadcast television networks. Cable news soon emerged to provide an alternative, but one that for the most part followed the same operating procedure for major nightly newscasts as the big networks. Late in the 1980s, talk radio, which had been around for some time, boomed in popularity and hosts such as Rush Limbaugh became household names. Hosts gleefully tweaked the mainstream media and embraced a much more aggressive, hard-hitting style that was explicitly ideological and partisan. There was, in this new forum, no pretense to being objective but, talk-radio fans would argue, the mainstream media were also not objective—they just pretended to be. News-oriented talk shows on cable followed the same pattern. The rise of the Internet in the 1990s was the most recent dramatic change in communications technology. Today, blogs receive most of the attention, with Twitter gaining ground, and sites such as YouTube make it possible for every misstep by a politician to be easily viewed by millions of viewers.

Major changes in communications technology have produced major changes in the practice of politics and the way people learn about government. Earlier technologies do not necessarily fade away, but their role changes and their dominance diminishes. Pamphlets, then newspapers, then radio, and then television all had their eras of ascendancy. All continued to play important roles when other technologies emerged. Political talk radio in the 1980s and 1990s, for example, gave new life to radio in the age of television, creating another kind of information exchange with which politicians had to become conversant. Inevitably, these technological shifts raise concerns that the new form of information dissemination will drive out some of the positive features of the previous technology.

Does the rise of new media inevitably mean that the old media must fade away? And if so, at what cost to democracy? In the excerpt of his article presented here, Tom Price provides background for analyzing these questions. He focuses particularly on the struggles facing newspapers, long the most significant location for news journalism. Even when Americans relied more on television than newspapers to get their news, newspaper coverage often influenced what was reported on TV. In addition to detailing the difficult environment for newspapers, Price presents concerns that newspaper supporters have raised about news gathering and presentation by new media. Fans of the new media argue that those media have the potential to provide a powerful check on politicians and to allow for a more participatory democracy. By combining the knowledge, memory, and energy of multitudes of contributors, blogs and new media such as Twitter can reveal faulty or absent reporting by the mainstream media. As Price notes, however, some observers are skeptical this promise will be fulfilled. Critics worry that blogs and other new media may gain increasing sway over politicians and the public while not being held to high journalistic standards and that they are as likely to generate misleading interpretations as uncover truth.

To Paul Starr, the decline of newspapers is a crisis for democracy. In his view, newspapers were uniquely able to hold government accountable and expose corruption. In large part, this was because the financial model that supported newspapers allowed extensive news staffs to be subsidized by advertisers, classified ads, and sections catering to sports and lifestyles. In the new media world, these components have become largely unbundled. News now has to be financially self-sustaining, which has proven to be a difficult task. Starr explores whether the idea that newspapers must make money has to be abandoned in favor of a model in which philanthropy subsidizes the news.

James Fallows discusses ways in which the new media and the old are mutually interdependent. In particular, Fallows focuses on concerns at Google:

because it thrives as a search engine when users find quality content, Google is concerned about the problems facing the news media, particularly newspapers. Fallows reports on Google's concerns and the ways in which the company is attempting to assist news organizations. According to company executives, there is no single big thing that will save newspapers, but lots of little things might.

Tom Price
Future of Journalism

Forty-three years ago, *Time* magazine posed a provocative question on its cover: "Is God Dead?" The answer turned out to be: "not so much."

This February, the magazine's cover pondered ways to stave off the death of newspapers. With the industry copiously bleeding red ink, reporters and editors losing jobs by the thousands and online news becoming increasingly popular—and controversial—*Time*'s editors aren't the only people wondering about journalism's future. Certainly the recent news has been grim:

• The *Rocky Mountain News* shut down on Feb. 27 after reporting about the Denver region for 150 years.
• The 146-year-old *Seattle Post-Intelligencer* turned off its presses on March 17, becoming a Web-only publication.
• *The Christian Science Monitor*, a highly regarded national daily newspaper since 1908, plans in April [2010] to become a Web and e-mail publication, offering only a weekly, magazine-like, printed edition.
• Thirty-three newspapers—including the *Los Angeles Times*, *Chicago Tribune* and *Philadelphia Inquirer*—sought Chapter 11 bankruptcy protection from December through February.
• Even the mighty *New York Times*, heavily in debt, in early 2009 borrowed an additional $250 million at 14 percent interest from Mexican billionaire Carlos Slim Helu, once described by *The Times* itself as having a "robber baron reputation."

Published in *CQ Researcher*, March 2009.

Newspapers across the country are declining in circulation, advertising and profitability. In 2008 alone, publicly traded newspaper stock prices fell 83 percent. The Fitch credit-rating service forecasts more newspaper closures this year and next, which could leave a growing number of cities with no newspaper at all.

* * *

Thomas Jefferson once famously remarked that, if he had to choose between government without newspapers or newspapers without government, he wouldn't hesitate to preserve newspapers. In the subsequent 222 years, Americans have had both, and newspapers have been citizens' primary source of information about government at all levels.

Many journalists, scholars, lobbyists and government officials worry that the decline of newspapers will leave citizens without sufficient information for effective self-government. They also worry that the fragmented nature of Internet and cable television audiences could turn the clock back to the late-18th and early-19th centuries, when a large number of partisan newspapers printed more opinion than news, and many readers read only publications with which they agreed.

As more Americans turn to the Internet and cable television for news, however, others are hopeful that new forms of journalism will fill the gaps. They envision cable news channels, bloggers, other online content providers and newspapers' own Web sites picking up the slack.

Ironically, newspapers' readership appears to be higher now than ever before as more and more readers access their papers online. U.S. daily newspapers sell about 51 million copies a day, while hosting nearly 75 million unique visitors on their Web sites each month. *The New York Times* sells about a million newspapers daily and about 1.4 million on Sunday, while its Web site attracts 20 million unique visitors monthly. Circulation and advertising revenues have been in a steady decline, however, and newspapers have not figured out how to profit from their Web sites. Only about 10 percent of newspaper advertising revenues are earned on the Internet.

Journalists, scholars, entrepreneurs and philanthropists are looking for ways to finance high-quality, comprehensive reporting online. In addition to the traditional for-profit model, they are experimenting with nonprofit news organizations and philanthropic support of journalistic enterprises. Some are discussing government funding.

* * *

* * * [M]ost news online is produced by newspapers or by organizations that are funded substantially by newspapers, such as the Associated Press. Many television organizations field significant newsgathering operations. But most lag far behind their newspaper counterparts—particularly at the local, regional and state levels—and they often follow newspapers' reporting leads.

"The decline of newspapers has a big ripple effect," says Peter Shane, executive director of the Knight Commission on the Information Needs of Communities in a Democracy, "because to a substantial extent television and radio news always has been based on local newspapers' reporting."

Yet, nearly across the board, newspapers are shrinking the government coverage that's most important to informing citizens in a democracy. Papers that remain in business are cutting staff, closing bureaus and reducing the number of reporters who cover public affairs full time.

Even as the United States is involved in an ever more globalized world—fighting wars in Iraq and Afghanistan, guarding against far-flung terrorist organizations, competing in a globalized economy—U.S. news organizations are bringing their foreign correspondents home.

And with a new administration shaking up Washington and the troubled global economy looking to Washington for leadership, newspapers are shrinking or closing their Washington bureaus. More than 40 regional correspondents—those who cover a particular community's interests in the nation's capital—lost their jobs over the last three years. Even major papers—including the *Los Angeles Times*, *Chicago Tribune* and *Baltimore Sun*—have cut the size of their Washington bureaus. Other publications have eliminated their Washington staffs entirely—notably *The San Diego Union* whose D.C. reporters won a 2006 Pulitzer Prize for exposing corrupt U.S. Rep. Randy "Duke" Cunningham, who now sits in jail. Newspapers in half the states now have no congressional correspondent.

Associated Press Senior Vice President Sue Cross lamented declining coverage of city, county and state governments as well—not just the number of reporters but their expertise. "Seasoned beat reporters are, in many cases, leaving the industry," she said.

Virginia's capital press corps shrank by half during the last decade, according to AP Richmond Correspondent Bob Lewis. Maryland media are sending half as many correspondents to Annapolis to cover state government as they did just two years ago, former AP reporter Tom Stukey said. In Broward County, Fla. (Fort Lauderdale), Commissioner John Rodstrom said, local newspapers have cut their county government coverage in half in a year.

* * *

The reduction in regional correspondents has generated particular concern in Washington. Regional reporters' importance goes beyond uncovering wrongdoing, according to Michael Gessel, a longtime congressional aide who now works as a Washington lobbyist for the Dayton Development Corp. in Ohio. "At least equally important is the day-to-day—and sometimes mundane—coverage of what our elected officials do that isn't scandalous," Gessel says.

Members of Congress often work hardest on matters that get the most coverage by news media in their districts, Gessel explains. Without a hometown reporter tracking the districts' interests in Washington, he says, those interests are likely to get less congressional attention.

Citizens also need to know when government does things well, he adds. "All democracies require consent of the governed. If people only hear about scandals, then that consent is withdrawn. Practically speaking, that means less willingness to have their tax dollars support government."

* * *

A Washington correspondent must know the actors and understand the processes of the federal government, Gessel says. "You can't get that by phone, by Internet or by e-mail."

As journalists, scholars and politicians try to navigate the new media environment, here are some of the questions they are asking about the future of democracy:

Can the Internet Fill the Reporting Gaps Caused by the Decline of Newspapers?

News-reporting sites are popping up on the Internet even faster than newspapers are losing circulation.

On Jan. 12, for instance, *GlobalPost* went online in an ambitious effort to do the kind of international journalism that newspapers and television networks have scaled back. Led by news veterans, the site promises comprehensive, frontline reporting by more than 60 freelance correspondents in more than 40 countries. The new operation hopes to turn a profit by selling advertising, syndicating its reporting to other news organizations and selling $199-a-year subscriptions to a premium service.

Two years earlier, other news veterans launched *Politico*, which quickly became a popular source of political news during the long campaign that carried Barack Obama to the White House. *Politico*—a Web site and a newspaper distributed free in Washington—is performing ahead of its business plan and expects to turn a profit this year, says Editor-in-Chief John Harris, a 21-year veteran of *The Washington Post*.

Across the country, countless sites have been created to cover local and regional communities. They range from highly professional organizations covering major metropolitan areas to primarily volunteer operations serving small communities to professional-amateur collaborations of all sizes.

MinnPost in Minnesota and *Voice of San Diego* have won widespread praise for practicing high-quality, professional journalism, for instance. Smaller, mostly amateur, sites contain little more than announcements from community organizations. *The New York Times* and the *Chicago Tribune* have assigned professionals to oversee networks of volunteers who report for Web sites operated by those papers, focusing on news about specific neighborhoods.

The Internet surpassed newspapers as Americans' favorite source of national and international news in late 2008. Both trailed television by a substantial margin among the population at large. But Americans younger than 30 turned to the Internet as often as to television—and twice as often as to newspapers. Readers still turn to newspapers more than to the Internet for local news.

Most of the news Americans obtain on the Web is not produced by online news organizations, however. On Election Day 2008, for instance, seven of the 10 most-popular Internet news sites belonged to CNN, MSNBC, Fox News, *The New York Times*, Tribune Newspapers, *The Washington Post* and *USA Today*. The others—Yahoo! News, AOL News and Google News—simply aggregate content produced by newsgathering organizations such as newspapers and television networks. Many other Web sites also link to reports produced by traditional news organizations.

*　*　*

Politico and *GlobalPost* are promising examples of niche sites that might succeed by attracting national or international audiences that advertisers want to reach. *Politico*, for instance, sells most of its ads to organizations that want to influence the federal government, and many of those ads appear in the printed edition, which targets an elite Washington audience.

* * *

"There's no sign anywhere of anything replacing the comprehensive metropolitan newspaper, replacing the kind of watchfulness that even a mediocre city newspaper might offer," says Tom Rosenstiel, director of the Project for Excellence in Journalism.

* * *

Others worry that online news sites can't serve Americans who don't have Internet access, a group that tends to be older and poorer than the general public. While nearly all young Americans go online, nearly three-quarters of Americans older than 75 do not. That also is true for a majority between 70 and 75, more than a third between 60 and 69, a quarter between 50 and 59 and a fifth between 45 and 49.

Business consultant James Moore—who advises newspapers to shut down their presses and become online-only operations—argues that publications can't afford to worry about those lost readers. "They are not the people advertisers reach out to," Moore says. "The people they're going after are people in the 35-to-45 category. You have to look to the future, and the future is the young."

Are the New Media Bad for Democracy?

On Oct. 3, 2008, CNN's *iReport* Internet site reported, incorrectly, that Apple CEO Steve Jobs had been rushed to the hospital after a heart attack. The account quickly was repeated on other Web sites, and Apple stock fell more than 9 percent in 12 minutes—a total loss of $9 billion in the company's value.

A month earlier, the Bloomberg financial Web site mistakenly posted a six-year-old report about United Airlines' 2002 bankruptcy filing. Thinking the airline was going bankrupt again, investors dumped the stock, which lost three-quarters of its value before the NASDAQ stock exchange halted trading. A financial newsletter had found the old newspaper story while doing a Google search and passed it on to Bloomberg believing it was current.

The credibility of the erroneous reports was enhanced by CNN's and Bloomberg's reputations as legitimate news organizations. But in both cases the reports appeared on the organizations' Web sites without being vetted.

The incidents illustrate some criticisms of Internet-based news operations.

Many bloggers—and even some traditional media—are cavalier about accuracy on the Web, critics complain. Moreover, they say, Internet public-affairs sites tend to publish more opinion than fact, much of it vicious, mean-spirited and profane. And they worry that fragmentation of the online audience can lead many Web surfers to experience a narrow, distorted view of the world in what some call the Internet "echo chamber."

Indeed, the Jobs story was repeated by blogger Henry Blodget on the widely read *Silicon Alley Insider* Web site. Blodget later unapologetically proclaimed he would do it again, noting he had warned readers he didn't know if the report was true.

"You, our readers, are smart enough to know the difference between rumors and facts, and you are smart enough to evaluate what we tell you," Blodget said. Posting unverified information "flushes out the truth," he argued. "We wouldn't want you to not tell us what everyone was talking about because you couldn't verify it."

That's an example of what Rosenstiel and Bill Kovach—former Washington bureau chief of *The New York Times* and former editor of *The Atlanta Journal-Constitution*—have termed "the journalism of assertion." Traditional journalistic ethics require that facts be confirmed before they're published, Rosenstiel and Kovach said. Many figures on talk radio, cable news and the Internet are "less interested in substantiating whether something is true and more interested in getting it into the public discussion." While they coined the phrase a decade ago, Rosenstiel says, it's even more true today.

CNN also defended its unverified *iReports* by noting the Web site carries a disclaimer that "the stories submitted by users are not edited, fact-checked or screened before they post."

CNN says it created *iReports* to extend CNN's newsgathering reach and to increase viewers' personal attachment to the cable network. It checks the accuracy of *iReporter*s' contributions only before using them in its telecasts.

A growing number of news organizations are recruiting volunteer, "citizen" journalists, especially online, as a way to compensate for cutbacks in their professional reporting staffs.

* * *

Journalism historian Anthony Fellow at California State University, Fullerton, is among those who worry about the fragmentation of the Internet audience among ideologically oriented sites. "We're back to the party press era" after the Revolutionary War, he says, "the viciousness that went on between the two camps, the name-calling."

* * *

City University of New York journalism Professor Jeff Jarvis rejects the echo-chamber charge. "We have more arguments than ever," he says. "The echo chamber was when there was one newspaper in town."

* * *

Most Americans aren't limiting themselves to partisan sites. Just 5 percent of the general public and 10 percent of conservatives say they listen to Limbaugh regularly, for instance. According to the Project for Excellence in Journalism's 2007 report on the "State of the News Media," two-thirds of Americans prefer to get their news from neutral sources, while just a quarter want sources that share their point of view.

* * *

Outlook

Newspapers Doomed?

A consensus is growing among journalists and scholars that newspapers as we've known them are doomed, but journalism always will be in demand.

What they don't know is when the last newspaper will dismantle its presses—or if a few will survive—and what kind of journalism will be preserved. * * *

* * *

Jay Smith, who retired last year as president of the Cox Newspapers chain, agrees that "far more important than the future of newspapers is the future of journalism." Smith expects printed newspapers to continue to shrink in size and circulation, while their online presence grows.

* * *

[Some observers] argue that newspapers will have to recruit amateur volunteers to provide comprehensive coverage, particularly at the local level. * * *

Others are less comfortable with that model. "So many public-policy stories today require not just going to meetings and listening to what people say but accessing records, acquiring data and analyzing that data," says Peter Shane at the Knight Commission on the Information Needs of Communities. "Amateurs are better than nothing, but they're not better than having trained people with experience and a deep knowledge of the community."

Similarly, Brian Tierney, CEO and publisher of *The Philadelphia Inquirer* and *Daily News*, scoffs: "The idea that citizen journalists are going to replace traditionally trained and paid journalists is like saying citizen surgeons are going to replace people who actually have a degree in medicine."

Niche Web sites with national audiences enjoy the best prospects, many say. So do sites with valuable information that some audiences will pay premium prices for.

* * *

But that prospect worries former *Atlanta Journal-Constitution* Editor Kovach and others. If general-circulation newspapers decline and important information is available only from expensive vendors, "the people get less information while the people in power get more information," he said. "If we talk about a government as Abraham Lincoln did—'of the people, by the people, for the people'—then that democracy is in trouble."

* * *

For his part, Tierney says the Philadelphia newspapers are exploring how to charge for online content. "We're going to have to find a way to encourage people to pay for quality journalism," he says. "To create great content, we've got to pay people. We just can't give it away."

* * *

Paul Starr

Goodbye to the Age of Newspapers
(Hello to a New Era of Corruption)

I.

We take newspapers for granted. They have been so integral a part of daily life in America, so central to politics and culture and business, and so powerful and profitable in their own right, that it is easy to forget what a remarkable historical invention they are. Public goods are notoriously under-produced in the marketplace, and news is a public good—and yet, since the mid-nineteenth century, newspapers have produced news in abundance at a cheap price to readers and without need of direct subsidy. More than any other medium, newspapers have been our eyes on the state, our check on private abuses, our civic alarm systems. It is true that they have often failed to perform those functions as well as they should have done. But whether they can continue to perform them at all is now in doubt.

* * *

II.

These developments raise practical questions for anyone concerned about the future of American democracy. * * * To answer those practical questions, it is necessary first to ponder a more theoretical one. Along with other new technology, the Internet was supposed to bring us a cornucopia of information, and in many respects it has done so. But if one of its effects is to shrink the production of professionally reported news, perhaps we need to understand the emerging framework of post-industrial society and politics somewhat differently.

* * *

Published in *The New Republic*, March 2009.

III.

Of course, a medium that 40 percent of the public still claim to read should not be pronounced dead yet. The situation is also a bit more complicated, and more hopeful, than these trends suggest. Total readership of news that originates from newspapers has probably at least stabilized. Online, many people read news items on blogs and other sites that take items from the press, and the news junkies among us are reading more news from more papers than they did before the Internet made the sampling of multiple publications so easy. And some newspapers are clearly gaining wider reach online.

* * *

Some critics of the companies wonder why they cannot adjust to lower profits and make do. The trouble is that the declines in print circulation and advertising are virtually certain to continue, and if newspapers try to maintain the size and the scope of their operations, they may not be able [to] make any profit even when the recession is over. Nor is it clear that they can cut deep enough fast enough while retaining enough readers to be profitable.

* * *

Among many journalists as well as investors, the hope has vanished that newspapers as we have known them can make the transition to a world of hybrid print-online publication. Like network TV news and weekly newsmagazines, newspapers have been living off aging audiences that acquired their media habits in earlier decades. A few years ago, it seemed that they could rely on that aging print readership to tide them over until revenue began gushing from the Web. But online ads still account for only 8 percent of ad sales, and their growth has stalled just as earnings from print have tumbled. The result is that newspapers are shrinking not just physically or in labor power, but in the most important dimension of all—their editorial mission.

* * *

Besides cutting back foreign, national, and state coverage, newspapers are also reducing space devoted to science and the arts, and laying off science and medical reporters, music critics, and book reviewers. But there is one type of coverage that newspapers have tried to protect, at least in the early phases of cutbacks. According to the 2008 Pew survey of news executives, they have devoted more resources to local news. The case for "hyperlocalism," as it is known, is that newspapers enjoy comparative advantage as sources of information about their immediate communities. But this strategy may not work commercially if it means moving downmarket. The less coverage of the wider world and cultural life that newspapers provide, the more they stand to lose readership among the relatively affluent who have those interests, and the less attractive newspapers will be to many advertisers. Hyperlocalism may be just a short step from hollowing out the newsroom to the point where most newspapers come to resemble the free tabloids distributed at supermarkets rather than the newspapers of the past.

* * *

* * * Many of the functions that were bundled together in the newspaper are being unbundled online. But if the emerging media environment favors niche journalism, how will public-service journalism be able to reach and influence the broad public that newspapers have had? There is no going back to the way things used to be. If independent news media capable of holding government accountable are going to flourish, they are going to have to do so in the new world of the news, not the one that used to exist.

IV.

After the dot-com bust, the effusive talk about the miracles of the information revolution thankfully went out of style. But the social transformation under way—and there ought to be no doubt that one is indeed underway—is breaking up old monopolies of communication and power and creating new possibilities for free expression and democratic politics. As in any upheaval, some effects are unanticipated, and not all of them are positive, and what is perhaps most confusing, the good and bad are often intertwined.

By vastly increasing the options for diversion as well as information, the Internet has extended a process that had already begun when cable began increasing the number of TV channels. And if the political scientist Markus Prior is right, that expansion of choice is partly responsible for one of the most worrisome trends in American life: diminished attention to the news and reduced engagement in civic life among a significant part of the public.

* * *

The decline of newspapers and the growth of the Internet as a source of news may have a similar impact. On the one hand, there is likely to be less incidental learning among those with low political interest. Like the entertainment-oriented TV viewers who learned about the world because they had no alternative except to sit through the national network news, many people who have bought a paper for the sports, the recipes, the comics, or the crossword puzzle have nonetheless learned something about the wider world because they have been likely at least to scan the front page. Online, by contrast, they do not necessarily see what would be front-page news in their city, and so they are likely to become less informed about news and politics as the reading of newspapers drops. * * *

But there is another side to the story. As Yochai Benkler argues in his brilliant book *The Wealth of Networks: How Social Production Transforms Markets and Freedom*, the new "networked information economy" has some critical advantages for realizing democratic values. The old "industrial model" mass media have required large investments of capital and provided a platform to speak to the public for a relatively small number of people, but now the falling costs of computers and communication have "placed the material means of information and cultural production in the hands of a significant fraction of the world's population—on the order of a billion people around the globe." Instead of being confined to a passive role, ordinary people can talk back to the media or circumvent them entirely and enter the public conversation.

The new public sphere, in Benkler's view, is also developing mechanisms for filtering information for reliability and relevance, organizing it into easily navigated paths, and raising it to higher levels of public debate, contrary to critics who have worried that the Internet would be a chaotic Babel or a polarized system of "echo chambers" (as Cass Sunstein argued in his book *Republic.com*). And, unlike the old mass media, the new digital environment facilitates decentralized individual and cooperative action, often organized on an open and voluntary basis. Benkler invests a great deal of hope in this type of non-market collaborative production—the kind that has generated new social media such as Wikipedia, which, amazingly, despite being an encyclopedia, has also become an important news medium because it is so rapidly updated.

Of course, some of these innovations are mixed blessings: people can now share their misinformation as well as their knowledge. Viral email, Twitter, and social network sites can be used to spread rumors and malice through channels hidden from the wider public and insulated from criticism. Benkler is right about the many important gains from new technology, but he does not adequately balance the gains against the losses that the emerging networked economy is also bringing about—among them the problems that Prior identifies, such as the diminished share of the public following the news, and perhaps most important, the toll on the institutions of professional journalism.

* * *

The non-market collaborative networks on the Web celebrated by Benkler represent an alternative way of producing information as a public good. Before Wikipedia was created, hardly anyone supposed it would work as well as it has. But it has severe limitations as a source of knowledge. Its entries, including news items, are rewritten from other sources, and it does not purport to offer original research or original reporting. The blogosphere and the news aggregators are also largely parasitic: they feed off the conventional news media. Citizen journalists contribute reports from the scene of far-flung events, but the reports may just be the propaganda of self-interested parties.

Voluntary networks cannot easily duplicate certain critical advantages that large-scale and professionally run media have had—the financial wherewithal to invest in trained reporters and editors and to assign them to beats and long projects, and a well-established system of professional norms that has been a source of conscientious motivation and restraint in the reporting of news. The new social media add value when they are a supplement to professional journalism. To the extent that they supplant it, however, the wildfires of rumor and malice will be harder to check.

* * *

V.

And this returns us to the central problem. If newspapers are no longer able to cross-subsidize public-service journalism and if the de-centralized, non-market forms of collaboration cannot provide an adequate substitute, how is that work going to be paid for? The answer, insofar as there is one, is that we are going to need much more philanthropic support for journalism than we have ever had in the United States.

When a society requires public goods, the solution is often to use government to subsidize them or to produce them directly. But if we want a press that is independent of political control, we cannot have government sponsoring or bailing out specific papers. In the late eighteenth and nineteenth centuries, besides using printing contracts to subsidize favored party organs, the federal government supported the press in what First Amendment lawyers today would call a "viewpoint-neutral" way—through cheap postal rates that were available to all newspapers. And since the 1960s, both the federal and state governments have aided public broadcasting, which has enabled public TV and radio stations to become important sources of news.

Public radio has been a particularly notable success. In a period when commercial radio stations have abandoned all but headline news, National Public Radio has become the last refuge of original reporting on the dial. But as Charles Lewis, a long-time leader in investigative reporting, has pointed out in the *Columbia Journalism Review*, public radio stations, for all their excellent work, have not done a lot of investigative stories. The dependence of many local stations on state government funding makes them vulnerable to political pressure and unlikely to fill the void left by the decline in newspaper coverage of the states. Virtually any proposal for government subsidies of the press today would likely fail on just these grounds: funding by the federal government or the states has too much potential for political manipulation. Elsewhere governments are subsidizing the press. In an effort to aid newspapers in France, President Nicolas Sarkozy recently announced a program to give eighteen-year-olds a free year-long subscription to a daily paper of their choice. In America this would be a joke, though depending on how many teenagers chose one of our racier tabloids, it could give added meaning to the concept of a "stimulus package."

The other standard means of supporting the production of public goods is through private non-profit organization. In fact, non-profit support of journalism has recently been increasing. But much of the discussion about non-profit journalism has failed to recognize that it can mean at least three different things. The first, though not necessarily the most relevant, is the conversion of newspapers from commercial to non-profit status as a way of preserving their public-service role. Florida's *St. Petersburg Times*, which is owned by a journalism school, the Poynter Institute for Media Studies, is often mistakenly cited as a model for this approach. In fact, the *Times* itself has been run at a profit, which has been used to build up the Poynter Institute into a major center for training in journalism. Today, however, the question is not whether to use a money-making newspaper to support philanthropy, but whether non-profit organizations can sustain newspapers that may be losing money. Britain's Guardian

Media Group, owned by the Scott Trust, comes closer to present demands. The trust uses profits from its money-making media subsidiaries to ensure the survival of the daily *Guardian*, which has lost money in recent years. But the *Guardian* model depends on having profitable subsidiaries to offset losses in a daily paper.

Before stopping the presses for the last time, the owners of some declining newspapers may try to convert them into non-profits in the hope of raising contributions to keep them in operation. I would not be surprised if some papers do have a devoted core of readers who would be willing to give more in tax-deductible contributions than they currently pay in subscriptions. But no paper has yet tested whether this option could raise enough money to stay in business.

Besides full non-profit operation of a newspaper, a second approach is philanthropic support of specific kinds of journalism, available through multiple outlets, whether they are commercial or non-profit. The best-known example of this solution is ProPublica, which describes itself as "an independent, non-profit newsroom that produces investigative journalism in the public interest." Publishing online as of last June, ProPublica also works in partnership on some stories with newspapers such as the *New York Times*. The partnerships enable newspapers to keep down the costs of investigative stories, and they give ProPublica access to mass distribution as well as a check on quality. Similarly, the Kaiser Family Foundation, which focuses on health policy, announced last fall that it would begin directly employing reporters to create a health policy news service. According to Drew Altman, Kaiser's president, besides making some stories freely available to newspapers and online, the news service will establish partnerships with newspapers for specific stories, which the papers will then have the right to release first. Some other foundations that focus on specific areas of policy may follow this approach as a way to promote public awareness of their concerns.

Both the non-profit operation of newspapers and the philanthropic subsidy of particular types of reporting are aimed at fostering forms of public-service journalism that would otherwise be in jeopardy. But there is yet a third use of non-profits—and it is for underwriting new models of journalism in the online environment. A good example of this approach is the Center for Independent Media, which, according to its director David Bennahum, receives about $4 million annually from seventy funders to support online political news sites in five states as well as one for national news, The Washington Independent.

Bennahum says that "the narrative voice of newspapers is not what [online] readers want" and that the sites his center finances are instead doing a kind of journalism that brings readers into dialogue.

The notion that the digital medium requires a more inclusive relationship with the "people formerly called the audience" is a common theme among online journalists. Joshua Micah Marshall, the founder of TalkingPoints Memo.com, which runs on a commercial basis, says that many of the stories on his site grow out of ideas and tips supplied by readers in thousands of emails daily. Any news operation has information flowing in and out; an online publication can productively open up this process to anyone who is able and prepared to help. Stories develop online incrementally, often through participation in a collaborative network, rather than being written behind the scenes and released only when checked and finished. This is entirely different from "citizen journalism," and has the potential to be just as rigorous as traditional journalistic practices.

In cities around the country, journalists are experimenting with a variety of strategies for building up Web-only news sites to make up for the shrinking newsrooms of local papers. MinnPost.com in Minneapolis-St. Paul, the most substantial of these ventures, hopes to attract a wide range of readers and sponsors with news coverage of relatively broad scope, according to its CEO and editor Joel Kramer. But its annual budget of $1.3 million cannot support an operation on the scale of a metropolitan daily; with only seven full-time staff, MinnPost.com relies primarily on freelancers, many of them journalists who have left St. Paul's *Pioneer Press* or Minneapolis's *Star-Tribune* (which in January filed for bankruptcy protection despite having cut its editorial staff by 25 percent). Another non-profit online metropolitan news site, the VoiceofSan Diego.org, developed as a response to scandals in the city and has specialized in investigative stories. Like public radio, these ventures raise money through individual membership contributions and grants from local foundations, though not from government.

Doubtful that they can ever achieve the scale of the big metros, Rosenstiel compares the Web-based city news sites to aggressive city magazines. If one major concern is keeping government accountable, that kind of aggressive reporting is certainly a valuable function and well worth supporting. But owing to their more limited economic basis, the non-profit news sites are unlikely to be able to offer the coverage, or to exert the influence, of a daily newspaper read by half the people in a city. The great metros did not emerge just because cities needed newspapers to inform citizens—after all, cities need lots of things that they are never able to develop. Newspapers flourished at the metropolitan level because their role as local market intermediaries enabled them to generate substantial advertising as well as circulation income and thereby to become strong and independent. Non-profit news sites that lack a strong advertising base depend on donors for their survival and are at risk of being destroyed by a single lawsuit, and so they are unlikely to be able to match the traditional power of the press.

Many people have been expecting the successors of newspapers to emerge on the Web. But there may be no successor, at least none like the papers we have known. The metropolitan daily may be a peculiar historical invention whose time is passing. We may be approaching not the end of newspapers, but the end of the age of newspapers—the long phase in history when newspapers published in major cities throughout the United States have been central to both the production of news and the life of their metropolitan regions.

Metropolitan newspapers have dominated news gathering, set the public agenda, served as the focal point of controversy, and credibly represented themselves as symbolizing and speaking for the cities whose names they have carried. They have tried to be everyone's source of news, appealing across the ideological spectrum, and to be comprehensive, providing their readers with whatever was of daily interest to them. Some newspapers, a smaller number than exist today, will survive the transition to the Web, but they probably will not possess the centrality, the scope, or the authoritative voice—much less the monopolies on metropolitan advertising—that newspapers have had.

* * *

For those with the skills and interest to take advantage of this new world of news, there should be much to be pleased with. Instead of being limited to a local paper, such readers already enjoy access to a broader range of publications and discussions than ever before. But without a local newspaper or even with a shrunken one, many other people will learn less about what is going on in the world. As of now, moreover, no source in any medium seems willing and able to pay for the general-interest reporting that newspapers are abandoning. Philanthropy can help to offset some of these cutbacks, but it is unlikely to make up fully for what we are losing.

News coverage is not all that newspapers have given us. They have lent the public a powerful means of leverage over the state, and this leverage is now at risk. If we take seriously the notion of newspapers as a fourth estate or a fourth branch of government, the end of the age of newspapers implies a change in our political system itself. Newspapers have helped to control corrupt tendencies in both government and business. If we are to avoid a new era of corruption, we are going to have to summon that power in other ways. Our new technologies do not retire our old responsibilities.

James Fallows

How to Save the News

Everyone knows that Google is killing the news business. Few people know how hard Google is trying to bring it back to life, or why the company now considers journalism's survival crucial to its own prospects.

Of course this overstates Google's power to destroy, or create. The company's chief economist, Hal Varian, likes to point out that perhaps the most important measure of the newspaper industry's viability—the number of subscriptions per household—has headed straight down, not just since Google's founding in the late 1990s but ever since World War II. In 1947, each 100 U.S. households bought an average of about 140 newspapers daily. Now they buy fewer than 50, and the number has fallen nonstop through those years. If Google had never been invented, changes in commuting patterns, the coming of 24-hour TV news and online information sites that make a newspaper's information stale before it appears, the general busyness of life, and many other factors would have created major problems for newspapers. Moreover, "Google" is shorthand for an array of other Internet-based pressures on the news business, notably the draining of classified ads to the likes of Craigslist and eBay. On the other side of the balance, Google's efforts to shore up news organizations are extensive and have recently become intense but are not guaranteed to succeed.

* * *

Let's start with the diagnosis: If you are looking at the troubled ecology of news from Google's point of view, how do you define the problem to be solved?

Published in *The Atlantic*, June 2010.

You would accept from the outset that something "historic," "epochal," "devastating," "unprecedented," "irresistible," and so on was happening to the news business—all terms I heard used in interviews to describe the challenges facing newspapers in particular and the journalism business more broadly.

"There really is no single cause," I was told by Josh Cohen, a former Webnews manager for Reuters who now directs Google's dealings with publishers and broadcasters, at his office in New York. "Rather, you could pick any single cause, and that on its own would be enough to explain the problems—except it's not on its own." The most obvious cause is that classified advertising, traditionally 30 to 40 percent of a newspaper's total revenue, is disappearing in a rush to online sites. "There are a lot of people in the business who think that in the not-too-distant future, the classified share of a paper's revenue will go to zero," Cohen said. "Stop right there. In any business, if you lose a third of your revenue, you're going to be in serious trouble."

You can't stop right there, Cohen said, and he went through the list of the other, related trends weighing on newspapers in particular, each pointing downward and each making the others worse. First, the relentless decline of circulation—"fewer people using your product," as he put it. Then, the consequent defection of advertisers from the lucrative "display" category—the big ads for cars, banks, airlines—as well as from classifieds. The typical newspaper costs much more to print and deliver than a subscriber pays. Its business rationale is as an advertising-delivery vehicle, with 80 percent of the typical paper's total revenue coming from ads. That's what's going away. In hopes of preserving that advertising model, newspapers have decided to defend their hold on the public's attention by giving away, online, the very information they were trying to sell in print. However that decision looks in the long run, for now it has created a rising generation of "customers" who are out of the habit of reading on paper and are conditioned to think that information should be free.

"It's the triple whammy," [Google CEO] Eric Schmidt said when I interviewed him. "Loss of classifieds, loss of circulation, loss of the value of display ads in print, on a per-ad basis. Online advertising is growing but has not caught up."

So far, this may sound familiar. To me, the interesting aspects of the Google diagnosis, which of course sets the stage for the proposed cure, were these:

First, it was strikingly not moralistic or mocking. This was a change, not simply from what I'd grown used to hearing at tech conferences over the past decade—the phrase "dead-tree edition" captures the tone—but also from the way Americans usually talk about distressed industries. Think of the connotations of "Big Auto" or "Rust Belt." * * *

Next in the Google assessment is the emphasis on "unbundling" as an insurmountable business problem for journalism. "Bundling" was the idea that all parts of the paper came literally in one wrapper—news, sports, comics, grocery-store coupons—and that people who bought the paper for one part implicitly subsidized all the rest. This was important not just because it boosted overall revenue but because it kept publishers from having to figure out whether enough people were reading stories from the statehouse or Mexico City to pay the costs of reporters there.

* * * The Internet has been one giant system for stripping away such cross-subsidies. Why look to the newspaper real-estate listings when you can get more up-to-date, searchable info on Zillow—or better travel deals on Orbitz, or a broader range of movie showtimes on Yahoo? Google has been the most powerful unbundling agent of all. It lets users find the one article they are looking for, rather than making them buy the entire paper that paid the reporter. It lets advertisers reach the one customer who is searching for their product, rather than making them advertise to an entire class of readers.

Next, and significantly for the company's vision of the future, nearly everyone at Google emphasized that prospects look bleak for the printed versions of newspapers—but could be bright for the news industry as a whole, including newspaper publishers. This could seem an artificial distinction, but it is fundamental to the company's view of how news organizations will support themselves.

* * *

Publishers would be overjoyed to stop buying newsprint—if the new readers they are gaining for their online editions were worth as much to advertisers as the previous ones they are losing in print. Here is a crucial part of the Google analysis: they certainly will be. The news business, in this view, is passing through an agonizing transition—bad enough, but different from dying. The difference lies in the assumption that soon readers will again pay for subscriptions, and online display ads will become valuable.

"Nothing that I see suggests the 'death of newspapers,'" Eric Schmidt told me. The problem was the high cost and plummeting popularity of their print versions. "Today you have a subscription to a print newspaper," he said. "In the future model, you'll have subscriptions to information sources that will have advertisements embedded in them, like a newspaper. You'll just leave out the print part. I am quite sure that this will happen." We'll get to the details in a moment, but the analytical point behind his conviction bears emphasis. "I observe that as print circulation falls, the growth of the online audience is dramatic," Schmidt said. "Newspapers don't have a demand problem; they have a business-model problem." Many of his company's efforts are attempts to solve this, so that newspaper companies can survive, as printed circulation withers away.

Finally, and to me most surprisingly, the Google analysis reveals something about journalism that people inside the business can't easily see about themselves. This involves a kind of inefficiency that a hard-pressed journalistic establishment may no longer be able to afford.

* * *

Except for an 18-month period when [Krishna] Bharat founded and ran Google's R&D center in Bangalore, his original hometown, he has been guiding Google News ever since. In this role, he sees more of the world's news coverage daily than practically anyone else on Earth. I asked him what he had learned about the news business.

He hesitated for a minute, as if wanting to be very careful about making a potentially offensive point. Then he said that what astonished him was the predictable and pack-like response of most of the world's news outlets to most stories. Or, more positively, how much opportunity he saw for anyone who was willing to try a different approach.

The Google News front page is a kind of air-traffic-control center for the movement of stories across the world's media, in real time. "Usually, you see essentially the same approach taken by a thousand publications at the same time," he told me. "Once something has been observed, nearly everyone says approximately the same thing." He didn't mean that the publications were linking to one another or syndicating their stories. Rather, their conventions and instincts made them all emphasize the same things. This could be reassuring, in indicating some consensus on what the "important" stories were. But Bharat said it also indicated a faddishness of coverage—when Michael Jackson dies, other things cease to matter—and a redundancy that journalism could no longer afford. "It makes you wonder, is there a better way?" he asked. "Why is it that a thousand people come up with approximately the same reading of matters? Why couldn't there be five readings? And meanwhile use that energy to observe something else, equally important, that is currently being neglected." He said this was not a purely theoretical question. "I believe the news industry is finding that it will not be able to sustain producing highly similar articles."

With the debut of Krishna Bharat's Google News in 2002, Google began its first serious interactions with news organizations. Two years later, it introduced Google Alerts, which sent e-mail or instant-message notifications to users whenever Google's relentless real-time indexing of the world's news sites found a match for a topic the user had flagged. Two years after that, in the fall of 2006, Google began scanning the paper or microfilmed archives of many leading publications so that articles from their pre-digital era could be indexed, searched for, and read online.

* * *

"About two years ago, we started hearing more and more talk about the decline of the press," Schmidt told me. "A set of people [inside the company] began looking at what might be the ways we could help newspapers."

Why should the company bother? Until recently, I would have thought that the answer was a combination of PR concerns and Schmidt's personal interest. * * *

Before this year, when I asked Google employees about the health of the news business, their answers often seemed dutiful. During my interviews this year, people sounded as if they meant it. Google is valuable, by the logic I repeatedly heard, because the information people find through it is valuable. If the information is uninteresting, inaccurate, or untimely, people will not want to search for it. How valuable would Google Maps be, if the directions or street listings were wrong?

Nearly everyone I spoke with made this point in some way. Nikesh Arora's version was that Google had a "deeply symbiotic relationship" with serious news organizations. "We help people find content," he told me. "We don't generate content ourselves. As long as there is great content, people will come looking for it. When there's no great content, it's very hard for people to be interested in finding it. That's what we do for a living." * * *

"For the last eight years, we mainly focused on getting the algorithms better," Krishna Bharat said, referring to the automated systems for finding and ranking items in Google News. "But lately, a lot of my time has gone into thinking about the basis on which the product"—news—"is built. A lot of our thinking now is focused on making the news sustainable."

So how can news be made sustainable? The conceptual leap in Google's vision is simply to ignore print. It's not that everyone at the company assumes "dead tree" newspapers and magazines will disappear. * * * No one I spoke with at Google went quite that far. But all of their plans for reinventing a business model for journalism involve attracting money to the Web-based news sites now available on computers, and to the portable information streams that will flow to whatever devices evolve from today's smart phones, iPods and iPads, Nooks and Kindles, and mobile devices of any other sort. This is a natural approach for Google, which is, except for its Nexus One phone, a strictly online company.

The three pillars of the new online business model, as I heard them invariably described, are distribution, engagement, and monetization. That is: getting news to more people, and more people to news-oriented sites; making the presentation of news more interesting, varied, and involving; and converting these larger and more strongly committed audiences into revenue, through both subscription fees and ads. Conveniently, each calls on areas of Google's expertise. "Not knowing as much about the news business as the newspapers do, it is unlikely that we can solve the problems better than they can," Nikesh Arora told me. "But we are willing to support any formal and informal effort that newspapers or journalists more generally want to make" to come up with new sources of money.

In practice this involves projects like the ones I'm about to describe, which share two other traits beyond the "distribution, engagement, monetization" strategy that officially unites them. One is the Google concept of "permanent beta" and continuous experimentation—learning what does work by seeing all the things that don't. "We believe that teams must be nimble and able to fail quickly," Josh Cohen told me. (I resisted making the obvious joke about the contrast with the journalism world, which believes in slow and statesmanlike failure.) "The three most important things any newspaper can do now are experiment, experiment, and experiment," Hal Varian said.

* * *

The other implicitly connecting theme is that an accumulation of small steps can together make a surprisingly large difference. The forces weighing down the news industry are titanic. In contrast, some of the proposed solutions may seem disappointingly small-bore. But many people at Google repeated a maxim from Clay Shirley, of New York University, in an essay last year about the future of the news: "Nothing will work, but everything might."

In all, Google teams are working with hundreds of news organizations, which range in scale from the Associated Press, the Public Broadcasting System, and *The New York Times* to local TV stations and papers. The last two efforts I'll mention are obviously different in scale and potential from all the others, but these examples give a sense of what "trying everything" means.

Living Stories

News reporting is usually incremental. Something happens in Kabul today. It's related to what happened there yesterday, plus 20 years ago, and further back. It has a bearing on what will happen a year from now. High-end news organizations reflect this continuous reality in hiring reporters and editors who (ideally) know the background of today's news and in the way they present it, usually with modest additions to the sum of established knowledge day by day.

The modest daily updating of the news—another vote in Congress, another debate among political candidates—matches the cycle of papers and broadcasts very well, but matches the Internet very poorly, in terms of both speed and popularity rankings. *The Financial Times* might have given readers better sustained coverage of European economic troubles than any other paper. But precisely because it has done so many incremental stories, no one of them might rise to the top of a Google Web search, compared with an occasional overview story somewhere else. By the standards that currently generate online revenue, better journalism gets a worse result.

This past winter, the Google News team worked with *The New York Times* and *The Washington Post* to run the Living Stories experiment, essentially a way to rig Google's search results to favor serious, sustained reporting. All articles about a big topic—the war in Afghanistan, health-care reform— were grouped on one page that included links to all aspects of the paper's coverage (history, videos, reader comments, related articles). "It is a repository of information, rather than ephemeral information," Krishna Bharat said, explaining that it was a repository designed to prosper in what he called "today's link economy." In February, Google called off the *Times-Post* experiment—and declared it a success, by making the source code available free online, for any organization that would like to create a Living Stories feature for its site.

* * *

Fast Flip

The Internet is a great way to get news but often a poor way to read it. Usually the longer the item, the worse the experience; a screenful is fine, clicking through thousands of words is an ordeal. * * *

The Fast Flip project, which began last summer and has now graduated to "official" status, is an attempt to approximate the inviting aspects of leafing through a magazine. It works by loading magazine pages not as collections of text but as highly detailed photos of pages as a whole, cached in Google's system so they load almost as quickly as a (human) reader can leaf through them. "It was an experiment in giving you a preview of an article that was more than just a link to the title," Krishna Bharat said. "It gives you a sense of the graphics, the emphasis, the quality, the feel. Whether you would like to spend time with it." Spending time with an article, whether in print or online, is of course the definition of "engagement" and the behavior advertisers seek. * * *

"We're not saying we have worked out exactly the right model," Krishna Bharat said when I asked about Fast Flip details. "We just want news to be available, fast, all over the place on the Internet."

YouTube Direct

Projects like Living Stories and Fast Flip are tactical in their potential. Google's hope is that broader use of YouTube videos could substantially boost a news organization's long-term ability to engage an audience. Amateur-produced video is perhaps the most powerful new tool of the Internet era in journalism, making the whole world a potential witness to dramas, tragedies, achievements almost anywhere. The idea behind the various YouTube projects is that the same newspapers that once commanded an audience with printed reports of local news, sports, crime, and weather could re-create their central role by becoming a clearinghouse for video reports.

* * * For instance, Google offers, for free, the source code for YouTube Direct, which any publication can put on its own Web site. Readers can then

easily send in their video clips, for the publication to review, censor, combine, or shorten before putting them up on its site. After a blizzard, people could send in clips of what they had seen outside. Same for a local football game, or a train wreck, or a city-council meeting, or any other event when many people would be interested in what their neighbors had seen. The advertising potential might be small, for YouTube and the local paper alike. The point would be engagement. Al Jazeera used YouTube Direct during the elections in Iraq this spring to show footage from around the country.

* * *

Another tool extends the lessons of the YouTube Debates during the 2008 presidential campaign, in which [Google] invited YouTube users from around the country to send in clips of brief questions for the candidates. Anderson Cooper of CNN then introduced YouTube clips of the questions CNN had chosen to use. They ranged from serious to silly and included one asking Barack Obama whether he was "black enough." YouTube has added a feature that lets users vote for the questions they want asked and has used the method effectively many times since then. . . .

Whatever comes of these experiments, two other broad initiatives are of unquestionable importance, because they address the two biggest business emergencies today's news companies face: they can no longer make enough money on display ads, and they can no longer get readers to pay. According to the Google view, these are serious situations, but temporary.

Display Ads

The idea for improving display-ad prospects begins with insignificant-sounding adjustments that have great potential payoff. For instance: Neal Mohan of Google pointed out that news organizations now typically sell their online ad space in two very different ways. Premium space—on the home page, facing certain featured articles or authors—is handled by "direct sales," through the publication's own sales staff. "Remnant" space, anything left over, is generally franchised out to a national sales network or "exchange" that digs up whatever advertisers it can. Publications decide on the division of space ahead of time, and hope the real-world results more or less fit.

One of Google's new systems does for online ad space what the airlines' dreaded "yield management" systems do for seats on a plane. Airlines constantly adjust the fares on a route, and the size of the planes that will fly it, toward the goal of making each plane as full as it can be before it takes off. The Google system does the same thing, allowing publishers to adjust the allocation of high- and low-priced space, second by second. "Your top salesperson might just have had dinner with the biggest client, who decides to run a big campaign," Mohan told me. The dynamic allocation system ensures that the publisher doesn't lose a penny of potential ad revenue to avoidable supply/demand glitches. If an advertiser wants to spend more on "premium" ads, the necessary space will be automatically redeployed from lower-value sections. * * * Yield management has allowed airlines to survive; according to Mohan, the advertising equivalent in Google's new system "has generated a lift for publishers of 130 percent, versus what they did when dividing the space themselves."

Mohan suggested a variety of other small but significant operational improvements, which together led to a proposal so revolutionary that it challenges all despairing conclusions about the economic future of the press. * * * Online display ads may not be so valuable now, he said, but that is because we're still in the drawn-out "transition" period. Sooner or later—maybe in two years, certainly in 10—display ads will, per eyeball, be worth more online than they were in print.

How could this be? In part, he said, today's discouraging ad results simply reflect a lag time. The audience has shifted dramatically from print to online. So has the accumulation of minutes people choose to spend each day reading the news. Wherever people choose to spend their time, Mohan said, they can eventually be "monetized"—the principle on which every newspaper and magazine (and television network) has survived until today.

* * *

* * * "The online world will be a lot more attuned to who you are and what you care about, and it will be interactive in a way it never has been before." Advertising has been around forever, Mohan said, "but until now it has always been a one-way conversation. Now your users can communicate back to you." His full argument is complex, but his conclusion is: eventually news operations will wonder why they worried so much about print display ads, since online display will be so much more attractive.

* * *

Designing the Paywall

The other hugely consequential effort Google is exploring involves reviving the idea of "subscriptions"—the quaint old custom of an audience paying for what it receives. Most Google people I spoke with had zero interest in the paywall question as an abstraction, because it seemed so obvious that different publications in different circumstances with different business models will make different decisions about how customers should pay.

* * *

"We don't want to encourage anyone to start charging for content, or not to charge for content," Chris Gaither said. "That is entirely up to them." But Google teams based in Mountain View and New York have been working with newspapers and magazines on the surprisingly complex details of making any kind of payment system work. Paywalls themselves come in a wide variety: absolute barriers to anyone who is not a subscriber, metered approaches that allow nonsubscribers a certain number of free views per day or month, "first click free" schemes to let anyone see the start of an article but reserve the full text for subscribers, and many more. Each involves twists in how the publication's results show up in Google searches and on Google News. For instance: if you are a paid subscriber to the *Financial Times*, any Web search you run should include FT results—and indeed rank them all the higher, since your status as a subscriber means you place extra value on the paper's reports. If you don't subscribe, those FT links should come lower in the search results, since you won't be able to read them—but the results should still appear, in case you decide you want them enough to subscribe. But when you run the search, how can Google tell whether or not you subscribe? How can it know that you are you, whether you're using your computer, or a friend's, or one at an Internet cafe, or an iPhone? And how can its Web crawlers index the FTs stories in the first place, if they're behind the paywall? All these questions have answers, but they're not always obvious.

"We often hear from publishers saying, 'We're thinking of this approach, and we want to understand it fully,'" Josh Cohen told me. "'We want to be sure this works the way we intend it to work. Can you give it a look?' We will tell them how their ideas would turn out with our system." Then, without giving the newspaper's name or the proprietary details of its specific plan, the Google team will also post its findings and advice on its public Web site. And for publications thinking of the "E-ZPass" approach—some automatic way to collect small per-article charges without slowing the user down or involving cumbersome forms—another Google team is working on the practicalities.

As for the very idea of paid subscriptions: How can they have a future in the Google-driven world of atomized spot information? "It is probable that unbundling has a limit," Eric Schmidt said. Something basic in human nature craves surprise and new sources of stimulation. Few people are "so monomaniacal," as he put it, that they will be interested only in a strict, predefined list of subjects. Therefore people will still want to buy subscriptions to sources of information and entertainment—"bundles," the head of the world's most powerful unbundler said—and advertisers will still want to reach them. His example:

"It's obvious that in five or 10 years, most news will be consumed on an electronic device of some sort. Something that is mobile and personal, with a nice color screen. Imagine an iPod or Kindle smart enough to show you stories that are incremental to a story it showed you yesterday, rather than just repetitive. And it knows who your friends are and what they're reading and think is hot. And it has display advertising with lots of nice color, and more personal and targeted, within the limits of creepiness. And it has a GPS and a radio network and knows what is going on around you. If you think about that, you get to an interesting answer very quickly, involving both subscriptions and ads."

This vision, which Schmidt presented as Utopian, helps illustrate the solution Google believes it will find; the problem it knows it can't solve; and another problem that goes well beyond its ambitions.

The solution is simply the idea that there can be a solution. The organization that dominates the online-advertising world says that much more online-ad money can be flowing to news organizations. The company whose standard price to consumers is zero says that subscribers can and will pay for news. The name that has symbolized disruption of established media says it sees direct self-interest in helping the struggling journalism business. In today's devastated news business, these are major and encouraging developments, all the more so for their contrast with what other tech firms are attempting.

The problem Google is aware of involves the disruption still ahead. Ten years from now, a robust and better-funded news business will be thriving. What next year means is harder to say. * * * But this is consistent with the way the news has always worked, rather than a threatening change. Fifteen years ago, Fox News did not exist. A decade ago, Jon Stewart was not known for political commentary. The news business has continually been reinvented by people in their 20s and early 30s. . . .

The challenge Google knows it has not fully coped with is a vast one, which involves the public function of the news in the broadest sense. The company views the survival of "premium content" as important to its own welfare. But Schmidt and his colleagues realize that a modernized news business might conceivably produce "enough" good content for Google's purposes even if no one has fully figured out how to pay for the bureau in Baghdad, or even at the statehouse. This is the next challenge, and a profound one, for a reinvented journalistic culture. The fluid history of the news business, along with today's technological pattern of Google-style continuous experimentation, suggests that there will be no one big solution but a range of partial remedies. Google's efforts may have bought time for a panicked, transitional news business to see a future for itself and begin discovering those new remedies and roles.

QUESTIONS

1. Which part or parts of the news media—newspapers, television, the Internet, blogs, radio, social networks, Twitter—do you rely on most? Which would you say you trust the most? Should all news-oriented media, whether new or old, use the same standards in determining what to broadcast or publish?

2. Imagine you are a blogger and you have come across some damaging information about a presidential candidate. Do you blog it? On one hand, it might not be true. On the other, if it is true, it is critical information that voters should know. Do you put the information into the blogosphere and trust it will be filtered and proven true or false by other media? Or do you approach it as mainstream media journalists traditionally would, requiring more corroboration for the story—which can take time to obtain—before presenting it to the public? Would your answer depend on how late in the campaign it is? Now imagine the same scenario, except that the office in question is an elected position in your hometown, where people know you. Would you handle this situation differently?

3. All three articles express concerns about the fate of newspapers. What are the key concerns? Do you share them? Why or why not?

4. What do you see as the strengths and weaknesses of the solutions described by Starr and Fallows for the problems facing newspapers?

10

Elections and Voting: Voter Identification

The last three national elections have raised many concerns about the voting system and the standards for administering elections in the United States. Charges of impropriety in voting procedures and vote counting as well as complaints that certain voting technologies were systematically likely to produce more voter error or not record voter choices were legion. Massive voter mobilization campaigns on both the political left and right registered millions of new voters. Huge sums were poured into campaign advertising, further stoking the interest of these newly registered voters and the public in general. In such a charged political environment, concerns about the integrity of the process took on a particular urgency. One issue on which battle lines are frequently drawn is voter identification, especially requiring voters to show a photo ID.

One argument, presented here by Chandler Davidson, contends that these complaints about fraud are part of a strategy to discourage or scare away potential voters. Voter ID laws are most likely to restrict turnout among minorities and the elderly, and the threat of fraud is minimal. To Davidson, voter ID laws are intended to promote the fortunes of the Republican party and are little different from other attempts to suppress voter turnout, such as the poll tax.

The opposing argument, presented here by Hans von Spakovsky, is that voter fraud is a reality. He points to voters registered in multiple locations, voting more than once, illegally registered, paid an inducement to vote, and to felons voting as symptomatic of the lack of control over the voting process. Spakovsky supports voter-ID laws and rejects the idea that they will systematically discriminate against minorities or other groups.

Edward Foley argues that conservatives and liberals both have valid points. Even if voting fraud is minimal, he writes, it is real and should be a concern, as conservatives argue. Similarly, liberals are right to be concerned that the cost of obtaining a photo ID might discourage some citizens from voting. Foley suggests the solution is to delink the photo ID from voting. Instead, potential voters would be able to get free digital photos from government offices if they do not have one. They would have to show this photo when they register to vote. When a voter arrives at the polls to vote, poll workers could pull up an electronic file of the photo and match it to the person standing in front of them. This solution, Foley argues, ensures that anyone who wants to register can, while also guaranteeing that the person voting at the polling place is the same person who is registered under that name.

Chandler Davidson

The Historical Context of Voter Photo-ID Laws

The issue before the U.S. Supreme Court in the *Crawford* case (*Crawford v. Marion County Election Bd.* 2008) was whether a law (Indiana Senate Enrolled Act No. 483) passed by the Indiana legislature requiring most voters to show a photo ID in order to cast a ballot violates the First and Fourteenth Amendments. Plaintiffs argued that it works an unfair hardship on many people who do not have the government-issued documents that count as a legitimate ID. They argued that the law, in effect, constitutes a poll tax, inasmuch as there are costs to obtain the right kind of photo ID, costs that unduly burden many eligible citizens wanting to exercise their right to vote.

Given the long history of legally sanctioned disfranchisement of large and disparate groups of citizens, from the founding of the Republic to the recent past, the case raised important questions to scholars of voting rights. Indeed, Indiana's new law brought to mind events during the half-century following the

Published in *Political Science & Politics*, January 2009.

Civil War, when the language of "progressive reform" cloaked the disfranchisement of blacks and poor whites in the South—those most likely to vote for Republican or Populist candidates. Actually adopted for partisan and racially discriminatory purposes, these laws were often presented as high-minded attacks on fraud—efforts to "purify" the electorate that would only inconvenience "vote sellers" or the ignorant and "shiftless."

To be sure, unlike today, when proponents of voter identification must strain mightily to find the rarest examples of fraud, particularly in-person voter fraud at the polls, in the nineteenth century there was widespread and readily admitted fraud. However, this was often committed against African Americans and the Republican Party to which they then overwhelmingly adhered. Louisiana senator and former governor Samuel D. McEnery stated in 1898 that his state's 1882 election law "was intended to make it the duty of the governor to treat the law as a formality and count in the Democrats." A leader of the 1890 Mississippi constitutional convention admitted that "it is no secret that there has not been a full vote and a fair count in Mississippi since 1875," which was the last year until 1967 in which blacks voted at all freely in the state. Nonetheless, these same Democrats invoked the language of reform in calling for a wide range of restrictions on the suffrage: registration acts, poll taxes, literacy and property tests, "understanding" qualifications, and white primaries, among others.

Between 1889 and 1913, for example, nine states outside the South made the ability to read English a prerequisite for voting. Literacy tests were said to reduce the influence of immigrants or African Americans who supported "bosses" and "demagogues." Moreover, between 1890 and 1908, seven of the 11 ex-Confederate states adopted state constitutional amendments allowing only literate voters or those with a certain amount of property to vote. There were sometimes loopholes like "understanding" qualifications or "grandfather" clauses that allowed some whites to vote who could not meet literacy or property tests. Shortly after passage of these amendments, less than 10% of African Americans managed to register to vote in most states, and no more than 15% in any.

The poll tax was one of the most notorious disfranchising mechanisms of its day. The current debate over the Indiana photo-ID requirement—as well as similar laws in other states—has led to claims that they are a "modern-day poll tax." This implies that the new Indiana law, too, falls within the ignominious American tradition of disfranchising laws passed under the guise of "good government" reform.

Frederick Ogden, perhaps the foremost scholar of the poll tax, wrote in the 1950s: "While critics of legalized restrictions on Negro voting may find it hard to discover any high moral tone in such activities, these restrictions reflected a movement for purifying the electoral process in southern states." Ogden quotes the editor of the *San Antonio Express* writing in 1902: "By requiring a poll tax receipt, secured six months previous to an election, fraudulent elections can be prevented almost entirely."

Other essays in this symposium address the nature and extent of burdens imposed on various subsets of Indiana citizens by the photo-ID law, and I shall forgo discussing them. Suffice it to say that the most accessible photo-ID in Indiana consists either of the state's driver's license or a state-issued ID card. Obtaining one or the other has been shown to be a good deal more difficult for some people than it might seem at first glance. At least 43,000 persons of voting age in Indiana are estimated to have neither.

The demographic characteristics of persons lacking the requisite ID are suggested by a November 2006 telephone survey of 987 randomly selected voting-age American citizens by the independent Opinion Research Corporation conducted for the Brennan Center for Justice at NYU School of Law: 11% did not have valid government-issued photo ID, while 18% of citizens 65 years of age or older lacked it, as did 25% of African Americans. The latter two demographic groups, the elderly and African Americans, are more likely to self-identify as Democrats—African-Americans disproportionately so. Elderly African Americans, who are even more unlikely than members of their ethnic group in general to have a photo ID, would be strongly predisposed to vote Democratic. In close elections, the additional burdens placed on both the elderly and African Americans by the photo-ID law could help elect Republican candidates. There is no reason to believe this national pattern is much different from that in Indiana.

Nonetheless, it is often asserted that such barriers should not prevent a truly motivated citizen from voting. In a classic article by Kelley, Ayres, and Bowen attempting to measure determinants of voter turnout, the authors make the following observation:

> A frequent objection to such efforts [to get out the vote] is that voters not interested enough to vote are not apt to vote wisely and so should be left alone. This view recalls the statement of a New York voter regarding the adequacy of the facilities for registering in New York City in 1964: "I sure

do want to vote against that man . . . but I don't think I hate him enough to stand on that line all day long." How much interest should a voter have to qualify him for voting? Enough to stand in line all day? For half a day? For two days? We cannot say, but those who think voting should be limited to the "interested" ought to be prepared to do so.

Their question, posed in terms of the burden of time alone, can also be posed with regard to money: particularly concerning the least well off, how large a monetary imposition should be placed on the right to vote before it becomes the functional equivalent of a poll tax? Regarding these twin burdens, two questions may be posed to help determine whether the Indiana photo-ID law should be interpreted according to the good-government language of its proponents: First, how will the application of the law help shape the Indiana electorate "to a size and composition deemed desirable by those in power," as Kelley, Ayres, and Bowen put it? In other words, to what extent is the law motivated by partisan efforts to disfranchise voters who are undesirable to Republicans and thus increase their chances of winning elections? Second, did supporters of the law demonstrate a significant degree of fraud of the kind the law was fashioned to prevent? Let us consider each question in turn.

While it is impossible to know the motives of those lawmakers who favored the photo-ID bill under consideration by the Indiana legislature in April 2005, we can ascertain whether it was passed by a partisan vote. Significantly, Indiana's photo-ID bill was one of at least 10 bills introduced by Republicans in state legislatures between 2005 and 2007 requiring voters to show a photo ID at the polls. Two of these states' bills were initially enjoined, and a second bill was introduced in one state. (Besides Indiana, the other states included Georgia, Florida, Missouri, Kansas, New Hampshire, Pennsylvania, Texas, and Wisconsin.) If the House and Senate votes for all 10 proposals are combined, 95.3% of the 1,222 Republicans voting and 2.1% of the 796 Democrats voting supported the bills. Moreover, in the five cases in which both houses passed a bill and a Republican was governor, he signed it. In the three cases in which both houses passed a bill and a Democrat was governor, he vetoed it. (In two cases, only one house passed a bill.) The Indiana vote was part of this pattern, although even more extreme. In the vote on Senate Bill 483, 85 Republicans voted for it and none against; 62 Democrats voted against it and none in favor. The Republican governor signed the bill into law.

Did supporters of the law demonstrate that there is a significant degree of fraud of the kind the law was fashioned to prevent? The debate over the extent and kind of vote fraud that exists in the United States today has been widespread and acerbic at least since the 2000 presidential election, and it shows no signs of abating. There are numerous kinds of vote fraud, and distinctions among them—which are necessary to determine the most effective means of their prevention—are often lost in popular debate. As critics of the Indiana law have asserted, the photo-ID requirement was implemented to prevent one type of fraud: voter impersonation at the polls on Election Day. Among the many kinds it does not prevent is that involving mail-in ballots, which some believe to be more common than impersonation at the polls. What makes the statute particularly suspect in the case of Indiana is the fact that there has not been a single prosecution for in-person vote fraud in the history of the state—a fact that Richard Posner, judge on the U.S. Court of Appeals for the Seventh Circuit and author of that court's split decision favoring Indiana, attributed to lax law enforcement.

Recent events in Texas are relevant in this regard. In both 2005 and 2007 Republicans in the legislature introduced photo-ID bills less restrictive than that in Indiana. In 2007, according to a newspaper reporter: "Republicans like the voter ID bill because they believe it will weaken Democrats, but can argue that it is a reasonable requirement" because it would prevent vote fraud. Not all Republicans, however, shared the belief that it would curtail fraud. Royal Masset, former political director of the Texas Republican Party, was one. He told the reporter he agreed that among his fellow Republicans it was "an article of religious faith that voter fraud is causing us to lose elections." He was not convinced. He did believe, however, that requiring photo IDs could cause enough of a drop-off in legitimate Democratic voting to add 3% to the Republican vote.

In January 2006, after his party's first failure to pass a photo-ID bill, Greg Abbott, the Republican attorney general of Texas, announced a "training initiative to identify, prosecute [and] prevent voter fraud." This was the most ambitious and costly effort in recent Texas history—perhaps ever—by the state's government to attack the alleged problem. "Vote fraud has been an epidemic in Texas for years, but it hasn't been treated like one," Abbott said. "It's time for that to change." He promised that his newly created Special Investigations Unit (SIU) would "help police departments, sheriff's offices, and district and county attorneys successfully identify, investigate and prosecute various types of voter fraud offences." Established with a $1.5 million grant from the governor's office, the SIU would have as one of its prime responsibilities investigating voter-fraud allegations, he said. Abbott targeted 44 counties containing 78% of registered voters in the state. According to the *Austin American-Statesman,* "Complaints originate from voting officials, district attorneys or citizens and are sent to the secretary of state or the attorney general. Each complaint is evaluated by a professional employee to determine whether the complaint is legitimate and warrants further investigation."

Such an initiative would seem to constitute a model of the aggressive, responsible, multi-level law-enforcement effort that Judge Posner seemed to believe had been lacking in Indiana. Moreover, given Republicans' desire to provide evidence of widespread voter fraud in order to justify new statutes criticized by Democrats and some media sources, one would expect Abbott to have conducted the effort with enthusiasm. What has been the result?

Texas is a large state, with thousands of elections occurring in a four-year period in its numerous governmental units. In 2006, there were 16.6 million persons of voting age, and of those, 13.1 million were registered to vote. An anti-immigration organization estimated that 1.7 million Texas inhabitants resided there illegally in 2007. Given these facts, one would expect an aggressive, centralized vote-fraud initiative by the state's highest law-enforcement officer to yield a sizable number of indictments during the more than 21 months of its existence if, in fact, vote fraud had reached "epidemic" proportions.

The data presented by Attorney General Abbot on his Web site told a different story. In the almost two years between the day the initiative was announced in late January 2006 and October 2007, 13 persons had either been indicted, found guilty, or sentenced for vote fraud, six on misdemeanor counts typically involving helping others with mail-in ballots. Of the 13, five were accused of having committed fraud before 2006, the year the initiative was announced, and the remaining eight in 2006. A total of 4.4 million Texans voted in the general elections for governor or U.S. senator that year, in addition to those who voted in primaries and local nonpartisan elections. At that point, six of the 13 persons mentioned above had not yet been found guilty. This, then, is the extent of vote fraud in Texas that has been uncovered after the announcement and implementation of the $1.5 million vote-fraud initiative. Moreover, of the seven found guilty and the six remaining under indictment, *none of the types of fraud they had been charged with would have been prevented by the photo-ID requirement advocated by Republicans in the 2007 legislative session.* That is to say, none involved voter impersonation at the polls. Most either involved political officials who were charged with engaging in illegal efforts to affect the election outcome, or persons who helped elderly or disabled friends with their mail-in ballots, apparently unaware of a law passed in 2003 requiring them to sign the envelope containing the friend's ballot before mailing it.

These data do not appear to be anomalous. A survey of the director or deputy director of all 88 Ohio boards of election in June 2005 found that a total of only four votes cast in the state's general elections in 2002 and 2004 (in which over nine million votes were cast) were judged ineligible and thus likely constituted actual voter fraud. Interviews by *New York Times* reporters with election-law-enforcement officials and academic experts suggest that the pattern in Ohio is not anomalous. Professor Richard L. Hasen, an election law expert at Loyola Law School, summed up knowledgeable opinion about vote fraud to the reporters as follows: "what we see is isolated, small-scale activities that often have not shown any kind of criminal intent."

While it is possible, as Judge Posner implied in his Seventh Circuit decision, that aggressive vote-fraud enforcement in Indiana might uncover its existence in the state, the Texas investigation suggests otherwise, and the burden of proof rests on those who allege that vote fraud there is widespread and of the kind that is deterred by a photo-ID requirement. Until that burden is responsibly shouldered by state authorities, the question of whether the Indiana voter-ID law has accomplished its ostensible purpose must be answered in the negative. When this conclusion is placed alongside our earlier findings that the legislative vote for the law was strictly along partisan lines and that the people most likely to be disfranchised by it are Democratic voters—particularly African Americans—Indiana's law appears to fit comfortably within the long and unsavory history of those in positions of power disfranchising blacks and less-well-off whites for partisan gain. Moreover, Indiana's attempt to justify its new law with claims of voter fraud is as dubious as those that justified the now unconstitutional poll tax.

A great deal of progress has been made over the past 50 years in combating racial discrimination in politics, thanks in part to such epochal events as passage of the Twenty-Fourth Amendment and the Voting Rights Act. However, race, class, and partisanship continue to be inextricably intertwined in the United States, just as they were from the end of Reconstruction to the Civil Rights Era. The 2005 Indiana voter-ID law, if the above analysis is correct, is an excellent example of this fact.

Hans von Spakovsky

Requiring Identification by Voters

Testimony Before the Texas Senate
Delivered March 10, 2009

I appreciate the invitation to be here today to discuss the importance of states such as Texas requiring individuals to authenticate their identity at the polls through photo and other forms of identification.

By way of background, I have extensive experience in voting matters, including both the administration of elections and the enforcement of federal voting rights laws. Prior to becoming a Legal Scholar at the Heritage Foundation, I was a member for two years of the Federal Election Commission. I spent four years at the Department of Justice as a career lawyer, including as Counsel to the Assistant Attorney General for Civil Rights. I also spent five years in Atlanta, Georgia, on the Fulton County Board of Registration and Elections, which is responsible for administering elections in the largest county in Georgia, a county that is almost half African-American. I have published extensively on election and voting issues, including on the subject of voter ID.

Guaranteeing the integrity of elections requires having security throughout the entire election process, from voter registration to the casting of votes to the counting of ballots at the end of the day when the polls have closed. For example, jurisdictions that use paper ballots seal their ballot boxes when all of the ballots have been deposited, and election officials have step-by-step procedures for securing election ballots and other materials throughout the election process.

I doubt any of you think that it would be a good idea for a county to allow world wide Internet access to the computer it uses in its election headquarters to tabulate ballots and count votes—we are today a computer-literate generation and you understand that allowing that kind of outside access to the software used for counting votes would imperil the integrity of the election.

Requiring voters to authenticate their identity at the polling place is part

Published by The Heritage Foundation, 2010.

and parcel of the same kind of security necessary to protect the integrity of elections. Every illegal vote steals the vote of a legitimate voter. Voter ID can prevent:

- impersonation fraud at the polls;
- voting under fictitious voter registrations;
- double voting by individuals registered in more than one state or locality; and
- voting by illegal aliens.

As the Commission on Federal Election Reform headed by President Jimmy Carter and Secretary of State James Baker said in 2005:

> The electoral system cannot inspire public confidence if no safeguards exist to deter or detect fraud or to confirm the identity of voters. Photo identification cards currently are needed to board a plane, enter federal buildings, and cash a check. Voting is equally important.

Voter fraud does exist, and criminal penalties imposed after the fact are an insufficient deterrent to protect against it. In the Supreme Court's voter ID case decided last year, the Court said that despite such criminal penalties:

> It remains true, however, that flagrant examples of such fraud in other parts of the country have been documented throughout this Nation's history by respected historians and journalists, that occasional examples have surfaced in recent years, and that [they] demonstrate that not only is the risk of voter fraud real but that it could affect the outcome of a close election.

The relative rarity of voter fraud prosecutions for impersonation fraud at the polls, as the Seventh Circuit Court of Appeals pointed out in the Indiana case, can be explained in part because the fraud cannot be detected without the tools—a voter ID—available to detect it. However, as I pointed out in a paper published by the Heritage Foundation last year, a grand jury in New York released a report in the mid-1980's detailing a widespread voter fraud conspiracy involving impersonation fraud at the polls that operated successfully for 14 years in Brooklyn without detection. That fraud resulted in thousands of fraudulent votes being cast in state and congressional elections and involved not only impersonation of legitimate voters at the polls, but voting under fictitious names that had been successfully registered without detection by local election officials. This fraud could have been easily stopped and detected if New York had required voters to authenticate their identity at the polls. According to the grand jury, the advent of mail-in registration was also a key factor in perpetrating the fraud. In recent elections, thousands of fraudulent voter registration forms have been detected by election officials. But given the minimal to nonexistent screening efforts engaged in by most election jurisdictions, there is no way to know how many others slipped through. In states without identification requirements, election officials have no way to prevent bogus votes from being cast by unscrupulous individuals based on fictitious voter registrations.

The problem of possible double voting by someone who is registered in two states is illustrated by one of the Indiana voters who was highlighted by the League of Women Voters in their amicus brief before the Supreme Court in the Indiana case. After an Indiana newspaper interviewed her, it turned out that the problems she encountered voting in Indiana stemmed from her trying to use a Florida driver's license to vote in Indiana. Not only did she have a Florida driver's license, but she was also registered to vote in Florida where she owned a second home. In fact, she had claimed residency in Florida by claiming a homestead exemption on her property taxes, which as you know is normally only available to residents. So the Indiana law worked perfectly as intended to prevent someone who could have illegally voted twice without detection.

I don't want to single out Texas, but just like Indiana, New York, and Illinois, Texas has a long and unfortunate history of voter fraud. In the late 1800's, for example, Harrison County was so infamous for its massive election fraud that the phrase "Harrison County Methods" became synonymous with election fraud. From Ballot Box 13 in Lyndon Johnson's 1948 Senate race, to recent reports of voting by illegal aliens in Bexar County, Texas does have individuals who are willing to risk criminal prosecution in order to win elections. I do not claim that there is massive voter fraud in Texas or anywhere else. In fact, as a former election official, I think we do a good job overall in administering our elections. But the potential for abuse exists, and there are many close elections that could turn on a very small number of votes. There are enough incidents of voter fraud to make it very clear that we must take the steps necessary to make it hard to commit. Requiring voter ID is just one such common sense step.

Not only does voter ID help prevent fraudulent voting, but where it has been implemented, it has not reduced turnout. There is no evidence that voter

ID decreases the turnout of voters or has a disparate impact on minority voters, the poor, or the elderly—the overwhelming majority of Americans have photo ID or can easily obtain one.

Numerous studies have borne this out. A study by a University of Missouri professor of turnout in Indiana showed that turnout actually increased by about two percentage points overall in Indiana after the voter ID law went into effect. There was no evidence that counties with higher percentages of minority, poor, elderly or less-educated populations suffered any reduction in voter turnout. In fact, "the only consistent and statistically significant impact of photo ID in Indiana is to increase voter turnout in counties with a greater percentage of Democrats relative to other counties."

The Heritage Foundation released a study in September of 2007 that analyzed 2004 election turnout data for all states. It found that voter ID laws do not reduce the turnout of voters, including African-Americans and Hispanics—such voters were just as likely to vote in states with ID as in states where just their name was asked at the polling place.

A study by professors at the Universities of Delaware and Nebraska-Lincoln examined data from the 2000, 2002, 2004, and 2006 elections. At both the aggregate and individual levels, the study found that voter ID laws do not affect turnout including across racial/ethnic/socioeconomic lines. The study concluded that "concerns about voter identification laws affecting turnout are much ado about nothing."

In 2007 as part of the MIT/CalTech Voter Project, an MIT professor did an extensive national survey of 36,500 individuals about Election Day practices. The survey found:

- overwhelming support for photo ID requirements across ethnic and racial lines with "over 70% of Whites, Hispanics and Blacks support[ing] the requirement"; and
- Only 23 people out of the entire 36,500 person sample said that they were not allowed to vote because of voter ID, although the survey did not indicate whether they were even eligible to vote or used provisional ballots.

A similar study by John Lott in 2006 also found no effect on voter turnout, and in fact, found an indication that efforts to reduce voter fraud such as voter ID may have a positive impact on voter turnout. That is certainly true in a case study of voter fraud in Greene County, Alabama that I wrote about recently for the Heritage Foundation. In that county, voter turnout went up after several successful voter fraud prosecutions instilled new confidence in local voters in the integrity of the election process.

Recent election results in Georgia and Indiana also confirm that the suppositions that voter ID will hurt minority turnout are incorrect. Turnout in both states went up dramatically in 2008 in both the presidential preference primary and the general election.

In Georgia, there was record turnout in the 2008 presidential primary election—over 2 million voters, more than twice as much as in 2004 when the voter photo ID law was not in effect. The number of African-Americans voting in the 2008 primary also doubled from 2004. In fact, there were 100,000 more votes in the Democratic Primary than in the Republican Primary. And the number of individuals who had to vote with a provisional ballot because they had not gotten the free photo ID available from the state was less that 0.01%.

In the general election, Georgia, with one of the strictest voter ID laws in the nation, had the largest turnout in its history—more than 4 million voters. Democratic turnout was up an astonishing 6.1 percentage points from the 2004 election. Overall turnout in Georgia went up 6.7 percentage points, the second highest increase of any state in the country. The black share of the state-wide vote increased from 25% in 2004 to 30% in 2008. By contrast, the Democratic turnout in the nearby state of Mississippi, also a state with a high percentage of black voters but without a voter ID requirement, increased by only 2.35 percentage points.

I should point out that the Georgia voter ID law was upheld in final orders issued by every state and federal court in Georgia that reviewed the law, including most recently by the Eleventh Circuit Court of Appeals. Just as in Texas, various organizations in Georgia made the specious claims that there were hundreds of thousands of Georgians without photo ID. Yet when the federal district court dismissed all of their claims, the court pointed out that after two years of litigation, none of the plaintiff organizations like the NAACP had been able to produce a single individual or member who did not have a photo ID or could not easily obtain one. The district court judge concluded that this "failure to identify those individuals is particularly acute in light of the Plaintiffs' contention that a large number of Georgia voters lack acceptable Photo ID . . . the fact that Plaintiffs, in spite of their efforts, have failed to uncover anyone who can attest to the fact that he/she will be prevented from voting provides significant support for a conclusion that the photo ID requirement does not unduly burden the right to vote."

In Indiana, which the Supreme Court said has the strictest voter ID law in the country, turnout in the Democratic presidential preference primary in 2008 quadrupled from the 2004 election when the photo ID law was not in effect—in fact, there were 862,000 more votes cast in the Democratic primary than the Republican primary. In the general election in November, the turnout of Democratic voters increased by 8.32 percentage points from 2004, the largest increase in Democratic turnout of any state in the nation. The neighboring state of Illinois, with no photo ID requirement and President Obama's home state, had an increase in Democratic turnout of only 4.4 percentage points—nearly half of Indiana's increase.

Just as in the federal case in Georgia, the federal court in Indiana noted the complete inability of the plaintiffs in that case to produce anyone who would not be able to vote because of the photo ID law:

> Despite apocalyptic assertions of wholesale vote disenfranchisement, Plaintiffs have produced not a single piece of evidence of any identifiable registered voter who would be prevented from voting pursuant to [the photo ID law] because of his or her inability to obtain the necessary photo identification.

One final point on the claims that requiring an ID, even when it is free, is a "poll tax" because of the incidental costs like possible travel to a registrar's office or obtaining a birth certificate that may be involved. That claim was also raised in Georgia. The federal court dismissed this claim, pointing out that such an "argument represents a dramatic overstatement of what fairly constitutes a 'poll tax'. Thus, the imposition of tangential burdens does not transform a regulation into a poll tax. Moreover, the cost of time and transportation cannot plausibly qualify as a prohibited poll tax because those same 'costs' also result from voter registration and in-person voting requirements, which one would not reasonably construe as a poll tax."

We are [the only] one of about one hundred democracies that do not uniformly require voters to present photo ID when they vote. All of those countries administer that law without any problems and without any reports that their citizens are in any way unable to vote because of that requirement. In fact, our southern neighbor Mexico, which has a much larger population in poverty than Texas or the United States, requires both a photo ID and a thumbprint to vote—and turnout has increased in their elections since this requirement went into effect in the 1990's.

Requiring voters to authenticate their identity is a perfectly reasonable and easily met requirement. It is supported by the vast majority of voters of all races and ethnic backgrounds. As the Supreme Court said, voter ID protects the integrity and reliability of the electoral process. Texas has a valid and legitimate state interest not only in deterring and detecting voter fraud, but in maintaining the confidence of its citizens in the security of its elections.

Edward B. Foley

Is There a Middle Ground in the Voter ID Debate?

The left and the right are increasingly trading accusations in the debate over new voter ID laws, and the rhetoric is heating up. Georgia's new law has been called the new "Jim Crow," although similar measures have recently been enacted in non-Southern states like Arizona and Indiana. (Wisconsin's legislature, too, has passed this kind of law, although it has been vetoed by Governor Doyle.) Defenders of such measures say opponents are willfully blind to the possibility of fraud unless a photo ID requirement is imposed.

Given that heels are digging in, it might seem naïve to search for a compromise. Yet it is imperative to do so. Election laws cannot serve their intended function unless they are accepted by both the left and the right as fair means for conducting the competition between these two political camps to win approval from the citizenry. If the right insists that a voter ID law is necessary to make the electoral process legitimate, while the left simultaneously says that the same ID law makes the electoral process illegitimate, then it becomes impossible for our society to settle upon rules of procedure for a fair contest between opposing political forces.

With that observation in mind, it is worth searching for a middle position on the voter ID issue, even if at the outset a successful conclusion to this endeavor is far from assured.

In principle, some form of identification requirement should not be objectionable to liberals. Voting is an activity that only the eligible are entitled to engage in, and so it is not unreasonable to ask citizens for some information to demonstrate their eligibility. For example, liberals do not generally object to the traditional requirements that voters provide their names, addresses, and signatures before casting their ballots.

Conservatives, however, say that these traditional requirements no longer suffice because an imposter easily could forge a signature and, in contemporary society, poll workers are unlikely to distinguish eligible from ineligible voters simply by looking at their visages. Therefore, according to these conservatives, a photo ID is necessary to show the voter's eligibility. The picture will show that the person standing before the poll worker is the same one who, according to the poll book, is registered to vote under that particular name and address.

Liberals object, however, to a photo ID requirement on the ground that it is burdensome to citizens who do not have a driver's license, passport, or comparable document. Part of the burden is cost, which can be addressed by making a valid photo ID free of charge. Another part of the burden is the difficulty of accessing locations where no-charge IDs may be obtained. That problem could be remedied by making them available at any post office, public library, or public school, as well as other social service agencies (hospitals, police stations, and so forth).

But a remaining concern of liberals is that, even if photo IDs are easily obtained, many voters will fail to bring them to the polls on Election Day. Public reminders may be issued, including public service announcements on TV. Still, some voters are forgetful, perhaps senior citizens more so than younger adults, and thus the obligation to carry an ID to the polls might serve as a barrier for these eligible citizens.

A potential solution to this problem is to break the connection with the photo requirement and the obligation to produce identification at the polls. Eligible citizens could be required to provide a photograph at the time they *register* to vote, and poll workers would match this photograph with the image of the person standing in front of them. Given the availability of digital photography, the photos of registered voters could be stored in electronic poll books and easily "pulled up" with a click of a computer mouse when voters sign in to vote.

These electronic photos should satisfy the anti-fraud concerns of conservatives as much as printed photos that citizens would be required to bring to the polls. After all, the purpose of a *photo* ID requirement—beyond the traditional requirement of providing one's name, address, and signature—is to compare the likeness of the person seeking to vote with the photograph that is linked to the name and address of the registered voter (whom the flesh-and-blood person purports to be). This function can just as easily occur by comparing the likeness of the person with the computerized photo in the electronic poll book, which was linked to the name and address of the registered voter at time of registration.

Of course, to satisfy the concerns of liberals, a requirement to provide a digital photograph at time of registration would have to address the cost and accessibility issues identified earlier. But, again, a system in which citizens could go to a wide variety of public offices (including post offices, libraries, and schools), where clerical officials would be authorized to take a digital photo of the citizen and then email it to the applicable board of election, without any cost to the citizen, would satisfactorily address these concerns. In addition, for those citizens seeking to register by mail, they could be permitted to email their own digital photos of themselves, if they conform to "passport style" specifications. In this way, nursing homes and other senior citizens centers could take "at home" digital photos of their elderly residents and email them to the board of election, without requiring these elderly citizens to travel to a post office, library, or other public building. (Another comparable approach would be to permit individuals to become a kind of "deputized notary public," trained to take the right sort of digital photo, so that other citizens could meet with any of these designated individuals whenever and wherever it would be convenient.) Moreover, as an alternative, those citizens who do not submit a digital photo at time of registration could provide the more conventional form of photo ID (like a driver's license) at time of voting, making either approach an equally available option, depending solely on which the particular citizen prefers.

Liberals might still complain that any form of photo ID requirement is unnecessary to reduce the risk of fraud and, in any event, will be ineffective if inapplicable to absentee voting. The point about absentee voting is surely a valid one. (For this reason, one wonders whether it is wise to expand the availability of at-home voting, as many states are doing.) If individuals sitting at home can vote without providing any form of photo ID, the opportunity for fraud exists even if voters who go to the polls are subject to a photograph requirement. One way around this discrepancy would be to require absentee voters to submit a photocopy of their photo ID when they mail in their absentee ballot. Or, if the digital photo proposal is adopted, absentee voters could mail with their ballot a printed copy of the digital photo they submitted as part of their registration. In the future, absentee voters might simply email a second copy of their digital photo when emailing their absentee ballots.

A liberal objection to any form of photo ID requirement is more difficult to sustain, particularly if the goal is a compromise acceptable to both sides. To be sure, the frequency of fraud at polling places that would be preventable by a photo ID requirement may be fairly low—there is clearly a debate between conservatives and liberals on this factual point—but it is not non-existent. Liberals acknowledge the possibility of fraudulent absentee voting, saying that its risk is greater than polling place voting. But if an imposter can obtain and submit an absentee ballot, he or she can show up at a polling place purporting to be someone else. Even if the latter is more difficult, the lack of a photo ID requirement makes this deceit easier than it otherwise would be.

Thus, an acceptable compromise must take the form of a photo ID requirement that is not unduly onerous. The proposal here, to permit voters to submit an easily obtainable and no-charge digital photo at the time they register, as an alternative to having to produce a driver's license or comparable photo ID when they go to the polls on Election Day, satisfies this objective. Pursuing this proposal would enable both sides to move beyond the vituperative rhetoric that increasingly, and unfortunately, is clouding the policy debate on this topic.

QUESTIONS

1. Would you approve of a proposal that all voters had to show photo identification at polling places? Do you think that would decrease turnout? If so, is that a reasonable cost?

2. Would you have any concerns with having voting conducted over the Internet or by mail (as is done in Washington and Oregon)? Are there benefits that outweigh these concerns?

3. What might be some possible objections raised against Foley's proposal by the two sides in the voter-ID debate?

4. As a general matter, do you believe there is a tradeoff between maximizing turnout and minimizing fraud? Or are these goals compatible? Why?

11

Political Parties: Red America versus Blue America—Are We Polarized?

In 1992, Patrick Buchanan famously stated at the Republican national convention that the United States was in the midst of a culture war that posited traditional, conservative social values against liberal, secular values. Bill Clinton's defeat of President George H. W. Bush seemed to defuse that idea: Clinton was a southern Democrat who had pushed his party toward the ideological center and, although garnering only 43 percent of the vote, he won states in all regions of the country. His 1996 victory was broader, adding states he had lost in 1992. In the 2000 presidential election, however, a striking regional pattern emerged in the results. Al Gore, the Democratic candidate, did well on the coasts and in the upper Midwest, while George W. Bush, the Republican candidate, picked up the remaining states. Many analysts were struck by this "red state/blue state" pattern—named after the coloring of the states on post-election maps—and suggested that it told us something more fundamental about American politics. Indeed, these analysts argued, Patrick Buchanan was in large measure right: the American public was deeply divided and polarized and in many respects living in two different worlds culturally. This polarization showed up not only in voting, but in presidential approval ratings, with the partisan gap in evaluations of Bill Clinton and George W. Bush being larger than for any previous presidents.

The 2004 presidential election looked very much like 2000: with a few exceptions, the red states stayed red and the blue states stayed blue. Eighty-five percent of conservatives voted for Bush; the same percentage of liberals voted for Kerry; and moderates split 54–45 percent for Kerry.

In 2008, Barack Obama campaigned on the idea of practicing a new kind of politics that set aside red-America/blue-America distinctions. His victory scattered the red/blue map, as he picked up nine states Bush won in 2004. Shortly into his presidency, however, Obama's policy plans became engulfed in deep partisan and ideological strife. Like those of Clinton and Bush before him, President Obama's approval ratings were sharply different among Democrats and Republicans. And like those two presidents, Obama invigorated his opponents. Where the Bush presidency played a major role in galvanizing the liberal blogosphere, Obama's contributed to the rise of the Tea Party, a political movement deeply skeptical about the effectiveness and growing size of American government.

Is America deeply polarized along partisan lines? Is there a culture war? Is the red-America/blue-America split real? Is there division on certain highly charged issues but not on most others? Are the divisions just artifacts of the way that survey questions are worded? In this debate, the political scientists James Q. Wilson and Morris Fiorina agree that the political elite—elected leaders, the news media, and interest groups—are polarized, but they disagree on the answers to the rest of the questions. Wilson argues that the cultural split is deep and is reflected in party competition and the public opinion of partisans within and across the red and blue states. Fiorina counters that the idea of a cultural war is vastly exaggerated—there might be a skirmish, but there is no war.

John Judis aligns more with Wilson. Clearly not a fan of the Tea Party, Judis nonetheless argues that it is a real movement with the potential for lasting influence. Its issues, anxieties, and ideological orientation, he states, draw on a deep populist tradition in American politics. As with other populist movements, supporters see the Tea Party as engaged in a struggle to define America, a struggle between "the people" and "the elites."

Morris P. Fiorina

What Culture Wars? Debunking the Myth of a Polarized America

> "There is a religious war going on in this country, a cultural war as critical to the kind of nation we shall be as the Cold War itself, for this war is for the soul of America."

With those ringing words insurgent candidate Pat Buchanan fired up his supporters at the 1992 Republican National Convention. To be sure, not all delegates cheered Buchanan's call to arms, which was at odds with the "kinder, gentler" image that George H.W. Bush had attempted to project. Election analysts later included Buchanan's fiery words among the factors contributing to the defeat of President Bush, albeit one of lesser importance than the slow economy and the repudiation of his "Read my lips, no new taxes" pledge.

In the years since Buchanan's declaration of cultural war, the idea of a clash of cultures has become a common theme in discussions of American politics. The culture war metaphor refers to a displacement of the classic economic conflicts that animated twentieth-century politics in the advanced democracies by newly emergent moral and cultural ones. The literature generally attributes Buchanan's inspiration to a 1991 book, *Culture Wars*, by sociologist James Davison Hunter, who divided Americans into the culturally "orthodox" and the culturally "progressive" and argued that increasing conflict was inevitable.

No one has embraced the concept of the culture war more enthusiastically than journalists, ever alert for subjects that have "news value." Conflict is high in news value. Disagreement, division, polarization, battles, and war make good copy. Agreement, consensus, moderation, compromise, and peace do not. Thus, the notion of a culture war fits well with the news sense of journalists who cover politics. Their reports tell us that contemporary voters are sharply divided on moral issues. As David Broder wrote in the *Washington Post* in November 2000, "The divide went deeper than politics. It reached into the nation's psyche. . . . It was the moral dimension that kept Bush in the race."

Published in *The Wall Street Journal*, July 2004.

Additionally, it is said that close elections do not reflect indifferent or ambivalent voters; rather, such elections reflect evenly matched blocs of deeply committed partisans. According to a February 2002 report in *USA Today*, "When George W. Bush took office, half the country cheered and the other half seethed"; some months later the *Economist* wrote that "such political divisions cannot easily be shifted by any president, let alone in two years, because they reflect deep demographic divisions. . . . The 50-50 nation appears to be made up of two big, separate voting blocks, with only a small number of swing voters in the middle."

The 2000 election brought us the familiar pictorial representation of the culture war in the form of the "red" and "blue" map of the United States. Vast areas of the heartland appeared as Republican red, while coastal and Great Lakes states took on a Democratic blue hue. Pundits reified the colors on the map, treating them as prima facie evidence of deep cultural divisions: Thus "Bush knew that the landslide he had wished for in 2000 . . . had vanished into the values chasm separating the blue states from the red ones" (John Kenneth White, in *The Values Divide*). In the same vein, the *Boston Herald* reported Clinton adviser Paul Begala as saying, on November 18, 2000, that "tens of millions of good people in Middle America voted Republican. But if you look closely at that map you see a more complex picture. You see the state where James Byrd was lynched—dragged behind a pickup truck until his body came apart—it's red. You see the state where Matthew Shepard was crucified on a split-rail fence for the crime of being gay—it's red. You see the state where right-wing extremists blew up a federal office building and murdered scores of federal employees—it's red."

Claims of bitter national division were standard fare after the 2000 elections, and few commentators publicly challenged them. On the contrary, the belief in a fractured nation was expressed even by high-level political operatives. Republican pollster Bill McInturff commented to the *Economist* in January 2001 that "we have two massive colliding forces. One is rural, Christian, religiously conservative. [The other] is socially tolerant, pro-choice, secular, living in New England and the Pacific Coast." And Matthew Dowd, a Bush reelection strategist, explained to the *Los Angeles Times* why Bush has not tried to expand his electoral base: "You've got 80 to 90 percent of the country that look at each other like they are on separate planets."

The journalistic drumbeat continues unabated. A November 2003 report from the Pew Research Center led E. J. Dionne Jr. of the *Washington Post* to comment: "The red states get redder, the blue states get bluer, and the political map of the United States takes on the coloration of the Civil War."

And as the 2004 election approaches, commentators see a continuation, if not an intensification, of the culture war. *Newsweek*'s Howard Fineman wrote in October 2003, "The culture war between the Red and Blue Nations has erupted again—big time—and will last until Election Day next year. Front lines are all over, from the Senate to the Pentagon to Florida to the Virginia suburbs where, at the Bush-Cheney 2004 headquarters, they are blunt about the shape of the battle: 'The country's split 50-50 again,' a top aide told me, 'just as it was in 2000.'"

In sum, observers of contemporary American politics have apparently reached a new consensus around the proposition that old disagreements about economics now pale in comparison to new divisions based on sexuality, morality, and religion, divisions so deep and bitter as to justify talk of war in describing them.

Yet research indicates otherwise. Publicly available databases show that the culture war script embraced by journalists and politicos lies somewhere between simple exaggeration and sheer nonsense. There is no culture war in the United States; no battle for the soul of America rages, at least none that most Americans are aware of.

Certainly, one can find a few warriors who engage in noisy skirmishes. Many of the activists in the political parties and the various cause groups do hate each other and regard themselves as combatants in a war. But their hatreds and battles are not shared by the great mass of Americans—certainly nowhere near "80–90 percent of the country"—who are for the most part moderate in their views and tolerant in their manner. A case in point: To their embarrassment, some GOP senators recently learned that ordinary Americans view gay marriage in somewhat less apocalyptic terms than do the activists in the Republican base.

If swing voters have disappeared, how did the six blue states in which George Bush ran most poorly in 2000 all elect Republican governors in 2002 (and how did Arnold Schwarzenegger run away with the 2003 recall in blue California)? If almost all voters have already made up their minds about their 2004 votes, then why did John Kerry surge to a 14-point trial-heat lead when polls offered voters the prospect of a Kerry-McCain ticket? If voter partisanship has hardened into concrete, why do virtually identical majorities in both red and blue states favor divided control of the presidency and Congress, rather than unified control by their party? Finally, and ironically, if voter positions have become so uncompromising, why did a recent CBS story titled "Polarization in America" report that 76 percent of Republicans, 87 percent of Democrats, and 86 percent of Independents would like to see elected officials compromise more rather than stick to their principles?

Still, how does one account for reports that have almost 90 percent of Republicans planning to vote for Bush and similarly high numbers of Democrats planning to vote for Kerry? The answer is that while voter *positions* have not polarized, their *choices* have. There is no contradiction here; positions and choices are not the same thing. Voter choices are functions of their positions and the positions and actions of the candidates they choose between.

Republican and Democratic elites unquestionably have polarized. But it is a mistake to assume that such elite polarization is equally present in the broader public. It is not. However much they may claim that they are responding to the public, political elites do not take extreme positions because *voters* make them. Rather, by presenting them with polarizing alternatives, elites make voters appear polarized, but the reality shows through clearly when voters have a choice of more moderate alternatives—as with the aforementioned Republican governors.

Republican strategists have bet the Bush presidency on a high-risk gamble. Reports and observation indicate that they are attempting to win in 2004 by getting out the votes of a few million Republican-leaning evangelicals who did not vote in 2000, rather than by attracting some modest proportion of 95 million other non-voting Americans, most of them moderates, not to mention moderate Democratic voters who could have been persuaded to back a genuinely compassionate conservative. Such a strategy leaves no cushion against a negative turn of events and renders the administration vulnerable to a credible Democratic move toward the center. Whether the Democrats can capitalize on their opportunity remains to be seen.

James Q. Wilson

How Divided Are We?

The 2004 election left our country deeply divided over whether our country is deeply divided. For some, America is indeed a polarized nation, perhaps more so today than at any time in living memory. In this view, yesterday's split over Bill Clinton has given way to today's even more acrimonious split between Americans who detest George Bush and Americans who detest John Kerry, and similar divisions will persist as long as angry liberals and angry conservatives continue to confront each other across the political abyss. Others, however, believe that most Americans are moderate centrists, who, although disagreeing over partisan issues in 2004, harbor no deep ideological hostility. I take the former view.

By polarization I do not have in mind partisan disagreements alone. These have always been with us. Since popular voting began in the 19th century, scarcely any winning candidate has received more than 60 percent of the vote, and very few losers have received less than 40 percent. Inevitably, Americans will differ over who should be in the White House. But this does not necessarily mean they are polarized.

By polarization I mean something else: an intense commitment to a candidate, a culture, or an ideology that sets people in one group definitively apart from people in another, rival group. Such a condition is revealed when a candidate for public office is regarded by a competitor and his supporters not simply as wrong but as corrupt or wicked; when one way of thinking about the world is assumed to be morally superior to any other way; when one set of political beliefs is considered to be entirely correct and a rival set wholly wrong. In extreme form, as defined by Richard Hofstadter in *The Paranoid Style in American Politics* (1965), polarization can entail the belief that the other side is in thrall to a secret conspiracy that is using devious means to obtain control over society. Today's versions might go like this: "Liberals employ their dominance of the media, the universities, and Hollywood to enforce a radically secular agenda"; or, "conservatives, working through the religious Right and the big

Reprinted from *Commentary*, February 2006.

corporations, conspired with their hired neocon advisers to invade Iraq for the sake of oil."

Polarization is not new to this country. It is hard to imagine a society more divided than ours was in 1800, when pro-British, pro-commerce New Englanders supported John Adams for the presidency while pro-French, pro-agriculture Southerners backed Thomas Jefferson. One sign of this hostility was the passage of the Alien and Sedition Acts in 1798; another was that in 1800, just as in 2000, an extremely close election was settled by a struggle in one state (New York in 1800, Florida in 2000).

The fierce contest between Abraham Lincoln and George McClellan in 1864 signaled another national division, this one over the conduct of the Civil War. But thereafter, until recently, the nation ceased to be polarized in that sense. Even in the half-century from 1948 to (roughly) 1996, marked as it was by sometimes strong expressions of feeling over whether the presidency should go to Harry Truman or Thomas Dewey, to Dwight Eisenhower or Adlai Stevenson, to John F. Kennedy or Richard Nixon, to Nixon or Hubert Humphrey, and so forth, opinion surveys do not indicate widespread detestation of one candidate or the other, or of the people who supported him.

Now they do. Today, many Americans and much of the press regularly speak of the President as a dimwit, a charlatan, or a knave. A former Democratic presidential candidate has asserted that Bush "betrayed" America by launching a war designed to benefit his friends and cor-porate backers. A senior Democratic Senator has characterized administration policy as a series of "lies, lies, and more lies" and has accused Bush of plotting a "mindless, needless, senseless, and reckless" war. From the other direction, similar expressions of popular disdain have been directed at Senator John Kerry (and before him at President Bill Clinton); if you have not heard them, that may be because (unlike many of my relatives) you do not live in Arkansas or Texas or other locales where the *New York Times* is not read. In these places, Kerry is widely spoken of as a scoundrel.

In the 2004 presidential election, over two-thirds of Kerry voters said they were motivated explicitly by the desire to defeat Bush. By early 2005, President Bush's approval rating, which stood at 94 percent among Republicans, was only 18 percent among Democrats—the largest such gap in the history of the Gallup poll. These data, moreover, were said to reflect a mutual revulsion between whole geographical sections of the country, the so-called Red (Republican) states versus the so-called Blue (Democratic) states. As summed up by the distinguished social scientist who writes humor columns under the name of Dave Barry, residents of Red states are "ignorant racist fascist knuckle-dragging NASCAR-obsessed cousin-marrying roadkill-eating tobacco-juice-dribbling gun-fondling religious fanatic rednecks," while Blue-state residents are "godless unpatriotic pierced-nose Volvo-driving France-loving leftwing Communist latte-sucking tofu-chomping holistic-wacko neurotic vegan weenie perverts."

To be sure, other scholars differ with Dr. Barry. To them, polarization, although a real enough phenomenon, is almost entirely confined to a small number of political elites and members of Congress. In *Culture War?*, which bears the subtitle "The Myth of a Polarized America," Morris Fiorina of Stanford argues that policy differences between voters in Red and Blue states are really quite small, and that most are in general agreement even on issues like abortion and homosexuality.

But the extent of polarization cannot properly be measured by the voting results in Red and Blue states. Many of these states are in fact deeply divided internally between liberal and conservative areas, and gave the nod to one candidate or the other by only a narrow margin. Inferring the views of individual citizens from the gross results of presidential balloting is a questionable procedure.

Nor does Fiorina's analysis capture the very real and very deep division over an issue like abortion. Between 1973, when *Roe v. Wade* was decided, and now, he writes, there has been no change in the degree to which people will or will not accept any one of six reasons to justify an abortion: (1) the woman's health is endangered; (2) she became pregnant because of a rape; (3) there is a strong chance of a fetal defect; (4) the family has a low income; (5) the woman is not married; and (6) the woman simply wants no more children. Fiorina may be right about that. Nevertheless, only about 40 percent of all Americans will support abortion for any of the last three reasons in his series, while over 80 percent will support it for one or another of the first three.

In other words, almost all Americans are for abortion in the case of maternal emergency, but fewer than half if it is simply a matter of the mother's preference. That split—a profoundly important one—has remained in place for over three decades, and it affects how people vote. In 2000 and again in 2004, 70 percent of those who thought abortion should always be legal voted for Al Gore or John Kerry, while over 70 percent of those who thought it should always be illegal voted for George Bush.

Division is just as great over other high-profile issues. Polarization over the war in Iraq, for example, is more pronounced than any war-related controversy in at least a half-century. In the fall of 2005, according to Gallup, 81 percent of Democrats but only 20 percent of Republicans thought the war in Iraq was a mistake. During the Vietnam war, by contrast, itself a famously contentious cause, there was more unanimity across party lines, whether for or against: in late 1968 and early 1969, about equal numbers of Democrats and Republicans thought the intervention there was a mistake. Pretty much the same was true of Korea: in early 1951, 44 percent of Democrats and 61 percent of Republicans thought the war was a mistake—a partisan split, but nowhere near as large as the one over our present campaign in Iraq.

Polarization, then, is real. But what explains its growth? And has it spread beyond the political elites to influence the opinions and attitudes of ordinary Americans?

The answer to the first question, I suspect, can be found in the changing politics of Congress, the new competitiveness of the mass media, and the rise of new interest groups.

That Congress is polarized seems beyond question. When, in 1998, the House deliberated whether to impeach President Clinton, all but four Republican members voted for at least one of the impeachment articles, while only five Democrats voted for even one. In the Senate, 91 percent of Republicans voted to convict on at least one article; every single Democrat voted for acquittal.

The impeachment issue was not an isolated case. In 1993, President Clinton's budget passed both the House and the Senate without a single Republican vote in favor. The same deep partisan split occurred over taxes and supplemental appropriations. Nor was this a blip: since 1950, there has been a steady increase in the percentage of votes in Congress pitting most Democrats against most Republicans.

In the midst of the struggle to pacify Iraq, Howard Dean, the chairman of the Democratic National Committee, said the war could not be won and Nancy Pelosi, the leader of the House Democrats, endorsed the view that American forces should be brought home as soon as possible. By contrast, although there was congressional grumbling (mostly by Republicans) about Korea and complaints (mostly by Democrats) about Vietnam, and although Senator George Aiken of Vermont famously proposed that we declare victory and withdraw, I cannot remember party leaders calling for unconditional surrender.

The reasons for the widening fissures in Congress are not far to seek. Each of the political parties was once a coalition of dissimilar forces: liberal

Northern Democrats and conservative Southern Democrats, liberal coastal Republicans and conservative Midwestern Republicans. No longer; the realignments of the South (now overwhelmingly Republican) and of New England (now strongly Democratic) have all but eliminated legislators who deviate from the party's leadership. Conservative Democrats and liberal Republicans are endangered species now approaching extinction. At the same time, the ideological gap between the parties is growing: if there was once a large overlap between Democrats and Republicans—remember "Tweedledum and Tweedledee"?—today that congruence has almost disappeared. By the late 1990s, virtually every Democrat was more liberal than virtually every Republican.

The result has been not only intense partisanship but a sharp rise in congressional incivility. In 1995, a Republican-controlled Senate passed a budget that President Clinton proceeded to veto; in the loggerhead that followed, many federal agencies shut down (in a move that backfired on the Republicans). Congressional debates have seen an increase not only in heated exchanges but in the number of times a representative's words are either ruled out of order or "taken down" (that is, written by the clerk and then read aloud, with the offending member being asked if he or she wishes to withdraw them).

It has been suggested that congressional polarization is exacerbated by new districting arrangements that make each House seat safe for either a Democratic or a Republican incumbent. If only these seats were truly competitive, it is said, more centrist legislators would be elected. That seems plausible, but David C. King of Harvard has shown that it is wrong: in the House, the more competitive the district, the more extreme the views of the winner. This odd finding is apparently the consequence of a nomination process dominated by party activists. In primary races, where turnout is low (and seems to be getting lower), the ideologically motivated tend to exercise a preponderance of influence.

All this suggests a situation very unlike the half-century before the 1990s, if perhaps closer to certain periods in the eighteenth and nineteenth centuries. Then, too, incivility was common in Congress, with members not only passing the most scandalous remarks about each other but on occasion striking their rivals with canes or fists. Such partisan feeling ran highest when Congress was deeply divided over slavery before the Civil War and over Reconstruction after it. Today the issues are different, but the emotions are not dissimilar.

Next, the mass media: Not only are they themselves increasingly polarized, but consumers are well aware of it and act on that awareness. Fewer people now subscribe to newspapers or watch the network evening news. Although some of this decline may be explained by a preference for entertainment over news, some undoubtedly reflects the growing conviction that the mainstream press generally does not tell the truth, or at least not the whole truth.

In part, media bias feeds into, and off, an increase in business competition. In the 1950s, television news amounted to a brief 30-minute interlude in the day's programming, and not a very profitable one at that; for the rest of the time, the three networks supplied us with westerns and situation comedies. Today, television news is a vast, growing, and very profitable venture by the many broadcast and cable outlets that supply news twenty-four hours a day, seven days a week.

The news we get is not only more omnipresent, it is also more competitive and hence often more adversarial. When there were only three television networks, and radio stations were forbidden by the fairness doctrine from broadcasting controversial views, the media gravitated toward the middle of the ideological spectrum, where the large markets could be found. But now that technology has created cable news and the Internet, and now that the fairness doctrine has by and large been repealed, many media outlets find their markets at the ideological extremes.

Here is where the sharper antagonism among political leaders and their advisers and associates comes in. As one journalist has remarked about the change in his profession, "We don't deal in facts [any longer], but in attributed opinions." Or, these days, in unattributed opinions. And those opinions are more intensely rivalrous than was once the case.

The result is that, through commercial as well as ideological self-interest, the media contribute heavily to polarization. Broadcasters are eager for stories to fill their round-the-clock schedules, and at the same time reluctant to trust the government as a source for those stories. Many media outlets are clearly liberal in their orientation; with the arrival of Fox News and the growth of talk radio, many are now just as clearly conservative.

The evidence of liberal bias in the mainstream media is very strong. The Center for Media and Public Affairs (CMPA) has been systematically studying television broadcasts for a quarter-century. In the 2004 presidential campaign, John Kerry received more favorable mentions than any presidential candidate in CMPA's history, especially during the month before election day. This is not new: since 1980 (and setting aside the recent advent of Fox News), the Democratic candidate has received more favorable mentions than the Republican candidate in every race except the 1988 contest between Michael Dukakis and George H. W. Bush. A similarly clear orientation characterizes weekly newsmagazines like *Time* and *Newsweek*.

For its part, talk radio is listened to by about one-sixth of the adult public, and that one-sixth is made up mostly of conservatives. National Public Radio has an audience of about the same size; it is disproportionately liberal. The same breakdown affects cable-television news, where the rivalry is between CNN (and MSNBC) and Fox News. Those who watch CNN are more likely to be Democrats than Republicans; the reverse is emphatically true of Fox. As for news and opinion on the Internet, which has become an important source for college graduates in particular, it, too, is largely polarized along political and ideological lines, emphasized even more by the culture that has grown up around news blogs.

At one time, our culture was only weakly affected by the media because news organizations had only a few points of access to us and were largely moderate and audience-maximizing enterprises. Today the media have many lines of access, and reflect both the maximization of controversy and the cultivation of niche markets. Once the media talked to us; now they shout at us.

And then there are the interest groups. In the past, the major ones—the National Association of Manufacturers, the Chamber of Commerce, and labor organizations like the AFL-CIO—were concerned with their own material interests. They are still active, but the loudest messages today come from very different sources and have a very different cast to them. They are issued by groups concerned with social and cultural matters like civil rights, managing the environment, alternatives to the public schools, the role of women, access to firearms, and so forth, and they directly influence the way people view politics.

Interest groups preoccupied with material concerns can readily find ways to arrive at compromise solutions to their differences; interest groups divided by issues of rights or morality find compromise very difficult. The positions taken by many of these groups and their supporters, often operating within the two political parties, profoundly affect the selection of candidates for office. In brief, it is hard to imagine someone opposed to abortion receiving the Democratic nomination for President, or someone in favor of it receiving the Republican nomination.

Outside the realm of party politics, interest groups also file briefs in important court cases and can benefit from decisions that in turn help shape the political debate. Abortion became a hot controversy in the 1970s not because the American people were already polarized on the matter but because their (mainly centrist) views were not consulted; instead, national policy was determined by the Supreme Court in a decision, *Roe v. Wade*, that itself reflected a definition of "rights" vigorously promoted by certain well-defined interest groups.

Polarization not only is real and has increased, but it has also spread to rank-and-file voters through elite influence.

In *The Nature and Origins of Mass Opinion . . .*, John R. Zaller of UCLA listed a number of contemporary issues—homosexuality, a nuclear freeze, the war in Vietnam, busing for school integration, the 1990–91 war to expel Iraq from Kuwait—and measured the views held about them by politically aware citizens. (By "politically aware," Zaller meant people who did well answering neutral factual questions about politics.) His findings were illuminating.

Take the Persian Gulf war. Iraq had invaded Kuwait in August 1990. From that point through the congressional elections in November 1990, scarcely any elite voices were raised to warn against anything the United States might contemplate doing in response. Two days after the mid-term elections, however, President George H. W. Bush announced that he was sending many more troops to the Persian Gulf. This provoked strong criticism from some members of Congress, especially Democrats.

As it happens, a major public-opinion survey was under way just as these events were unfolding. Before criticism began to be voiced in Congress, both registered Democrats and registered Republicans had supported Bush's vaguely announced intention of coming to the aid of Kuwait; the more politically aware they were, the greater their support. After the onset of elite criticism, the support of Republican voters went up, but Democratic support flattened out. As Bush became more vigorous in indicating his aims, politically aware voters began to differ sharply, with Democratic support declining and Republican support increasing further.

Much the same pattern can be seen in popular attitudes toward the other issues studied by Zaller. As political awareness increases, attitudes split apart, with, for example, highly aware liberals favoring busing and job guarantees and opposing the war in Vietnam, and highly aware conservatives opposing busing and job guarantees and supporting the war in Vietnam.

But why should this be surprising? To imagine that extremist politics has been confined to the chattering classes is to believe that Congress, the media, and American interest groups operate in an ideological vacuum. I find that assumption implausible.

As for the extent to which these extremist views have spread, that is probably best assessed by looking not at specific issues but at enduring political values and party preferences. In 2004, only 12 percent of Democrats approved of George Bush; at earlier periods, by contrast, three to four times as many Democrats approved of Ronald Reagan, Gerald Ford, Richard Nixon, and Dwight D. Eisenhower. Over the course of about two decades, in other words, party affiliation had come to exercise a critical influence over what people thought about a sitting President.

The same change can be seen in the public's view of military power. Since the late 1980s, Republicans have been more willing than Democrats to say that "the best way to ensure peace is through military strength." By the late 1990s and on into 2003, well over two-thirds of all Republicans agreed with this view, but far fewer than half of all Democrats did. In 2005, three-fourths of all Democrats but fewer than a third of all Republicans told pollsters that good diplomacy was the best way to ensure peace. In the same survey, two-thirds of all Republicans but only one fourth of all Democrats said they would fight for this country "whether it is right or wrong."

Unlike in earlier years, the parties are no longer seen as Tweedledum and Tweedledee. To the contrary, as they sharpen their ideological differences, attentive voters have sharpened their ideological differences. They now like either the Democrats or the Republicans more than they once did, and are less apt to feel neutral toward either one.

How deep does this polarization reach? As measured by opinion polls, the gap between Democrats and Republicans was twice as great in 2004 as in 1972. In fact, rank-and-file Americans disagree more strongly today than did politically active Americans in 1972.

To be sure, this mass polarization involves only a minority of all voters, but the minority is sizable, and a significant part of it is made up of the college-educated. As Marc Hetherington of Vanderbilt puts it: "people with the greatest ability to assimilate new information, those with more formal education, are most affected by elite polarization." And that cohort has undeniably grown.

In 1900, only 10 percent of all young Americans went to high school. My father, in common with many men his age in the early twentieth century, dropped out of school after the eighth grade. Even when I graduated from college, the first in my family to do so, fewer than one-tenth of all Americans over the age of twenty-five had gone that far. Today [2006], 84 percent of adult Americans have graduated from high school and nearly 27 percent have graduated from college. This extraordinary growth in schooling has produced an ever larger audience for political agitation.

Ideologically, an even greater dividing line than undergraduate education is postgraduate education. People who have proceeded beyond college seem to be very different from those who stop with a high-school or college diploma. Thus, about a sixth of all voters describe themselves as liberals, but the figure for those with a postgraduate degree is well over a quarter. In mid-2004, about half of all voters trusted George Bush; less than a third of those with a postgraduate education did. In November of the same year, when over half of all college graduates voted for Bush, well over half of the smaller cohort who had done postgraduate work voted for Kerry. According to the Pew Center for Research on the People and the Press, more than half of all Democrats with a postgraduate education supported the antiwar candidacy of Howard Dean.

The effect of postgraduate education is reinforced by being in a profession. Between 1900 and 1960, write John B. Judis and Ruy Teixeira in *The Emerging Democratic Majority* . . . , professionals voted pretty much the same way as business managers; by 1988, the former began supporting Democrats while the latter supported Republicans. On the other hand, the effect of postgraduate education seems to outweigh the effect of affluence. For most voters, including college graduates, having higher incomes means becoming more conservative; not so for those with a postgraduate education, whose liberal predilections are immune to the wealth effect.

The results of this linkage between ideology, on the one hand, and congressional polarization, media influence, interest-group demands, and education on the other are easily read in the commentary surrounding the 2004 election. In their zeal to denigrate the President, liberals, pronounced one conservative pundit, had "gone quite around the twist." According to liberal spokesmen, conservatives with their "religious intolerance" and their determination to rewrite the Constitution had so befuddled their fellow Americans that a "great nation was felled by a poisonous nut."

If such wholesale slurs are not signs of polarization, then the word has no meaning. To a degree that we cannot precisely measure, and over issues that we cannot exactly list, polarization has seeped down into the public, where it has assumed the form of a culture war. The sociologist James Davison Hunter, who has written about this phenomenon in a mainly religious context, defines culture war as "political and social hostility rooted in different systems of moral understanding." Such conflicts, he writes, which can involve "fundamental ideas about who we are as Americans," are waged both across the religious/secular divide and within religions themselves, where those with an "orthodox" view of moral authority square off against those with a "progressive" view.

To some degree, this terminology is appropriate to today's political situation as well. We are indeed in a culture war in Hunter's sense, though I believe this war is itself but another component, or another symptom, of the larger ideological polarization that has us in its grip. Conservative thinking on political issues has religious roots, but it also has roots that are fully as secular as anything on the Left. By the same token, the liberal attack on conservatives derives in part from an explicitly "progressive" religious orientation—liberal Protestantism or Catholicism, or Reform Judaism—but in part from the same secular sources shared by many conservatives.

But what, one might ask, is wrong with having well-defined parties arguing vigorously about the issues that matter? Is it possible that polarized politics is a good thing, encouraging sharp debate and clear positions? Perhaps that is true on those issues where reasonable compromises can be devised. But there are two limits to such an arrangement.

First, many Americans believe that unbridgeable political differences have prevented leaders from addressing the problems they were elected to address. As a result, distrust of government mounts, leading to an alienation from politics altogether. The steep decline in popular approval of our national officials has many causes, but surely one of them is that ordinary voters agree among themselves more than political elites agree with each other—and the elites are far more numerous than they once were.

In the 1950s, a committee of the American Political Science Association (APSA) argued the case for a "responsible" two-party system. The model the APSA had in mind was the more ideological and therefore more "coherent" party system of Great Britain. At the time, scarcely anyone thought our parties could be transformed in such a supposedly salutary direction. Instead, as Governor George Wallace of Alabama put it in his failed third-party bid for the presidency, there was not a "dime's worth of difference" between Democrats and Republicans.

What Wallace forgot was that, however alike the parties were, the public liked them that way. A half-century ago, Tweedledum and Tweedledee enjoyed the support of the American people; the more different they have become, the greater has been the drop in popular confidence in both them and the federal government.

A final drawback of polarization is more profound. Sharpened debate is arguably helpful with respect to domestic issues, but not for the management of important foreign and military matters. The United States, an unrivaled super-power with unparalleled responsibilities for protecting the peace and defeating terrorists, is now forced to discharge those duties with its own political house in disarray.

We fought World War II as a united nation, even against two enemies (Germany and Italy) that had not attacked us. We began the wars in Korea and Vietnam with some degree of unity, too, although it was eventually whittled away. By the early 1990s, when we expelled Iraq from Kuwait, we had to do so over the objections of congressional critics; the first President Bush avoided putting the issue to Congress altogether. In 2003 we toppled Saddam Hussein in the face of catcalls from many domestic leaders and opinion-makers. Now, in stabilizing Iraq and helping that country create a new free government, we have proceeded despite intense and mounting criticism, much of it voiced by politicians who before the war agreed that Saddam Hussein was an evil menace in possession of weapons of mass destruction and that we had to remove him.

Denmark or Luxembourg can afford to exhibit domestic anguish and uncertainty over military policy; the United States cannot. A divided America encourages our enemies, disheartens our allies, and saps our resolve—potentially to fatal effect. What General Giap of North Vietnam once said of us is even truer today. America cannot be defeated on the battlefield, but it can be defeated at home. Polarization is a force that can defeat us.

Polarized America?

February 21, 2006

To the editor:
James Q. Wilson (February) takes issue with my demonstration in *Culture War? The Myth of a Polarized America* (with Samuel Abrams and Jeremy Pope) that the polarization evident among the members of the American political

Published in *Commentary*, May 2006.

class has only a faint reflection in the American public. As a long-time admirer of Wilson's work I am naturally concerned when his take on some aspect of American politics differs from mine. But I believe that his criticisms are a result of misunderstanding. I would like to address two of them.

First, Wilson discounts our red state-blue state comparisons with the comment that "Inferring the views of individual citizens from the gross results of presidential balloting is a questionable procedure." Indeed it is, which is why we did not do that. As we wrote in the book, inferring polarization from close elections is precisely what pundits have done and why their conclusions have been wrong. In contrast, we report detailed analyses of the policy views expressed by voters in 2000 and 2004 and contrary to the claims of Garry Wills, Maureen Dowd, and other op-ed columnists, we find surprisingly small differences between the denizens of the blue states and the red states. As we show in the book and emphasize repeatedly, people's *choices* (as expressed, say, in presidential balloting) can be polarized while their *positions* are not, and the evidence strongly indicates that this is the case.

Moreover, we report that not only are red and blue state citizens surprisingly similar in their views, but other studies find little evidence of growing polarization no matter how one slices and dices the population—affluent v. poor, white v. black v. brown, old v. young, well educated v. the less educated, men v. women, and so on. Like many before him, Wilson confuses partisan *sorting* with polarization—the Democrats have largely shed their conservative southern wing while Republicans have largely shed their liberal Rockefeller wing, resulting in more distinct parties, even while the aggregate distribution of ideology and issue stances among the citizenry remains much the same as in the past.

Second, Wilson criticizes our analysis of Americans' views on the specific issue of abortion, contending that the small numerical differences expressed by people on a General Social Survey scale constitute a significantly larger substantive difference. Although we disagree, even if one accepted Wilson's contention, it would not apply to our supporting analysis of a differently-worded Gallup survey item that yields the same conclusions, or to numerous other survey items that clearly show that most Americans are "pro-choice, buts."

For example, Wilson notes that "70 percent of those who thought abortion should always be legal voted for Al Gore or John Kerry, while over 70 percent of those who thought it should always be illegal voted for George Bush." True enough, but he does not mention that Gallup repeatedly finds that a majority of the American people place themselves between those polar categories—they think abortion should be "legal only under certain circumstances." Even limiting the analysis to avowed partisans, in 2005 only 30 percent of Democrats thought abortion should always be legal, and fewer than 30 percent of Republicans thought it should always be illegal. One can raise questions about every survey item that has ever been asked, but the cumulative weight of the evidence on Americans' abortion views is overwhelming. Contrary to the wishes of the activists on both sides, the American people prefer a middle ground on abortion, period.

Wilson approvingly cites James Davison Hunter, whose book, *Culture War*, inspired Patrick Buchanan's 1992 speech at the Republican National Convention. In a forthcoming Brookings Institution volume, Hunter now limits his thesis to "somewhere between 10 and 15 percent who occupy these opposing moral and ideological universes." That leaves more than 80 percent of the American public not engaged in the moral and ideological battles reveled in by the political class. Note that Wilson's examples of incivil discourse reference "the press," "a former Democratic presidential candidate," "a senior Democratic Senator," "liberal spokesmen," and "one conservative pundit." Absent from this list are well-intentioned, ordinary working Americans not given to the kind of incendiary remarks that get quoted by journalists.

I share Wilson's concern with the potentially harmful consequences of polarization. But the first step in addressing those concerns is to get the facts correct. I remain convinced that we have done that. If Americans are offered competent, pragmatic candidates with a problem-solving orientation, the shallow popular roots of political polarization will be exposed for all to see.

Morris P. Fiorina
Stanford, California

John B. Judis

Tea Minus Zero

Liberals have responded to the Tea Party movement by reaching a comforting conclusion: that there is no way these guys can possibly be for real. The movement has variously been described as a "front group for the Republican party" and a "media creation"; Paul Krugman has called Tea Party rallies "AstroTurf (fake grass roots) events, manufactured by the usual suspects."

I can understand why liberals would want to dismiss the Tea Party movement as an inauthentic phenomenon; it would certainly be welcome news if it were. The sentiments on display at Tea Party rallies go beyond run-of-the-mill anti-tax, anti-spending conservatism and into territory that rightly strikes liberals as truly disturbing. Among the signs I saw at an April 15 protest in Washington: "IF IT SOUNDS LIKE MARX AND ACTS LIKE STALIN IT MUST BE OBAMA," "STOP OBAMA'S BROWNSHIRT INFILTRAITORS," and "OBAMA BIN LYIN," which was accompanied by an illustration of the president looking like a monkey.

But the Tea Party movement is not inauthentic, and—contrary to the impression its rallies give off—it isn't a fringe faction either. It is a genuine popular movement, one that has managed to unite a number of ideological strains from U.S. history—some recent, some older. These strains can be described as many things, but they cannot be dismissed as passing phenomena. Much as liberals would like to believe otherwise, there is good reason to think the Tea Party movement could exercise considerable influence over our politics in the coming years.

The movement essentially began on February 19, 2009, when CNBC commentator Rick Santelli, speaking from the floor of the Chicago Mercantile Exchange, let loose against the Obama administration's plan to help homeowners who could no longer pay their mortgages. "This is America!" Santelli exclaimed. "How many of you people want to pay for your neighbors' mortgage that has an extra bathroom and can't pay their bills?" Santelli called for a "Chicago Tea Party" to protest the administration's plan.

Santelli's appeal was answered by a small group of bloggers, policy wonks,

Published by *The New Republic*, May 2010.

and Washington politicos who were primarily drawn from the libertarian wing of the conservative movement. They included John O'Hara from the Illinois Policy Institute (who has written a history of the movement, titled *A New American Tea Party*); Brendan Steinhauser of FreedomWorks, a Washington lobbying group run by former Representative Dick Armey; and blogger Michael Patrick Leahy, a founder of Top Conservatives on Twitter. The initial round of Tea Party protests took place at the end of February in over 30 cities. There were more protests in April, and, by the time of the massive September 12 protest last year, the Tea Party movement had officially arrived as a political force.

Like many American movements, the Tea Parties are not tightly organized from above. They are a network of local groups and national ones (Tea Party Patriots, Tea Party Express, Tea Party Nation), Washington lobbies and quasi-think tanks (FreedomWorks, Americans for Prosperity), bloggers, and talk-show hosts. There are no national membership lists, but extensive polls done by Quinnipiac, the Winston Group, and Economist/YouGov suggest that the movement commands the active allegiance of between 13 percent and 15 percent of the electorate. That is a formidable number, and, judging from other polls that ask whether someone has a "favorable" view of the Tea Parties, the movement gets a sympathetic hearing from as much as 40 percent of the electorate.

Tea Partiers' favorite politician is undoubtedly Sarah Palin—according to the Economist/YouGov poll, 71 percent of Tea Partiers think Palin "is more qualified to be president than Barack Obama" (and another 15 percent are "not sure")—but, more than anyone else, the movement takes its cues from Glenn Beck. Unlike fellow talkers Rush Limbaugh and Sean Hannity, Beck has never been a conventional Republican; he calls himself a conservative rather than a member of the GOP. While Limbaugh has attempted to soft-pedal his personal failings, the baby-faced Beck makes his into a story of redemption. He is, in his own words, an "average, everyday person." You need to have followed Beck's conspiratorial meanderings to understand what preoccupies many members of the Tea Party movement. At the Washington demonstration in April, for instance, there were people holding signs attacking Frances Fox Piven and Richard Cloward, two 1960s-era Columbia University sociologists who, Beck claims, were the brains behind both the community group ACORN and Obama's attempt to destroy capitalism by bankrupting the government through national health care reform.

In the last year, the movement's focus has shifted from demonstrations to elections. Currently, Tea Party groups are backing Republican Senate candidates in Kentucky, Utah, and Florida, while trying to knock off Democratic Senators Harry Reid in Nevada and Arlen Specter in Pennsylvania. In some places, Tea Party organizations have begun to displace the state GOP. Last month, Action is Brewing, the northern Nevada Tea Party affiliate, hosted a televised debate for the Republican gubernatorial and senatorial candidates. In addition, numerous candidates are running for Congress as Tea Party supporters.

The Tea Parties are the descendants of a number of conservative insurgencies from the past two generations: the anti-tax rebellion of the late '70s, the Moral Majority and Christian Coalition of the '80s and '90s, and Pat Buchanan's presidential runs. Like the Tea Partiers I saw in Washington—and the picture of the Tea Partiers put forward by the Winston and Quinnipiac polls—these movements have been almost entirely white, disproportionately middle-aged or older, and more male than female (though parts of the Christian right are an exception on this count). A majority of their adherents generally are not college-educated, with incomes in the middle range—attributes that also closely match the Tea Party movement's demographic profile. (A misleading picture of Tea Partiers as college-educated and affluent came from a *New York Times*/CBS poll of people who merely "support," but don't necessarily have anything to do with, the Tea Party movement. The other polls surveyed people who say they are "part of" the movement.)

Sociologists who have studied these earlier movements describe their followers as coming from the "marginal segments of the middle class." That's a sociological, but also a political, fact. These men and women look uneasily upward at corporate CEOs and investment bankers, and downward at low-wage service workers and laborers, many of whom are minorities. And their political outlook is defined by whether they primarily blame those below or above for the social and economic anxieties they feel. In the late nineteenth and early twentieth century, the marginal middle class was the breeding ground for left-wing attacks against Wall Street. For the last half-century, it has nourished right-wing complaints about blacks, illegal immigrants, and the poor.

It isn't just demography that the Tea Parties have in common with recent conservative movements; it's also politics. To be sure, some of the original Tea Party organizers were young libertarians, many of whom, like Brendan Steinhauser, voted for Ron Paul in 2008 and have rediscovered Ayn Rand's ethic of rational selfishness. They remain part of the movement—one sign I saw at the Washington rally read, "WE ARE JOHN GALT," referring to the hero of *Atlas Shrugged*—but, as the movement has grown, its adherents have become more conventionally conservative. As Grover Norquist likes to point out, what distinguishes one conservative group from another is not their members' overall views, but what "moves" them to demonstrate or to vote. The Christian right, for instance, went to the barricades over abortion and gay marriage, yet most members also hold conservative economic views. Likewise, the Tea Partiers have been moved to action by economic issues, but they share the outlook of social conservatives. According to the Economist/YouGov poll, 74 percent of Tea Party members think abortion is "murder," and 81 percent are against gay marriage. Sixty-three percent are in favor of public school students learning that "the Book of Genesis in the Bible explains how God created the world"; 62 percent think that "the only way to Heaven is through Jesus Christ." These beliefs are on display at rallies: In Washington, one demonstrator in clerical garb held a sign saying, "GOD HATES TAXES." Moreover, aside from the followers of Ron Paul, Tea Party members also share the post-September 11 national security views of the GOP. When Tea Partiers were asked to name the "most important issue" to them, terrorism came in third out of ten, behind only the economy and the budget deficit.

If you look at the people who are running as pro–Tea Party candidates, you discover that some of them have simply graduated from one stage of the conservative movement to another. Jason Meade, who is running for Congress in Ohio, was just out of school, working in his father's business and playing music, when he "returned to the church and left the music world behind." Now 38, he sees his participation in Tea Party politics as a continuation of his twelve subsequent years in ministry school. "I decided to try and minister in a new way; by trying to be involved in the protection of the freedoms and liberty that God has given us and that have been woven into the fabric of our country," he wrote on his website. Jason Sager, 36, who is running in a Republican congressional primary northeast of Tampa, got into conservative politics in the wake of September 11. A Navy veteran, he joined a group called Protest Warrior that staged counter-demonstrations at antiwar rallies, and he was a volunteer in George W. Bush's 2004 campaign. After Obama's election, he got involved with Glenn Beck's 912 Project and, then, with the local Tea Parties.

But the Tea Parties' roots in U.S. history go back much further than the conservative movements of recent decades. The Tea Parties are defined by three general ideas that have played a key role in U.S. politics since the country's early days. The first is an obsession with decline. This idea, which traces back to the outlook of New England Puritans during the seventeenth century, consists of a belief that a golden age occurred some time ago; that we are now in a period of severe social, economic, or moral decay; that evil forces and individuals are the cause of this situation; that the goal of politics is to restore the earlier period; and that the key to doing so is heeding a special text that can serve as a guidebook for the journey backward. (The main difference between the far right and far left is that the left locates the golden age in the future.) The Puritans were trying to reproduce the circumstances of early Christianity in New England, using the Bible as their guiding text. Their enemies were Catholics and the Church of England, who they believed had corrupted the religion. For the Tea Partiers, the golden age is the time of the Founders, and adherence to the Constitution is the means to restore this period in the face of challenges from secular humanism, radical Islam, and especially socialism.

Beck has been instrumental in sacralizing the Constitution. He has touted the works of the late W. Cleon Skousen, a John Birch Society defender who projected his ultraconservative views back onto the Founding Fathers. In *The 5000 Year Leap*, which has been reissued with a foreword by Beck, Skousen claimed that the Founders "warned against the 'welfare state'" and against "the drift toward the collectivist left."

In Arizona, Tea Party members hand out copies of the Constitution at political meetings the way a missionary group might hand out Bibles. The San Antonio Tea Party group has demanded that politicians sign a "contract with the Constitution." In speeches, Tea Partiers cite articles and amendments from the Constitution the same way that clerics cite Biblical verses. Speaking at the Lakeland Tea Party rally on tax day, Jason Sager said, "You are now able to see the most pressing issue that faces our nation and our society. Do you know what that issue is? We are now witnessing the fundamental breakdown of the republican form of government that we are guaranteed in Article Four, Section Four of our Constitution." In typical fashion, Sager did not go on to explain what Article Four, Section Four was. (You can look it up. I had to.)

Just as the Puritans believed Catholics and the Church of England were undermining Christianity, the Tea Partiers have fixated on nefarious individuals and groups—Saul Alinsky, ACORN, and, of course, Obama himself—who they believe are destroying the country. (According to the Economist/YouGov poll, 52 percent of Tea Party members think ACORN stole the 2008 election from John McCain; another 24 percent are still not sure.) "America has let thieves into her home," writes Beck, "and that nagging in your gut is a final warning that our country is about to be stolen." Their determination to locate the threat outside the United States accounts for their emphasis on Obama being a socialist, Marxist, communist, or even fascist—all of which are foreign faiths—rather than what he is: a conventional American liberal. It also helps explain the repeated references to Obama's African father. And it explains why some Tea Partiers continue to believe, in the face of incontrovertible evidence, that Obama was born outside the United States. The Economist/YouGov poll found that 34 percent of Tea Party members think he was not born in the United States, and another 34 percent are not sure.

But how could a movement that cultivates such crazy, conspiratorial views be regarded favorably by as much as 40 percent of the electorate? That is where the Tea Party movement's second link to early U.S. history comes in. The Tea Partiers may share the Puritans' fear of decline, but it is what they share with Thomas Jefferson that has far broader appeal: a staunch anti-statism. What began as a sentiment of the left—a rejection of state monopolies—became, after the industrial revolution and the rise of the labor movement, a weapon against progressive reforms. The basic idea—that government is a "necessary evil"—has retained its power, and, when the economy has faltered, Americans have been quick to blame Washington, perhaps even before they looked at Wall Street or big corporations. It happened in the late '70s under Jimmy Carter and in the early '90s under George H. W. Bush; and it has happened again during Obama's first 18 months in office. According to a Pew poll, the percentage of Americans "angry" with government has risen from 10 percent in February 2000 to 21 percent today, while another 56 percent are "frustrated" with government.

Of course, during Franklin Roosevelt's first term, most voters didn't blame the incumbent administration for the Great Depression. Roosevelt was able to deflect blame for the depression back onto the Hoover administration and the "economic royalists" of Wall Street and corporate America. But Roosevelt took office at the nadir of the Great Depression, and his policies achieved dramatic improvements in unemployment and economic growth during his first term. Obama took office barely four months after the financial crisis visibly hit, and he has had to preside over growing unemployment.

Simmering economic frustration also accounts for the final historical strain that defines the Tea Parties: They are part of a tradition of producerism that dates to Andrew Jackson. Jacksonian Democrats believed that workers should enjoy the fruits of what they produce and not have to share them with the merchants and bankers who didn't actually create anything. The Populists of the late nineteenth century invoked this ethic in denouncing the Eastern bankers who held their farms hostage. Producerism also underlay Roosevelt's broadsides against economic royalists and Bill Clinton's promise to give priority to those who "work hard and play by the rules."

During the 1970s, conservatives began invoking producerism to justify their attacks on the welfare state, and it was at the core of the conservative tax revolt. While the Jacksonians and Populists had largely directed their anger upward, conservatives directed their ire at the people below who were beneficiaries of state programs—from the "welfare queens" of the ghetto to the "illegal aliens" of the barrio. Like the attack against "big government," this conservative producerism has most deeply resonated during economic downturns. And the Tea Parties have clearly built their movement around it.

Producerism was at the heart of Santelli's rant against government forcing the responsible middle class to subsidize those who bought homes they couldn't afford. In his history of the Tea Party movement, O'Hara described an America divided between "moochers, big and small, corporate and individual, trampling over themselves with their hands out demanding endless bailouts" and "disgusted, hardworking citizens getting sick of being played for chumps and punished for practicing personal responsibility." The same theme recurs in the Tea Partiers' rejection of liberal legislation. Beck dismissed Obama's health care reform plan as "good old socialism . . . raping the pocketbooks of the rich to give to the poor." Speaking to cheers at the April 15 rally in Washington, Armey denounced the progressive income tax in the same terms. "I can't steal your money and give it to this guy," he declared. "Therefore, I shouldn't use the power of the state to steal your money and give it to this guy."

The Tea Parties are not managed by the Republican National Committee, and they are not really a wing of the GOP. It is telling that Beck devoted his February speech at the Conservative Political Action Conference to bashing Republicans—and that, in a survey of 50 Tea Party leaders, the Sam Adams Alliance found that 28 percent identify themselves as Independents and 11 percent as Tea Party members rather than Republicans. Still, the Tea Partiers' political objective is clearly to push the GOP to the right. They agitated last summer for a Republican party-line vote against health care reform and are now arguing that states have a constitutional right to refuse to comply with it.

They have been calling the offices of Republican senators to demand that they oppose a bipartisan compromise on financial regulatory reform. In South Carolina, they have attacked Senator Lindsey Graham, who is also a favorite Beck target, for backing a cap-and-trade [environmental] bill. The Arizona Tea Party pressured Governor Jan Brewer to sign the now-infamous bill targeting illegal immigrants. And Tea Party Nation has issued a "Red Alert" to prevent Congress from adopting "amnesty" legislation.

If the GOP wins back at least one house of Congress in November, the Tea Parties will be able to claim victory and demand a say in Republican congressional policies. That could lead to a replay of the Newt Gingrich Congress of 1995–1996, from which the country was lucky to escape relatively unscathed. But, beyond this, it's hard to say what will become of the movement. If the economy improves in a significant way next year, it is likely to fade. That is what happened to the tax revolt, which peaked from 1978 to 1982 and then subsided. But, if the economy limps along—say, in the manner of Japan over the last 15 years—then the Tea Parties will likely remain strong, and may even become a bigger force in U.S. politics than they are now.

For all of its similarities to previous insurgencies, the Tea Party movement differs in one key respect from the most prominent conservative movement of recent years, the Christian right: The Tea Parties do not have the same built-in impediments to growth. The Christian right looked like it was going to expand in the early '90s, but it ran up against the limit of its politics, which were grounded ultimately in an esoteric theology and a network of churches. If it strayed too far from the implications of that theology, it risked splitting its membership. But, if it articulated it—as Pat Robertson and others did at various inopportune moments—then it risked alienating the bulk of Americans. The Tea Parties do not have the same problem. They have their own crazy conspiracy theories, but even the wackiest Tea Partiers wouldn't demand that a candidate seeking their endorsement agree that ACORN fixed the election or that Obama is foreign-born. And their core appeal on government and spending will continue to resonate as long as the economy sputters. None of this is what liberals want to hear, but we might as well face reality: The Tea Party movement—firmly grounded in a number of durable U.S. political traditions and well-positioned for a time of economic uncertainty—could be around for a while.

QUESTIONS

1. According to Wilson and Judis, what are the chief factors contributing to polarization and cultural division in the United States? Are these factors likely to change anytime soon? What part, if any, of Wilson's and Judis's arguments would Fiorina agree with?

2. Based on the articles and other information you might have, do you think Fiorina is right that the American public is not deeply split on a range of issues and that they tend to favor more moderate solutions to problems? Can you think of issues for which this would be true?

3. If you were an adviser for one of the two major parties, how would you advise them to address the issue of polarization or culture war? Should they emphasize issues where broader consensus might be possible? Or is it the job of political parties to emphasize precisely those issues that might be the most divisive in order to appeal to their strongest supporters? Which is better for voters—a focus on consensus or on contrasts?

4. Party strategists often talk about changing a party's public image. In your view, what would a party have to do to change its public image significantly? What would convince you that a party had changed?

12

Groups and Interests: Was Madison Right?

In his famous essay *Federalist* 10, the future president James Madison expressed concern about the "mischief of factions." It was natural, he argued, for people to organize around a principle or interest they held in common, and the most common motivation for organizing such factions was property—those who had it versus those who did not, creditors versus lenders. The danger in such efforts, however, was that a majority faction might usurp the rights of a minority. In a small direct democracy, where a majority of the people could share a "common passion," the threat was very real. Expand the geographic size of the country, however, and replace direct democracy with a system of elected representatives, separation of powers, and checks and balances, and the threat diminished. The likelihood of any one faction appealing to a majority of citizens in a large republic governed by representatives from diverse geographic regions was remote. To Madison, factions were a natural outgrowth of the differences between people, and the only way to eliminate factions would be to eliminate liberty. Eliminating factions might not be possible or desirable, but the mischief of factions could be controlled with a system of representation based upon varied constituencies that embraced multiple, diverse interests. From the competition of diverse interests would arise compromise and balanced public policy.

Madison's concerns about interests and particularly organized interests have resonated throughout American history. At various times in U.S. history, the public has seemed to become especially concerned with the power of interests in politics. One political scientist refers to this as the "ideals vs. institutions" gap: there are times when "what is" is so different from what Americans believe "should be" that pressure mounts to reform lobbying laws, campaign regulations, business practices, and so on. Positions on these issues do not always neatly sort out into the typical liberal and conservative categories. For example, in the early 2000s, a Democratic senator (Russ Feingold) and a Republican senator (John McCain) joined forces to lead the effort for campaign finance reform, but since then liberal and conservative interest groups have frequently joined forces to challenge the constitutionality of some of the new law's limits on interest-group campaign advertising as well as the constitutionality of other campaign-finance laws and regulations.

Was Madison right about the benefits that would emerge from the competition of interests? In the following excerpt from *The Governmental Process*, David Truman answers with an emphatic Yes! Despite the popular criticism of "special" interests that seem to taint the political process with their dominant influence, Truman argues that such groups have been a common and inevitable feature of American government. Groups form to give individuals a means of self-expression and to help individuals find security in an uncertain world. In fact, the uncertainty of the social environment, and the resulting threat to one's interests, is a chief motivation for groups to form, and "taming" this environment is a central concern for group members. Truman suggests that rather than leading to a system ruled by a few dominant powers, the reality is much more fluid. What the critics of group influence fail to recognize is that people have "multiple or overlapping membership" in groups so that "no tolerable normal person is totally absorbed in any group in which he participates." There is balance, in other words, to the views any one member brings to the organization and ultimately to the political process. Further, the potential for a group to form is always present, and "[s] ometimes it may be this possibility of organization that alone gives the potential group a minimum of influence in the political process." Just because someone is not a member of an organized group does not obviate the influence he or she can bring to bear on the political process. The result, as Madison argued, is a balanced approach to the diverse interests that must compromise to form public policy.

Writing in 1960, about a decade after Truman, E. E. Schattschneider finds much to lament in Truman's group-oriented theory of politics. That approach,

Schattschneider argues, attributes almost all of the outcomes in politics to the actions of groups. Thus, group-oriented theory misses much that is important in politics. First, Schattschneider writes, the political process matters. The relative advantages that one group has over another can be lost as opinions and options change. You cannot simply determine the relative power advantage of one group over another and believe you have either explained past outcomes or can predict future ones. Second, by omitting the political process, the group theory ignores the majority by focusing on the narrow interests that are battling over an issue. But the fact that an issue is now on the public agenda is itself highly significant. Politics is the "socialization of conflict," Schattschneider writes. Because they are dominant, powerful interests would be content to leave conflicts private. Seemingly weaker groups aim to widen (i.e., socialize) conflict by bringing it into the political process, where the fight is no longer limited to two relatively narrow interests. And last, the relationships among interest groups and political parties are interdependent. Using the example of the Republican party and business, Schattschneider analyzes how each finds the other useful. He also notes that once an interest group such as business enters into activity with a political party, it loses some control, because the party has to satisfy a majority of the population if it is to win elections. To Schattschneider, strong political parties are a crucial element of a properly working American political system. To weaken parties is to strengthen the influences of narrow special interests.

Jonathan Rauch views with pessimism the ever-expanding number of interest groups in the political process. Whether groups claim to represent narrow economic interests or a broader public interest, Rauch does not see balance and compromise as the result of their competition in the political arena. Rather, he sees a nation suffering from "hyperpluralism," or the explosion of groups making claims on government power and resources. When elected officials attempt to reduce budget deficits or to establish new priorities and refocus expenditures, they are overwhelmed by the pressures of a wide range of groups. As a result, government programs are not terminated or restructured; tough budget cuts or tax changes are rarely made; and a very rich democratic country and its government becomes immobilized. Rather than the dynamic system of change and compromise Truman envisioned, Rauch sees a system characterized primarily by inertia because of the power of groups to prevent government action.

David B. Truman

The Alleged Mischiefs of Faction, from *The Governmental Process*

Most accounts of American legislative sessions—national, state, or local—are full of references to the maneuverings and iniquities of various organized groups. Newspaper stories report that a legislative proposal is being promoted by groups of business men or school teachers or farmers or consumers or labor unions or other aggregations of citizens. Cartoonists picture the legislature as completely under the control of sinister, portly, cigar-smoking individuals labeled "special interests," while a diminutive John Q. Public is pushed aside to sulk in futile anger and pathetic frustrations. A member of the legislature rises in righteous anger on the floor of the house or in a press conference to declare that the bill under discussion is being forced through by the "interests," by the most unscrupulous high-pressure "lobby" he has seen in all his years of public life. An investigating committee denounces the activities of a group as deceptive, immoral, and destructive of our constitutional methods and ideals. A chief executive attacks a "lobby" or "pressure group" as the agency responsible for obstructing or emasculating a piece of legislation that he has recommended "in the public interest."

* * *

Such events are familiar even to the casual student of day-to-day politics, if only because they make diverting reading and appear to give the citizen the "low-down" on his government. He tends, along with many of his more sophisticated fellow citizens, to take these things more or less for granted, possibly because they merely confirm his conviction that "as everybody knows, politics is a dirty business." Yet at the same time he is likely to regard the activities of organized groups in political life as somehow outside the proper and normal processes of government, as the lapses of his weak contemporaries whose moral fiber is insufficient to prevent their defaulting on the great traditions of the Founding Fathers. These events appear to be a modern pathology.

Published in *The Governmental Process*, 1971.

Group Pressure and the Founding Fathers

Group pressures, whatever we may wish to call them, are not new in America. One of the earliest pieces of testimony to this effect is essay number 10 of *The Federalist*, which contains James Madison's classic statement of the impact of divergent groups upon government and the reasons for their development. He was arguing the virtues of the proposed Union as a means to "break and control the violence of faction," having in mind, no doubt, the groups involved in such actions of the debtor or propertyless segment of the population as Shays's Rebellion. He defined faction in broader terms, however, as "a number of citizens, whether amounting to a majority or minority of the whole, who are united and actuated by some common impulse of passion, or of interest. . . ."

* * *

[Madison's] analysis is not just the brilliant generalization of an armchair philosopher or pamphleteer; it represents as well the distillation from Madison's years of acquaintance with contemporary politics as a member of the Virginia Assembly and of [the Continental] Congress. Using the words "party" and "faction" almost interchangeably, since the political party as we know it had not yet developed, he saw the struggles of such groups as the essence of the political process. One need not concur in all his judgments to agree that the process he described had strong similarities to that of our own day.

The entire effort of which *The Federalist* was a part was one of the most skillful and important examples of pressure group activity in American history. The State ratifying conventions were handled by the Federalists with a skill that might well be the envy of a modern lobbyist. It is easy to overlook the fact that "unless the Federalists had been shrewd in manipulation as they were sound in theory, their arguments could not have prevailed."

* * *

Alexis de Tocqueville, perhaps the keenest foreign student ever to write on American institutions, noted as one of the most striking characteristics of the nation the penchant for promoting a bewildering array of projects through organized societies, among them those using political means. "In no country in the world," he observed, "has the principle of association been more successfully used or applied to a greater multitude of objects than in America." De Tocqueville [sic] was impressed by the organization of such groups and by their tendency to operate sometimes upon and sometimes parallel to the formal institutions of government. Speaking of the similarity between the representatives of such groups and the members of legislatures, he stated: "It is true that they [delegates of these societies] have not the right, like the others, of making the laws; but they have the power of attacking those which are in force and of drawing up beforehand those which ought to be enacted."

Since the modern political party was, in the Jackson period, just taking the form that we would recognize today, De Tocqueville does not always distinguish sharply between it and other types of political interest groups. In his discussion of "political associations," however, he gives an account of the anti-tariff convention held in Philadelphia in October of 1831, the form of which might well have come from the proceedings of a group meeting in an American city today:

> Its debates were public, and they at once assumed a legislative character; the extent of the powers of Congress, the theories of free trade, and the different provisions of the tariff were discussed. At the end of ten days the Convention broke up, having drawn up an address to the American people in which it declared: (1) that Congress had not the right of making a tariff, and that the existing tariff was unconstitutional; (2) that the prohibition of free trade was prejudicial to the interests of any nation, and to those of the American people especially.

Additional evidence might be cited from many quarters to illustrate the long history of group politics in this country. Organized pressures supporting or attacking the charter of the Bank of the United States in Jackson's administration, the peculations surrounding Pendleton's "Palace of Fortune" in the pre–Civil War period, the operations of the railroads and other interests in both national and state legislatures in the latter half of the last century, the political activities of farm groups such as the Grange in the same period—these and others indicate that at no time have the activities of organized political interests not been a part of American politics. Whether they indicate pathology or not, they are certainly not new.

* * *

The political interest group is neither a fleeting, transitory newcomer to the political arena nor a localized phenomenon peculiar to one member of the family of nations. The persistence and the dispersion of such organizations indicate rather that we are dealing with a characteristic aspect of our society. That such groups are receiving an increasing measure of popular and technical attention suggests the hypothesis that they are appreciably more significant in the complex and interdependent society of our own day than they were in the simpler, less highly developed community for which our constitutional arrangements were originally designed.

Many people are quite willing to acknowledge the accuracy of these propositions about political groups, but they are worried nevertheless. They are still concerned over the meaning of what they see and read of the activities of such organizations. They observe, for example, that certain farm groups apparently can induce the Government to spend hundreds of millions of dollars to maintain the price of food and to take "surplus" agricultural produce off the market while any urban residents are encountering painful difficulty in stretching their food budgets to provide adequately for their families. They observe that various labor organizations seem to be able to prevent the introduction of cheaper methods into building codes, although the cost of new housing is already beyond the reach of many. Real estate and contractors' trade associations apparently have the power to obstruct various governmental projects for slum clearance and low-cost housing. Veterans' organizations seem able to secure and protect increases in pensions and other benefits almost at will. A church apparently can prevent the appropriation of Federal funds to public schools unless such funds are also given to the schools it operates in competition with the public systems. The Government has declared that stable and friendly European governments cannot be maintained unless Americans buy more goods and services abroad. Yet American shipowners and seamen's unions can secure a statutory requirement that a large proportion of the goods purchased by European countries under the Marshall Plan* must be carried in American ships. Other industries and trade associations can prevent the revision of tariff rates and customs regulations that restrict imports from abroad.

In all these situations the fairly observant citizen sees various groups slugging it out with one another in pursuit of advantages from the Government. Or he sees some of them co-operating with one another to their mutual benefit. He reads of "swarms" of lobbyists "putting pressure on" congressmen and administrators. He has the impression that any group can get what it wants in

---

*The Marshall Plan was the U.S. European Recovery Plan after World War II [Editors].

Washington by deluging officials with mail and telegrams. He may then begin to wonder whether a governmental system like this can survive, whether it can carry its responsibilities in the world and meet the challenges presented by a ruthless dictatorship. He wants to see these external threats effectively met. The sentimental nonsense of the commercial advertisements aside, he values free speech, free elections, representative government, and all that these imply. He fears and resents practices and privileges that seem to place these values in jeopardy.

A common reaction to revelations concerning the more lurid activities of political groups is one of righteous indignation. Such indignation is entirely natural. It is likely, however, to be more comforting than constructive. What we seek are correctives, protections, or controls that will strengthen the practices essential in what we call democracy and that will weaken or eliminate those that really threaten that system. Uncritical anger may do little to achieve that objective, largely because it is likely to be based upon a picture of the governmental process that is a composite of myth and fiction as well as of fact. We shall not begin to achieve control until we have arrived at a conception of politics that adequately accounts for the operations of political groups. We need to know what regular patterns are shown by group politics before we can predict its consequences and prescribe for its lapses. We need to re-examine our notions of how representative government operates in the United States before we can be confident of our statements about the effects of group activities upon it. Just as we should not know how to protect a farm house from lightning unless we knew something of the behavior of electricity, so we cannot hope to protect a governmental system from the results of group organization unless we have an adequate understanding of the political process of which these groups are a part.

* * *

There are two elements in this conception of the political process in the United States that are of crucial significance and that require special emphasis. These are, first, the notion of multiple or overlapping membership and, second, the function of unorganized interests, or potential interest groups.

The idea of overlapping membership stems from the conception of a group as a standardized pattern of interactions rather than as a collection of human units. Although the former may appear to be a rather misty abstraction, it is actually far closer to complex reality than the latter notion. The view of a group as an aggregation of individuals abstracts from the observable fact that in any society, and especially a complex one, no single group affiliation accounts for all of the attitudes or interests of any individual except a fanatic or a compulsive neurotic. No tolerably normal person is totally absorbed in any group in which he participates. The diversity of an individual's activities and his attendant interests involve him in a variety of actual and potential groups. Moreover, the fact that the genetic experiences of no two individuals are identical and the consequent fact that the spectra of their attitudes are in varying degrees dissimilar means that the members of a single group will perceive the group's claims in terms of a diversity of frames of reference. Such heterogeneity may be of little significance until such time as these multiple memberships conflict. Then the cohesion and influence of the affected group depend upon the incorporation or accommodation of the conflicting loyalties of any significant segment of the group, an accommodation that may result in altering the original claims. Thus the leaders of a Parent-Teacher Association must take some account of the fact that their proposals must be acceptable to members who also belong to the local taxpayers' league, to the local chamber of commerce, and to the Catholic Church.

* * *

We cannot account of an established American political system without the second crucial element in our conception of the political process, the concept of the unorganized interest, or potential interest group. Despite the tremendous number of interest groups existing in the United States, not all interests are organized. If we recall the definition of an interest as a shared attitude, it becomes obvious that continuing interaction resulting in claims upon other groups does not take place on the basis of all such attitudes. One of the commonest interest groups forms, the association, emerges out of severe or prolonged disturbances in the expected relationships of individuals in similar institutionalized groups. As association continues to function as long as it succeeds in ordering these disturbed relationships, as a labor union orders the relationships between management and workers. Not all such expected relationships are simultaneously or in a given short period sufficiently disturbed to produce organization. Therefore only a portion of the interests or attitudes involved in such expectations are represented by organized groups. Similarly, many organized groups—families, businesses, or churches, for example—do not operate continuously as interest groups or as political interest groups.

Any mutual interest, however, any shared attitude, is a potential group. A disturbance in established relationships and expectations anywhere in the society may produce new patterns of interaction aimed at restricting or eliminating he disturbance. Sometimes it may be this possibility of organization that alone gives the potential group a minimum of influence in the political process. Thus . . . the Delta planters in Mississippi "must speak for their Negroes in such programs as health and education," although the latter are virtually unorganized and are denied the means of active political participation.*

* * *

Obstacles to the development of organized groups from potential ones may be presented by inertia or by the activities of opposed groups, but the possibility that severe disturbances will be created if these submerged, potential interests should organize necessitates some recognition of the existence of these interests and gives them at least a minimum of influence.

More important for present purposes than the potential groups representing separate minority elements are those interests or expectations that are so widely held in the society and are so reflected in the behavior of almost all citizens that they are, so to speak, taken for granted. Such "majority" interests are significant not only because they may become the basis for organized interest groups overlaps extensively the memberships of the various organized interest groups. The resolution of conflicts between the claims of such unorganized interests and those of organized interest groups must grant recognition to the former not only because affected individuals may feel strongly attached to them but even more certainly because these interests are widely shared and are a part of many established patterns of behavior the disturbance of which would be difficult and painful. They are likely to be highly valued.

* * *

It is thus multiple memberships in potential groups based on widely held and accepted interests that serve as a balance wheel in a going political system like that of the United States. To some people this observation may appear to be a truism and to others a somewhat mystical notion. It is neither. In the first place, neglect of this function of multiple memberships in most discussions of

*Until the 1960s, most Southern black people were denied the right to vote [Editors].

organized interest groups indicates that the observation is not altogether commonplace. Secondly, the statement has no mystical quality; the effective operation of these widely held interests is to be inferred directly from verbal and other behavior in the political sphere. Without the notion of multiple memberships in potential groups it is literally impossible to account for the existence of a viable polity such as that in the United States or to develop a coherent conception of the political process. The strength of these widely held but largely unorganized interests explains the vigor with which propagandists for organized groups attempt to change other attitudes by invoking such interests. Their importance is further evidenced in the recognized function of the means of mass communication, notably the press, in reinforcing widely accepted norms of "public morality."

* * *

Thus it is only as the effects of overlapping memberships and the functions of unorganized interests and potential groups are included in the equation that it is accurate to speak of governmental activity as the product or resultant of interest group activity. As [political scientist Arthur F.] Bentley has put it:

> There are limits to the technique of the struggle, this involving also limits to the group demands, all of which is solely a matter of empirical observation. . . . Or, in other words, when the struggle proceeds too harshly at any point there will become insistent in the society a group more powerful than either of those involved which tends to suppress the extreme and annoying methods of the groups in the primary struggle. It is within the embrace of these great lines of activity that the smaller struggles proceed, and the very word struggle has meaning only with reference to its limitations.

To assert that the organization and activity of powerful interest groups constitutes a threat to representative government without measuring their relation to and effects upon the widespread potential groups is to generalize from insufficient data and upon an incomplete conception of the political process. Such an analysis would be as faulty as one that ignoring differences in national systems, predicted identical responses to a given technological change in the United States, Japan, and the Soviet Union.

E. E. Schattschneider

The Scope and Bias of the Pressure System, from *The Semisovereign People*

A Critique of Group Theories of Politics

It is extremely unlikely that the vogue of group theories of politics would have attained its present status if its basic assumptions had not been first established by some concept of economic determinism. The economic interpretation of politics has always appealed to those political philosophers who have sought a single prime mover, a sort of philosopher's stone of political science around which to organize their ideas. The search for a single, ultimate cause has something to do with the attempt to explain *everything* about politics in terms of group concepts. The logic of economic determinism is to *identify the origins of conflict and to assume the conclusion*. This kind of thought has some of the earmarks of an illusion. The somnambulatory quality of thinking in this field appears also in the tendency of research to deal only with successful pressure campaigns or the willingness of scholars to be satisfied with having placed pressure groups on the scene of the crime without following through to see if the effect can really be attributed to the cause. What makes this kind of thinking remarkable is the fact that in political contests there are as many failures as there are successes. Where in the literature of pressure politics are the failures?

Students of special-interest politics need a more sophisticated set of intellectual tools than they have developed thus far. The theoretical problem involved in the search for a single cause is that all power relations in a democracy are reciprocal. Trying to find the original cause is like trying to find the first wave of the ocean.

Can we really assume that we know all that is to be known about a conflict if we understand its *origins?* Everything we know about politics suggests that a conflict is likely to change profoundly as it becomes political. It is a rare individual who can confront his antagonists without changing his opinions to some degree. Everything changes once a conflict gets into the political arena—*who* is

Published in *Semi-Sovereign People*, 1961.

involved, *what* the conflict is about, the resources available, etc. It is extremely difficult to predict the outcome of a fight by watching its beginning because we do not even know who else is going to get into the conflict. The logical consequence of the exclusive emphasis on the determinism of the private origins of conflict is to assign zero value to the political process.

The very expression "pressure politics" invites us to misconceive the role of special-interest groups in politics. The word "pressure" implies the use of some kind of force, a form of intimidation, something other than reason and information, to induce public authorities to act against their own best judgment. In Latham's famous statement already quoted the legislature is described as a "referee" who "ratifies" and "records" the "balance of power" among the contending groups.

It is hard to imagine a more effective way of saying that Congress has no mind or force of its own or that Congress is unable to invoke new forces that might alter the equation.

Actually the outcome of political conflict is not like the "resultant" of opposing forces in physics. To assume that the forces in a political situation could be diagrammed as a physicist might diagram the resultant of opposing physical forces is to wipe the slate clean of all remote, general and public considerations for the protection of which civil societies have been instituted.

* * *

Moreover, the notion of "pressure" distorts the image of the power relations involved. *Private conflicts are taken into the public arena precisely because someone wants to make certain that the power ratio among the private interests most immediately involved shall not prevail. To treat a conflict as a mere test of the strength of the private interests is to leave out of the most significant factors.* This is so true that it might indeed be said that the only way to preserve private power ratios is to keep conflicts out of the public arena.

The assumption that it is only the "interested" who count ought to be reexamined in view of the foregoing discussion. The tendency of the literature of pressure politics has been to neglect the low-tension force of large numbers because it *assumes that the equation of forces is fixed at the outset.*

Given the assumptions made by the group theorists, the attack on the idea of the majority is completely logical. The assumption is that conflict is monopolized narrowly by the parties immediately concerned. There is no room for a majority when conflict is defined so narrowly. It is a great deficiency of the group theory that it has found no place in the political system for the majority. The force of the majority is of an entirely different order of magnitude something not to be measured by pressure-group standards.

Instead of attempting to exterminate all political forms, organizations and alignments that do not qualify as pressure groups, would it not be better to attempt to make a synthesis, covering the whole political system and finding a place for all kinds of political life?

One possible synthesis of pressure politics and party politics might be produced by *describing politics as the socialization of conflict*. That is to say, the political process is a sequence; conflicts are initiated by highly motivated, high-tension groups so directly and immediately involved that it is difficult for them to see the justice of competing claims. As long as the conflicts of these groups remain *private* (carried on in terms of economic competition, reciprocal denial of goods and services, private negotiations and bargaining, struggles for corporate control or competition for membership), no political process is initiated. Conflicts become political only when an attempt is made to involve the wider public. Pressure politics might be described as a stage in the socialization of conflict. This analysis makes pressure politics an integral part of all politics, including party politics.

One of the characteristic points of origin of pressure politics is a breakdown of the discipline of the business community. The flight to government is perpetual. Something like this is likely to happen wherever there is a point of contact between competing power systems. It is the *losers in intrabusiness conflict who seek redress from public authority. The dominant business interests resist appeals to the government.* The role of the government as the patron of the defeated private interest sheds light on its function as the critic of private power relations.

Since the contestants in private conflicts are apt to be unequal in strength, it follows that *the most powerful special interests want private settlements* because they are able to dictate the outcome as long as the conflict remains private. If A is a hundred times as strong as B he does not welcome the intervention of a third party because he expects to impose his own terms on B; he wants to isolate B. He is especially opposed to the intervention of public authority, because public authority represents the most overwhelming form of outside intervention. Thus, if $\dfrac{A}{B} = \dfrac{1}{100}$, it is obviously not to A's advantage to involve a third party a million times as strong as A and B combined. Therefore, it is the weak, not the strong, who appeal to public authority for relief. It is the weak who want to socialize conflict, i.e., to involve more and more people in the conflict until the balance of forces is changed. In the school yard it is not the bully, but the defenseless smaller boys who "tell the teacher." When the teacher intervenes the balance of power in the school yard is apt to change drastically. It is the function of public authority to *modify private power relations by enlarging the scope of conflict.* Nothing could be more mistaken than to suppose that public authority merely registers the dominance of the strong over the weak. The mere existence of public order has already ruled out a great variety of forms of private pressure. Nothing could be more confusing than to suppose that the refugees from the business community who come to Congress for relief and protection *force* Congress to do their bidding.

Evidence of the truth of this analysis may be seen in the fact that the big private interests do not necessarily win if they are involved in public conflicts with petty interests. The image of the lobbyists as primarily the agents of big business is not easy to support on the face of the record of congressional hearings, for example. The biggest corporations in the country tend to avoid the arena in which pressure groups and lobbyists fight it out before congressional committees. To describe this process exclusively in terms of an effort of business to intimidate congressmen is to misconceive what is actually going on.

It is probably a mistake to assume that pressure politics is the typical or even the most important relation between government and business. The pressure group is by no means the perfect instrument of the business community. What does big business want? The *winners* in intrabusiness strife want (1) to be let alone (they want autonomy) and (2) to preserve the solidarity of the business community. For these purposes pressure politics is not a wholly satisfactory device. The most elementary considerations of strategy call for the business community to develop some kind of common policy more broadly based than any special-interest group is likely to be.

The political influence of business depends on the kind of solidarity that, on the one hand, leads all business to rally to the support of *any* businessman in trouble with the government, and on the other hand, keeps internal business disputes out of the public arena. In this system businessmen resist the impulse to attack each other in public and discourage the efforts of individual members of the business community to take intrabusiness conflicts into politics.

The attempt to mobilize a united front of the whole business community does not resemble the classical concept of pressure politics. The logic of business politics is to keep peace within the business community by supporting as far as possible all claims that business groups make for themselves. The tendency is to support all businessmen who have conflicts with the government and support all businessmen in conflict with labor. In this way *special-interest politics can be converted into party policy.* The search is for a broad base of political mobilization grounded on the strategic need for political organization on a wider scale than is possible in the case of the historical pressure group. Once the business community begins to think in terms of a larger scale of political organization the Republican party looms large in business politics.

It is a great achievement of American democracy that business has been forced to form a political organization designed to win elections, i.e., has been forced to compete for power in the widest arena in the political system. On the other hand, *the power of the Republican party to make terms with business rests on the fact that business cannot afford to be isolated.*

The Republican party has played a major role in *the political organization of the business community*, a far greater role than many students of politics seem to have realized. The influence of business in the Republican party is great, but it is never absolute because business is remarkably dependent on the party. The business community is too small, it arouses too much antagonism, and its aims are too narrow to win the support of a popular majority. The political education of business is a function of the Republican party that can never be done so well by anyone else.

In the management of the political relations of the business community, the Republican party is much more important than any combination of pressure groups ever could be. The success of special interests in Congress is due less to the "pressure" exerted by these groups than it is due to the fact that Republican members of Congress are committed in advance to a general probusiness attitude. The notion that business groups coerce Republican congressmen into voting for their bills underestimates the whole Republican posture in American politics.

It is not easy to manage the political interests of the business community because there is a perpetual stream of losers in intrabusiness conflicts who go to the government for relief and protection. It has not been possible therefore to maintain perfect solidarity, and when solidarity is breached the government is involved almost automatically. The fact that business has not become hopelessly divided and that it has retained great influence in American politics has been due chiefly to the over-all mediating role played by the Republican party. There has never been a pressure group or a combination of pressure groups capable of performing this function.

Jonathan Rauch

The Hyperpluralism Trap

Anyone who believes Washington needs to get closer to the people ought to spend a little time with Senator Richard Lugar, the Indiana Republican. "Take a look at the people coming into my office on a normal Tuesday and Wednesday," Lugar said in a speech not long ago [1994]. "Almost every organization in our society has a national conference. The typical way of handling this is to come in on a Monday, rev up the troops, give them the bill number and send them up to the Hill. If they can't get in on Tuesday, strike again on Wednesday. I regularly have on Tuesday as many as fifteen constituent groups from Indiana, all of whom have been revved up by some skillful person to cite bills that they don't understand, have never heard of prior to that time, but with a score sheet to report back to headquarters whether I am for or against. It is so routine, it is so fierce, that at some point you [can't be] immune to it."

This is the reality of modern government. The rhetoric of modern politics, alas, is a little different. Take today's standard-issue political stem-winder, which goes something like this: "I think perhaps the most important thing that we understand here in the heartland . . . is the need to reform the political system, to reduce the influence of special interests and give more influence back to the kind of people that are in this crowd tonight by the tens of thousands." That stream of boilerplate is from Bill Clinton (from his election-night speech), but it could have come from almost any politician. It's pitched in a dominant key of political rhetoric today: *standard populism*—that is, someone has taken over the government and "we" must take it back, restore government to the people, etc. But who, exactly, are those thousands of citizens who troop weekly through Senator Lugar's suite, clutching briefing packets and waving scorecards? Standard populism says they are the "special interests," those boils on the skin of democracy, forever interposing themselves between the American people and the people's servants in Washington.

Well, fifty years ago that analysis may have been useful, but not anymore. In America today, the special interests and "the people" have become objectively indistinguishable. Groups are us. As a result, the populist impulse to blame special interests, big corporations and political careerists for our

Published in *National Journal*, March 2009.

problems—once a tonic—has become Americans' leading political narcotic. Worse, it actually abets the lobbying it so righteously denounces.

Begin with one of the best known yet most underappreciated facts of our time: over the past three or four decades we have busily organized ourselves into interest groups—lobbies, loosely speaking—at an astonishing rate. Interest groups were still fairly sparse in America until about the time of World War II. Then they started proliferating, and in the 1960s the pace of organizing picked up dramatically.

Consider, for instance, the numbers of groups listed in Gale Research's *Encyclopedia of Associations*. The listings have grown from fewer than 5,000 in 1956 to well over 20,000 today. They represent, of course, only a small fraction of America's universe of interest groups. Environmental organizations alone number an estimated 7,000, once you count local clean-up groups and the like; the Washington *Blade*'s resource directory lists more than 400 gay groups, up from 300 at the end of 1990. Between 1961 and 1982 the number of corporate offices in Washington increased tenfold. Even more dramatic was the explosion in the number of public-interest organizations and grass-roots groups. These barely existed at all before the 1960s; today they number in the tens of thousands and collect more than $4 billion per year from 40 million individuals, according to political scientist Ronald Shaiko of American University.

Well, so what? Groups do many good things—provide companionship for the like-minded, collect and disseminate information, sponsor contests, keep the catering industry solvent. Indeed, conventional political theory for much of the postwar period was dominated by a strain known as pluralism, which holds that more groups equals more representation equals better democracy. Yet pluralism missed something. It assumed that the group-forming process was self-balancing and stable, as opposed to self-feeding and unstable. Which is to say, it failed to grasp the danger of what American University political scientist James Thurber aptly calls hyperpluralism.

In economics, inflation is a gradual increase in the price level. Up to a point, if the inflation rate is stable, people can plan around it. But if the rate starts to speed up, people start expecting more inflation. They hoard goods and dump cash, driving the inflation still faster. Eventually, an invisible threshold is crossed: the inflation now feeds on its own growth and undermines the stability of the whole economic system.

What the pluralists missed is that something analogous can happen with interest groups. People see that it pays to organize into groups and angle for benefits, so they do it. But as more groups make more demands, and as even more hungry groups form to compete with all the other groups, the process begins to feed on itself and pick up momentum. At some point there might be so many groups that they choke the political system, sow contention and conflict, even erode society's governability. That's hyperpluralism. And if it is less destabilizing than hyperinflation, it may be more insidious.

The pattern is most visible in smaller social units, such as local school districts, where groups colonize the curriculum—sex education for liberals, values instruction for conservatives, recycling lessons for environmentalists, voluntary silent prayer for Christians. But even among the general population the same forces are at work. Fifty years ago the phrase "the elderly" denoted a demographic category; today, thanks largely to federal pension programs and the American Association of Retired Persons (AARP), it denotes a giant and voracious lobby. In the 1930s the government set up farm-subsidy programs, one per commodity; inevitably, lobbies sprang up to defend each program, so that today American agriculture is fundamentally a collection of interest groups. With the help of group organizers and race-based benefits, loose ethnic distinctions coalesce into hard ethnic lobbies. And so on.

Even more depressing, any attempt to fight back against the proliferating mass of subdivision is foiled by the rhetoric of standard populism and its useful stooge: the special interest. The concept of a "special interest" is at the very core of standard populism—the "them" without which there can be no "us." So widely accepted is this notion, and so useful is it in casual political speech, that most of us talk routinely about special interests without a second thought. We all feel we know a special interest when we see one, if only because it is a group of which we are not a member. Yet buried in the special interest idea is an assumption that is no longer true.

The concept of the special interest is not based on nothing. It is, rather, out of date, an increasingly empty relic of the time of machine politics and political bosses, when special interests were, quite literally, special. Simply because of who they were, they enjoyed access that was available to no one else. But the process of everyone's organizing into more and more groups can go only so far before the very idea of a special interest loses any clear meaning. At some point one must throw up one's hands and concede that the hoary dichotomy between special interests and "us" has become merely rhetoric.

According to a 1990 survey conducted for the American Society of Association Executives, seven out of ten Americans belong to at least one association, and one in four Americans belongs to four or more. Practically everyone who reads these words is a member of an interest group, probably several. Moreover, formal membership tallies omit many people whom we ordinarily think of as being represented by lobbies. For example, the powerful veterans' lobbies enroll only perhaps one-seventh of American veterans, yet the groups lobby on behalf of veterans as a class, and all 27 million veterans share in the benefits. Thus the old era of lobbying by special interests—by a well-connected, plutocratic few—is as dead now as slavery and Prohibition. We Americans have achieved the full democratization of lobbying: influence-peddling for the masses.

The appeal of standard populism today comes precisely from the phony reassurance afforded by its real message: "Other people's groups are the special interests. Less for them—more for you!" Spread that sweet manure around and the natural outgrowth is today's tendency, so evident in the Clinton style, to pander to interest groups frantically while denouncing them furiously. It is the public's style, too: sending ever more checks to the AARP and the National Rifle Association and the National Federation of Independent Business and the National Wildlife Federation and a million others, while railing against special interests. Join and join, blame and blame.

So hyperpluralism makes a hash of the usual sort of standard populist prescription, which calls for "the people" to be given more access to the system, at the expense of powerful Beltway figures who are alleged to have grown arrogant or corrupt or out of touch. Activists and reformers who think the answer to democracy's problems is more access for more of the people need to wake up. Uncontrolled access only breeds more lobbies. It is axiomatic that "the people" (whatever that now means) do not organize to seek government benefits; lobbies do. Every new door to the federal treasury is an opportunity for new groups to queue up for more goodies.

Populists resolutely refuse to confront this truth. Last year, for example, Republicans and the editors of *The Wall Street Journal* campaigned fiercely—and successfully—for new congressional rules making it easier for legislators and groups to demand that bottled-up bills be discharged from committee. The idea was to bring Congress closer to "the people" by weakening the supposedly high-handed barons who rule the Hill. But burying the Free Christmas Tree for Every American Act (or whatever) in committee—while letting members of Congress say they *would* have voted for it—was one of the few remaining ways to hold the door against hungry lobbies clamoring for gifts.

A second brand of populism, *left-populism*, is even more clueless than the standard brand, if that's possible. Many liberals believe the problem is that the wrong groups—the rich, the elites, the giant corporations, etc.—have managed to out-organize the good guys and take control of the system. One version of this model was elaborated by William Greider in his book *Who Will Tell the People*. The New Deal legacy, he writes, "rests upon an idea of interest group bargaining that has gradually been transformed into the random deal-making and permissiveness of the present. The alterations in the system are decisive and . . . the ultimate effects are anti-democratic. People with limited resources, with no real representation in the higher levels of politics, are bound to lose in this environment." So elaborate is the Washington machine of lobbyists, consultants, P.R. experts, political action committees and for-hire think tanks, says Greider, that "powerful economic interests," notably corporations and private wealth, inevitably dominate.

What's appealing about this view is the truism from which it springs: the wealthy enjoy a natural advantage in lobbying, as in almost everything else. Thus many lobbies—even liberal lobbies—are dominated by the comfortable and the wealthy. Consider the case of environmental groups. Anyone who doubts they are major players in Washington today need only look at the massive 1990 Clean Air Act, a piece of legislation that business gladly would have done without. Yet these groups are hardly battalions of the disfranchised. "Readers of *Sierra*, the magazine of the Sierra Club, have household incomes twice that of the average American," notes Senior Economist Terry L. Anderson of the Political Economy Research Center. And *The Economist* notes that "in 1993 the Nature Conservancy, with $915 million in assets, drew 73 percent of its income from rich individuals." When such groups push for emissions controls or pesticide rules, they may be reflecting the priorities of people who buy BMWs and brie more than the priorities of people who buy used Chevies and hamburger. So left-populism's claim to speak for "the people" is often suspect, to say the least.

The larger problem with left-populism, however, is its refusal to see that it is feeding the very problem it decries. Left-populism was supposed to fix the wealth-buys-power problem by organizing the politically disadvantaged into groups: unions, consumer groups, rainbow coalitions and so on. But the strategy has failed. As the left (the unions, the environmentalists) has organized ever more groups, the right (the bosses, the polluters) has followed suit. The group-forming has simply spiralled. This makes a joke of the left-populist prescription, which is to form more "citizens' groups" on the Naderite model, supposedly reinvigorating representative democracy and giving voice to the weak and the silenced. Greider proposes giving people subsidies to spend on political activism: "Giving individual citizens the capacity to deploy political money would inevitably shift power from existing structures and disperse it among the ordinary millions who now feel excluded."

Inevitably, it would do no such thing. Subsidies for activism would perforce go straight into the waiting coffers of (what else?) interest groups, new and old. That just makes matters worse, for if one side organizes more groups, the other side simply redoubles its own mobilization ad infinitum. That escalating cycle is the story of the last three decades. The only winner is the lobbying class. Curiously, then, left-populism has come to serve the very lobbying elites—the Washington lawyers and lobby shops and P.R. pros and interest group execs—whom leftists ought, by rights, to loathe.

The realization that the lobbying class is, to a large extent, both entrepreneurial and in business for itself has fed the third brand of populism, *right-populism*. In the right-populist model, self-serving political careerists have hijacked government and learned to manipulate it for profit. In refreshing contrast to the other two brands of populism, however, this one is in touch with reality. Washington *is* in business for itself, though not only for itself. Legislators and lobbies have an interest in using the tax code to please their constituents, but they also have an interest in churning the tax code to generate campaign contributions and lobbying fees. Luckily for them, those two imperatives generally coincide: the more everyone hunts for tax breaks, the more lobbying jobs there are. Right-populism has tumbled to the fact that so-called public interest and citizens' groups are no more immune to this self-serving logic of lobbying—create conflict, reap rewards—than is any other sort of professional lobby.

Yet right-populism fails to see to the bottom of the problem. It looks into the abyss but flinches. This is not to say that term limits and other procedural fine-tunes may not help; such reforms are no doubt worth trying. But even if noodling with procedures succeeded in diluting the culture of political careerism, it would help (or hurt) mainly at the margins. No, tinkering with the process isn't the answer. What we must do is go straight at the beast itself. We must attack and weaken the lobbies—that is, the *people*'s lobbies.

It sounds so simple: weaken the lobbies! Shove them aside, reclaim the government! "It's just that simple," twinkles Ross Perot. But it's not that simple. Lobbies in Washington have clout because the people who scream when "special interests" are attacked are Medicare recipients defending benefits, farmers defending price supports, small businesses defending subsidized loans, racial groups defending set-asides and so on. Inherently, challenging these groups is no one's idea of fun, which is why politicians so rarely propose to do it. The solution is to strip away lobbies' protections and let competition hammer them. In practice, that means:

Balance the federal budget. It is a hackneyed prescription, but it is the very first thing we should do to curtail the lobbies' ability to rob the future. Deficits empower lobbies by allowing them to raid the nation's scarce reserves of investment capital. Deprived of that ability, they will be forced to compete more fiercely for money, and they'll be unable to steal from the future.

Cut the lobbies' lifelines. Eliminate subsidies and programs, including tax loopholes, by the hundreds. Killing a program here or there is a loser's game; it creates a political uproar without actually making a noticeable difference. The model, rather, should be the 1986 tax reform measure, which proved that a wholesale housecleaning really is possible. Back then, tax loopholes were cleared away by the truckload. The trick was—and is—to do the job with a big package of reforms that politicians can tout back home as real change. That means ditching whole Cabinet departments and abolishing virtually all industry-specific subsidies. Then go after subsidies for the non-needy—wholesale, not retail.

*Promote domestic perestroika.** Lobbies live to lock benefits in and competition out, so government restraints on competition should be removed—not indiscriminately, but determinedly. President Carter's deregulation of transportation industries and interest rates, though imperfectly executed, were good examples. Air travel, trucking and rail shipping are cheaper *and* safer. The affected industries have been more turbulent, but that's exactly the point. Domestic competition shakes up interest groups that settle cozily into Washington.

Encourage foreign competition. This is most important of all. The forces that breed interest groups never abate, and so fighting them requires a constant counterforce. Foreign competition is such a counterforce. Protection invariably benefits the industries and groups with the sharpest lobbyists and the fattest political action committees; stripping away protection forces them to focus more on modernizing and less on lobbying.

No good deed, they say, goes unpunished. We sought to solve pressing social problems, so we gave government vast power to reassign resources. We also

---

*1980s Soviet Union program of political and economic reform [*Editors*].

sought to look out for ourselves and bring voices to all of our many natures and needs, so we built countless new groups to seek government's resources. What we did not create was a way to control the chain reaction we set off. Swarming interest groups excited government to perpetual activism, and government activism drew new groups to Washington by the thousands. Before we knew it, society itself was turning into a collection of ravenous lobbies.

Why was this not always a problem? Because there used to be control rods containing the chain reaction. Smoke-filled rooms, they were called. On Capitol Hill or in Tammany Hall, you needed to see one of about six people to have any hope of getting what you wanted, and those six people dispensed (and conserved) favors with parsimonious finesse. Seen from today's vantage, smoke-filled rooms and political machines did a creditable job of keeping a lid on the interest group frenzy—they just didn't do it particularly fairly. That's why we opened up access to anyone who wants to organize and lobby, and opened up power to subcommittee chairs and caucus heads and even junior legislators. In doing so, we abolished the venal gatekeepers. But that was only the good news. The bad news was that we also abolished the gate.

No, we shouldn't go back to smoke-filled rooms. But the way forward is harder than it ever was before. The maladies that now afflict government are ones in which the public is wholly, enthusiastically implicated. Still, there are sprigs and shoots of encouragement all around. There was the surprisingly strong presidential bid of former Senator Paul Tsongas, which built something of a constituency for straight talk. There's the rise of a school of Democrats in Congress—among them Senator Bob Kerrey and retiring Representative Tim Penny—who are willing to drag the White House toward sterner fiscal measures. There was the Clinton-led triumph of NAFTA [North American Free Trade Agreement] last year. Those developments show promise of a political movement that is counterpopulist yet also popular. Maybe—is it too much to hope?—they point beyond the desert of populism.

QUESTIONS

1. Can you think of any examples of overlapping group memberships—that is, situations where members of a group are also likely to be members of other groups that may have different public policy positions? How about an example of a new organization that had a significant impact on a recent policy debate? Can you think of instances in which, counter to Truman, a new organization surprisingly did not emerge, leaving a group unrepresented?

2. Rauch complains that interest groups slow down the policy-making process, but isn't this what the Framers of the Constitution intended? Is the interest-group system as portrayed by Rauch a danger to democracy? Or is it in fact implementing the principles implicit in the Constitution?

3. Think of two examples of recent policy debates where one side or the other attempted to socialize conflict. That is, one side sought to widen the issue, to bring in more participants, to have the debates be about a broader rather than a narrower set of concerns. Would you agree with Schattschneider that this tactic was adopted by the side that seemed to be in a weaker position?

4. Does Rauch's analysis conform or argue against Schattschneider's points about the benefits of political parties in the interest-group process?

13

Politics and Policy: How Should We Address Global Warming?

Policy analysts often make distinctions between what are called Type I and Type II errors. Type I errors occur when a problem exists and policy makers fail to respond. Type II errors occur when there is no problem, but policy makers still respond as if there were.

If ever there was a policy for which we had to have the right policy response, it would be global warming. The question is whether emissions of carbon dioxide, which result primarily from the burning of fossil fuels, are contributing to a rise in global temperature. There is little doubt the earth is warming (a conclusion not substantially affected by the 2009 controversy over leaked e-mails from climate researchers at Britain's East Anglia University, suggesting that climate scientists were suppressing dissenting scientific views and had tinkered with temperature readings to get the desired results). If human-caused (anthropogenic) global warming is real, and if the threat is as serious as some claim, failure to act could have catastrophic worldwide consequences: mass extinction, permanent expansion of deserts, massive shifts in the distribution of arable land, rising sea levels that could wipe out coastal cities. Some of the scenarios are nearly apocalyptic. And yet, if the threat is *not* so bad as claimed—if the recent increase in global temperatures is due to natural variation in climate or the result of poor measurements, or if nothing we do will have much effect on temperature change—and we still impose the sorts of draconian solutions that some insist are necessary, then we will have invested hundreds of billions of dollars, perhaps trillions, with nothing to show for it. We will be poorer, but still warmer.

The debate is acrimonious; Al Gore, who won an Academy Award for his documentary *An Inconvenient Truth* and the 2007 Nobel Peace Prize for his environmental work, declares the science "settled" and says questioning anthropogenic global warming is no different from insisting that the earth is flat. Skeptics argue that models of global climate are far too complex and poorly understood to allow accurate forecasts fifty or one hundred years into the future. A nonexpert has little chance of truly assessing the evidence, because the science is complicated and often poorly communicated. Efforts to take collective action, such as the 2009 Copenhagen Conference, have failed, mostly because of disagreements between the industrialized world and developing nations. Developing nations say it is unfair to ask them to reduce their carbon emissions (which are a byproduct of economic growth) when the wealthy nations have already benefitted from cheap energy and unrestrained carbon emissions.

In this section we offer competing perspectives on how to handle global warming. Bill McKibben, who also calls the science settled, addresses arguments against global warming. He declares that we are out of time, and that it indeed may be too late to stop significant temperature increases. He notes that it will be expensive to shift toward a green-energy economy but claims that the costs are bearable. Some of the changes, he argues, would even save money, though he concedes nobody is sure of the total costs. But, he insists, doing nothing would impose unbearable costs; he cites several potentially catastrophic consequences, including famine, wars, droughts, floods, and disease.

Bjørn Lomborg, a Danish scholar, takes a pure cost-benefit approach to the problem. He begins by dismissing the apocalyptic visions promoted by (among others) Al Gore, and claims that most of the solutions proposed will produce minimal benefit at enormous cost. Using Gore's main proposals as his examples—setting global targets for carbon dioxide emissions, raising the costs of fossil fuels—Lomborg estimates that they would cost $800 billion over the next ninety years but reduce temperatures by only a fraction of a degree over the same period. We will have spent an enormous amount of money to little avail.

Instead of forcing reductions in fossil fuel use, Lomborg urges much higher spending on research and development. Research into alternative renewable energy will produce far more benefits that setting arbitrary caps on carbon emissions.

Finally, Lomborg argues that global warming is far from the greatest threat to the globe. Millions of people die from indoor air pollution, malaria, malnutrition, and accidents. We would be better off, Lomborg argues, by spending that $800 billion on those problems.

Bill McKibben

Climate Change

"Scientists Are Divided"

No, they're not. In the early years of the global warming debate, there was great controversy over whether the planet was warming, whether humans were the cause, and whether it would be a significant problem. That debate is long since over. Although the details of future forecasts remain unclear, there's no serious question about the general shape of what's to come.

Every national academy of science, long lists of Nobel laureates, and in recent years even the science advisors of President George W. Bush have agreed that we are heating the planet. Indeed, there is a more thorough scientific process here than on almost any other issue: Two decades ago, the United Nations formed the Intergovernmental Panel on Climate Change (IPCC) and charged its scientists with synthesizing the peer-reviewed science and developing broad-based conclusions. The reports have found since 1995 that warming is dangerous and caused by humans. The panel's most recent report, in November 2007, found it is "very likely" (defined as more than 90 percent certain, or about as certain as science gets) that heat-trapping emissions from human activities have caused "most of the observed increase in global average temperatures since the mid-20th century."

If anything, many scientists now think that the IPCC has been too conservative—both because member countries must sign off on the conclusions and because there's a time lag. Its last report synthesized data from the early part of the decade, not the latest scary results, such as what we're now seeing in the Arctic.

In the summer of 2007, ice in the Arctic Ocean melted. It melts a little

Published in *Foreign Policy*, January/February 2009.

every summer, of course, but this time was different—by late September, there was 25 percent less ice than ever measured before. And it wasn't a one-time accident. By the end of the summer season in 2008, so much ice had melted that both the Northwest and Northeast passages were open. In other words, you could circumnavigate the Arctic on open water. The computer models, which are just a few years old, said this shouldn't have happened until sometime late in the 21st century. Even skeptics can't dispute such alarming events.

"We Have Time"

Wrong. Time might be the toughest part of the equation. That melting Arctic ice is unsettling not only because it proves the planet is warming rapidly, but also because it will help speed up the warming. That old white ice reflected 80 percent of incoming solar radiation back to space; the new blue water left behind absorbs 80 percent of that sunshine. The process amps up. And there are many other such feedback loops. Another occurs as northern permafrost thaws. Huge amounts of methane long trapped below the ice begin to escape into the atmosphere; methane is an even more potent greenhouse gas than carbon dioxide.

Such examples are the biggest reason why many experts are now fast-forwarding their estimates of how quickly we must shift away from fossil fuel. Indian economist Rajendra Pachauri, who accepted the 2007 Nobel Peace Prize alongside Al Gore on behalf of the IPCC, said recently that we must begin to make fundamental reforms by 2012 or watch the climate system spin out of control; NASA scientist James Hansen, who was the first to blow the whistle on climate change in the late 1980s, has said that we must stop burning coal by 2030. Period.

All of which makes the Copenhagen climate change talks that are set to take place in December 2009 more urgent than they appeared a few years ago. At issue is a seemingly small number: the level of carbon dioxide in the air. Hansen argues that 350 parts per million is the highest level we can maintain "if humanity wishes to preserve a planet similar to that on which civilization developed and to which life on Earth is adapted." But because we're already past that mark—the air outside is currently about 387 parts per million and growing by about 2 parts annually—global warming suddenly feels less like a huge problem, and more like an Oh-My-God Emergency.

"Climate Change Will Help as Many Places as It Hurts"

Wishful thinking. For a long time, the winners-and-losers calculus was pretty standard: Though climate change will cause some parts of the planet to flood or shrivel up, other frigid, rainy regions would at least get some warmer days every year. Or so the thinking went. But more recently, models have begun to show that after a certain point almost everyone on the planet will suffer. Crops might be easier to grow in some places for a few decades as the danger of frost recedes, but over time the threat of heat stress and drought will almost certainly be stronger.

A 2003 report commissioned by the Pentagon forecasts the possibility of violent storms across Europe, megadroughts across the Southwest United States and Mexico, and unpredictable monsoons causing food shortages in China. "Envision Pakistan, India, and China—all armed with nuclear weapons— skirmishing at their borders over refugees, access to shared rivers, and arable land," the report warned. Or Spain and Portugal "fighting over fishing rights— leading to conflicts at sea."

Of course, there are a few places we used to think of as possible winners— mostly the far north, where Canada and Russia could theoretically produce more grain with longer growing seasons, or perhaps explore for oil beneath the newly melted Arctic ice cap. But even those places will have to deal with expensive consequences—a real military race across the high Arctic, for instance.

Want more bad news? Here's how that Pentagon report's scenario played out: As the planet's carrying capacity shrinks, an ancient pattern of desperate, all-out wars over food, water, and energy supplies would reemerge. The report refers to the work of Harvard archaeologist Steven LeBlanc, who notes that wars over resources were the norm until about three centuries ago. When such conflicts broke out, 25 percent of a population's adult males usually died. As abrupt climate change hits home, warfare may again come to define human life. Set against that bleak backdrop, the potential upside of a few longer growing seasons in Vladivostok doesn't seem like an even trade.

"It's China's Fault"

Not so much. China is an easy target to blame for the climate crisis. In the midst of its industrial revolution, China has overtaken the United States as the world's biggest carbon dioxide producer. And everyone has read about the one-a-week pace of power plant construction there. But those numbers are misleading, and not just because a lot of that carbon dioxide was emitted to build products for the West to consume. Rather, it's because China has four times the population of the United States, and per capita is really the only way to think about these emissions. And by that standard, each Chinese person now emits just over a quarter of the carbon dioxide that each American does. Not only that, but carbon dioxide lives in the atmosphere for more than a century. China has been at it in a big way less than 20 years, so it will be many, many years before the Chinese are as responsible for global warming as Americans.

What's more, unlike many of their counterparts in the United States, Chinese officials have begun a concerted effort to reduce emissions in the midst of their country's staggering growth. China now leads the world in the deployment of renewable energy, and there's barely a car made in the United States that can meet China's much tougher fuel-economy standards.

For its part, the United States must develop a plan to cut emissions—something that has eluded Americans for the entire two-decade history of the problem. Although the U.S. Senate voted down the last such attempt, Barack Obama has promised that it will be a priority in his administration. He favors some variation of a "cap and trade" plan that would limit the total amount of carbon dioxide the United States could release, thus putting a price on what has until now been free.

Despite the rapid industrialization of countries such as China and India, and the careless neglect of rich ones such as the United States, climate change is neither any one country's fault, nor any one country's responsibility. It will require sacrifice from everyone. Just as the Chinese might have to use somewhat more expensive power to protect the global environment, Americans will have to pay some of the difference in price, even if just in technology. Call it a Marshall Plan for the environment. Such a plan makes eminent moral and practical sense and could probably be structured so as to bolster emerging green energy industries in the West. But asking Americans to pay to put up windmills in China will be a hard political sell in a country that already thinks China is prospering at its expense. It could be the biggest test of the country's political maturity in many years.

"Climate Change Is an Environmental Problem"

Not really. Environmentalists were the first to sound the alarm. But carbon dioxide is not like traditional pollution. There's no Clean Air Act that can solve it. We must make a fundamental transformation in the most important part of our economies, shifting away from fossil fuels and on to something else. That means, for the United States, it's at least as much a problem for the Commerce and Treasury departments as it is for the Environmental Protection Agency.

And because every country on Earth will have to coordinate, it's far and away the biggest foreign-policy issue we face. (You were thinking terrorism? It's hard to figure out a scenario in which Osama bin Laden destroys Western civilization. It's easy to figure out how it happens with a rising sea level and a wrecked hydrological cycle.)

Expecting the environmental movement to lead this fight is like asking the USDA to wage the war in Iraq. It's not equipped for this kind of battle. It may be ready to save Alaska's Arctic National Wildlife Refuge, which is a noble undertaking but on a far smaller scale. Unless climate change is quickly de-ghettoized, the chances of making a real difference are small.

"Solving It Will Be Painful"

It depends. What's your definition of painful? On the one hand, you're talking about transforming the backbone of the world's industrial and consumer system. That's certainly expensive. On the other hand, say you manage to convert a lot of it to solar or wind power—think of the money you'd save on fuel.

And then there's the growing realization that we don't have many other possible sources for the economic growth we'll need to pull ourselves out of our current economic crisis. Luckily, green energy should be bigger than IT and biotech combined.

Almost from the moment scientists began studying the problem of climate change, people have been trying to estimate the costs of solving it. The real answer, though, is that it's such a huge transformation that no one really knows for sure. The bottom line is, the growth rate in energy use worldwide could be cut in half during the next 15 years and the steps would, net, save more money than they cost. The IPCC included a cost estimate in its latest five-year update on climate change and looked a little further into the future. It found that an attempt to keep carbon levels below about 500 parts per million would shave a little bit off the world's economic growth—but only a little. As in, the world would have to wait until Thanksgiving 2030 to be as rich as it would have been on January 1 of that year. And in return, it would have a much-transformed energy system.

Unfortunately though, those estimates are probably too optimistic. For one thing, in the years since they were published, the science has grown darker. Deeper and quicker cuts now seem mandatory.

But so far we've just been counting the costs of fixing the system. What about the cost of doing nothing? Nicholas Stern, a renowned economist commissioned by the British government to study the question, concluded that the costs of climate change could eventually reach the combined costs of both world wars and the Great Depression. In 2003, Swiss Re, the world's biggest reinsurance company, and Harvard Medical School explained why global warming would be so expensive. It's not just the infrastructure, such as sea walls against rising oceans, for example. It's also that the increased costs of natural disasters begin to compound. The diminishing time between monster storms in places such as the U.S. Gulf Coast could eventually mean that parts of "developed countries would experience developing nation conditions for prolonged periods." Quite simply, we've already done too much damage and waited too long to have any easy options left.

"We Can Reverse Climate Change"

If only. Solving this crisis is no longer an option. Human beings have already raised the temperature of the planet about a degree Fahrenheit. When people first began to focus on global warming (which is, remember, only 20 years ago), the general consensus was that at this point we'd just be standing on the threshold of realizing its consequences—that the big changes would be a degree or two and hence several decades down the road. But scientists seem to have systematically underestimated just how delicate the balance of the planet's physical systems really is.

The warming is happening faster than we expected, and the results are more widespread and more disturbing. Even that rise of 1 degree has seriously perturbed hydrological cycles: Because warm air holds more water vapor than cold air does, both droughts and floods are increasing dramatically. Just look at the record levels of insurance payouts, for instance. Mosquitoes, able to survive in new places, are spreading more malaria and dengue. Coral reefs are dying, and so are vast stretches of forest.

None of that is going to stop, even if we do everything right from here on out. Given the time lag between when we emit carbon and when the air heats up, we're already guaranteed at least another degree of warming.

The only question now is whether we're going to hold off catastrophe. It won't be easy, because the scientific consensus calls for roughly 5 degrees more warming this century unless we do just about everything right. And if our behavior up until now is any indication, we won't.

Bjørn Lomborg

Mr. Gore, Your Solution to Global Warming Is Wrong

I. A False Choice

On a family visit to Kenya long before he became president of the United States, Barack Obama declared that he wanted to go on safari. His Kenyan half sister, Auma, chided him for being a neocolonialist.

"Why should all that land be set aside for tourists," she asked, "when it could be used for farming? These wazungu [white people] care more about one dead elephant than they do for a hundred black children." Obama had no answer to her question, he would later write in *Dreams from My Father.* Why are rich countries more concerned about poor nations' nature reserves than about farms that would ward off starvation?

The safari story calls to mind the current preoccupation with global warming in the Western world. The financial crisis notwithstanding, many people—including President Obama—believe that global warming is among the most urgent issues of our time, and that cutting CO_2 emissions is the most virtuous thing we can do about it. In fact, many say that doing so is perhaps the greatest moral obligation of the current inhabitants of planet earth. And they frame any discussion on warming by telling us that if we don't radically alter the way we live, the worst problems of humanity—chiefly disease and hunger—will become

Published in *Esquire,* August 2009.

devastatingly worse. Before long, they say—perhaps a decade if we do not act immediately—it will be too late for us.

These apocalyptic visions are not at all supported by the available evidence. And to me, the solutions prescribed by those leading the charge are akin to building more safari parks instead of farms to feed the hungry. Campaigners in rich countries are pushing politicians to spend a great fortune on an ineffective solution to climate change instead of tackling the real problems of today—or looking for better responses to warming.

President Obama and other world leaders face a clear choice. They can continue on their current path—what we might call the "Gore solution" to climate change, given that the former vice-president is the fiercest advocate of cutting CO_2 emissions, whether through a carbon tax or a cap-and-trade scheme.

Or, here's the truth: There are better, more cost-effective ways to fight global warming. And if we want to fight the problems that will be made worse by global warming, the solutions have very little to do with cutting CO_2 emissions.

II. The Real Moral Imperative

The effort to cut carbon emissions is generally cast as a moral imperative necessary to avert the human consequences of warming. In reality, however, it does very little at very high cost. It is also politically complicated, because it requires every nation on earth to agree to reduction targets and then reach them. Even if this were somehow achievable, the plan's meager effects on global temperatures are simply not worth all the pain: If we spent $800 billion over the next ninety years solely on the Gore solution of mitigating carbon emissions, we would rein in temperature increases by just 0.3 degrees by the end of this century. That was the finding reached recently by some of the world's top climate economists at a gathering called the Copenhagen Consensus, where the ramifications of this response to climate change were calculated.

In addition to calculating the effect on temperature of reducing carbon emissions, these economists calculated the environmental and humanitarian benefits that would accrue from this reduction in the rate of warming. Through models, they have estimated the benefits of a wide range of effects, from fewer heat deaths and less malaria to fewer floods and more preserved wetlands. Converting all these benefits into monetary terms—i.e., What would societies be willing to pay for such benefits?—means that we don't have to guess; we can actually compare the costs of climate policies with the benefits.

And, simply put, when we count up all the expected benefits from this ever-so-slight reduction in temperature, they are significantly less than the costs. In fact, it turns out that—at best—each dollar spent on the Gore solution would achieve just ninety cents' worth of good. And this assumes that every cent of the $800 billion is maximized. If we factor in more realistic expectations—allowing, say, for some of the money to be used in less efficient ways, as is the case with the EU's new climate policies—every dollar of the hypothetical $800 billion spent on the Gore solution to global warming could achieve as little as four cents of good.

Worse than that, it means there's much less money available to respond to the big problems facing developing countries today.

There is another way to respond to climate change. Instead of putting arbitrary, expensive caps on carbon emissions, we can and should immediately spend more money on researching and developing alternative energy. This means renewable sources of energy like wind, solar, geothermal, and wave. These are all promising but in their current forms are incredibly inefficient compared with fossil fuels. It also means developing second-generation biofuel from biomass. It also means investing in energy efficiency, fission and fusion, and carbon capture and storage. Unless we make a much bigger investment in these areas right now, fossil fuels are going to maintain their stranglehold on all the economies of the world.

Spending more on research will mean that we can shift away from carbon-heavy energy much faster. It gives us the possibility of a low-carbon, high-wealth future—something the Gore solution rules out because of its primary focus on trying to make fossil fuels more expensive. We will never succeed in making fossil fuels so expensive that they become unappealing by following the Gore approach—but we can succeed if we focus on making alternative energy sources so cheap that they become competitive.

When we calculate the costs and benefits of this alternative solution, we discover that each time we invest a dollar, we create benefits worth sixteen dollars—at least eighteen times and possibly four hundred times better than the Gore approach. This is because the money spent on research and development will make alternatives to fossil fuels cheaper sooner, and make for a genuine transition to a low-carbon future, with all its benefits accruing sooner and at lower costs.

So where does President Obama stand on the choice between these two paths? He has promised to spend $150 billion over the next decade on clean technology. This could do a lot of good, if he uses it primarily to invest in creating new technologies, rather than simply subsidizing existing ones (which is much easier politically). Investing in current-day solar panels costs a lot for little benefit. Germany is the leading consumer of solar panels and will end up spending about $150 billion on them, yet the effect will be to delay global warming by one hour by the end of the century. However, investing in the creation of an entirely new way to harness the energy of the sun that can become competitive with fossil fuels will mean that everyone, including China and India, can shift to a low-carbon economy sooner rather than later.

Unfortunately, it looks like much of the $150 billion proposed by the president will be going to the existing technologies with the loudest lobbyists. Likewise, the Obama administration seems more inclined to go for the Gore-like solution of fixing climate change through an ambitious cap-and-trade policy. This will do little for the climate, and it will cost Americans dearly.

It is a very good thing that President Obama accepts that global warming is real and man-made; his predecessor's reluctance or inability to recognize the issue was an embarrassment. However, making rational decisions on global warming has become incredibly difficult. Discussion has been warped by politics and by a polarizing, irrelevant debate between those who believe that the problem is not real and those who believe that it is the worst problem humanity has ever faced. So we must both ignore the blithe deniers of science and overthrow the regime of hysterical solutions on the other side—and consider this simple truth: For once, the sensible approach and the most moral approach are one and the same.

III. A Matter of Simple Economics

Malaria will claim more than one million lives this year. It undermines entire societies, making them less productive and even poorer. The economic toll runs to tens of billions of dollars.

Campaigners for drastic CO_2 emission cuts will tell President Obama and other world leaders that the Gore solution is especially critical because global warming will mean more malaria. In warmer, wetter conditions, mosquitoes can expand their range. Models reveal that global warming will put 3 percent more of the earth's population at risk of catching malaria by the end of the century.

But this is a perfect demonstration of the problem with the Gore solution. Even if we continued with worldwide Kyoto Protocol–style CO_2 emission cuts for the rest of this century, with its inconsequential 0.3 degree reduction in temperatures by the year 2100, we would cut the malaria risk by only 0.2 percent. On the other hand, for $3 billion—2 percent of the annual cost of the Kyoto Protocol—we could invest in mosquito nets and medicine today and cut malaria cases by half within one decade.

Put another way: Every time the Gore solution of CO_2 reduction saves one person from dying from malaria in the future, the same money could save thirty-six thousand people today.

Tell me, which approach makes the most sense?

Of course, an increase in malaria is not the only result of global warming. Malnutrition is another issue that has prompted calls for drastic CO_2 emission cuts. In isolation, global warming will probably cause the number of malnourished people to increase by twenty-eight million by the end of the century. Yet the much more important point is that there are more than nine hundred million malnourished people on earth right now.

Tackling hunger through climate-change policy would be amazingly inefficient. For $180 billion each year, Kyoto Protocol–style CO_2 emission cuts would reduce the number of hungry people globally by two million by the end of the century. Alternatively, just $10 billion spent on direct malnutrition-reduction programs would save 229 million people now.

President Obama has a stark choice to make. Whatever is spent on climate policies to save one person from hunger in one hundred years could instead save five thousand people today.

Often I hear the argument that if so little is achieved by cutting CO_2, then obviously we just need to make bigger cuts. Unfortunately, this would only transform an implausible solution into a ridiculous one. Even Kyoto was overly ambitious; by 2010, the world will probably end up implementing less than 5 percent of the originally envisioned cuts. If we decided to increase the size of the reductions tenfold, the costs would increase much more than ten times, whereas the benefits would increase much less. This is because we do not have cost-effective replacements for burning carbon. Using carbon, particularly coal, is helping lift millions of people from poverty in India and China. Massive carbon cuts just now are not a smart solution, and not at all plausible. And that is not a matter of political opinion; it is a matter of simple economics.

IV. Sometimes, We Need to Burn More Fossil Fuels

I did not always look at the world this way. There was a time when I would have eagerly climbed onto the bandwagon calling for CO_2 emission cuts.

Twenty years ago, I took it for granted that the world was in a terrible environmental state. I supported Greenpeace and lobbied my friends on environmental issues. I am from Denmark, and was particularly upset during the 1980s when our government allowed ocean die-off zones to expand because of agricultural runoff. I thought that political leaders were criminal for not prioritizing longer-term environmental concerns. Later, when I was a university lecturer, my students and I set out to counter what we believed were far-fetched arguments that global environmental conditions were actually improving.

My thinking started to change when I analyzed the data. It was clear that many things were indeed getting better, not worse. It is obvious, for instance, that air pollution in most developed countries is much better than it was thirty or forty years ago.

Another important lesson I learned was that when poor countries battle to raise their living standards, they give very little priority to environmental concerns. In these circumstances, pollution rises. But once a country achieves a certain standard of living, with their kids healthy and educated, citizens invariably begin to shift their focus toward the environment, and pollution starts to fall.

This effect is called the Kuznets curve, named after the Nobel-prize-winning [sic] economist who developed it, and it tells us that one of the pivotal things we can do to help the environment is to help poor countries get richer.

And so it is a paradox that today rich countries care more about global warming than about virtually any other global problem, whereas in the developing world, the biggest environmental challenge is simply the pollution caused by too many people trying to survive in one small space. There is a lack of public awareness of sustainable agricultural practices. There is illegal logging, soil erosion, habitat loss for animals and plants, and disruption of water flow.

When we look across poor nations, the biggest environmental issue is actually indoor air pollution. In developing countries, 2.5 billion people rely on biomass such as wood, waste, and dung to cook and keep warm. Each year, indoor air pollution kills about 1.3 million people, most of them women and children. In this case, a switch from biomass to fossil fuels would dramatically improve the lives of almost half the world's population.

There are plenty of other major global problems that have reasonably cheap solutions. One billion people lack clean drinking water. Two billion lack sanitation. Three billion lack basic micronutrients. One quarter of all deaths each year are caused by infectious diseases that we could easily combat.

The Gore solution will do nothing to reduce those stunning numbers. In fact, the Global Fund to Fight AIDS, Tuberculosis and Malaria has acknowledged that billions of dollars could potentially be redirected to global warming at the expense of diseases that are the biggest killers in poor countries.

V. The Debate Starts Now

The Copenhagen Consensus Center, which we started in 2004, put my conclusion about the Gore solution to the severest test. First, we commissioned independent research on solutions to ten of the planet's biggest challenges: problems like hunger, conflict, global warming, and barriers to education. World experts were asked to identify the best ways to spend $50 billion in their field. The findings, published in academic papers, were reviewed by a second team of specialists.

The point of the project wasn't simply to identify good ways to spend money—it was to promote prioritization between competing options. We gathered a team of the best economists in the world, including several Nobel laureates. We asked this group to consider, test, and debate all the research and identify the best and worst ways that a limited pool of money could be spent.

Economists are experts in prioritization. The massive media hype about certain problems is irrelevant to them; they focus simply on where limited funds could achieve the most good.

In 2004—and again last year, when we repeated the global project—the world's top minds did not select CO_2 emission cuts as the best use of money. In fact, both times, CO_2 emission reductions came out at the bottom of their lists. In 2008, the top priority the Nobel-laureate economists identified was providing micronutrients to developing countries.

Three billion people—about half the world's population—lack one or more micronutrients, such as vitamin A, iron, iodine, or zinc. About two billion—or almost one third of the world's population—lack iron, a deficiency that causes physical and mental impairment. On average, a person with iron deficiency is 17 percent weaker and loses 8 IQ points.

We could so easily right this wrong. At a cost of less than $400 million a year, we could permanently help almost half the world get stronger and smarter. In monetary terms, for every dollar we spend, we could do more than twenty dollars' worth of good in the world.

Interestingly, also in 2008, the assembled experts heard from a lead author for the Intergovernmental Panel on Climate Change, the very group that shared the Nobel Peace Prize with Al Gore, that the Gore approach of spending even $800 billion on carbon cuts would slow the pace of global warming—and this bears repeating—by just 0.3 degrees over the next ninety years.

It is vital that decision makers pay heed to these facts, so that better responses to global warming can be more seriously considered immediately. But the atmosphere has become one in which the "good guys" fight for more money for global warming against foes real and imagined. And this polarization stops us from seeing that we need to tackle climate change the same way that we tackle most public-policy problems—by weighing benefits and costs.

Let me offer this analogy: Just as we know that global warming is real and serious, we also know that speed kills. Globally, 1.2 million people die in traffic accidents and 50 million are injured every year. By 2020, the World Health Organization estimates that traffic deaths will be the second-biggest killer in the world. About 90 percent of traffic deaths occur in Third World countries. Politicians could instantly save all these lives and eliminate $500 billion worth of damage by simply lowering global speed limits to five miles per hour. Of course, that won't happen, because the benefits from driving moderately fast vastly outweigh the costs. Traffic interconnects our societies, brings people together, and delivers goods at competitive prices to wherever we happen to live. A world trudging along at five miles per hour is a world gone medieval.

Just like traffic fatalities, global warming is caused by man. Just like traffic fatalities, we have the technology to effectively eliminate the problem—in this case by making massive cuts in CO_2 emissions. But this is not sensible. The benefits from moderate use of fossil fuels vastly outweigh the costs. Fossil fuels give us low-cost light, heat, food, communication, and travel. We can eat fruits and vegetables year-round, and air-conditioning means that people in the United States no longer die in droves during heat waves. Communication and cheap flights give ever more people the opportunity to experience other cultures and forge global friendships. Carbon has powered growth in China and India, allowing millions of workers to escape poverty.

To stretch the traffic analogy slightly further: We don't ignore the impact of speed, nor should we disregard global warming. Countries set speed limits at a sensible level. We should do the same thing with taxes on CO_2 emissions. When it comes to reducing carbon emissions, President Obama should talk realistically about setting a price on carbon that reflects its damage. Economic estimates show that the cost is about seven dollars per ton of CO_2—or about six cents on the gallon of gas. Yet, though such a tax can be used to raise funds to tackle global warming smartly, we should not have any illusions that it will in itself reduce global warming. As we have shown above, it will have virtually no impact, even a hundred years from now.

Underlying these economic arguments is a basic moral one: With limited resources, carbon cuts shouldn't be our top priority. I hope that President Obama will not be swayed by the loud, well-meaning, but mistaken appeals from climate-change activists, and instead identify the obvious areas that need more urgent attention. It would be grossly immoral to knowingly squander colossal sums of money achieving almost nothing, while comparatively tiny sums could save millions of lives right now.

But the United States should not go it alone. Every country should agree to spend 0.05 percent of its GDP on low-carbon energy R&D. The total global cost would be ten times greater than current spending on this research, yet ten times less than the cost of the Kyoto Protocol. Such an agreement could be the new Kyoto treaty for the world—only this protocol would actually make a difference.

President Obama stands at the juncture of two very different paths. One would be enormously expensive and is destined to end in failure. The other would recapture a vision that has become lost amid pessimistic, alarmist rhetoric: that of a world that is both low-carbon and high-income. Debate about the science is over.

But the debate over a sensible solution starts now.

QUESTIONS

1. "I'll believe it's a crisis when the people who say it's a crisis act as if it's a crisis. Al Gore tells us that we have to drastically cut our energy use, but he flies around the world in a private jet and has a mansion 10 times the size of the average American house. He's a hypocrite, and he's not the only one." Is this a valid argument? Can we draw any inferences about the nature of the evidence from the behavior of global warming proponents? What if the proponents of curbing global warming would benefit from the policies that they are urging, such as carbon offsets or particular technologies in which they have a stake?

2. What level of certainty should be required before major international action is taken? Is it enough to be 75 percent sure that anthropogenic global warming is real? 80 percent? 95 percent? Is there a way to assess these uncertainties reasonably? Or is too much at stake?

3. Is Lomborg right that global warming must be addressed in the context of other issues of global health and safety? Where would you rank global warming on the list of most important problems?

4. What is your view of global warming? How did you come to your view? How well do you think you understand the science? How certain are you that you are right? What would change your mind?

14

Government and the Economy: Bailing Out Wall Street

The economic meltdown of 2008–2009 resulted in the deepest economic recession since the Great Depression. As the housing market collapsed, financial mainstays such as Bear Stearns, Lehman Brothers, Merrill Lynch, Washington Mutual, and Wachovia went bankrupt or were acquired in fire sales by other institutions. Other troubled institutions such as American International Group (AIG), which was at the center of the financial crisis, and the mortgage-lending giants Fannie Mae and Freddie Mac were deemed "too big to fail" and were essentially taken over by the federal government. Stock markets collapsed and the United States and European banks lost more than $1 trillion on toxic assets from the subprime mortgage market and from other bad loans. Since peaking in the second quarter of 2007, household wealth in the United States was down a staggering $14 trillion due to a 25-percent plunge in the value of homes, as well as shrunken savings and retirement accounts.

In the face of this economic crisis, Congress, the Federal Reserve, and the U.S. Treasury took unprecedented actions to shore up the financial system. Congress created the Troubled Asset Relief Program (TARP), which authorized the Treasury to invest $700 billion to shore up the financial system. The Federal Reserve (the Fed) intervened in the short-term "commercial paper" market (which supplies short-term loans to businesses), shored up money market funds, and provided emergency loans to troubled banks. Was this unprecedented set of measures necessary to thaw out the frozen credit markets and get the financial system working again? Or was it a "bailout hustle" that rewarded Wall Street insiders' risky behavior?

Matt Taibbi is clearly outraged at what he sees as the unjustified bailout of Wall Street. Especially galling were the $16.2 billion in salaries and bonuses that Goldman Sachs employees received in 2009 (and the $140 billion for executive compensation at the nation's six largest banks) as the rest of the country was just starting to climb out of the recession and nearly 10 percent of Americans remained unemployed. Taibbi sees this compensation as troubling because it would not have been possible without the help of the federal government. Even worse, financial institutions seem not to have learned from the experience of 2008–2009 and have gone right back to their same risky behavior. Taibbi compares the Wall Street bailout with con men's old-fashioned hustles with colorful names such as the "swoop and squat" and the "pig in the poke." The clear winners of this hustle are the big financial institutions of Wall Street. The bag holders are the American taxpayers and the little investors.

Treasury Secretary Timothy Geithner obviously has a different take on the situation. In his testimony before the Congressional Oversight Panel that monitors the expenditure of the TARP funds, Geithner had an upbeat assessment of the impact that the government's actions had on averting a worse economic crisis. Geithner is in a difficult spot because the main success is something that *didn't* happen: as bad as things got in 2008–2009, it could have been much worse if more financial institutions had been allowed to fail. Geithner makes two central points: first, the programs worked just as expected to stabilize financial markets and promote economic growth. Second, TARP will cost the taxpayers far less than the $700 billion that was authorized. As of the Treasury's last statement in November 2010, only $389 billion had been paid out and nearly all of that money will be recovered. Some of the Fed's programs, such as the rescue of money market funds, have actually turned a profit. Although Geithner does not directly address some of Taibbi's criticisms, his response in part would be, "Yes, the banks came out very nicely after all of our initiatives. *That was the point—to stabilize the financial sector.*"

Matt Taibbi

Wall Street's Bailout Hustle

On January 21st, Lloyd Blankfein left a peculiar voicemail message on the work phones of his employees at Goldman Sachs. * * * In his message, Blankfein addressed his plan to pay out gigantic year-end bonuses amid widespread controversy over Goldman's role in precipitating the global financial crisis.

The bank had already set aside a tidy $16.2 billion for salaries and bonuses—meaning that Goldman employees were each set to take home an average of $498,246, a number roughly commensurate with what they received during the bubble years. Still, the troops were worried: There were rumors that Dr. [Blankfein], bowing to political pressure, might be forced to scale the number back. After all, the country was broke, 14.8 million Americans were stranded on the unemployment line, and Barack Obama and the Democrats were trying to recover the populist high ground after their whipping in Massachusetts by calling for a "bailout tax" on banks. Maybe this wasn't the right time for Goldman to be throwing its annual Roman bonus orgy.

Not to worry, Blankfein reassured employees. "In a year that proved to have no shortage of story lines," he said, "I believe very strongly that performance is the ultimate narrative."

Translation: We made a s***load of money last year because we're so amazing at our jobs, so f*** all those people who want us to reduce our bonuses.

Goldman wasn't alone. The nation's six largest banks—all committed to this balls-out, I drink your milkshake! strategy of flagrantly gorging themselves as America goes hungry—set aside a whopping $140 billion for executive compensation last year, a sum only slightly less than the $164 billion they paid themselves in the pre-crash year of 2007. In a gesture of self-sacrifice, Blankfein himself took a humiliatingly low bonus of $9 million, less than the 2009 pay of elephantine New York Knicks washout Eddy Curry. But in reality, not much had changed. "What is the state of our moral being when Lloyd Blankfein taking a $9 million bonus is viewed as this great act of contrition, when every penny of it was a direct transfer from the taxpayer?" asks Eliot Spitzer, who

Published in *Rolling Stone*, March 2010.

tried to hold Wall Street accountable during his own ill-fated stint as governor of New York.

Beyond a few such bleats of outrage, however, the huge payout was met, by and large, with a collective sigh of resignation. Because beneath America's populist veneer, on a more subtle strata of the national psyche, there remains a strong temptation to not really give a s***. The rich, after all, have always made way too much money; what's the difference if some fat cat in New York pockets $20 million instead of $10 million?

The only reason such apathy exists, however, is because there's still a widespread misunderstanding of how exactly Wall Street "earns" its money, with emphasis on the quotation marks around "earns." The question everyone should be asking, as one bailout recipient after another posts massive profits—Goldman reported $13.4 billion in profits last year, after paying out that $16.2 billion in bonuses and compensation—is this: In an economy as horrible as ours, with every factory town between New York and Los Angeles looking like those hollowed-out ghost ships we see on History Channel documentaries like *Shipwrecks of the Great Lakes*, where in the hell did Wall Street's eye-popping profits come from, exactly? Did Goldman go from bailout city to $13.4 billion in the black because, as Blankfein suggests, its "performance" was just that awesome? A year and a half after they were minutes away from bankruptcy, how are these ***holes not only back on their feet again, but hauling in bonuses at the same rate they were during the bubble?

The answer to that question is basically twofold: They raped the taxpayer, and they raped their clients.

The bottom line is that banks like Goldman have learned absolutely nothing from the global economic meltdown. In fact, they're back conniving and playing speculative long shots in force—only this time with the full financial support of the U.S. government. In the process, they're rapidly re-creating the conditions for another crash, with the same actors once again playing the same crazy games of financial chicken with the same toxic assets as before.

That's why this bonus business isn't merely a matter of getting upset whether or not Lloyd Blankfein buys himself one tropical island or two on his next birthday. The reality is that the post-bailout era in which Goldman thrived has turned out to be a chaotic frenzy of high-stakes con-artistry, with taxpayers and clients bilked out of billions using a dizzying array of old-school hustles that, but for their ponderous complexity, would have fit well in slick grifter movies like *The Sting* and *Matchstick Men*. There's even a term in con-man lingo for what some of the banks are doing right now, with all their cosmetic gestures of scaling back bonuses and giving to charities. In the grifter world, calming down a mark so he doesn't call the cops is known as the "Cool Off."

To appreciate how all of these (sometimes brilliant) schemes work is to understand the difference between earning money and taking scores, and to realize that the profits these banks are posting don't so much represent national growth and recovery, but something closer to the losses one would report after a theft or a car crash. Many Americans instinctively understand this to be true. * * * In that spirit, a brief history of the best 18 months of grifting this country has ever seen:

Con #1: The Swoop and Squat

By now, most people who have followed the financial crisis know that the bailout of AIG was actually a bailout of AIG's "counterparties"—the big banks like Goldman to whom the insurance giant owed billions when it went belly up.

What is less understood is that the bailout of AIG counterparties like Goldman and Société Générale, a French bank, actually began before the collapse of AIG, before the Federal Reserve paid them so much as a dollar. Nor is it understood that these counterparties actually accelerated the wreck of AIG in what was, ironically, something very like the old insurance scam known as "Swoop and Squat," in which a target car is trapped between two perpetrator vehicles and wrecked, with the mark in the game being the target's insurance company—in this case, the government.

This may sound far-fetched, but the financial crisis of 2008 was very much caused by a perverse series of legal incentives that often made failed investments worth more than thriving ones. Our economy was like a town where everyone has juicy insurance policies on their neighbors' cars and houses. In such a town, the driving will be suspiciously bad, and there will be a lot of fires.

AIG was the ultimate example of this dynamic. At the height of the housing boom, Goldman was selling billions in bundled mortgage-backed securities—often toxic crap of the no-money-down, no-identification-needed variety of home loan—to various institutional suckers like pensions and insurance companies, who frequently thought they were buying investment-grade instruments. At the same time, in a glaring example of the perverse incentives that existed and still exist, Goldman was also betting against those same sorts of securities—a practice that one government investigator compared to "selling a car with faulty brakes and then buying an insurance policy on the buyer of those cars."

Goldman often "insured" some of this garbage with AIG, using a virtually unregulated form of pseudoinsurance called credit-default swaps. Thanks in large part to deregulation pushed by Bob Rubin, former chairman of Goldman, and Treasury secretary under Bill Clinton, AIG wasn't required to actually have the capital to pay off the deals. As a result, banks like Goldman bought more than $440 billion worth of this bogus insurance from AIG, a huge blind bet that the taxpayer ended up having to eat.

Thus, when the housing bubble went crazy, Goldman made money coming and going. They made money selling the crap mortgages, and they made money by collecting on the bogus insurance from AIG when the crap mortgages flopped.

Still, the trick for Goldman was: how to collect the insurance money. As AIG headed into a tailspin that fateful summer of 2008, it looked like the beleaguered firm wasn't going to have the money to pay off the bogus insurance. So Goldman and other banks began demanding that AIG provide them with cash collateral. In the 15 months leading up to the collapse of AIG, Goldman received $5.9 billion in collateral. Société Générale, a bank holding lots of mortgage-backed crap originally underwritten by Goldman, received $5.5 billion. These collateral demands squeezing AIG from two sides were the "Swoop and Squat" that ultimately crashed the firm. "It put the company into a liquidity crisis," says Eric Dinallo, who was intimately involved in the AIG bailout as head of the New York State Insurance Department.

It was a brilliant move. When a company like AIG is about to die, it isn't supposed to hand over big hunks of assets to a single creditor like Goldman; it's supposed to equitably distribute whatever assets it has left among all its creditors. Had AIG gone bankrupt, Goldman would have likely lost much of the $5.9 billion that it pocketed as collateral. "Any bankruptcy court that saw those collateral payments would have declined that transaction as a fraudulent conveyance," says Barry Ritholtz, the author of *Bailout Nation*. Instead, Goldman and the other counterparties got their money out in advance—putting a torch to what was left of AIG. Fans of the movie *Goodfellas* will recall Henry Hill and Tommy DeVito taking the same approach to the Bamboo Lounge nightclub they'd been gouging. Roll the Ray Liotta narration: "Finally, when there's nothing left, when you can't borrow another buck . . . you bust the joint out. You light a match."

And why not? After all, according to the terms of the bailout deal struck when AIG was taken over by the state in September 2008, Goldman was paid 100 cents on the dollar on an additional $12.9 billion it was owed by AIG—again, money it almost certainly would not have seen a fraction of had AIG proceeded to a normal bankruptcy. Along with the collateral it pocketed, that's $19 billion in pure cash that Goldman would not have "earned" without massive state intervention. How's that $13.4 billion in 2009 profits looking now? And that doesn't even include the direct bailouts of Goldman Sachs and other big banks, which began in earnest after the collapse of AIG.

Con #2: The Dollar Store

In the usual "Dollar Store" or "Big Store" scam—popularized in movies like *The Sting*—a huge cast of con artists is hired to create a whole fake environment into which the unsuspecting mark walks and gets robbed over and over again. A warehouse is converted into a makeshift casino or off-track betting parlor, the fool walks in with money, leaves without it.

The two key elements to the Dollar Store scam are the whiz-bang theatrical redecorating job and the fact that everyone is in on it except the mark. In this case, a pair of investment banks were dressed up to look like commercial banks overnight, and it was the taxpayer who walked in and lost his shirt, confused by the appearance of what looked like real Federal Reserve officials minding the store.

Less than a week after the AIG bailout, Goldman and another investment bank, Morgan Stanley, applied for, and received, federal permission to become bank holding companies—a move that would make them eligible for much greater federal support. The stock prices of both firms were cratering, and there was talk that either or both might go the way of Lehman Brothers, another once-mighty investment bank that just a week earlier had disappeared from the face of the earth under the weight of its toxic assets. By law, a five-day waiting period was required for such a conversion—but the two banks got them overnight, with final approval actually coming only five days after the AIG bailout.

Why did they need those federal bank charters? This question is the key to understanding the entire bailout era—because this Dollar Store scam was the big one. Institutions that were, in reality, high-risk gambling houses were al-lowed to masquerade as conservative commercial banks. As a result of this new designation, they were given access to a virtually endless tap of "free money" by unsuspecting taxpayers. The $10 billion that Goldman received under the better-known TARP bailout was chump change in comparison to the smorgas-bord of direct and indirect aid it qualified for as a commercial bank.

When Goldman Sachs and Morgan Stanley got their federal bank charters, they joined Bank of America, Citigroup, J. P. Morgan Chase and the other banking titans who could go to the Fed and borrow massive amounts of money at interest rates that, thanks to the aggressive rate-cutting policies of Fed chief Ben Bernanke during the crisis, soon sank to zero percent. The ability to go to the Fed and borrow big at next to no interest was what saved Goldman, Mor-gan Stanley and other banks from death in the fall of 2008. "They had no other way to raise capital at that moment, meaning they were on the brink of insolvency," says Nomi Prins, a former managing director at Goldman Sachs. "The Fed was the only shot."

In fact, the Fed became not just a source of emergency borrowing that en-abled Goldman and Morgan Stanley to stave off disaster—it became a source of long-term guaranteed income. Borrowing at zero percent interest, banks like Goldman now had virtually infinite ways to make money. In one of the most common maneuvers, they simply took the money they borrowed from the government at zero percent and lent it back to the government by buying Trea-sury bills that paid interest of three or four percent. It was basically a license to print money—no different than attaching an ATM to the side of the Federal Reserve.

"You're borrowing at zero, putting it out there at two or three percent, with hundreds of billions of dollars—man, you can make a lot of money that way," says the manager of one prominent hedge fund. "It's free money."

Which goes a long way to explaining Goldman's enormous profits last year. But all that free money was amplified by another scam:

Con #3: The Pig in the Poke

At one point or another, pretty much everyone who takes drugs has been burned by this one, also known as the "Rocks in the Box" scam or, in its more elaborate variations, the "Jamaican Switch." Someone sells you what looks like an eightball of coke in a baggie, you get home and, you dumbass, it's baby powder.

The scam's name comes from the Middle Ages, when some fool would be sold a bound and gagged pig that he would see being put into a bag; he'd miss the switch, then get home and find a tied-up cat in there instead. Hence the expression "Don't let the cat out of the bag."

The "Pig in the Poke" scam is another key to the entire bailout era. After the crash of the housing bubble—the largest asset bubble in history—the economy was suddenly flooded with securities backed by failing or near-failing home loans. In the cleanup phase after that bubble burst, the whole game was to get taxpayers, clients and shareholders to buy these worthless cats, but at pig prices.

One of the first times we saw the scam appear was in September 2008, right around the time that AIG was imploding. That was when the Fed changed some of its collateral rules, meaning banks that could once borrow only against sound collateral, like Treasury bills or AAA-rated corporate bonds, could now borrow against pretty much anything—including some of the mortgage-backed sewage that got us into this mess in the first place. In other words, banks that once had to show a real pig to borrow from the Fed could now show up with a cat and get pig money. "All of a sudden, banks were allowed to post absolute s*** to the Fed's balance sheet," says the manager of the prominent hedge fund.

The Fed spelled it out on September 14th, 2008, when it changed the collateral rules for one of its first bailout facilities—the Primary Dealer Credit Facility, or PDCF. The Fed's own write-up described the changes: "With the Fed's action, all the kinds of collateral then in use . . . including non-investment-grade securities and equities . . . became eligible for pledge in the PDCF."

Translation: We now accept cats.

The Pig in the Poke also came into play in April of last year, when Congress pushed a little-known agency called the Financial Accounting Standards Board, or FASB, to change the so-called "mark-to-market" accounting rules. Until this rule change, banks had to assign a real-market price to all of their assets. If they had a balance sheet full of securities they had bought at $3 that were now only worth $1, they had to figure their year-end accounting using that $1 value. In other words, if you were the dope who bought a cat instead of a pig, you couldn't invite your shareholders to a slate of pork dinners come year-end accounting time.

But last April, FASB changed all that. From now on, it announced, banks could avoid reporting losses on some of their crappy cat investments simply by declaring that they would "more likely than not" hold on to them until they recovered their pig value. In short, the banks didn't even have to actually hold on to the toxic s*** they owned—they just had to sort of promise to hold on to it.

That's why the "profit" numbers of a lot of these banks are really a joke. In many cases, we have absolutely no idea how many cats are in their proverbial bag. What they call "profits" might really be profits, only minus undeclared millions or billions in losses.

"They're hiding all this stuff from their shareholders," says Ritholtz, who was disgusted that the banks lobbied for the rule changes. "Now, suddenly banks that were happy to mark to market on the way up don't have to mark to market on the way down."

Con #4: The Rumanian Box

One of the great innovations of Victor Lustig, the legendary Depression-era con man who wrote the famous "Ten Commandments for Con Men," was a thing called the "Rumanian Box." This was a little machine that a mark would put a blank piece of paper into, only to see real currency come out the other side. The brilliant Lustig sold this Rumanian Box over and over again for vast sums—but he's been outdone by the modern barons of Wall Street, who managed to get themselves a real Rumanian Box.

How they accomplished this is a story that by itself highlights the challenge of placing this era in any kind of historical context of known financial crime. What the banks did was something that was never—and never could have been—thought of before. They took so much money from the government, and then did so little with it, that the state was forced to start printing new cash to throw at them. Even the great Lustig in his wildest, horniest dreams could never have dreamed up this one.

The setup: By early 2009, the banks had already replenished themselves with billions if not trillions in bailout money. It wasn't just the $700 billion in TARP cash, the free money provided by the Fed, and the untold losses obscured by accounting tricks. Another new rule allowed banks to collect interest on the cash they were required by law to keep in reserve accounts at the

Fed—meaning the state was now compensating the banks simply for guaranteeing their own solvency. And a new federal operation called the Temporary Liquidity Guarantee Program let insolvent and near-insolvent banks dispense with their deservedly ruined credit profiles and borrow on a clean slate, with FDIC backing. Goldman borrowed $29 billion on the government's good name, J. P. Morgan Chase $38 billion, and Bank of America $44 billion. "TLGP," says Prins, the former Goldman manager, "was a big one."

Collectively, all this largesse was worth trillions. The idea behind the flood of money, from the government's standpoint, was to spark a national recovery: We refill the banks' balance sheets, and they, in turn, start to lend money again, recharging the economy and producing jobs. "The banks were fast approaching insolvency," says Rep. Paul Kanjorski, a vocal critic of Wall Street who nevertheless defends the initial decision to bail out the banks. "It was vitally important that we recapitalize these institutions."

But here's the thing. Despite all these trillions in government rescues, despite the Fed slashing interest rates down to nothing and showering the banks with mountains of guarantees, Goldman and its friends had still not jump-started lending again by the first quarter of 2009. That's where those [bonuses] of Lloyd Blankfein came into play, as Goldman and other banks basically threatened to pick up their bailout billions and go home if the government didn't fork over more cash—a lot more. "Even if the Fed could make interest rates negative, that wouldn't necessarily help," warned Goldman's chief domestic economist, Jan Hatzius. "We're in a deep recession mainly because the private sector, for a variety of reasons, has decided to save a lot more."

Translation: You can lower interest rates all you want, but we're still not f****** lending the bailout money to anyone in this economy. Until the government agreed to hand over even more goodies, the banks opted to join the rest of the "private sector" and "save" the taxpayer aid they had received—in the form of bonuses and compensation.

The ploy worked. In March of last year, the Fed sharply expanded a radical new program called quantitative easing, which effectively operated as a real-live Rumanian Box. The government put stacks of paper in one side, and out came $1.2 trillion "real" dollars.

The government used some of that freshly printed money to prop itself up by purchasing Treasury bonds—a desperation move, since Washington's demand for cash was so great post-Clusterf*** '08 that even the Chinese couldn't buy U.S. debt fast enough to keep America afloat. But the Fed used most of the new cash to buy mortgage-backed securities in an effort to spur home lending—instantly creating a massive market for major banks.

And what did the banks do with the proceeds? Among other things, they bought Treasury bonds, essentially lending the money back to the government, at interest. The money that came out of the magic Rumanian Box went from the government back to the government, with Wall Street stepping into the circle just long enough to get paid. And once quantitative easing ends, as it is scheduled to do in March, the flow of money for home loans will once again grind to a halt. The Mortgage Bankers Association expects the number of new residential mortgages to plunge by 40 percent this year.

Con #5: The Big Mitt

All of that Rumanian Box paper was made even more valuable by running it through the next stage of the grift. Michael Masters, one of the country's leading experts on commodities trading, compares this part of the scam to the poker game in the Bill Murray comedy *Stripes*. "It's like that scene where John Candy leans over to the guy who's new at poker and says, 'Let me see your cards,' then starts giving him advice," Masters says. "He looks at the hand, and the guy has bad cards, and he's like, 'Bluff me, come on! If it were me, I'd bet everything!' That's what it's like. It's like they're looking at your cards as they give you advice."

In more ways than one can count, the economy in the bailout era turned into a "Big Mitt," the con man's name for a rigged poker game. Everybody was indeed looking at everyone else's cards, in many cases with state sanction. Only taxpayers and clients were left out of the loop.

At the same time the Fed and the Treasury were making massive, earth-shaking moves like quantitative easing and TARP, they were also consulting regularly with private advisory boards that include every major player on Wall Street. The Treasury Borrowing Advisory Committee has a J.P. Morgan executive as its chairman and a Goldman executive as its vice chairman, while the board advising the Fed includes bankers from Capital One and Bank of New York Mellon. That means that, in addition to getting great gobs of free money, the banks were also getting clear signals about when they were getting that money, making it possible to position themselves to make the appropriate investments.

One of the best examples of the banks blatantly gambling, and winning, on government moves was the Public-Private Investment Program, or PPIP. In this bizarre scheme cooked up by goofball-geek Treasury Secretary Tim Geithner, the government loaned money to hedge funds and other private investors to buy up the absolutely most toxic horses*** on the market—the same kind of high-risk, high-yield mortgages that were most responsible for triggering the financial chain reaction in the fall of 2008. These satanic deals were the basic currency of the bubble: Jobless dope fiends bought houses with no money down, and the big banks wrapped those mortgages into securities and then sold them off to pensions and other suckers as investment-grade deals. The whole point of the PPIP was to get private investors to relieve the banks of these dangerous assets before they hurt any more innocent bystanders.

But what did the banks do instead, once they got wind of the PPIP? They started buying that worthless crap again, presumably to sell back to the government at inflated prices! In the third quarter of last year, Goldman, Morgan Stanley, Citigroup and Bank of America combined to add $3.36 billion of exactly this horses*** to their balance sheets.

This brazen decision to gouge the taxpayer startled even hardened market observers. According to Michael Schlachter of the investment firm Wilshire Associates, it was "absolutely ridiculous" that the banks that were supposed to be reducing their exposure to these volatile instruments were instead loading up on them in order to make a quick buck. "Some of them created this mess," he said, "and they are making a killing undoing it."

* * *

Con artists have a word for the inability of their victims to accept that they've been scammed. They call it the "True Believer Syndrome." That's sort of where we are, in a state of nagging disbelief about the real problem on Wall Street. It isn't so much that we have inadequate rules or incompetent regulators, although both of these things are certainly true. The real problem is that it doesn't matter what regulations are in place if the people running the economy are rip-off artists. The system assumes a certain minimum level of ethical behavior and civic instinct over and above what is spelled out by the regulations. If those ethics are absent—well, this thing isn't going to work, no matter what we do. Sure, mugging old ladies is against the law, but it's also easy. To prevent it, we depend, for the most part, not on cops but on people making the conscious decision not to do it.

That's why the biggest gift the bankers got in the bailout was not fiscal but psychological. "The most valuable part of the bailout," says Rep. Sherman, "was the implicit guarantee that they're Too Big to Fail." Instead of liquidating and prosecuting the insolvent institutions that took us all down with them in a giant Ponzi scheme, we have showered them with money and guarantees and all sorts of other enabling gestures. And what should really freak everyone out is the fact that Wall Street immediately started skimming off its own rescue money. If the bailouts validated anew the crooked psychology of the bubble, the recent profit and bonus numbers show that the same psychology is back, thriving, and looking for new disasters to create. "It's evidence," says Rep. Kanjorski, "that they still don't get it."

More to the point, the fact that we haven't done much of anything to change the rules and behavior of Wall Street shows that we still don't get it. Instituting a bailout policy that stressed recapitalizing bad banks was like the addict coming back to the con man to get his lost money back. Ask yourself how well that ever works out. And then get ready for the reload.

Timothy F. Geithner

Written Testimony before the Congressional Oversight Panel

Introduction

Chair Warren, Representative Hensarling, and members Neiman, Silvers and Atkins, thank you for the opportunity to testify before you again.

Since I last appeared before this panel, U.S. financial and economic conditions have continued to improve. Borrowing costs have fallen, and businesses have raised substantial capital from private sources. The contraction in bank lending has moderated. Residential mortgage lending by banks actually expanded last month. The economy started growing again in the third quarter, a trend that private economists predict will continue. And the pace of deterioration in the labor market has moderated.

These improvements are remarkable. One year ago, we faced one of the most severe financial crises of the past century, and the economy was contracting sharply. Fear of a possible depression froze markets and spurred businesses to lay off workers and pull back from investment.

A coordinated government response turned this around. Action taken last fall by the Department of the Treasury, the Federal Reserve, the FDIC, and other government agencies averted a catastrophic collapse of our financial system. As your latest report states, the Troubled Asset Relief Program (TARP), which was established by Congress in the Emergency Economic Stabilization Act of 2008 (EESA), played a significant role in that success. But when the Obama Administration took office, the financial system was still extremely fragile, and the economy was shrinking rapidly. The Administration swiftly initiated financial and fiscal policies to address both challenges. In particular, the Financial Stability Plan helped to shore up confidence in our financial institutions and markets, while mobilizing private capital. The Administration also redirected public support from large financial institutions to households, small banks, and small businesses.

As a result of these policies, confidence in our financial system has improved, credit is flowing, and the economy is growing. Moreover, the government is exiting from its emergency financial policies and taxpayers are being repaid. Indeed, the ultimate cost of those policies is likely to be significantly lower than previously expected. In particular, while EESA provided the Secretary of the Treasury with the authority to invest $700 billion, it is clear today that TARP will not cost taxpayers $700 billion. Banks have already repaid nearly half of TARP funds they received over the past year, and we now expect a positive return from the government's investments in banks. We also plan to use significantly less than the full $700 billion in EESA authority. As a result, we now expect that TARP will cost taxpayers at least $200 billion less than was projected in the August Mid-Session Review of the President's Budget.

This week, Treasury published the first annual financial statements for the Office of Financial Stability, which implements TARP. Audited by the GAO, these statements discuss the impact of the program and provide cost estimates for it. Today, I will provide highlights from these statements.

I will also discuss the significant financial and economic challenges that remain and what the Administration is doing to address them. We need to continue to find ways to help mitigate foreclosures for responsible homeowners and to get credit to small businesses. We also must maintain the capacity to address potential threats to our financial system, which could undermine the recovery we have seen to date. Further, we need to reform our laws to provide stronger, more effective regulation of our financial system and to protect consumers. Doing so will decrease the need for future intervention.

In this context, I will lay out an exit strategy for TARP. There are four broad elements to that strategy:

1. terminating and winding down programs that have supported large financial institutions;
2. limiting new investments to housing, small business, and securitization markets that facilitate consumer and small business loans;
3. maintaining the capacity to respond to potential financial threats; and
4. continuing to manage equity investments acquired through TARP in a commercial manner, while protecting taxpayers and unwinding those investments as soon as practicable.

Extending TARP authority is necessary for this strategy to succeed. Therefore, earlier this week I extended that authority until October 3, 2010. While we work to return taxpayer dollars, this Administration will not waver in its commitment to preserve the stability of our financial system and to help restore economic opportunity for American families and small businesses.

TARP Performance

The primary purpose of TARP was to restore the liquidity and stability of our financial system. That system plays a critical role in our economy, for example, by helping businesses raise funds and pay employees, providing consumers with convenient forms of credit, financing education, and allowing millions of Americans to own homes. The success or failure of TARP must be evaluated first and foremost on whether it has achieved that primary purpose.

Second, EESA required that TARP be used in a manner that maximized overall returns to taxpayers, while preserving home ownership and promoting jobs and economic growth.

As I will discuss, TARP has been successful by each measure, although challenges remain that require us to refocus initiatives, particularly toward mitigating foreclosure and getting credit to small businesses.

Impact on the Financial System

Measuring the impact of TARP in isolation is challenging. The health of the overall system and its impact on the U.S. economy are the most important metrics by which we can measure the effectiveness of these policies. However, the cost of the financial system collapse that was averted by TARP and the other government actions taken in the fall of 2008 and since then will never be known. Moreover, it is difficult to measure separately the impact of TARP, as it was part of a coordinated government response to restore confidence in our financial system. Nevertheless, a few TARP programs were uniquely targeted to specific markets and institutions. In those instances, we can measure performance more directly.

At a broad level, confidence in the stability of our financial markets and institutions has improved dramatically over the past year. Interbank lending rates, which reflect stress in the banking system, have returned to levels associated with more stable times. Credit-default swap spreads for financial institutions, which measure investor confidence in their health, have also fallen significantly.

At the same time, borrowing costs have declined for many businesses, homeowners, and municipalities, allowing them to raise substantial capital from private sources. Corporations, for example, have raised over $1 trillion from bond issuance this year. While much of the issuance early this year was supported by government guarantees, private investors have funded most new corporate debt without public support in recent months. Importantly, banks have raised substantial funds from private sources since federal regulators released the results of their "stress test" of major U.S. financial institutions. As a result, the U.S. banking system is better capitalized today. TARP investments provided our financial institutions with an important bridge to critical access to private capital.

More narrowly targeted programs have also had a significant impact. Securitization markets that provide important channels of credit for consumers and small businesses have improved, in large part because of the government's Term Asset-Backed Securities Loan Facility (TALF). Spreads in these markets have narrowed considerably in response to announcements and actions through the program. New issuance has picked up and is shifting from public support to purely private financing. Prices for impaired securities on bank balance sheets have improved significantly this year. Announcements for the Public-Private Investment Program have contributed to these improvements, and the recently-formed Public-Private Investment Funds have started to purchase troubled assets from banks. Meanwhile, housing markets are showing some signs of stabilizing. Thanks in part to federal government financial policies, mortgage rates remain near historic lows, and home prices and sales are increasing. Millions of Americans have refinanced their mortgages since we announced the Making Home Affordable program, and over 650,000 trial modifications have been initiated under the Home Affordable Modification Program, which is largely funded by TARP.

As credit conditions have improved, the U.S. economy has started to grow again, and job losses have slowed. These are significant improvements from where we were last year.

However, the financial and economic recovery still faces significant headwinds. Unemployment remains very high, along with foreclosure and delinquency rates, and housing markets are still overwhelmingly dependent on government support. Lending standards are tight and bank lending continues to contract overall, although the pace of contraction has moderated and residential mortgage lending by banks has stabilized. Commercial real estate losses weigh heavily on many small banks, impairing their ability to extend new loans. Further, although securitization markets have improved, parts of those markets are still impaired, especially for securities backed by commercial mortgages. These conditions place enormous pressure on American families, homeowners, and small businesses, which rely heavily on bank lending. Later, I will describe how we are refocusing EESA-funded programs to mitigate this pressure.

In sum, TARP has largely succeeded in achieving its primary goal, and we are winding down many initiatives established under the program. However, four tasks remain for TARP: preserving financial stability, which is essential for long-term economic growth; mitigating foreclosure for responsible American homeowners; getting credit to small businesses; and supporting securitization markets that facilitate consumer and small business loans.

Financial Returns and Expected Cost

The expected cost of using TARP to stabilize our financial system has fallen dramatically. While EESA provided the Secretary of the Treasury with the authority to invest $700 billion, the ultimate cost for taxpayers will undoubtedly be far less.

One way of evaluating the program's cost is its impact on the Federal deficit. We now expect that TARP's contribution to Federal deficits will be at least $200 billion less than was projected in the August Mid-Session Review of the President's Budget, which assumed a $341 billion cost. And the expected budgetary impact of $364 billion in funds disbursed in Fiscal Year 2009 has fallen from $151 billion to $42 billion.

This improvement is driven by two factors: (1) investments are generating higher returns than previously anticipated, and (2) we do not anticipate using the full spending authority granted by EESA. We now expect to make—not lose—money on $245 billion of investments in banks. We estimate that in the aggregate, major bank stabilization programs funded through TARP will yield a positive net return of over $19 billion, thanks to dividends, interest, early repayments, and the sale of warrants.* In short, taxpayers are being repaid at a substantial profit by banks.

Repayments are already substantial. To date, banks have returned $116 billion in taxpayer investments—nearly one-third of all TARP disbursements to date. Further, we anticipate that total repayments could reach $175 billion by the end of next year; that is, nearly half of TARP disbursements to date.

These early repayments are testaments to the success of the government's efforts to stabilize and rehabilitate our financial system. Private investors now have much greater confidence in the prospects of our major financial institutions. This is reflected in the significant private fundraising by banks this year. Just last week, Bank of America raised $19.3 billion in common equity—after it announced that it would repay $45 billion of government investments. More broadly, the largest U.S. banks have raised over $110 billion in common equity and other regulatory capital since we announced the results of the "stress test" in May. That nearly matches the $116 billion in repayments we have received.

TARP programs have already generated significant income—roughly $15 billion—which has been used to pay down the debt. Our outstanding equity investments continue to generate substantial income through dividends. And

---

*Warrants are a financial instrument that allows the holder to buy stock in the future at a fixed price. Banks provided the government warrants (basically an equity stake in the bank) in exchange for financial support [*Editors*].

we are adding to the taxpayer's return by auctioning warrants. Last week, for example, we raised nearly $150 million from the sale of Capital One warrants. We expect substantial income from additional warrant sales over the next few weeks.

However, we do not expect all TARP investments to generate positive returns. There is a significant likelihood that we will not be repaid for the full value of our investments in AIG, GM, and Chrysler. But here too the outlook has improved. We now expect these institutions to repay $14 billion more than was originally projected.

Furthermore, expenditures through the Home Affordable Modification Program were never intended to generate revenue. Consistent with the mandate of EESA, this program was created to help mitigate foreclosure for responsible but at-risk homeowners. The program requires mortgage lenders to share the financial burden of meeting that goal.

In sum, the ultimate return on TARP investments will depend on how the economy and financial markets evolve, and whether we can reform financial regulation and consumer protection in meaningful, efficient ways. But the bottom line is as follows. In combination with other government programs, TARP helped prevent a financial collapse that would likely have plunged this country into a much deeper recession, led to staggering job losses, and further reduced tax revenue. The financial system continues to improve, private capital is replacing public support, and the economy is growing again. Taxpayers should get back the vast majority of funds invested through TARP. And the ultimate fiscal cost of the program will be substantially less than originally expected, thereby reducing the burden on current and future taxpayers.

Exit Strategy for TARP

Next, I will lay out our exit strategy for TARP. There are four broad elements to that strategy.

First, we will continue terminating and winding down many of the government programs put in place to address the crisis. That process is already well underway. In September, Treasury ended its Money Market Fund Guarantee Program, which guaranteed at its peak over $3 trillion of assets. The program incurred no losses, and generated $1.2 billion in fees. New issuance under the FDIC's Temporary Liquidity Guarantee Program (TLGP) ended in October. Credit extended through Federal Reserve liquidity programs has declined substantially as market conditions have improved, and most of these programs are scheduled to expire at the beginning of February.

With respect to TARP, support for large financial institutions is coming to an end. The Capital Purchase Program, under which the bulk of support to banks has been provided, is effectively closed. Before this Administration took office, nearly $240 billion in TARP funds had been committed to banks. Since January 20, we have committed approximately $7 billion to banks, much of which went to small institutions. Major U.S. banks subject to the "stress test" conducted last spring have raised over $110 billion in high-quality capital from the private sector. And banks have repaid $116 billion of TARP funds.

Second, we must fulfill EESA's mandate to preserve home ownership, stimulate liquidity for small businesses, and promote jobs and economic growth. To do so, we will limit new commitments in 2010 to three areas.

- We will continue to mitigate foreclosure for responsible American homeowners as we take the steps necessary to stabilize our housing market.
- We recently launched initiatives to provide capital to small and community banks, which are important sources of credit for small businesses. We are also reserving funds for additional efforts to facilitate small business lending.
- Finally, we may increase our commitment to the Term Asset-Backed Securities Loan Facility (TALF), which is improving securitization markets that facilitate consumer and small business loans, as well as commercial mortgage loans. We expect that increasing our commitment to TALF would not result in additional cost to taxpayers.

Third, beyond these limited new commitments, we will not use remaining EESA funds unless necessary to respond to an immediate and substantial threat to the economy stemming from financial instability. As a nation we must maintain capacity to respond to such a threat. Banks are still experiencing significant new credit losses, and the pace of bank failures, which tend to lag economic cycles, remains elevated. At the same time, many of the Federal Reserve and FDIC programs that have complemented TARP investments are ending. This creates a financial environment in which new shocks could have an outsized effect—especially if an adequate financial stability reserve is not maintained. As we wind down many of the government programs launched initially to address the crisis, it is imperative that we maintain this capacity to respond if financial conditions worsen and threaten our economy. However, before using EESA funds to respond to new financial threats, I would consult with the President and Chairman of the Federal Reserve Board and submit written notification to Congress. This capacity will bolster confidence and improve financial stability, thereby decreasing the probability that it will need to be used.

* * *

By stabilizing our financial system, assisting responsible homeowners, and getting credit to small businesses, EESA authority will continue to improve the outlook for our economy and American workers. And it will do so within the limits established by Congress in EESA. Further, while we are extending the $700 billion program, we do not expect to deploy more than $550 billion. We also expect up to $175 billion in repayments by the end of next year, and substantial additional repayments thereafter. The combination of the reduced scale of TARP commitments and substantial repayments should allow us to commit significant resources to pay down the federal debt over time.

Fourth, we will continue to manage the equity investments acquired through EESA in a commercial manner, while protecting taxpayers and unwinding those investments as soon as practicable. We will exercise our voting rights only on core issues such as election of directors, and not interfere in the day to day management of individual companies. In addition, as the steward of taxpayers' funds, Treasury will manage investments in a manner that ensures accountability, transparency and oversight. And we will work with recipients of EESA funds and their supervisors to accelerate repayment where appropriate. We want to see the capital base of our financial system return to private hands as quickly as possible, while preserving financial stability and promoting economic recovery.

Conclusion

In conclusion, I can report significant improvements in our financial markets and economy, as well as the positive financial results of our TARP programs. However, our job is far from finished. History suggests that exiting too soon from policies designed to contain a financial crisis can significantly prolong an economic downturn. While we exit our emergency financial policies, we must not waver in our resolve to ensure the stability of the financial system and to support the nascent recovery that the Administration and Congress have worked so hard to achieve. Improvements in the financial performance of TARP programs put us in a better position to address the financial and economic challenges that many Americans still face. The Department of the Treasury looks forward to continuing to work with you and the Congress to achieve these goals.

* * *

QUESTIONS

1. Which of the "hustles" Taibbi describes strike you as the most outrageous? Which seem as if they may have been necessary to stabilize the financial sector?

2. Imagine a debate between Secretary Geithner and Taibbi on a Sunday morning talk show. How do you think Geithner would defend the various "hustles"?

3. How could Congress reform the financial system to prevent the type of crisis the economy suffered in 2008–2009? What could have been done differently to get us out of the crisis?

15

Government and Society: Health Care Reform

Every president since Theodore Roosevelt who attempted comprehensive health care reform failed until Barack Obama's success in 2010. Most recently, Bill Clinton's attempt at reform in 1993–94 was unable to win support in Congress even when Democrats controlled both the House and the Senate. Obama faced an uphill battle as well, with unified opposition from Republicans and splits within his own party about the direction of reform. Through the first eight months in office, Obama remained out of the legislative fray in an effort to avoid the centralized micromanaging that had doomed President Clinton's attempt. After poll numbers showed the public turning against health care reform and a series of angry town-hall meetings in August 2009, in which members of Congress faced questions about "death panels" and a government takeover of health care, Obama decided he needed to regain control of the debate. In a nationally televised speech before a joint session of Congress, Obama outlined his priorities, answered his critics, and urged Congress to action. Obama said, "I am not the first President to take up this cause, but I am determined to be the last."

The priorities outlined in this speech—achieving as close to universal coverage as possible; a set of programs that would not "add a dime to the federal deficit;" preventing health insurance companies from denying coverage to people with preexisting health conditions or dropping policy holders when they get ill;

and holding down health care costs by adopting "best practices," encouraging competition between health care providers and insurers, and computerizing health records—all became part of the final legislation.

Health care experts surveyed by the nonpartisan *National Journal* gave the law a mixed report card. Marilyn Werber Serfani tried to "craft survey questions to elicit objective assessments rather than partisan or ideological views." Overall, the experts were most impressed with its progress toward universal coverage, with 31 million of the 47 million uninsured Americans gaining health insurance by the time the law is fully implemented. They were less impressed with the impact the law will have on the quality of care, with the greatest hope for improvement coming from computerized records. The lowest scores came on cost control; many experts were disappointed with the delay (until 2018) in and reduction of the "Cadillac tax" that could have had a bigger impact on expensive and unnecessary medical procedures.

Although the *National Journal*'s experts were measured in their critiques, opponents of the bill promised to repeal the law and used this pledge as a central part of their campaign strategy in the 2010 midterm elections. Yuval Levin writes, "Because Obamacare embodies a rejection of incrementalism, it cannot be improved in small steps. Fixing our health care systems in the wake of the program's enactment will require a big step—repeal of the law before most of it takes hold—followed by incremental reforms addressing the public's real concerns." Levin argues that the health care plan will not control costs, will require people to buy insurance they cannot afford, and will bankrupt the country. Given the law's comprehensive scope, affecting one-sixth of the economy, things are bound to go wrong that will produce a host of unanticipated problems. He believes that more market-based solutions would provide the competition to hold down costs.

Barack Obama

Address to Congress on Health Care Reform

Madame Speaker, Vice President Biden, Members of Congress, and the American people:

* * *

* * * We came to build a future. So tonight, I return to speak to all of you about an issue that is central to that future—and that is the issue of health care.

I am not the first President to take up this cause, but I am determined to be the last. It has now been nearly a century since Theodore Roosevelt first called for health care reform. And ever since, nearly every President and Congress, whether Democrat or Republican, has attempted to meet this challenge in some way. A bill for comprehensive health reform was first introduced by John Dingell Sr. in 1943. Sixty-five years later, his son continues to introduce that same bill at the beginning of each session.

Our collective failure to meet this challenge—year after year, decade after decade—has led us to a breaking point. Everyone understands the extraordinary hardships that are placed on the uninsured, who live every day just one accident or illness away from bankruptcy. These are not primarily people on welfare. These are middle-class Americans. Some can't get insurance on the job. Others are self-employed, and can't afford it, since buying insurance on your own costs you three times as much as the coverage you get from your employer. Many other Americans who are willing and able to pay are still denied insurance due to previous illnesses or conditions that insurance companies decide are too risky or expensive to cover.

We are the only advanced democracy on earth—the only wealthy nation—that allows such hardships for millions of its people. There are now more than thirty million American citizens who cannot get coverage. In just a two year period, one in every three Americans goes without health care coverage at some point. And every day, 14,000 Americans lose their coverage. In other words, it can happen to anyone.

But the problem that plagues the health care system is not just a problem of the uninsured. Those who do have insurance have never had less security and stability than they do today. More and more Americans worry that if you move, lose your job, or change your job, you'll lose your health insurance too. More and more Americans pay their premiums, only to discover that their insurance company has dropped their coverage when they get sick, or won't pay the full cost of care. It happens every day.

One man from Illinois lost his coverage in the middle of chemotherapy because his insurer found that he hadn't reported gallstones that he didn't even know about. They delayed his treatment, and he died because of it. Another woman from Texas was about to get a double mastectomy when her insurance company canceled her policy because she forgot to declare a case of acne. By the time she had her insurance reinstated, her breast cancer more than doubled in size. That is heart-breaking, it is wrong, and no one should be treated that way in the United States of America.

Then there's the problem of rising costs. We spend one-and-a-half times more per person on health care than any other country, but we aren't any healthier for it. This is one of the reasons that insurance premiums have gone up three times faster than wages. It's why so many employers—especially small businesses—are forcing their employees to pay more for insurance, or are dropping their coverage entirely. It's why so many aspiring entrepreneurs cannot afford to open a business in the first place, and why American businesses that compete internationally—like our automakers—are at a huge disadvantage. And it's why those of us with health insurance are also paying a hidden and growing tax for those without it—about $1000 per year that pays for somebody else's emergency room and charitable care.

Finally, our health care system is placing an unsustainable burden on taxpayers. When health care costs grow at the rate they have, it puts greater pressure on programs like Medicare and Medicaid. If we do nothing to slow these skyrocketing costs, we will eventually be spending more on Medicare and Medicaid than every other government program combined. Put simply, our health care problem is our deficit problem. Nothing else even comes close.

These are the facts. Nobody disputes them. We know we must reform this system. The question is how.

There are those on the left who believe that the only way to fix the system is through a single-payer system like Canada's, where we would severely restrict the private insurance market and have the government provide coverage for everyone. On the right, there are those who argue that we should end the employer-based system and leave individuals to buy health insurance on their own.

I have to say that there are arguments to be made for both approaches. But either one would represent a radical shift that would disrupt the health care most people currently have. Since health care represents one-sixth of our economy, I believe it makes more sense to build on what works and fix what doesn't, rather than try to build an entirely new system from scratch. And that is precisely what those of you in Congress have tried to do over the past several months.

* * *

The plan I'm announcing tonight would meet three basic goals:

It will provide more security and stability to those who have health insurance. It will provide insurance to those who don't. And it will slow the growth of health care costs for our families, our businesses, and our government. It's a plan that asks everyone to take responsibility for meeting this challenge—not just government and insurance companies, but employers and individuals. And it's a plan that incorporates ideas from Senators and Congressmen; from Democrats and Republicans—and yes, from some of my opponents in both the primary and general election.

Here are the details that every American needs to know about this plan:

First, if you are among the hundreds of millions of Americans who already have health insurance through your job, Medicare, Medicaid, or the VA, nothing in this plan will require you or your employer to change the coverage or the doctor you have. Let me repeat this: nothing in our plan requires you to change what you have.

What this plan will do is to make the insurance you have work better for you. Under this plan, it will be against the law for insurance companies to deny you coverage because of a pre-existing condition. As soon as I sign this bill, it will be against the law for insurance companies to drop your coverage when you get sick or water it down when you need it most. They will no longer be able to place some arbitrary cap on the amount of coverage you can receive in a given year or a lifetime. We will place a limit on how much you can be charged for out-of-pocket expenses, because in the United States of America, no one should go broke because they get sick. And insurance companies will be required to cover, with no extra charge, routine checkups and preventive care, like mammograms and colonoscopies—because there's no reason we shouldn't be catching diseases like breast cancer and colon cancer before they get worse. That makes sense, it saves money, and it saves lives.

That's what Americans who have health insurance can expect from this plan—more security and stability.

Now, if you're one of the tens of millions of Americans who don't currently have health insurance, the second part of this plan will finally offer you quality, affordable choices. If you lose your job or change your job, you will be able to get coverage. If you strike out on your own and start a small business, you will be able to get coverage. We will do this by creating a new insurance exchange—a marketplace where individuals and small businesses will be able to shop for health insurance at competitive prices. Insurance companies will have an incentive to participate in this exchange because it lets them compete for millions of new customers. As one big group, these customers will have greater leverage to bargain with the insurance companies for better prices and quality coverage. This is how large companies and government employees get affordable insurance. It's how everyone in this Congress gets affordable insurance. And it's time to give every American the same opportunity that we've given ourselves.

For those individuals and small businesses who still cannot afford the lower-priced insurance available in the exchange, we will provide tax credits, the size of which will be based on your need. And all insurance companies that want access to this new marketplace will have to abide by the consumer protections I already mentioned. This exchange will take effect in four years, which will give us time to do it right. In the meantime, for those Americans who can't get insurance today because they have pre-existing medical conditions, we will immediately offer low-cost coverage that will protect you against financial ruin if you become seriously ill. This was a good idea when Senator John McCain proposed it in the campaign, it's a good idea now, and we should embrace it.

Now, even if we provide these affordable options, there may be those—particularly the young and healthy—who still want to take the risk and go without coverage. There may still be companies that refuse to do right by their workers. The problem is, such irresponsible behavior costs all the rest of us money. If there are affordable options and people still don't sign up for health insurance, it means we pay for those people's expensive emergency room visits. If some businesses don't provide workers health care, it forces the rest of us to pick up the tab when their workers get sick, and gives those businesses an unfair advantage over their competitors. And unless everybody does their part, many of the insurance reforms we seek—especially requiring insurance companies to cover pre-existing conditions—just can't be achieved.

That's why under my plan, individuals will be required to carry basic health insurance—just as most states require you to carry auto insurance. Likewise, businesses will be required to either offer their workers health care, or chip in to help cover the cost of their workers. There will be a hardship waiver for those individuals who still cannot afford coverage, and 95% of all small businesses, because of their size and narrow profit margin, would be exempt from these requirements. But we cannot have large businesses and individuals who can afford coverage game the system by avoiding responsibility to themselves or their employees. Improving our health care system only works if everybody does their part.

While there remain some significant details to be ironed out, I believe a broad consensus exists for the aspects of the plan I just outlined: consumer protections for those with insurance, an exchange that allows individuals and small businesses to purchase affordable coverage, and a requirement that people who can afford insurance get insurance.

And I have no doubt that these reforms would greatly benefit Americans from all walks of life, as well as the economy as a whole. Still, given all the misinformation that's been spread over the past few months, I realize that many Americans have grown nervous about reform. So tonight I'd like to address some of the key controversies that are still out there.

Some of people's concerns have grown out of bogus claims spread by those whose only agenda is to kill reform at any cost. The best example is the claim, made not just by radio and cable talk show hosts, but prominent politicians, that we plan to set up panels of bureaucrats with the power to kill off senior citizens. Such a charge would be laughable if it weren't so cynical and irresponsible. It is a lie, plain and simple.

There are also those who claim that our reform effort will insure illegal immigrants. This, too, is false—the reforms I'm proposing would not apply to those who are here illegally. And one more misunderstanding I want to clear up—under our plan, no federal dollars will be used to fund abortions, and federal conscience laws will remain in place.

* * *

[*Here President Obama discusses the "public option"—a Medicare-type health insurance plan that would have been available to those without insurance. However, the public option was not included as part of the final law—Editors.*]

Finally, let me discuss an issue that is a great concern to me, to members of this chamber, and to the public—and that is how we pay for this plan.

Here's what you need to know. First, I will not sign a plan that adds one dime to our deficits—either now or in the future. Period. And to prove that I'm serious, there will be a provision in this plan that requires us to come forward with more spending cuts if the savings we promised don't materialize. Part of the reason I faced a trillion dollar deficit when I walked in the door of the White House is because too many initiatives over the last decade were not paid for—from the Iraq War to tax breaks for the wealthy. I will not make that same mistake with health care.

Second, we've estimated that most of this plan can be paid for by finding savings within the existing health care system—a system that is currently full of waste and abuse. Right now, too much of the hard-earned savings and tax dollars we spend on health care doesn't make us healthier. That's not my judgment—it's the judgment of medical professionals across this country. And this is also true when it comes to Medicare and Medicaid.

In fact, I want to speak directly to America's seniors for a moment, because Medicare is another issue that's been subjected to demagoguery and distortion during the course of this debate.

More than four decades ago, this nation stood up for the principle that after a lifetime of hard work, our seniors should not be left to struggle with a pile of medical bills in their later years. That is how Medicare was born. And it remains a sacred trust that must be passed down from one generation to the next. That is why not a dollar of the Medicare trust fund will be used to pay for this plan.

The only thing this plan would eliminate is the hundreds of billions of dollars in waste and fraud, as well as unwarranted subsidies in Medicare that go to insurance companies—subsidies that do everything to pad their profits and nothing to improve your care. And we will also create an independent commission of doctors and medical experts charged with identifying more waste in the years ahead.

These steps will ensure that you—America's seniors—get the benefits you've been promised. They will ensure that Medicare is there for future generations. And we can use some of the savings to fill the gap in coverage that forces too many seniors to pay thousands of dollars a year out of their own pocket for prescription drugs. That's what this plan will do for you. So don't pay attention to those scary stories about how your benefits will be cut—especially since some of the same folks who are spreading these tall tales have fought against Medicare in the past, and just this year supported a budget that would have essentially turned Medicare into a privatized voucher program. That will never happen on my watch. I will protect Medicare.

Now, because Medicare is such a big part of the health care system, making the program more efficient can help usher in changes in the way we deliver health care that can reduce costs for everybody. We have long known that some places, like the Intermountain Healthcare in Utah or the Geisinger Health System in rural Pennsylvania, offer high-quality care at costs below average. The commission can help encourage the adoption of these common-sense best practices by doctors and medical professionals throughout the system—everything from reducing hospital infection rates to encouraging better coordination between teams of doctors.

Reducing the waste and inefficiency in Medicare and Medicaid will pay for most of this plan. Much of the rest would be paid for with revenues from the very same drug and insurance companies that stand to benefit from tens of millions of new customers. This reform will charge insurance companies a fee for their most expensive policies, which will encourage them to provide greater value for the money—an idea which has the support of Democratic and Republican experts. And according to these same experts, this modest change could help hold down the cost of health care for all of us in the long-run.

Finally, many in this chamber—particularly on the Republican side of the aisle—have long insisted that reforming our medical malpractice laws can help bring down the cost of health care. I don't believe malpractice reform is a silver bullet, but I have talked to enough doctors to know that defensive medicine may be contributing to unnecessary costs. So I am proposing that we move forward on a range of ideas about how to put patient safety first and let doctors focus on practicing medicine. I know that the Bush Administration considered authorizing demonstration projects in individual states to test these issues. It's a good idea, and I am directing my Secretary of Health and Human Services to move forward on this initiative today.

Add it all up, and the plan I'm proposing will cost around $900 billion over ten years—less than we have spent on the Iraq and Afghanistan wars, and less than the tax cuts for the wealthiest few Americans that Congress passed at the beginning of the previous administration. Most of these costs will be paid for with money already being spent—but spent badly—in the existing health care system. The plan will not add to our deficit. The middle-class will realize greater security, not higher taxes. And if we are able to slow the growth of health care costs by just one-tenth of one percent each year, it will actually reduce the deficit by $4 trillion over the long term.

This is the plan I'm proposing. It's a plan that incorporates ideas from many of the people in this room tonight—Democrats and Republicans. And I will continue to seek common ground in the weeks ahead. If you come to me with a serious set of proposals, I will be there to listen. My door is always open.

* * *

[Here President Obama talks about Ted Kennedy and his role in health care reform—Editors.]

That large-heartedness—that concern and regard for the plight of others—is not a partisan feeling. It is not a Republican or a Democratic feeling. It, too, is part of the American character. Our ability to stand in other people's shoes. A recognition that we are all in this together; that when fortune turns against one of us, others are there to lend a helping hand. A belief that in this country, hard work and responsibility should be rewarded by some measure of security and fair play; and an acknowledgement that sometimes government has to step in to help deliver on that promise.

This has always been the history of our progress. In 1933, when over half of our seniors could not support themselves and millions had seen their savings wiped away, there were those who argued that Social Security would lead to socialism. But the men and women of Congress stood fast, and we are all the better for it. In 1965, when some argued that Medicare represented a government takeover of health care, members of Congress, Democrats and Republicans, did not back down. They joined together so that all of us could enter our golden years with some basic peace of mind.

You see, our predecessors understood that government could not, and should not, solve every problem. They understood that there are instances when the gains in security from government action are not worth the added constraints on our freedom. But they also understood that the danger of too much government is matched by the perils of too little; that without the leavening hand of wise policy, markets can crash, monopolies can stifle competition, and the vulnerable can be exploited. And they knew that when any government measure, no matter how carefully crafted or beneficial, is subject to scorn; when any efforts to help people in need are attacked as un-American; when facts and reason are thrown overboard and only timidity passes for wisdom, and we can no longer even engage in a civil conversation with each other over the things that truly matter—that at that point we don't merely lose our capacity to solve big challenges. We lose something essential about ourselves.

What was true then remains true today. I understand how difficult this health care debate has been. I know that many in this country are deeply skeptical that government is looking out for them. I understand that the politically safe move would be to kick the can further down the road—to defer reform one more year, or one more election, or one more term.

But that's not what the moment calls for. That's not what we came here to do. We did not come to fear the future. We came here to shape it. I still believe we can act even when it's hard. I still believe we can replace acrimony with civility, and gridlock with progress. I still believe we can do great things, and that here and now we will meet history's test.

Because that is who we are. That is our calling. That is our character. Thank you, God Bless You, and may God Bless the United States of America.

Marilyn Werber Serafini

Grading Health Reform: Experts Assess Whether the Bill Delivers on Its Promises

The primary objectives of health care reform were clear long before Congress took up the issue last year: slow the growth of health care spending, insure more people, improve the quality of care—and do it all without busting the federal budget. *National Journal* this week asked 20 health care experts across the political spectrum how the bill that President Obama signed into law on Tuesday measures up against those yardsticks.

Published in *National Journal*, March 2010.

The experts generally agreed that the new law comes close to achieving the objective of providing insurance to all Americans and does a fairly good job of making coverage affordable and available to consumers. But the experts also said that the law falls short of promises to lower skyrocketing health care spending, and they concluded that it doesn't do enough to improve the quality of health care.

* * *

Our judges gave each candidate's plan a series of numerical grades, from 1 to 10, depending on how close they thought it would come to achieving a given goal, such as covering the uninsured. A score of 10 indicated that the plan would come extremely close to reaching the goal, while a score of 1 meant that it would not come at all close.

National Journal tried to craft the survey questions to elicit objective assessments rather than partisan or ideological views. Regarding the uninsured, for example, we asked the judges how close each proposal would come to providing health insurance for all Americans. *NJ* did not want answers that reflected the judges' political leanings or personal views about whether a given plan was the best—or even a good—approach.

* * *

A Big Step Toward Universal Coverage

The Congressional Budget Office estimates that the health care reform law will provide coverage to 31 million of the 47 million Americans currently uninsured. Many of the people who won't be covered are illegal immigrants who are ineligible for federal assistance in obtaining insurance.

None of the 20 experts gave the law a perfect score of 10 for providing coverage, although all but two gave it high marks. Indeed, in this category, President Obama received the same grade that he did as a candidate.

During the campaign Obama recommended a narrower mandate requiring only that parents purchase insurance for their children; in contrast, the new law requires many adults to also get coverage. Most people without health insurance will have to pay one of two penalties, whichever is greater: either a fixed fine, starting at $95 in 2014, rising to $325 in 2015, and to $695 in 2016; or a percentage of taxable income, starting at 1.0 percent in 2014 and rising to 2.5 percent in 2016.

People with annual incomes below 100 percent of the federal poverty line ($10,830 for an individual and $22,050 for a family of four) are exempt from the penalties.

The law will significantly expand Medicaid, the federal-state health care program for the poor, to as many as 13 million additional beneficiaries. Beginning in 2014, Medicaid eligibility will extend to people with annual earnings lower than 133 percent of the federal poverty line ($14,440 for an individual).

Some judges took 1 or 2 points off their scores in this category because they advocated tougher penalties for failure to purchase insurance. Paul Ginsburg, president of the Center for Studying Health System Change, said, "I expect that the mandate will be refined in response to experience."

Ed Howard, executive vice president of the Alliance for Health Reform, called the law "a good start," and Jeffrey Levi, executive director of the Trust for America's Health, agreed. "Clearly, a significant group of people will be left out of this reform," he said. "But the addition of over 30 million Americans to the insurance roll is a monumental step of major proportions. But those who are left out will continue to need a safety net—hence the importance of the provisions expanding funding for community health centers and public health."

Gail Wilensky, a senior fellow at Project Hope who was Medicare administrator during the presidency of George H. W. Bush, noted that according to CBO estimates, "the percentage of people without insurance would drop from the current 15 percent to 5 percent, which is two-thirds of the way to universal coverage."

Elizabeth McGlynn, associate director of the health program at Rand, said that based on her think tank's microsimulation modeling, the percentage of uninsured would be reduced by 53 to 57 percent. She called that "a substantial improvement," although she added that it "would not achieve universal coverage." McGlynn concluded, "A large portion of the uninsured would be eligible for, but not enrolled in, Medicaid."

The Lewin Group actuary, John Sheils, said that his firm's model indicates that the law covers 60 percent of the uninsured population but only 43 percent of care that is currently uncompensated. "Very-low-income people exempt from the mandate account for much of this," he said.

According to Joe Antos, an American Enterprise Institute scholar, the goal shouldn't be reducing the number of uninsured but increasing the number of people who have access to appropriate care. "There is nothing in the bill that assures this," he said. Over time, Heritage Foundation Vice President Stuart Butler cautioned, although almost all citizens and legal residents will get coverage, "it may not be of the type, cost, and quality that they would like."

Some conservative opponents argue that an insurance mandate is unconstitutional and sets a worrisome precedent for government power. More than a dozen states have already filed lawsuits challenging the constitutionality of the requirement.

Many health reform advocates are also concerned, but for different reasons. They worry that some people will ignore the mandate—especially those who are young and healthy and see little need for health insurance. America's Health Insurance Plans, which represents insurers, shares this apprehension. Insurers agreed early on to stop denying policies to people with pre-existing conditions and in poor health in exchange for universal coverage.

Minor Impact on Quality of Care

Many of National Journal's health care experts are disappointed that the new law won't do more to improve the quality of health care. "The main focus of the legislation is on coverage expansion, not on improving quality or consumer decision-making," said Elizabeth McGlynn, associate director of the health program at Rand. "The bill contains provisions that would increase the information available to consumers; however, there are no direct incentives for consumers to use that information or to change the decisions they would have otherwise made."

The key, said Paul Ginsburg, president of the Center for Studying Health System Change, is implementing research into medical effectiveness. The new law funds research on so-called comparative effectiveness to evaluate the success of various medical treatments.

But American Enterprise Institute scholar Joe Antos worries that even the most-sophisticated [sic] consumers will have trouble interpreting and applying comparative-effectiveness results. "Sensible consumers will continue to rely on the advice of their doctors, which depends on the community standard of practice, the patient's specific circumstances, how services are paid for, and other factors. Patients are increasingly also seeking information on the Internet, which can lead some to demand inappropriate treatments."

Jeffrey Levi, executive director of Trust for America's Health, shares Antos's concern. "It's one thing to do the comparative-effectiveness research and quality assessment; it's another for consumers to take that information to heart and apply it to their own situations."

Quality may also differ for those getting insurance through an exchange and those in employer-sponsored plans, said Heritage Foundation Vice President Stuart Butler. Those in exchanges will have "a lot more choice and information," he said, predicting that employers will react to extra fees by restricting coverage and shifting costs.

Few experts were optimistic that doctors, hospitals, and other medical providers will gain the tools to improve care using best practices. "The bill promotes comparative-effectiveness research but does nothing to increase adherence to guidelines," said Lewin Group actuary John Sheils. "Adherence is the problem. There is overwhelming evidence in the literature showing that doctors do not follow guidelines."

Former Senate Majority Leader Tom Daschle noted that changes resulting from the research will not come "for some time." And even when the results of comparative-effectiveness research are more readily available, "probably past the 10-year mark," according to Antos, "their appropriate application depends critically on the specific patient's circumstances. Judgment will remain the driving factor, unless future Congresses attempt to impose uniform standards on medical practice."

Grace-Marie Turner, president of the Galen Institute, worries that comparative-effectiveness studies "are historically out of date long before the studies are finalized." What may have a greater effect on quality of care is the funding that President Obama included in last year's economic stimulus law to encourage doctors to adopt electronic medical records. "Considerable work must be done to help physicians who are in solo and small group practice use emerging tools," she said.

Although former Medicare Administrator Gail Wilensky called the law's direction positive, she stressed that much depends on what happens with pilot and demonstration projects that the law establishes for Medicare. The law authorizes pilot projects to test so-called accountable care organizations and the bundling of payments to medical providers. The idea is to get medical providers to better coordinate patient care. The government and private insurers, in turn, could then more effectively base payments on performance.

The experts were somewhat skeptical that the reforms will encourage medical providers to compete for patients based on quality and price. Conservatives were especially critical, but liberals didn't give high scores either.

Competition will change, Butler said, but not to meet that goal. "In Medicaid, Medicare, and in the more regulated private system, the incentive will increase to compete by cutting costs and avoiding certain patients to achieve a reasonable return amid tighter fee schedules," he said.

Bill Gets Low Score For Cost Control

Bringing health care spending in line with the economy's growth rate has been a priority since Washington began talking about health reform decades ago. During the 2008 presidential campaign, judges gave Barack Obama's proposal a score of only 3 for controlling costs.

In rating the newly passed reforms, the scores were nearly as low. Former Medicare Administrator Gail Wilensky noted that the law will institute some "promising" pilot projects for coordinating medical care in Medicare and for testing ways to pay doctors and hospitals. Still, Heritage Foundation Vice President Stuart Butler said that the law will increase, not decrease, the growth rate of total health spending.

"While the bill contains provisions that may ultimately lead to reductions," Elizabeth McGlynn, Rand health program associate director said, her think tank's projections indicate that, "with the exception of payment reform options, most would have a relatively small effect on the growth rate in health spending."

The actuary for the Centers for Medicare and Medicaid Services "reports that health spending will continue to grow faster than the economy, even assuming that future Congresses cut Medicare spending as prescribed in the bill," American Enterprise Institute scholar Joe Antos contended, adding, "This objective is probably impossible to meet even over the long term given the aging populace."

Brookings Institution senior fellow Henry Aaron is more optimistic about the long-term forecast; and Ed Howard, executive vice president of the Alliance for Health Reform, said that "most of what is possible is at least put in place, but will take time to have impact."

Many health care economists had high hopes for a so-called Cadillac tax to discourage employers from offering overly generous benefits. With less coverage, the theory goes, people will have to pay more out of their own pockets and thus become thriftier about purchasing medical services. But the final law watered down the tax and delayed its implementation. The tax on high-end insurance plans will apply to health plan premiums greater than $10,200 for individual coverage and $27,500 for families; it won't kick in until 2018.

Scores were somewhat higher, although mixed, when National Journal asked whether the federal government will get its money's worth from the law. "In terms of government spending per net newly insured individual, the expected value of the services obtained should exceed the cost to the federal government," McGlynn responded.

Butler, however, argued that the law is based on a "very high taxpayer cost for coverage expansions that could have been achieved at much lower cost." In scoring the law on its cost, Butler wanted to know whether zero was an option. "It has been 'funded' with new taxes and 'savings' that will not materialize. It is thus actually being funded with debt obligations on future generations."

Grace-Marie Turner, president of the Galen Institute, particularly worries about Medicare savings, which mostly come from decreasing payments to the Medicare Advantage program.

One-quarter of Medicare recipients get their insurance coverage from health maintenance organizations, preferred provider groups, and even some private fee-for-service plans as part of Medicare Advantage. But the program has been controversial because the government pays participating insurers about 14 percent more per beneficiary than it pays for the care of seniors in Medicare's traditional fee-for-service program.

"Richard Foster, Medicare's chief actuary, warned Congress that making the deep cuts to Medicare contained in the Senate bill 'represent an exceedingly difficult challenge' and, if sustained, would cause one out of five hospitals and nursing homes to become unprofitable," Turner said. "Congress is highly unlikely to allow this to happen, requiring even more tax dollars and deficit spending. This legislation is not paid for, even with half a trillion dollars in cuts to Medicare and half a trillion in new taxes. Political pressures will intensify to provide ever larger subsidies to more and more people and to impose strict price controls on providers. Coverage restrictions inevitably will follow. So, no, reform is not funded with existing health care dollars."

Paul Ginsburg, president of the Center for Studying Health System Change, countered that the government would have cut Medicare Advantage costs even if reform legislation had not passed, "although perhaps less sharply."

Yuval Levin

Repeal: Why and How Obamacare Must Be Undone

In the days since the enactment of their health care plan, Democrats in Washington have been desperately seeking to lodge the new program in the pantheon of American public-policy achievements. House Democratic whip James Clyburn compared the bill to the Civil Rights Act of 1964. Vice President Biden argued it vindicates a century of health reform efforts by Democrats and Republicans alike. House speaker Nancy Pelosi said "health insurance reform will stand alongside Social Security and Medicare in the annals of American history."

Even putting aside the fact that Social Security and Medicare are going broke and taking the rest of the government with them, these frantic forced analogies are preposterous. The new law is a ghastly mess, which began as a badly misguided technocratic pipe dream and was then degraded into ruinous incoherence by the madcap process of its enactment.

The appeals to history are understandable, however, because the Democrats know that the law is also exceedingly vulnerable to a wholesale repeal effort: Its major provisions do not take effect for four years, yet in the interim it is likely to begin wreaking havoc with the health care sector—raising insurance premiums, health care costs, and public anxieties. If those major provisions do take effect, moreover, the true costs of the program will soon become clear, and its unsustainable structure will grow painfully obvious. So, to protect it from an angry public and from Republicans armed with alternatives, the new law must be made to seem thoroughly established and utterly irrevocable—a fact on the ground that must be lived with; tweaked, if necessary, at the edges, but at its core politically untouchable.

But it is no such thing. Obamacare starts life strikingly unpopular and looks likely to grow more so as we get to know it in the coming months and years. The entire House of Representatives, two-thirds of the Senate, and the president will be up for election before the law's most significant provisions become fully active. The American public is concerned about spending, deficits,

Published in *The Weekly Standard*, April 2010.

debt, taxes, and overactive government to an extent seldom seen in American history. The excesses of the plan seem likely to make the case for alternative gradual and incremental reforms only stronger.

And the repeal of Obamacare is essential to any meaningful effort to bring down health care costs, provide greater stability and security of coverage to more Americans, and address our entitlement crisis. Both the program's original design and its contorted final form make repairs at the edges unworkable. The only solution is to repeal it and pursue genuine health care reform in its stead.

From Bad to Worse

To see why nothing short of repeal could suffice, we should begin at the core of our health care dilemma.

Conservative and liberal experts generally agree on the nature of the problem with American health care financing: There is a shortage of incentives for efficiency in our methods of paying for coverage and care, and therefore costs are rising much too quickly, leaving too many people unable to afford insurance. We have neither a fully public nor quite a private system of insurance, and three key federal policies—the fee-for-service structure of Medicare, the disjointed financing of Medicaid, and the open-ended tax exclusion for employer-provided insurance—drive spending and costs ever upward.

The disagreement about just how to fix that problem has tended to break down along a familiar dispute between left and right: whether economic efficiency is best achieved by the rational control of expert management or by the lawful chaos of open competition.

Liberals argue that the efficiency we lack would be achieved by putting as much as possible of the health care sector into one big "system" in which the various irregularities could be evened and managed out of existence by the orderly arrangement of rules and incentives. The problem now, they say, is that health care is too chaotic and answers only to the needs of the insurance companies. If it were made more orderly, and answered to the needs of the public as a whole, costs could be controlled more effectively.

Conservatives argue that the efficiency we lack would be achieved by allowing price signals to shape the behavior of both providers and consumers, creating more savings than we could hope to produce on purpose, and allowing competition and informed consumer choices to exercise a downward pressure on prices. The problem now, they say, is that third-party insurance (in which employers buy coverage or the government provides it, and consumers almost never pay doctors directly) makes health care too opaque, hiding the cost of everything from everyone and so making real pricing and therefore real economic efficiency impossible. If it were made more transparent and answered to the wishes of consumers, prices could be controlled more effectively.

That means that liberals and conservatives want to pursue health care reform in roughly opposite directions. Conservatives propose ways of introducing genuine market forces into the insurance system—to remove obstacles to choice and competition, pool risk more effectively, and reduce the inefficiency in government health care entitlements while helping those for whom entry to the market is too expensive (like Americans with preexisting conditions) gain access to the same high quality care. Such targeted efforts would build on what is best about the system we have in order to address what needs fixing.

Liberals, meanwhile, propose ways of moving Americans to a more fully public system, by arranging conditions in the health care sector (through a mix of mandates, regulations, taxes, and subsidies) to nudge people toward public coverage, which could be more effectively managed. This is the approach the Democrats originally proposed last year. The idea was to end risk-based insurance by making it essentially illegal for insurers to charge people different prices based on their health, age, or other factors; to force everyone to participate in the system so that the healthy do not wait until they're sick to buy insurance; to align various insurance reforms in a way that would raise premium costs in the private market; and then to introduce a government-run insurer that, whether through Medicare's negotiating leverage or through various exemptions from market pressures, could undersell private insurers and so offer an attractive "public option" to people being pushed out of employer plans into an increasingly expensive individual market.

Conservatives opposed this scheme because they believed a public insurer could not introduce efficiencies that would lower prices without brutal rationing of services. Liberals supported it because they thought a public insurer would be fairer and more effective.

But in order to gain 60 votes in the Senate last winter, the Democrats were forced to give up on that public insurer, while leaving the other components of their scheme in place. The result is not even a liberal approach to escalating costs but a ticking time bomb: a scheme that will build up pressure in our private insurance system while offering no escape. Rather than reform a system that everyone agrees is unsustainable, it will subsidize that system and compel participation in it—requiring all Americans to pay ever-growing premiums to insurance companies while doing essentially nothing about the underlying causes of those rising costs.

Liberal health care mavens understand this. When the public option was removed from the health care bill in the Senate, Howard Dean argued in the *Washington Post* that the bill had become merely a subsidy for insurance companies, and failed completely to control costs. Liberal health care blogger Jon Walker said, "The Senate bill will fail to stop the rapidly approaching meltdown of our health care system, and anyone is a fool for thinking otherwise." Markos Moulitsas of the Daily Kos called the bill "unconscionable" and said it lacked "any mechanisms to control costs."

Indeed, many conservatives, for all their justified opposition to a government takeover of health care, have not yet quite seen the full extent to which this bill will exacerbate the cost problem. It is designed to push people into a system that will not exist—a health care bridge to nowhere—and so will cause premiums to rise and encourage significant dislocation and then will initiate a program of subsidies whose only real answer to the mounting costs of coverage will be to pay them with public dollars and so increase them further. It aims to spend a trillion dollars on subsidies to large insurance companies and the expansion of Medicaid, to micromanage the insurance industry in ways likely only to raise premiums further, to cut Medicare benefits without using the money to shore up the program or reduce the deficit, and to raise taxes on employment, investment, and medical research.

The case for averting all of that could hardly be stronger. And the nature of the new law means that it must be undone—not trimmed at the edges. Once implemented fully, it would fairly quickly force a crisis that would require another significant reform. Liberals would seek to use that crisis, or the prospect of it, to move the system toward the approach they wanted in the first place: arguing that the only solution to the rising costs they have created is a public insurer they imagine could outlaw the economics of health care. A look at the fiscal collapse of the Medicare system should rid us of the notion that any such approach would work, but it remains the left's preferred solution, and it is their only plausible next move—indeed, some Democrats led by Iowa senator Tom Harkin have already begun talking about adding a public insurance option to the plan next year.

Because Obamacare embodies a rejection of incrementalism, it cannot be improved in small steps. Fixing our health care system in the wake of the program's enactment will require a big step—repeal of the law before most of it takes hold—followed by incremental reforms addressing the public's real concerns.

The Case for Repeal

That big step will not be easy to take. The Democratic party has invested its identity and its future in the fate of this new program, and Democrats control the White House and both houses of Congress. That is why the conservative health care agenda must now also be an electoral agenda—an effort to refine, inform, and build on public opposition to the new program and to the broader trend toward larger and more intrusive, expensive, and fiscally reckless government in the age of Obama. Obamacare is the most prominent emblem of that larger trend, and its repeal must be at the center of the conservative case to voters in the coming two election cycles.

The design of the new law offers some assistance. In an effort to manipulate the program's Congressional Budget Office score so as to meet President Obama's goal of spending less than $1 trillion in its first decade, the Democrats' plan will roll out along a very peculiar trajectory. No significant entitlement benefits will be made available for four years, but some significant taxes and Medicare cuts—as well as regulatory reforms that may begin to push premium prices up, especially in the individual market—will begin before then. And the jockeying and jostling in the insurance sector in preparation for the more dramatic changes that begin in 2014 will begin to be felt very soon.

To blunt the effects of all this, the Democrats have worked mightily to give the impression that some attractive benefits, especially regarding the rules governing insurance companies, will begin immediately. This year, they say, insurance companies will be prevented from using the preexisting medical condition of a child to exclude that child's parents from insurance coverage, and a risk-pool program will be established to help a small number of adults who are excluded too. Additionally, insurance policies cannot be cancelled retroactively when someone becomes sick, some annual and lifetime limits on coverage are prohibited, and "children" may stay on their parents' insurance until they turn 26. Obamacare's champions hope these reforms might build a constituency for the program.

But these benefits are far too small to have that effect. The preexisting condition exclusion prohibits only the refusal to cover treatment for a specific disease, not the exclusion of a family from coverage altogether, and applies only in the individual market, and so affects almost no one. More than half the states already have laws allowing parents to keep adult children on their policies—through ages varying from 24 to 31. And the other new benefits, too, may touch a small number of people (again, mostly in the individual market, where premiums will be rising all the while), but will do nothing to affect the overall picture of American health care financing. CBO scored these immediate reforms as having no effect on the number of uninsured or on national health expenditures.

The bill will also have the government send a $250 check to seniors who reach the "donut hole" gap in Medicare prescription drug coverage this year—and the checks will go out in September, just in time for the fall elections. But the checks will hardly make up for the significant cuts in Medicare Advantage plans that allow seniors to choose among private insurers for their coverage. Those cuts begin in 2011, but the millions of seniors who use the program will start learning about them this year—again, before the election—as insurance companies start notifying their beneficiaries of higher premiums or cancelled coverage.

We are also likely to see some major players in health insurance, including both large employers and large insurers, begin to take steps to prepare for the new system in ways that employees and beneficiaries will find disconcerting. Verizon, for instance, has already informed its employees that insurance premiums will need to rise in the coming years and retiree benefits may be cut. Caterpillar has said new taxes and rules will cost the company $100 million in just the next year, and tractor maker John Deere has said much the same. Such announcements are likely to be common this year, and many insurers active in the individual market are expected to begin curtailing their offerings as that market looks to grow increasingly unprofitable under new rules.

These early indications will help opponents of the new law make their case. But the case will certainly need to focus most heavily on what is to come in the years after this congressional election: spending, taxes, rising health care costs, cuts in Medicare that don't help save the program or reduce the deficit, and a growing government role in the management of the insurance sector.

The numbers are gargantuan and grim—even as laid out by the Congressional Budget Office, which has to accept as fact all of the legislation's dubious premises and promises. If the law remains in place, a new entitlement will begin in 2014 that will cost more than $2.4 trillion in its first 10 years, and will grow faster than either Medicare or private-sector health care spending has in the past decade.

Rather than reducing costs, Obamacare will increase national health expenditures by more than $200 billion, according to the Obama administration's own HHS actuary. Premiums in the individual market will increase by more than 10 percent very quickly, and middle-class families in the new exchanges (where large numbers of Americans who now receive coverage through their employers will find themselves dumped) will be forced to choose from a very limited menu of government-approved plans, the cheapest of which, CBO estimates, will cost more than $12,000. Some Americans—those earning up to four times the federal poverty level—will get subsidies to help with some of that cost, but these subsidies will grow more slowly than the premiums, and those above the threshold will not receive them at all. Many middle-class families will quickly find themselves spending a quarter of their net income on health insurance, according to a calculation by Scott Gottlieb of the American Enterprise Institute.

Through the rules governing the exchanges and other mechanisms (including individual and employer insurance mandates, strict regulation of plan benefit packages, rating rules, and the like), the federal government will begin micromanaging the insurance sector in an effort to extend coverage and control costs. But even CBO's assessment does not foresee a reduction in costs and therefore an easing of the fundamental source of our health care woes.

To help pay for the subsidies, and for a massive expansion of Medicaid, taxes will rise by about half a trillion dollars in the program's first 10 years— hitting employers and investors especially hard, but quickly being passed down to consumers and workers. And the law also cuts Medicare, especially by reducing physician and hospital payment rates, by another half a trillion dollars—cuts that will drastically undermine the program's operation as, according to the Medicare actuary, about 20 percent of doctors and other providers who participate in the program "could find it difficult to remain profitable and, absent legislative intervention, might end their participation." And all of this, CBO says, to increase the portion of Americans who have health insurance from just under 85 percent today to about 95 percent in 10 years.

Of course, this scenario—for all the dark prospects it lays out—assumes things will go more or less as planned. CBO is required to assume as much. But in a program so complex and enormous, which seeks to take control of a sixth of our economy but is profoundly incoherent even in its own terms, things will surely not always go as planned. The Medicare cuts so essential to funding the new entitlement, for instance, are unlikely to occur. Congress has shown itself thoroughly unwilling to impose such cuts in the past, and if it fails to follow through on them in this case, Obamacare will add hundreds of billions of additional dollars to the deficit. By the 2012 election, we will have certainly begun to see whether the program's proposed funding mechanism is a total sham, or is so unpopular as to make Obamacare toxic with seniors. Neither option bodes well for the program's future.

Some of the taxes envisioned in the plan, especially the so-called Cadillac tax on high-cost insurance, are also unlikely to materialize quite as proposed, adding further to the long-term costs of the program. And meanwhile, the bizarre incentive structures created by the law (resulting in part from the elimination of the public insurance plan which was to have been its focus) are likely to cause massive distortions in the insurance market that will further increase costs. The individual market will quickly collapse, since new regulations will put it at an immense disadvantage against the new exchanges. We are likely to see significant consolidation in the insurance sector, as smaller insurers go out of business and the larger ones become the equivalent of subsidized and highly regulated public utilities. And the fact that the exchanges will offer subsidies not available to workers with employer-based coverage will mean either that employers will be strongly inclined to stop offering insurance, or that Congress will be pressured to make subsidies available to employer-based coverage. In either case, the program's costs will quickly balloon.

Perhaps worst of all, the law not only shirks the obligation to be fiscally responsible, it will also make it much more difficult for future policymakers to do something about our entitlement and deficit crisis. Obamacare constructs a new entitlement that will grow more and more expensive even more quickly than Medicare itself. Even if the program were actually deficit neutral, which it surely won't be, that would just mean that it would keep us on the same budget trajectory we are on now—with something approaching trillion-dollar deficits in each of the next 10 years and a national debt of more than $20 trillion by 2020—but leave us with much less money and far fewer options for doing anything about it.

In other words, Obamacare is an unmitigated disaster—for our health care system, for our fiscal future, and for any notion of limited government. But it is a disaster that will not truly get under way for four years, and therefore a disaster we can avert.

This is the core of the case the program's opponents must make to voters this year and beyond. If opponents succeed in gaining a firmer foothold in Congress in the fall, they should work to begin dismantling and delaying the program where they can: denying funding to key provisions and pushing back implementation at every opportunity. But a true repeal will almost certainly require yet another election cycle, and another president.

The American public is clearly open to the kind of case Obamacare's opponents will need to make. But keeping voters focused on the problems with the program, and with the reckless growth of government beyond it, will require a concerted, informed, impassioned, and empirical case. This is the kind of case opponents of Obamacare have made over the past year, of course, and it persuaded much of the public—but the Democrats acted before the public could have its say at the polls. The case must therefore be sustained until that happens. The health care debate is far from over.

Toward Real Reform

Making and sustaining that case will also require a clear sense of what the alternatives to Obamacare might be—and how repeal could be followed by sensible incremental steps toward controlling health care costs and thereby increasing access and improving care.

Without a doubt, the Democrats' program is worse than doing nothing. But the choice should not be that program or nothing. The problems with our health care system are real, and conservatives must show the public how repealing Obamacare will open the way to a variety of options for more sensible reforms—reforms that will lower costs and help those with preexisting conditions or without affordable coverage options, but in ways that do not bankrupt the country, or undermine the quality of care or the freedom of patients and doctors to make choices for themselves.

Republicans this past year offered a variety of such approaches, which varied in their ambitions, costs, and forms. A group led by representatives Paul Ryan and Devin Nunes and senators Tom Coburn and Richard Burr proposed a broad measures that included reforms of Medicare, Medicaid, the employer-based coverage tax exclusion, and malpractice liability and would cover nearly all of the uninsured. The House Republican caucus backed a more modest first step to make high-risk pools available to those with preexisting conditions, enable insurance purchases across state lines, pursue tort reform, and encourage states to experiment with innovative insurance regulation. Former Bush administration official Jeffrey Anderson has offered an approach somewhere between the two, which pursues incremental reforms through a "small bill." Other conservatives have offered numerous other proposals, including ways of allowing small businesses to pool together for coverage, the expansion of Health Savings Accounts and consumer-driven health care (which Obamacare would thoroughly gut), and various reforms of our entitlement system.

All share a basic commitment to the proposition that our health care dilemmas should be addressed through a series of discrete, modest, incremental solutions to specific problems that concern the American public, and all agree that the underlying cause of these problems is the cost of health coverage and care, which would be best dealt with by using market forces to improve efficiency and bring down prices.

The approach to health care just adopted by President Obama and the Democratic Congress thoroughly fails to deal with efficiency and cost, and stands in the way of any meaningful effort to do so. It is built on a fundamental conceptual error, suffers from a profound incoherence of design, and would make a bad situation far worse. It cannot be improved by tinkering. It must be removed before our health care crisis can be addressed.

If we are going to meet the nation's foremost challenges—ballooning debt, exploding entitlements, out of control health care costs, and the task of keeping America strong and competitive—we must begin by making Obamacare history. We must repeal it, and then pursue real reform.

QUESTIONS

1. Do you think that President Obama was effective in laying out the case for comprehensive reform and in answering his critics? If you were his speechwriter, what would you have changed?

2. The health care experts surveyed by *National Journal* were most impressed with the law's progress on universal coverage and most concerned about costs. What do you see as the strengths and weaknesses of the law?

3. Do you agree with Yuval Levin that repeal is the only answer? One practical point that Levin does not address is that many popular parts of the law are already in effect, such as allowing young adults to stay on their parents' policies until they are twenty-six, fixing the Medicare drug plan "donut hole," prohibiting insurers from charging copayments or deductibles for preventive care on all new insurance plans, and preventing insurers from dropping policyholders when they get sick. Could these popular parts of the law be kept without a more comprehensive approach?

16

Foreign Policy: The National Security Strategy of the United States

Writing down a "National Security Strategy" may seem like an obvious exercise—what is there to say after, "We will respond to attacks on our homeland or allies; we will defend our interests?"—but the obvious parts are merely the starting points. What are our interests? What do we see as the major threats? How will we respond? When will we use military force, and when will we rely on softer forms of power, such as economic sanctions or diplomatic negotiations? When will we act unilaterally, and when will we act only in concert with other nations? The documents state for the public record how the United States defines its national security interests and how it will protect them. The documents do not have any legal force.

The two readings in this section are selections from the national security strategy documents issued by the George W. Bush administration in September 2002 and by the Obama administration in May 2010. Both contain "boilerplate" language—neutral, content-light language that says the obvious. But when read closely, the documents reveal the differences between the approaches each administration took in its effort to safeguard American security. The most provocative aspect of the Bush strategy was its use of "preemptive war." International law has long held that nations do not have to wait until they are attacked to use military force against a threat. But nations are required, under the doctrine of preemptive war, to act only when a threat is immediate—as in the case of a country within days or hours of attacking the United States. The Bush strategy expanded the scope of preemptive war, stating that the United States would use military force to prevent a threat from emerging. (International relations scholars would call this a doctrine of "preventive war," a subtle but important distinction.) This expansion of the circumstances in which the United States would resort to war alarmed the administration's critics, who saw in that language an aggressive unilateralism. The administration's defenders responded that it was a necessary change in an environment in which a single attack, say a nuclear device in a city, could result in millions of deaths.

In his campaign, Obama promised a less unilateral and aggressive national security posture. These themes are reflected in the selection from his administration's national security strategy. It emphasizes collective action and makes far fewer mentions of war or the use of military force. Indeed, the policy on military force is in a separate text box, rather than worked into the language of the strategy document itself.

George W. Bush

The National Security Strategy of the United States: V. Prevent Our Enemies from Threatening Us, Our Allies, and Our Friends with Weapons of Mass Destruction

The nature of the Cold War threat required the United States—with our allies and friends—to emphasize deterrence of the enemy's use of force, producing a grim strategy of mutual assured destruction. With the collapse of the Soviet Union and the end of the Cold War, our security environment has undergone profound transformation.

Having moved from confrontation to cooperation as the hallmark of our relationship with Russia, the dividends are evident: an end to the balance of terror that divided us; an historic reduction in the nuclear arsenals on both sides; and cooperation in areas such as counterterrorism and missile defense that until recently were inconceivable.

But new deadly challenges have emerged from rogue states and terrorists.

None of these contemporary threats rival the sheer destructive power that was arrayed against us by the Soviet Union. However, the nature and motivations of these new adversaries, their determination to obtain destructive powers hitherto available only to the world's strongest states, and the greater likelihood that they will use weapons of mass destruction against us, make today's security environment more complex and dangerous.

In the 1990s we witnessed the emergence of a small number of rogue states that, while different in important ways, share a number of attributes. These states:

- brutalize their own people and squander their national resources for the personal gain of the rulers;
- display no regard for international law, threaten their neighbors, and callously violate international treaties to which they are party;
- are determined to acquire weapons of mass destruction, along with other advanced military technology, to be used as threats or offensively to achieve the aggressive designs of these regimes;
- sponsor terrorism around the globe; and
- reject basic human values and hate the United States and everything for which it stands.

At the time of the Gulf War, we acquired irrefutable proof that Iraq's designs were not limited to the chemical weapons it had used against Iran and its own people, but also extended to the acquisition of nuclear weapons and biological agents. In the past decade North Korea has become the world's principal purveyor of ballistic missiles, and has tested increasingly capable missiles while developing its own WMD arsenal. Other rogue regimes seek nuclear, biological, and chemical weapons as well. These states' pursuit of, and global trade in, such weapons has become a looming threat to all nations.

We must be prepared to stop rogue states and their terrorist clients before they are able to threaten or use weapons of mass destruction against the United States and our allies and friends. Our response must take full advantage of strengthened alliances, the establishment of new partnerships with former adversaries, innovation in the use of military forces, modern technologies, including the development of an effective missile defense system, and increased emphasis on intelligence collection and analysis.

Our comprehensive strategy to combat WMD includes:

- *Proactive counterproliferation efforts.* We must deter and defend against the threat before it is unleashed. We must ensure that key capabilities—detection, active and passive defenses, and counterforce capabilities—are integrated into our defense transformation and our homeland security systems. Counterproliferation must also be integrated into the doctrine, training, and equipping of our forces and those of our allies to ensure that we can prevail in any conflict with WMD-armed adversaries.
- *Strengthened nonproliferation efforts to prevent rogue states and terrorists from acquiring the materials, technologies, and expertise necessary for weapons of mass destruction.* We will enhance diplomacy, arms control, multilateral export controls, and threat reduction assistance that impede states and terrorists seeking WMD, and when necessary, interdict enabling technologies and materials. We will continue to build coalitions to support these efforts, encouraging their increased political and financial support for nonproliferation and threat reduction programs. The recent G-8 agreement to commit up to $20 billion to a global partnership against proliferation marks a major step forward.
- *Effective consequence management to respond to the effects of WMD use, whether by terrorists or hostile states.* Minimizing the effects of WMD use against our people will help deter those who possess such weapons and dissuade those who seek to acquire them by persuading enemies that they cannot attain their desired ends. The United States must also be prepared to respond to the effects of WMD use against our forces abroad, and to help friends and allies if they are attacked.

It has taken almost a decade for us to comprehend the true nature of this new threat. Given the goals of rogue states and terrorists, the United States can no longer solely rely on a reactive posture as we have in the past. The inability to deter a potential attacker, the immediacy of today's threats, and the magnitude of potential harm that could be caused by our adversaries' choice of weapons, do not permit that option. We cannot let our enemies strike first.

- In the Cold War, especially following the Cuban missile crisis, we faced a generally status quo, risk-averse adversary. Deterrence was an effective defense.

But deterrence based only upon the threat of retaliation is less likely to work against leaders of rogue states more willing to take risks, gambling with the lives of their people, and the wealth of their nations.

- In the Cold War, weapons of mass destruction were considered weapons of last resort whose use risked the destruction of those who used them. Today, our enemies see weapons of mass destruction as weapons of choice. For rogue states these weapons are tools of intimidation and military aggression against their neighbors. These weapons may also allow these states to attempt to blackmail the United States and our allies to prevent us from deterring or repelling the aggressive behavior of rogue states. Such states also see these weapons as their best means of overcoming the conventional superiority of the United States.

- Traditional concepts of deterrence will not work against a terrorist enemy whose avowed tactics are wanton destruction and the targeting of innocents; whose so-called soldiers seek martyrdom in death and whose most potent protection is statelessness. The overlap between states that sponsor terror and those that pursue WMD compels us to action.

For centuries, international law recognized that nations need not suffer an attack before they can lawfully take action to defend themselves against forces that present an imminent danger of attack. Legal scholars and international jurists often conditioned the legitimacy of preemption on the existence of an imminent threat—most often a visible mobilization of armies, navies, and air forces preparing to attack.

We must adapt the concept of imminent threat to the capabilities and objectives of today's adversaries. Rogue states and terrorists do not seek to attack us using conventional means. They know such attacks would fail. Instead, they rely on acts of terror and, potentially, the use of weapons of mass destruction—weapons that can be easily concealed, delivered covertly, and used without warning.

The targets of these attacks are our military forces and our civilian population, in direct violation of one of the principal norms of the law of warfare. As was demonstrated by the losses on September 11, 2001, mass civilian casualties is the specific objective of terrorists and these losses would be exponentially more severe if terrorists acquired and used weapons of mass destruction.

The United States has long maintained the option of preemptive actions to counter a sufficient threat to our national security. The greater the threat, the greater is the risk of inaction—and the more compelling the case for taking anticipatory action to defend ourselves, even if uncertainty remains as to the time and place of the enemy's attack. To forestall or prevent such hostile acts by our adversaries, the United States will, if necessary, act preemptively.

The United States will not use force in all cases to preempt emerging threats, nor should nations use preemption as a pretext for aggression. Yet in an age where the enemies of civilization openly and actively seek the world's most destructive technologies, the United States cannot remain idle while dangers gather.

We will always proceed deliberately, weighing the consequences of our actions. To support preemptive options, we will:

- build better, more integrated intelligence capabilities to provide timely, accurate information on threats, wherever they may emerge;
- coordinate closely with allies to form a common assessment of the most dangerous threats; and
- continue to transform our military forces to ensure our ability to conduct rapid and precise operations to achieve decisive results.

The purpose of our actions will always be to eliminate a specific threat to the United States or our allies and friends. The reasons for our actions will be clear, the force measured, and the cause just.

Barack Obama

The National Security Strategy of the United States: III. Advancing Our Interests

* * *

Security

* * *

The threats to our people, our homeland, and our interests have shifted dramatically in the last 20 years. Competition among states endures, but instead of a single nuclear adversary, the United States is now threatened by the potential spread of nuclear weapons to extremists who may not be deterred from using them. Instead of a hostile expansionist empire, we now face a diverse array of challenges, from a loose network of violent extremists to states that flout international norms or face internal collapse. In addition to facing enemies on traditional battlefields, the United States must now be prepared for asymmetric threats, such as those that target our reliance on space and cyberspace.

This Administration has no greater responsibility than protecting the American people. Furthermore, we embrace America's unique responsibility to promote international security—a responsibility that flows from our commitments to allies, our leading role in supporting a just and sustainable international order, and our unmatched military capabilities.

The United States remains the only nation able to project and sustain large-scale military operations over extended distances. We maintain superior capabilities to deter and defeat adaptive enemies and to ensure the credibility of security partnerships that are fundamental to regional and global security. In this way, our military continues to underpin our national security and global leadership, and when we use it appropriately, our security and leadership is reinforced. But when we overuse our military might, or fail to invest in or deploy complementary tools, or act without partners, then our military is overstretched, Americans bear a greater burden, and our leadership around the world is too narrowly identified with military force. And we know that our enemies aim to overextend our Armed Forces and to drive wedges between us and those who share our interests.

Therefore, we must continue to adapt and rebalance our instruments of statecraft. At home, we are integrating our homeland security efforts seamlessly with other aspects of our national security approach, and strengthening our preparedness and resilience. Abroad, we are strengthening alliances, forging new partnerships, and using every tool of American power to advance our objectives—including enhanced diplomatic and development capabilities with the ability both to prevent conflict and to work alongside our military. We are strengthening international norms to isolate governments that flout them and to marshal cooperation against nongovernmental actors who endanger our common security.

Strengthen Security and Resilience at Home

At home, the United States is pursuing a strategy capable of meeting the full range of threats and hazards to our communities. These threats and hazards include terrorism, natural disasters, large-scale cyber attacks, and pandemics. As we do everything within our power to prevent these dangers, we also recognize that we will not be able to deter or prevent every single threat. That is why we must also enhance our resilience—the ability to adapt to changing conditions and prepare for, withstand, and rapidly recover from disruption. To keep Americans safe and secure at home, we are working to:

Enhance Security at Home: Security at home relies on our shared efforts to prevent and deter attacks by identifying and interdicting threats, denying hostile actors the ability to operate within our borders, protecting the nation's critical infrastructure and key resources, and securing cyberspace. That is why we are pursuing initiatives to protect and reduce vulnerabilities in critical infrastructure, at our borders, ports, and airports, and to enhance overall air, maritime, transportation, and space and cyber security. Building on this foundation, we recognize that the global systems that carry people, goods, and data around the globe also facilitate the movement of dangerous people, goods, and data. Within these systems of transportation and transaction, there are key nodes—for example, points of origin and transfer, or border crossings—that represent opportunities for exploitation and interdiction. Thus, we are working with partners abroad to confront threats that often begin beyond our borders. And we are developing lines of coordination at home across Federal, state, local, tribal, territorial, nongovernmental, and private-sector partners, as well as individuals and communities.

Effectively Manage Emergencies: We are building our capability to prepare for disasters to reduce or eliminate long-term effects to people and their property from hazards and to respond to and recover from major incidents. To improve our preparedness, we are integrating hazard planning at all levels of government and building key capabilities to respond to emergencies. We continue to collaborate with communities to ensure preparedness efforts are integrated at all levels of government with the private and nonprofit sectors. We are investing in operational capabilities and equipment, and improving the reliability and interoperability of communications systems for first responders. We are encouraging domestic regional planning and integrated preparedness programs and will encourage government at all levels to engage in long-term recovery planning. It is critical that we continually test and improve plans using exercises that are realistic in scenario and consequences.

Empowering Communities to Counter Radicalization: Several recent incidences of violent extremists in the United States who are committed to fighting here and abroad have underscored the threat to the United States and our interests posed by individuals radicalized at home. Our best defenses against this threat are well informed and equipped families, local communities, and institutions. The Federal Government will invest in intelligence to understand this threat and expand community engagement and development programs to empower local communities. And the Federal Government, drawing on the expertise and resources from all relevant agencies, will clearly communicate our policies and intentions, listening to local concerns, tailoring policies to address regional concerns, and making clear that our diversity is part of our strength—not a source of division or insecurity.

Improve Resilience Through Increased Public-Private Partnerships: When incidents occur, we must show resilience by maintaining critical operations and functions, returning to our normal life, and learning from disasters so that their lessons can be translated into pragmatic changes when necessary. The private sector, which owns and operates most of the nation's critical infrastructure, plays a vital role in preparing for and recovering from disasters. We must, therefore, strengthen public-private partnerships by developing incentives for government and the private sector to design structures and systems that can withstand disruptions and mitigate associated consequences, ensure redundant systems where necessary to maintain the ability to operate, decentralize critical operations to reduce our vulnerability to single points of disruption, develop and test continuity plans to ensure the ability to restore critical capabilities, and invest in improvements and maintenance of existing infrastructure.

Engage with Communities and Citizens: We will emphasize individual and community preparedness and resilience through frequent engagement that provides clear and reliable risk and emergency information to the public. A key part of this effort is providing practical steps that all Americans can take to protect themselves, their families, and their neighbors. This includes transmitting information through multiple pathways and to those with special needs. In addition, we support efforts to develop a nationwide public safety broadband network. Our efforts to inform and empower Americans and their communities recognize that resilience has always been at the heart of the American spirit.

Disrupt, Dismantle, and Defeat Al-Qa'ida and Its Violent Extremist Affiliates in Afghanistan, Pakistan, and Around the World

The United States is waging a global campaign against al-Qa'ida and its terrorist affiliates. To disrupt, dismantle and defeat al-Qa'ida and its affiliates, we are pursuing a strategy that protects our homeland, secures the world's most dangerous weapons and material, denies al-Qa'ida safe haven, and builds positive partnerships with Muslim communities around the world. Success requires a broad, sustained, and integrated campaign that judiciously applies every tool of American power—both military and civilian—as well as the concerted efforts of like-minded states and multilateral institutions.

We will always seek to delegitimize the use of terrorism and to isolate those who carry it out. Yet this is not a global war against Islam. We are at war with a specific network, al-Qa'ida, and its terrorist affiliates who support efforts to attack the United States, our allies, and partners.

Prevent Attacks on and in the Homeland: To prevent acts of terrorism on American soil, we must enlist all of our intelligence, law enforcement, and homeland security capabilities. We will continue to integrate and leverage state and major urban area fusion centers that have the capability to share classified information; establish a nationwide framework for reporting suspicious activity; and implement an integrated approach to our counterterrorism information systems to ensure that the analysts, agents, and officers who protect us have access to all relevant intelligence throughout the government. We are improving information sharing and cooperation by linking networks to facilitate Federal, state, and local capabilities to seamlessly exchange messages and information, conduct searches, and collaborate. We are coordinating better with foreign partners to identify, track, limit access to funding, and prevent terrorist travel. Recognizing the inextricable link between domestic and transnational security, we will collaborate bilaterally, regionally, and through international institutions to promote global efforts to prevent terrorist attacks.

Strengthen Aviation Security: We know that the aviation system has been a particular target of al-Qa'ida and its affiliates. We must continue to bolster aviation security worldwide through a focus on increased information collection and sharing, stronger passenger vetting and screening measures, the development of advanced screening technologies, and cooperation with the international community to strengthen aviation security standards and efforts around the world.

Deny Terrorists Weapons of Mass Destruction: To prevent acts of terrorism with the world's most dangerous weapons, we are dramatically accelerating and intensifying efforts to secure all vulnerable nuclear materials by the end of 2013, and to prevent the spread of nuclear weapons. We will also take actions to safeguard knowledge and capabilities in the life and chemical sciences that could be vulnerable to misuse.

Deny Al-Qa'ida the Ability to Threaten the American People, Our Allies, Our Partners and Our Interests Overseas: Al-Qa'ida and its allies must not be permitted to gain or retain any capacity to plan and launch international terrorist attacks, especially against the U.S. homeland. Al Qa'ida's core in Pakistan remains the most dangerous component of the larger network, but we also face a growing threat from the group's allies worldwide. We must deny these groups the ability to conduct operational plotting from any locale, or to recruit, train, and position operatives, including those from Europe and North America.

Afghanistan and Pakistan: This is the epicenter of the violent extremism practiced by al Qa'ida. The danger from this region will only grow if its security slides backward, the Taliban controls large swaths of Afghanistan, and al-Qa'ida is allowed to operate with impunity. To prevent future attacks on the United States, our allies, and partners, we must work with others to keep the pressure on al-Qa'ida and increase the security and capacity of our partners in this region.

In Afghanistan, we must deny al-Qa'ida a safe haven, deny the Taliban the ability to overthrow the government, and strengthen the capacity of Afghanistan's security forces and government so that they can take lead responsibility for Afghanistan's future. Within Pakistan, we are working with the government to address the local, regional, and global threat from violent extremists.

We will achieve these objectives with a strategy comprised of three components.

- First, our military and International Security Assistance Force (ISAF) partners within Afghanistan are targeting the insurgency, working to secure key population centers, and increasing efforts to train Afghan security forces.

These military resources will allow us to create the conditions to transition to Afghan responsibly. In July 2011, we will begin reducing our troops' responsibility, taking into account conditions on the ground. We will continue to advise and assist Afghanistan's Security Forces so that they can succeed over the long term.

- Second, we will continue to work with our partners, the United Nations, and the Afghan Government to improve accountable and effective governance. As we work to advance our strategic partnership with the Afghan Government, we are focusing assistance on supporting the President of Afghanistan and those ministries, governors, and local leaders who combat corruption and deliver for the people. Our efforts will be based upon performance, and we will measure progress. We will also target our assistance to areas that can make an immediate and enduring impact in the lives of the Afghan people, such as agriculture, while supporting the human rights of all of Afghanistan's people—women and men. This will support our long-term commitment to a relationship between our two countries that supports a strong, stable, and prosperous Afghanistan.

- Third, we will foster a relationship with Pakistan founded upon mutual interests and mutual respect. To defeat violent extremists who threaten both of our countries, we will strengthen Pakistan's capacity to target violent extremists within its borders, and continue to provide security assistance to support those efforts. To strengthen Pakistan's democracy and development, we will provide substantial assistance responsive to the needs of the Pakistani people, and sustain a long-term partnership committed to Pakistan's future. The strategic partnership that we are developing with Pakistan includes deepening cooperation in a broad range of areas, addressing both security and civilian challenges, and we will continue to expand those ties through our engagement with Pakistan in the years to come.

Deny Safe Havens and Strengthen At-Risk States: Wherever al-Qa'ida or its terrorist affiliates attempt to establish a safe haven—as they have in Yemen, Somalia, the Maghreb, and the Sahel—we will meet them with growing pressure. We also will strengthen our own network of partners to disable al-Qa'ida's financial, human, and planning networks; disrupt terrorist operations before they mature; and address potential safe-havens before al-Qa'ida and its terrorist affiliates can take root. These efforts will focus on information-sharing, law enforcement cooperation, and establishing new practices to counter evolving adversaries. We will also help states avoid becoming terrorist safe havens by helping them build their capacity for responsible governance and security through development and security sector assistance.

Deliver Swift and Sure Justice: To effectively detain, interrogate, and prosecute terrorists, we need durable legal approaches consistent with our security and our values. We adhere to several principles: we will leverage all available information and intelligence to disrupt attacks and dismantle al-Qa'ida and affiliated terrorist organizations; we will bring terrorists to justice; we will act in line with the rule of law and due process; we will submit decisions to checks and balances and accountability; and we will insist that matters of detention and secrecy are addressed in a manner consistent with our Constitution and laws. To deny violent extremists one of their most potent recruitment tools, we will close the prison at Guantanamo Bay.

Resist Fear and Overreaction: The goal of those who perpetrate terrorist attacks is in part to sow fear. If we respond with fear, we allow violent extremists to succeed far beyond the initial impact of their attacks, or attempted attacks— altering our society and enlarging the standing of al-Qa'ida and its terrorist affiliates far beyond its actual reach. Similarly, overreacting in a way that creates fissures between America and certain regions or religions will undercut our leadership and make us less safe.

Contrast Al-Qa'ida's Intent to Destroy with Our Constructive Vision: While violent extremists seek to destroy, we will make clear our intent to build. We are striving to build bridges among people of different faiths and religions. We will continue to work to resolve the Arab-Israeli conflict, which has long been a source of tension. We will continue to stand up for the universal rights of all people, even for those with whom we disagree. We are developing new partnerships in Muslim communities around the world on behalf of health, education, science, employment, and innovation. And through our broader emphasis on Muslim engagement, we will communicate our commitment to support the aspirations of all people for security and opportunity. Finally, we reject the notion that al-Qa'ida represents any religious authority. They are not religious leaders, they are killers; and neither Islam nor any other religion condones the slaughter of innocents.

Use of Force

Military force, at times, may be necessary to defend our country and allies or to preserve broader peace and security, including by protecting civilians facing a grave humanitarian crisis. We will draw on diplomacy, development, and international norms and institutions to help resolve disagreements, prevent conflict, and maintain peace, mitigating where possible the need for the use of force. This means credibly underwriting U.S. defense commitments with tailored approaches to deterrence and ensuring the U.S. military continues to have the necessary capabilities across all domains—land, air, sea, space, and cyber. It also includes helping our allies and partners build capacity to fulfill their responsibilities to contribute to regional and global security.

While the use of force is sometimes necessary, we will exhaust other options before war whenever we can, and carefully weigh the costs and risks of action against the costs and risks of inaction. When force is necessary, we will continue to do so in a way that reflects our values and strengthens our legitimacy, and we will seek broad international support, working with such institutions as NATO and the U.N. Security Council.

The United States must reserve the right to act unilaterally if necessary to defend our nation and our interests, yet we will also seek to adhere to standards that govern the use of force. Doing so strengthens those who act in line with international standards, while isolating and weakening those who do not. We will also outline a clear mandate and specific objectives and thoroughly consider the consequences—intended and unintended—of our actions. And the United States will take care when sending the men and women of our Armed Forces into harm's way to ensure they have the leadership, training, and equipment they require to accomplish their mission.

QUESTIONS

1. Who do you think is the intended audience for these documents? Is it the U.S. electorate? The international community? Potential adversaries?

2. What other differences can you find between the documents? How would you connect them to what you know about the other characteristics of the George W. Bush and the Obama administrations?

3. Critics of the Bush strategy argued that it was too aggressive and unilateral. Critics of the Obama strategy say it places too much emphasis on diplomacy and subordinating U.S. interests to international opinion. What do you see as the strengths and weaknesses of these documents?

4. Is there an ideal national security strategy? Is it possible to construct a strategy that everyone would agree with?

Permissions Acknowledgments

Judis, John B.: "Tea Minus Zero," *The New Republic*, May 27, 2010. Reprinted by permission of *The New Republic*, © 2010 TNR II, LLC.

Lane, Eric and Michael Oreskes: From *The Genius of America: How the Constitution Saved Our Country and Why It Can Again*. Copyright © 2007 by Eric Lane and Michael Oreskes. Reprinted by permission of Bloomsbury USA.

Levin, Yuval: "Repeal: Why and How Obamacare Must Be Undone." This article is reprinted with permission of *The Weekly Standard*, where it first appeared on 4/5-12/2010. For more information visit www.weeklystandard.com.

Levinson, Sanford: chapter 1, "The Ratification Referendum," *Our Undemocratic Constitution: Where the Constitution Goes Wrong (And How We the People Can Correct It)* by Sanford Levinson, pp. 11–24. Copyright © 2006 by Oxford University Press, Inc. Reprinted with permission of Oxford University Press.

Lomborg, Bjørn: "Mr. Gore, Your Solution to Global Warming Is Wrong," *Esquire*, August 2009, vol. 152, issue 2, pp. 104–107. Reprinted by permission of the author.

Lowry, Rich and Ramesh Ponnuru: "An Exceptional Debate," *National Review*, March 8, 2010, pp. 31–38. © 2010 by National Review, Inc., 215 Lexington Avenue, New York, NY 10016. Reprinted by permission.

McKibben, Bill: "Climate Change," *Foreign Policy*, January/February 2009, pp. 32–38. © 2009 The Slate Group, LLC. www.foreignpolicy.com. Reprinted by permission via Copyright Clearance Center.

Price, Tom: "The Future of Journalism," *CQ Researcher*, March 27, 2009, vol. 19, no. 12, pp. 275–279, 290–291. Reprinted by permission of CQ Press.

Rauch, Jonathan: "Earmarks Are a Model, Not a Menace." Reprinted with permission from *National Journal*, March 14, 2009. Copyright 2010 by National Journal Group, Inc. All rights reserved.

——— "The Hyperpluralism Trap," *The New Republic*, June 6, 1994, pp. 22–25. Copyright Jonathan Rauch. Reprinted by permission of the author.

Schattschneider, E. E.: "A Critique of Group Theories of Politics." From *Semi-Sovereign People*, 1E. Copyright © 1961 Wadsworth, a part of Cengage Learning, Inc. Reproduced by permission. www.cengage.com/permissions

Serafini, Marilyn: "Grading Reform." Excerpted with permission from *National Journal*, March 27, 2010. Copyright 2010 by National Journal Group, Inc. All rights reserved.

Smith, Bradley: "*Citizens United* We Stand," *The American Spectator*, vol. 43, no. 4, May 2010, pp. 14–17. Reprinted by permission of *The American Spectator* and Spectator.org.

Song, Sarah: "What Does It Mean to Be an American?", *Daedalus*, 138:2 (Spring, 2009), pp. 31–40. © 2009 by the American Academy of Arts and Sciences. Reprinted by permission of MIT Press Journals.

von Spakowsky, Hans: "Requiring Identification by Voters," Testimony before the Texas Senate, Delivered March 10, 2009. © 2010, The Heritage Foundation. Reprinted by permission of The Heritage Foundation.

Starr, Paul: "Goodbye to the Age of Newspapers (Hello to a New Era of Corruption)," *The New Republic*, March 4, 2009. Reprinted by permission of *The New Republic*, © 2009 TNR II, LLC.

Taibbi, Matt: "Wall Street Bailout Hustle." Article by Matt Taibbi. From *Rolling Stone* issue dated, March 4, 2010. © Rolling Stone LLC 2010. All Rights Reserved. Reprinted by Permission.

Truman, David B.: "The Alleged Mischiefs of Faction" from *The Governmental Process* (Knopf, 1971). Reprinted with permission of Edwin M. Truman.

vanden Heuvel, Katrina and Robert Borosage: "Change Won't Come Easy." Reprinted with permission from the February 1, 2010 issue of *The Nation*. For subscription information, call 1-800-333-8536. Portions of each week's magazine can be accessed at http://www.thenation.com.

Warshawsky, Steven M.: "What Does It Mean to Be an American?," *American Thinker*, July 2, 2007. Reprinted by permission of the author.

Wilentz, Sean: "States of Anarchy," *The New Republic*, April 29, 2010. Reprinted by permission of *The New Republic*, © 2010 TNR II, LLC.

Wilson, James Q.: "How Divided Are We?" Reprinted from *Commentary*, February 2006, by permission; copyright © 2006 by Commentary, Inc.